FIRE IN
THE VALLEY

FIRE IN THE VALLEY

The Making of the Personal Computer

Second Edition

PAUL FREIBERGER

MICHAEL SWAINE

McGraw-Hill

New York   San Francisco   Washington, D.C.   Auckland   Bogotá
Caracas   Lisbon   London   Madrid   Mexico City   Milan
Montreal   New Delhi   San Juan   Singapore
Sydney   Tokyo   Toronto

Library of Congress Catalog Card Number: 99-075973

McGraw-Hill

A Division of The **McGraw·Hill** Companies

First Edition: Copyright © 1984 by McGraw-Hill, Inc. All rights reserved.

2 3 4 5 6 7 8 9 0   DOC/DOC   0 9 8 7 6 5 4 3 2 1 0

ISBN 0-07-135892-7

This book was set in Fairfield LH Medium by North Market Street Graphics.

Printed and bound by R. R. Donnelley & Sons Company.

McGraw-Hill books are available at special quantity discounts to use as premiums
and sales promotions, or for use in corporate training programs. For more information, please write to the Director of Special Sales, Professional Publishing, McGraw-
Hill, Two Penn Plaza, New York, NY 10121-2298. Or contact your local bookstore.

To our moms and in memory of our dads:
Ida and Norman Freiberger
Barbara and Earl Swaine
and
To Jeanne and Nancy

CONTENTS

FOREWORD

Paul Freiberger, Michael Swaine, and I arrived at about the same time in late 1981 at a funky little publication that had recently been renamed *InfoWorld.* Until the summer of 1981, *InfoWorld* had been known as the *Intelligent Machines Journal,* a hobbyist journal written for a small but rapidly growing community of computing enthusiasts.

The *Intelligent Machines Journal* had been founded by Jim Warren, an itinerant former school teacher who had also created the West Coast Computer Faire. When he decided to sell his then quasi-academic publication, he found an eager buyer in Patrick McGovern, the chairman of the International Data Corporation, whose flagship weekly *ComputerWorld* was the unofficial organ of the mainframe computer industry.

McGovern had his ear to the ground, and he had realized early on that a new computer industry was emerging that had little in common with the stuffy East Coast–based computer companies. The transformation of *Intelligent Machines Journal* was just one in a series of events between 1977 and 1981 that marked the evolution of a hobbyist sub-culture into the world's most dynamic industry.

The three of us couldn't have arrived at a better time. The PC hobbyist era was ending, but in its place was thriving an equally wild, absolutely out-of-control group of small businesses—populated by remarkable and quirky characters—on their way to becoming major corporations.

Overnight, *InfoWorld* became a perfect perch from which to watch history take place. Everything was moving rapidly, and the publication we had found ourselves working for was attempting to define itself while the world was being turned upside down by the microprocessor. One moment *InfoWorld* tried to be a *Rolling Stone* to the personal computer industry; the next moment it set out to be a *Sports Illustrated*.

Few of us were trained journalists, but like the fledgling industry we were covering, we made it up as we went along. It was soon obvious that the world was taking notice of the PC. On an almost weekly basis, people from around the country would simply appear at our offices in downtown Palo Alto, having made their way to the Mecca of Silicon Valley looking for jobs or connections.

At *InfoWorld* we were close to history in the making—sometimes too close. One day I walked into Paul Freiberger's office, a small windowless corridor, only to find him in a tense conversation with Steven Jobs. Jobs was yelling at him because Paul was about to break the story of the Lisa and the Macintosh, and Jobs was accusing him of helping the Japanese take over the American computer industry.

Indeed, it is the proximity of its authors to the enterprises that gave birth to the microcomputer industry that sets *Fire in the Valley* apart from the now dozens of other attempts to tell the story of the computing revolution. Paul and Michael lived through a remarkable period of history, and their book captures the spirit of the personal computer revolution.

Originally published in 1984, *Fire in the Valley* was the first, and is still the best, account of the people who created what venture capitalist John Doerr has called the "single largest legal accumulation of wealth in the century."

More recent histories of the personal computer have tended to devolve into accounts of the legends of William Gates, Steven Jobs, and the Xerox Palo Alto Research Center. What sets *Fire in the Valley* apart is that it succeeds in telling the story of what came before. Freiberger and Swaine's account of the history of the Homebrew Computer Club still stands as the definitive tale of a remarkable anarchist assembly of engineers, hackers, and fellow travelers that began as a genuine counter-culture and ended by changing the world.

There is also a trend in computer histories today to reject the impact of culture and politics in the development of the personal computer. But even a casual reading of *Fire in the Valley* clearly demonstrates that the personal computer industry, and its emergence in Silicon Valley in the 1970s, was a direct outgrowth of a remarkable period in the suburban region that surrounds Stanford University.

It was a particular chemistry—not just greed and not just engineering, but also a strain of passionate political purity best expressed by young people such as Lee Felsenstein, the inventor of the Sol and designer of the Osborne I—that gave rise to the personal computer industry.

Now a decade and a half after its first publication, this new edition of *Fire in the Valley* has been expanded with both additional reporting and new chapters. This revised edition brings the history of Apple Computer up to date and adds more depth to the life and impact of CP/M designer Gary Kildall. It also explores the contribution of Douglas Engelbart and the researchers at the Xerox Palo Alto Research Center. This new edition of *Fire in the Valley* also adds the most recent developments in the history of the personal computer: Sun Microsystems and Netscape and the rise of the Internet and the World Wide Web.

Fire in the Valley has stood the test of time well. It remains a great adventure that gives the reader a sense of being close to a historical movement that is still playing itself out.

John Markoff
The New York Times
San Francisco, September 1999

PREFACE

How do you convey the magic of a new dawn?

It was a time when cranks and dreamers saw the power they dreamed of drop into their hands and used it to change the world. It was a turning point when multinational corporations lost their way and kitchen-table entrepreneurs seized the banner and pioneered the future for everyone. It was a moment when nerds laughed in bullies' faces, idealism paid off, and you could *feel* the pace of change. Hobbyists became visionaries, and visionaries became multimillionaires. It was a bona fide revolution, bred of those things that drive people to greatness: greed and idealism, pride and love, the thrill of achieving what nobody else has ever done before, the adrenaline rush of riding a big wave—and yes, throw in Buddhism, *est*, and transcendental meditation, too.

So what you do is, you tell the stories. You report what happened, what the players did, and what they had to say about what they did, and in the process hope you convey some sense of what it was like to be there. That's what we attempted in 1984 with the first edition of this book and what we hope to do in this one.

In the early 1980s, we were two young and eager reporters for *InfoWorld,* the first news weekly to cover the personal computer industry, although the word *industry* probably conveys the wrong impression.

We were reporting on what comes before an industry. We were reporting on a revolution. Caught up in the pitch of events, we felt a part of them. It was an exhilarating time, watching and chronicling history in the making.

Like interviewing Bill Gates in the bleachers above the show floor at an early West Coast Computer Faire. Dining with his partner Paul Allen in a high-rise in Seattle. Driving the back roads of Georgia to talk with Ed Roberts, the guy who started it all, now in "retirement" as a country doctor. Sitting with Woz on the floor of the apartment he occupied while he attended U.C. Berkeley under the pseudonym of "Rocky Raccoon Clark." Visiting an elementary school and discussing creativity with Alan Kay. Watching night fall in Jim Warren's aerie in the Santa Cruz Mountains and hearing about his early computer shows and publications and hot tub parties that *Playboy* covered. Scuba diving with Captain Crunch, the king of the phone phreaks. Mooching a gourmet meal from programmer Alan Cooper. Getting well oiled with early computer makers Lee Felsenstein and Bob Marsh in a tiny Palo Alto flat. Dining in the Apple cafeteria with Steve Jobs and *finally* getting the interview.

We talked shop with them all as part of our work, but we noticed a palpable shift in atmosphere when we put aside the business of the day, laid down our *InfoWorld* notebooks, and said, "Now tell us how you got started." And tell us they did—often at great length, and frequently with astonishing candor.

When the previous edition of this book was published in 1984, it recorded a history still in the making. So much so that the book preceded most people's understanding of the personal computer's importance. We ourselves didn't guess how huge the phenomenon would become. Since that time, others have added pieces to this story, and the mainstream press now covers it daily. But we had a privileged vantage point back then. We are slightly awed now as we recall having lived close enough to the principals to absorb their energy, excitement, ambition, and dreams.

It's 16 years later. So much has happened since the beginning that the birth of the personal computer seems half-mythical, like a tale of King Arthur. We want the words on these pages to bring that time alive for those who missed it. Because it lit a fire that changed society.

Today, personal computers pervade the workplace, the home, and our culture. Every day people compose letters, print statements, calculate figures, update spreadsheets, buy and sell goods, and exchange e-mail, all on the same glowing screen. While many feared computers would eliminate jobs, the opposite has proved true: the industry has created millions of jobs and given the economy a major boost.

The personal computer has entered our homes, sometimes disguised as a game machine, telephone, television, or microwave oven. More than 50 percent of the homes in the United States now have personal computers. Even as recently as 16 years ago it would have taken some courage to predict that personal computer use would spread so rapidly.

The events since 1984 give perspective to the stories we told in the first edition, and endow some with piquant irony, even tragedy. We can count the winners and losers now, but the story continues. The venture capitalists and angel investors have learned to take the nerds, the hackers, and the quiet engineers very seriously and are writing checks to accelerate change. Politicians strive to ally themselves with Silicon Valley leaders, and kids come out of college expecting to get rich writing software. Many will. The personal computer—and the Internet and other technologies that have been built on it—is changing the world as profoundly as the printing press or the Industrial Revolution. Yes, it's that big.

And it's all the more amazing when you think about how it got started.

In bringing this book up to date, we talked to many of the people we interviewed for the first edition and numerous others, revisited every line on every page, corrected errors and omissions, expanded on some stories, and added new ones. We also wrote new chapters on developments in the personal computer field since 1984 and added many additional photos to help tell the story. But we've tried not to lose the flavor of those early days.

Even with the perspective of 16 years and evidence of the extraordinary changes this little box has wrought, it's hard to believe we've come so far so fast. That's why we think it's important to know where it began, what it felt like then, and how we all have been changed. This new edition of *Fire in the Valley* is our effort to tell that story.

ACKNOWLEDGMENTS

The personal computer idea continues to spread even as our story ends. Our research grew into hundreds of hours of interviews with most of the principals, as each interview led to others and drew us deeper into the story. Many of the people we interviewed graciously supplied us with documents, records, letters, diaries, time lines, and photographs.

Among others, we are grateful to the following individuals:

Scott Adams, Todd Agulnick, David Ahl, Alice Ahlgren, Bob Albrecht, Paul Allen, Bill Baker, Steve Ballmer, Rob Barnaby, John Barry, Allen Baum, John Bell, Tim Berners-Lee, Tim Berry, Ray Borrill, Stewart Brand, Dan Bricklin, Keith Britton, David Bunnell, David Carlick, Douglas Carlston, Mark Chamberlain, Hal Chamberlin, Alan Cooper, Sue Cooper, Ben Cooper, John Craig, Andy Cunningham, Eddie Curry, Steve Dompier, John Draper, John Dvorak, Doug Engelbart, Chris Espinosa, Gordon Eubanks, Ed Faber, Federico Faggin, Lee Felsenstein, Bill Fernandez, Todd Fischer, Richard Frank, Bob Frankston, Paul Franson, Nancy Freitas, Don French, Gordon French, Howard Fulmer, Dan Fylstra, Mark Garetz, Harry Garland, Jean-Louis Gassée, Bill Gates, Bill Godbout, Chuck Grant, Wayne Green, Dick Heiser, Carl Helmers, Kent Hensheid, Andy Hertzfeld, Ted Hoff, Thom Hogan, Rod Holt, Randy Hyde, Peter Jennings, Steve Jobs, Bill Joy, Philippe Kahn,

Mitch Kapor, Vinod Khosla, Gary Kildall, Joe Killian, Dan Kottke, Barbara Krause, Tom Lafleur, Phil Lemons, Andrea Lewis, Bill Lohse, Dorothy McEwen, Regis McKenna, Mike Markkula, Bob Marsh, Patty McCracken, Scott McNealy, Roger Melen, Seymour Merrin, Edward Metro, Jill Miller, Dick Miller, Michael Miller, Fred Moore, Gordon Moore, Lyall Morrill, George Morrow, Jeanne Morrow, Robert Noyce, Tom and Molly O'Neill, Terry Opdendyk, Adam Osborne, Chuck Peddle, Harvard Pennington, Joel Pitt, Fred "Chip" Poode, Frank and Susan Raab, Jeff Raikes, Jef Raskin, Ed Roberts, Tom Rolander, Phil Roybal, Seymour Rubinstein, Sue Runfola, Chris Rutkowski, Paul Saffo, Art Salsberg, Wendell Sanders, Ed Sawicki, Joel Schwartz, John Sculley, Jon Shirley, John Shoch, Richard Shoup, Michael Shrayer, Bill Siler, Les Solomon, Alan Stein, Barney Stone, Don Tarbell, George Tate, Paul Terrell, Larry Tesler, Glenn Theodore, John Torode, Jack Tramiel, Bruce Van Natta, Jim Warren, Larry Weiss, Randy Wigginton, Margaret Wozniak, Steve Wozniak, Greg Yob, and Pierluigi Zappacosta.

Thanks to Steven Haft, producer of *Pirates of Silicon Valley,* for seeing the movie possibilities in the book.

We also benefited from discussions and comments from many knowledgeable friends and colleagues. Our friends Eva Langfeldt and John Barry read our initial proposal; Dave Needle provided timely research assistance; Thom Hogan offered useful suggestions; Dan McNeill often found just the right word; Nancy Groth brought grace with a red pencil; Nelda Cassuto offered sweet support in the form of zabaglione and editing; Levi Thomas and Laura Dimario lent photographic expertise; Amy Hyams provided patient research and friendly conversation; Carol Moran opened secret doors; Scott Kildall gave his trust; John Markoff provided knowledge and insight generously whenever we asked; Jason Lewis shared software wizardry; David Reed made corrections from his kitchen on the other coast; Charlie Athanas provided timely and generous insights; former colleagues Judy Canter, Phil Bronstein, and Richard Paoli of the *San Francisco Examiner* opened photo archives; Howard Bailen gave years of enthusiastic support; our editor at McGraw-Hill, Michelle Reed, had vision, energy, and quick and perceptive editing skill. Thanks to Roger Kasunic and his production team at McGraw. Thanks to editors Nancy DelFavero, Stefan Grunwedel, Rich Aden, and Ami Knox. Our agents on this project,

David Fugate and William Gladstone, had just the right combination of persistence and patience and we are grateful.

On a most personal note, there are some special people that gave their love and support and sacrificed to help make this book possible: Nancy Groth, Jeanne L. Freiberger, Edan Freiberger, and Max Freiberger.

PORTENTS

In the late 1960s, just outside Seattle, a group of teenagers met after school each day and biked to a local company. As it closed for the day and its employees began heading home, the boys were just getting started. They thought of themselves as the firm's unofficial night shift, and in fact they routinely worked till long after dark, pounding the keys of the company's DEC computer and gorging on carry-out pizza and soft drinks.

The two leaders of the group were considered a little odd by their classmates. They were "computer nuts," completely absorbed in the technology. All the boys worked for free, but Paul Allen, a soft-spoken 15-year-old, would have paid for the experience. His friend Bill Gates, who was 13 and looked even younger, was a math whiz and hooked on programming.

Computer Center Corporation, which they called "C Cubed," let them come in to find errors in the DEC computer's programming. C Cubed was more than happy to have them around. According to its contract with DEC, as long as C Cubed could show that DEC's programs had bugs (errors that caused the programs to malfunction or "crash"), the firm didn't have to pay DEC for using the computer. The kids were postponing the day when C Cubed would have to pay its bill.

DEC's arrangement with C Cubed was a common one for tracking down subtle bugs in complex programs. The DEC software was new and intricate, so everyone knew it would have at least a few errors. But the kids discovered plenty, and young Bill Gates found more than his share. The Problem Report Book, as the boys entitled their bug journal, grew and grew and grew to 300 pages. Finally, DEC called a halt to the proceedings. As Gates later recalled, DEC told C Cubed, "These guys are going to find bugs forever."

Allen and Gates stayed on with C Cubed for months after the other boys lost interest and they eventually drew pay for their work. They were privileged—and they knew it. Few teenagers at the time had ever seen, much less programmed, a computer. And the computer they were using was a marvel of modern engineering. DEC pioneered the *minicomputer*, which shrank the computer from a mammoth wall of circuitry affordable only to the federal government and the largest companies, into a refrigerator-sized box that smaller firms, factories, and universities could buy. But the minicomputer was just one step on the path of miniaturization that would lead to the personal computer. Having the C Cubed machine largely to themselves after hours, Allen and Gates dreamed of the day when they would actually own their own computers. "It's going to happen," Paul Allen would tell his friend.

It did happen, of course. And more has happened than those gifted teenagers, or anyone else back then, could possibly have imagined. Virtually nonexistent until 1974, personal computers are now in offices, homes, laboratories, schools, on airplanes, and at the beach. Retail outlets for PCs are now as common as bookstores. Computers sit on desktops, ride in briefcases, and slip into coat pockets. When it comes to information storage, they make encyclopedias seem like telegrams, and their capacities are protean. They act at once as a typewriter, calculator, accounting system, spreadsheet, telephone, library, drafting board, theater, tutor, and toy. And with the Internet, they allow access to an instant postal system and a dazzling, worldwide array of information, entertainment, and commercial sites. A revolution has indeed taken place.

Yet personal computers themselves did not arise from expensive, well-equipped labs staffed by an army of research and development specialists. They began outside the corporate and academic establishment, built by amateur business owners and hobbyists like Bill Gates, Paul Allen, Lee Felsenstein, Alan Cooper, Steve Dompier, Gary Kildall, Gordon Eubanks, Steve Jobs, and Steve Wozniak working after-hours in garages, warehouses, basements, and bedrooms.

These hobbyists brought about this revolution through their own fascination with this technology. Their story is as strange and remarkable as any in modern business. It is a tale of overnight millionaires bewildered by their sudden success, populist engineers holed up in garages soldering together machines that would forever change lives, manufacturers afflicted with consumerism, consumers who accepted faulty merchandise for the fun of fixing it themselves, and a spirit of sharing hard-won technical insights—a spirit rare in any industry, but essential for the creation of the personal computer.

The flames of the personal computer revolution were ignited in many places during the mid-1970s, but nowhere did the fire burn as brightly as it did in Silicon Valley, California's high-tech development center. This is the history of that revolution in the Valley and beyond.

1970
- Xerox opens the Palo Alto Research Center (PARC)

1971
- Intel develops the 8008 microprocessor
- Niklaus Wirth invents the Pascal programming language
- Steve Wozniak and Bill Fernandez build their "Cream Soda Computer"

1972
- Gary Kildall writes PL/M, the first programming language for the 4004
- Bob Albrecht founds People's Computer Company (PCC)
- Bill Gates and Paul Allen found Traf-O-Data in Seattle
- Steve Wozniak and Steve Jobs begin selling "blue boxes" (devices to subvert the phone system and make free calls)

1973
- André Thi Truong creates the Micral industrial microcomputer based on the 8008 chip
- Steve Wozniak joins Hewlett-Packard
- The Community Memory Project begins in the San Francisco Bay Area
- Radio Electronics publishes an article by Don Lancaster describing a "TV Typewriter"
- Gary Kildall and Ben Cooper build their astrology forecasting machine
- Bob Metcalfe invents Ethernet

1967
- IBM makes the first floppy disk

1968
- Ed Roberts founds an electronics company called Micro Instrumentation Telemetry Systems (MITS)
- Robert Noyce and Gordon Moore found Intel Corporation
- Doug Engelbart delivers "The Mother of All Demos" at the Fall Joint Computer Conference in San Francisco

1924
- Computing-Tabulating-Recording becomes International Business Machines

1930
- Claude Shannon's Ph.D. thesis explains how electrical switching circuits can model Boolean logic

1936
- Benjamin Burack builds the first electric logic machine

1955
- William Shockley founds Shockley Semiconductor Laboratory in Palo Alto, California

1956
- John Bardeen, Walter Brattain, and William Shockley share the Nobel Prize in physics for the transistor

1962
- Tandy Corporation buys the chain of Radio Shack electronics stores
- Steve Wozniak builds an addition and subtraction machine that wins a prize in a local science fair

1963
- Doug Engelbart invents the computer mouse

1823
- Charles Babbage begins work on the first of his machines to mechanize solutions to general mathematical problems

---

1800   **1900**   **1950**   **1960**   **1970**

1885
- Allan Marquand designs the first electric logic machine

1890
- Herman Hollerith designs the first tabulating machine

1940
- John Atanasoff and Clifford Berry design the first computer with vacuum tubes as switching units

1945
- John Mauchley and J. Presper Eckert build ENIAC, the first all-electronic digital computer
- Vannevar Bush writes essay envisioning information-processing technology as an extension of human intellect

1947
- The transistor is perfected

1957
- Fairchild Semiconductor is founded
- Kenneth Olsen founds Digital Equipment Corporation

1959
- Lee Felsenstein fails in his first attempt to design a computer
- National Semiconductor is founded

1964
- Control Data Corporation releases the CDC6600 supercomputer, designed by Seymour Cray
- Professors John Kemeney and Thomas Kurtz develop the first BASIC programming language at Dartmouth College

1965
- Digital Equipment Corporation releases the PDP-8 minicomputer
- IBM introduces its System/360 line of computers

1969
- Intel is commissioned to produce integrated circuits for a line of Japanese calculators
- Lee Felsenstein leaves Ampex to write for the Berkeley Barb
- Data General releases the Nova computer
- Intel decides to build the first microprocessor, the 4004; Ted Hoff, Federico Faggin, and Stan Mazor execute the project
- David Ahl goes to work for Digital Equipment Corporation
- Dennis Ritchie and Ken Thompson develop the Unix operating system

1974
- Ted Nelson publishes Computer Lib
- Intel releases the 8080
- Xerox releases the Alto
- John Torode and Gary Kildall begin selling a microcomputer with a disk operating system
- Radio Electronics publishes an article calling the Mark-8 "your personal minicomputer"
- David Ahl founds Creative Computing, the first home computer hobby magazine

1975
- Microsoft (formerly Traf-O-Data) writes the first BASIC language for the Altair
- Popular Electronics publishes an article describing the MITS Altair
- Bob Marsh and Lee Felsenstein rent garage space in Berkeley, California, to conduct electronics projects
- Harry Garland and Roger Melen found Cromemco in Los Altos, California
- Homebrew Computer Club holds its first meeting in Menlo Park, California
- Amateur Computer Group of New Jersey holds its first meeting
- Bob Marsh and Gary Ingram found Processor Technology
- Southern California Computer Society holds its first meeting in Los Angeles
- Dick Heiser opens the first retail personal computer outlet, The Computer Store, in Los Angeles, California
- First issue of Byte magazine is published
- Paul Terrell opens the first Byte Shop in Mountain View, California

1976

- Ed Faber joins IMSAI as director of sales; IMSAI begins shipping its first computers
- Bill Gates's "Open Letter to Hobbyists" lamenting software piracy appears in the Homebrew Computer Club newsletter
- George Morrow founds Microstuf
- The first issue of Dr. Dobb's Journal is published
- Ray Borrill founds Data Domain
- World Altair Computer Conference is held in Albuquerque, New Mexico
- Gary Kildall founds Intergalactic Digital Research (later Digital Research)
- Trenton (New Jersey) Computer Festival is held
- Chuck Grant and Mark Greenberg found Kentucky Fried Computers in Berkeley
- Midwest Area Computer Club conference is held
- Steve Leininger and Don French begin work on Radio Shack's first microcomputer
- Processor Technology's Sol computer appears on the cover of Popular Electronics
- Steve Wozniak demonstrates the Apple I at the Homebrew Computer Club
- Personal Computing Festival held in Atlantic City, New Jersey
- Harry Garland and Roger Melen name the S100 bus
- Ed Faber founds ComputerLand
- Mike Markkula visits Steve Jobs's garage
- Gary Kildall makes his first sale of CP/M to IMSAI
- Michael Shrayer creates Electric Pencil

1980

- Hewlett-Packard releases the HP-85
- Apple announces the Apple III
- Microsoft signs a consulting agreement with IBM to produce an operating system

1981

- Osborne Computer Corporation incorporates and a short time later introduces the Osborne 1, the first portable computer
- Steve Wozniak suffers a plane crash
- "Black Wednesday" firings occur at Apple
- Xerox releases the 8010 Star and the 820 computers
- IBM announces its Personal Computer
- Rod Canion, Jim Harris, and Bill Murto found Compaq in Houston, Texas

1982

- Apple announces the Lisa
- Vinod Khosla, Bill Joy, Andy Bechtolsheim, and Scott McNealy found Sun Microsystems
- Lotus Development Corp. announces Lotus 1-2-3
- DEC announces a line of personal computers

1990

- Tim Berners-Lee invents the World Wide Web by creating HTTP and HTML
- John Perry Barlow and Mitch Kapor found the Electronic Frontier Foundation

1991

- Disney signs a three-picture deal with Pixar, including a movie to be called Toy Story
- Apple and IBM sign a joint development agreement
- Novell buys Digital Research
- Sun developes Java
- Linus Torvalds releases Linux version of Unix operating system

1992

- Microsoft releases Windows 3.1

1993

- John Sculley departs Apple; Michael Spindler becomes CEO
- Eric Bina and Marc Andreessen develop the Mosaic Web browser

1994

- Gary Kildall dies
- Marc Andreessen and James Clark found Netscape

1995

- Netscape files its IPO
- Microsoft commits to the Internet
- Toy Story is released
- Pixar files its IPO, making Steve Jobs a billionaire

1980 1990 2001

1977

- Jonathan Rotenberg founds Boston Computer Society
- David Bunnell begins publishing Personal Computing
- Seymour Rubinstein joins IMSAI as software product marketing manager
- The first ComputerLand franchise store opens in Morristown, New Jersey, under the name ComputerShack
- Apple Computer opens its first offices in Cupertino, California
- Lee Felsenstein (with others) founds Community Memory
- The first West Coast Computer Faire is held in San Francisco, California
- Apple introduces the Apple II
- Commodore introduces the PET computer
- Ed Roberts sells MITS to Pertec
- Tandy/Radio Shack announces its first TRS-80 microcomputer
- Scott Adams founds Adventure International
- Bob Miner, Ed Oates, and Larry Ellison found Software Development Laboratories (later Oracle Corporation)

1978

- Apple introduces and begins shipping disk drives for the Apple II
- Apple initiates Lisa research and development projects
- Bill Joy and others develop BSD version of Unix operating system

1979

- IMSAI files for bankruptcy
- Steve Jobs visits Xerox PARC
- Processor Technology closes
- MicroPro releases WordStar
- Tandy/Radio Shack announces the TRS-80 Model II
- IMSAI closes its doors
- Personal Software introduces VisiCalc

1983

- IBM announces the PCjr
- Compaq begins shipping its Portable PC
- Tandy/Radio Shack announces its notebook TRS-80 Model 100
- John Sculley is Apple CEO
- Osborne Computer Corporation files Chapter 11 bankruptcy
- Philippe Kahn founds Borland International

1984

- Apple announces the Macintosh and runs its "1984" TV commercial during the Super Bowl
- Michael Dell starts Dell Computer
- Borland ships Turbo Pascal

1985

- Apple grants Microsoft a license to some of its graphical user interface (windowing) features
- Steve Jobs leaves Apple and founds NeXT Inc.
- Microsoft ships Windows 1.0

1986

- Steve Jobs purchases Pixar
- Microsoft ships Windows 2.0

1987

- National Semiconductor buys Fairchild Semiconductor

1988

- Apple sues Microsoft and Hewlett-Packard for copyright infringement
- NeXT unveils its first computer
- Pixar's Tin Toy is the first computer-animated film to receive an Academy Award for best animated short film

1996

- Gilbert Amelio replaces Michael Spindler as Apple CEO
- Apple buys NeXT Inc.
- Steve Jobs returns to Apple

1997

- Microsoft Internet Explorer passes Netscape Communicator in browser market share
- Steve Jobs takes control of Apple as interim CEO

1998

- Apple releases the iMac
- Compaq buys Digital Equipment Corporation
- U.S. Justice Department and the attorneys general of some twenty states file an antitrust suit against Microsoft
- Netscape makes the source code to its browser freely available
- America Online buys Netscape in a $4.2 billion stock swap
- Linux becomes the second-fastest-growing operating system

1999

- IBM CEO Lou Gerstner announces "the PC era is over," in terms of PCs driving customer buying decisions and being the primary platform for application development
- In response to market pressure from Intel, National Semiconductor bows out of the microchip business

FIRE IN
THE VALLEY

CHAPTER 1

TINDER FOR THE FIRE

*I think there is a world market
for maybe five computers.*

THOMAS WATSON
Chairman of IBM, 1943

Steam

*I wish to God these calculations
had been executed by steam.*

CHARLES BABBAGE
Nineteenth-century inventor, bewailing
the drudgery of hand calculation

THE PERSONAL COMPUTER SPRANG TO LIFE IN THE MID-1970S, BUT ITS historical roots reach back to the giant electronic "brains" of the 1950s and well before that to the "thinking" machines of nineteenth-century fiction. Can a machine really be programmed to think? This was a tantalizing and frightening thought for the intellectuals of a century or two ago.

Two past observers of the changes being wrought by science, the poets Lord Byron and Percy Bysshe Shelley, sat around one rainy summer day in Switzerland discussing artificial life and artificial thought, and wondered whether "the component parts of a creature might be manufactured, brought together, and endued with vital warmth." On hand to take mental notes of their conversation was Mary Wollstonecraft Shelley, Percy's wife and author of the novel *Frankenstein*. She expanded on the theme of artificial life in her famous novel. Mary Shelley's monster presented a genuinely disturbing allegory to readers of the Steam Age. The early part of the nineteenth century introduced the age of mechanization, and the main symbol of mechanical power was the steam engine. It was then that the steam engine was first mounted on wheels, and by 1825 the first public railway was in operation. Steam power held the same sort of mystique that electricity and atomic power would have in later generations. In 1833, when British mathematician, astronomer, and inventor Charles Babbage spoke of executing calculations by steam and then actually designed machines that he claimed could mechanize calculation, even mechanize thought, many saw him as a real-life Dr. Frankenstein. Although he never implemented his designs, Babbage was no idle dreamer; he worked on what he called his "Analytical Engine," drawing on the most advanced thinking in logic and mathematics, until his death in 1871. Babbage intended that the machine would free people from repetitive and boring mental tasks, just as the new machines of that era were freeing people from physical drudgery.

Babbage's colleague, patroness, and scientific chronicler was Augusta Ada Byron, daughter of Lord Byron, pupil of algebraist Augustus De Morgan, and the future Lady Lovelace. A writer herself and an amateur mathematician, Ada was able through her articles and papers to explain Babbage's ideas to the more educated members of the public and to potential patrons among the British nobility. She also wrote sets of instructions that told Babbage's Analytical Engine how to solve advanced mathematical problems. Because of this work, many regard Ada as the first computer programmer. The U.S. Department of Defense recognized her role in anticipating the discipline of computer programming by naming its Ada programming language after her in the early 1980s.

No doubt thinking of the public's fear of technology that Mary Shelley had alluded to in *Frankenstein*, Ada figured she'd better reassure her readers that Babbage's Analytical Engine did not actually think for itself. She assured them that the machine could only do what people instructed it to do. Nevertheless, the Analytical Engine was very close to being a true computer in the modern sense of the word, and "what people instructed it to do" presaged what we today call *computer programming*.

The Analytical Engine that Babbage designed would have been a huge, loud, outrageously expensive, gleaming steel and brass machine. Numbers were to be stored in registers composed of toothed wheels, and the adding and carrying over of numbers was done through cams and ratchets. It was supposed to be capable of storing up to 1000 numbers with a limit of 50 digits each. This internal storage capacity would be described today in terms of the machine's *memory* size. By modern standards, the Analytical Engine would have been absurdly slow—capable of less than one addition operation per second—but it actually had more memory than the first useful computers of the 1940s and 1950s and the early microcomputers of the 1970s.

Although he came up with three separate, highly detailed plans for his Analytical Engine, Babbage never constructed that machine, nor his simpler but also enormously ambitious Difference Engine. For over a century, it was thought that the machining technology of his time was simply inadequate to produce the thousands of precision parts that the machines required. Then in 1991, Doron Swade, senior curator of computing for the Science Museum of London, succeeded in constructing Babbage's Difference Engine using only the technology, techniques, and materials available to Babbage in his time. Swade's achievement revealed the great irony of Babbage's life. A century before anyone would attempt the task again, he had succeeded in designing a computer, his machines would in fact have worked, and could have been built. The reasons for Babbage's failure to carry out his dream all have to do with his inability to get sufficient funding, due largely to his propensity for alienating those in a position to provide that funding.

If Babbage had been less confrontational or if Lord Byron's daughter had been a wealthier woman, there may have been an enormous steam-engine computer belching clouds of logic over Dickens's London, balancing the books of some real-life Scrooge, or playing chess with Charles Darwin or another of Babbage's celebrated intellectual friends. But—as Mary Shelley had predicted—electricity was the force required to bring the thinking machine to life.

In the 1860s, the American logician Charles Sanders Peirce began lecturing on the work of George Boole, the fellow who gave his name to Boolean algebra. In doing so, Peirce brought symbolic logic to the United States and radically redefined and expanded Boole's algebra in the process. Boole had brought logic and mathematics together in a particularly cogent way, and Peirce probably knew more about Boolean algebra than anyone else in the mid-nineteenth century.

By the 1880s, Peirce figured out that Boolean algebra could be used as the model for electrical switching circuits. The true/false distinction of Boolean logic mapped exactly to the way current flowed through the on/off switches of complex electrical circuits. Logic, in other words, could be represented by electrical circuitry. Therefore, electrical calculating machines and logic machines could, in principle, be built. One of Peirce's students, Allan Marquand, actually designed, but did not build, an electric machine to perform simple logic operations in 1885.

The switching circuit (also know as a switching unit, switching organ, or relay organ—many names exist for it) that Peirce planned to use to implement Boolean algebra in electric circuitry is one of the fundamental elements of a computer. The unique feature of such a device is that it manipulates information, as opposed to electrical currents or locomotives.

The substitution of electrical circuitry for mechanical switches allowed for, among other benefits, smaller computing devices. In fact, the first electric logic machine ever made was a portable device built by Benjamin Burack, which he designed to be carried in a briefcase. Burack's logic machine, built in 1936, could process statements made in the form of syllogisms. For example, given "All men are mortal, Socrates is a man," it would then accept "Socrates is mortal" and reject "Socrates is a woman." Such erroneous deductions closed circuits and lit up the machine's warning lights, indicating the kind of logical error committed.

Burack's device was a special-purpose machine with limited capabilities. Nevertheless, most of the special-purpose computing devices built around that time dealt with only numbers, and not logic. Decades earlier, Herman Hollerith had designed a tabulating machine that was used to compute the U.S. census of 1890. Hollerith's company was eventually absorbed by an enterprise that came to be called the International Business Machines Corporation. By the late 1920s, IBM was making money selling special-purpose calculating machines to businesses, enabling those businesses to automate routine numerical tasks. The IBM machines weren't computers, nor were they logic machines like Burack's, but simply big, glorified calculators.

Spurred by Claude Shannon's Ph.D. thesis at MIT, which explained how electrical switching circuits could be used to model Boolean logic (as Peirce had demonstrated 50 years earlier), IBM executives agreed in the 1930s to finance a large computing machine based on electromechanical relays. Although they later regretted it, IBM executives gave Howard Aiken, a Harvard professor, the then-huge sum of $500,000 to develop the Mark I, a calculating device largely inspired by Babbage's Analytical Engine. Babbage, though, had designed a purely mechanical machine. The Mark I, by comparison, was an electro-mechanical machine with electrical relays serving as the switching units and banks of relays serving as space for number storage. Calculation was a noisy affair; the electrical relays clacked open and shut incessantly. When the Mark I was completed in 1944, it was widely hailed as the electronic brain of science fiction fame made real. But IBM executives were less than pleased when, as they saw it, Aiken failed to acknowledge IBM's contribution at the unveiling of the Mark I. And IBM had other reasons to regret its investment. Even before work began on the Mark I device, technological developments elsewhere had made it obsolete.

Electricity was making way for the emergence of electronics. Just as others had earlier replaced Babbage's steam-driven wheels and cogs with electrical relays, John Atanasoff, a professor of mathematics and physics at Iowa State College, saw how electronics could replace the relays. Shortly before the American entry into World War II, Atanasoff, with the help of Clifford Berry, designed the ABC, the Atanasoff-Berry Computer, a device whose switching units were to be vacuum tubes rather than relays. This substitution was an important technological advance. Vacuum tube machines could, in principle, do calculations considerably faster and more efficiently than relay machines. The ABC, like Babbage's Analytical Engine, was never completed, probably because Atanasoff got less than $7,000 in grant money to build it. Atanasoff and Berry did assemble a simple prototype, a mass of wires and tubes that resembled a primitive desk calculator. But by using tubes as switching elements, Atanasoff greatly advanced the development of the computer. The added efficiency of vacuum tubes over relay switches would make the computer a reality.

The vacuum tube is a glass tube with the air removed. Thomas Edison discovered that electricity travels through the vacuum under certain conditions, and Lee De Forest turned vacuum tubes into electrical switches using this "Edison effect." In the 1950s, vacuum tubes were used extensively in electronic devices from televisions to computers. Today you still see them in the form of computer displays and television picture tubes.

By the 1930s, the advent of computing machines was apparent. It also seemed that computers were destined to be huge and expensive special-purpose devices. It took decades before they became much smaller and cheaper, but they were already on their way to becoming more than special-purpose machines.

It was British mathematician Alan Turing who envisioned a machine designed for no other purpose than to read coded instructions for any describable task and to follow the instructions to complete the task: because it could perform any task described in the instructions, such a machine would be a true general-purpose device. Within a decade, Turing's visionary idea became reality. The instructions became programs, and his concept, in the hands of another mathematician, John Von Neumann, became the general-purpose computer.

In 1943, at the Moore School of Engineering in Philadelphia, John Mauchley and J. Presper Eckert proposed the idea for and began supervising the building of ENIAC, which was to be the first all-electronic digital computer. With the exception of the peripheral machinery it needed for information input and output, ENIAC was purely a vacuum tube machine, perhaps based in part on ideas Mauchley hatched during a visit to John Atanasoff. Mauchley and Eckert attracted a number of bright mathematicians to the ENIAC project, including John Von Neumann. Von Neumann became involved with the project and made various—and variously reported—contributions to building the ENIAC, and in addition offered an outline for a more sophisticated machine called EDVAC. Because of Von Neumann, the emphasis at the Moore School swung from technology to logic. He saw EDVAC as more than a calculating device. He felt that it should be able to perform logical as well as arithmetic operations and be able to operate on coded symbols. Its instructions for operating on—and for interpreting—the symbols should themselves be symbols that are coded into the machine and operated on. This was the last fundamental insight in the conception of the modern computer. By specifying that EDVAC should be programmable by instructions that were themselves fed to the machine as data, Von Neumann created the specifications for the stored-program computer.

After World War II, Von Neumann proposed a method for turning ENIAC into a programmable computer like EDVAC, and Adele Goldstine wrote the 55-operation language that made the machine easier to operate. After that, no one ever again used ENIAC in its original mode of operation.

When development on ENIAC was finished in early 1946, it ran 1000 times faster than its electromechanical counterparts. But electronic or not, it still made noise. ENIAC was a roomful of clanking teletype machines and whirring tape drives, in addition to the walls of relatively silent electronic circuitry. It had 20,000 switching units, weighed 30 tons, and dissipated 150,000 watts of energy. Despite all that electrical power, ENIAC could handle only 20 numbers of 10 decimal digits each at a time. But even before construction was completed on ENIAC, it was put to significant use. In 1945, ENIAC performed calculations used in the atomic bomb testing at Los Alamos, New Mexico.

A new industry emerged after World War II. Building computers became a business, and by the very nature of the equipment, it became a *big* business. With the help of engineers John Mauchley and J. Presper Eckert, who were fresh from their ENIAC triumph, the Remington Typewriter Company became Sperry Univac. For a few years, the name "Univac" was synonymous with computers, just as the name Kleenex came to be synonymous with facial tissues. Sperry Univac had some formidable competition. IBM executives recovered from the disappointment of the Mark I and began building general-purpose computers. The two companies developed distinctive operating styles: IBM was the land of blue pinstripe suits, whereas the halls of Sperry Univac were filled with young academics in sneakers. Whether because of its image or business savvy, before long IBM took the industry leader position away from Sperry Univac.

Soon, most computers were IBM machines, and the company's share of the market continued to grow.

Meanwhile, the entire market grew. Other companies emerged, typically under the guidance of engineers who had been trained at IBM or Sperry Univac. Control Data Corporation in Minneapolis spun off from IBM, and soon computers were made by Honeywell, Burroughs, General Electric, RCA, and NCR. Within a decade, eight companies came to dominate the growing computer market, but with IBM so far ahead of the others in revenues, they were often referred to as Snow White (IBM) and the Seven Dwarfs. But IBM and the other seven were about to be taught a lesson by some brash upstarts. A new kind of computer emerged in the 1960s—smaller, cheaper, and referred to as, in imitation of the popular miniskirt, the minicomputer. Among the most significant companies producing smaller computers were Digital Equipment Corporation (DEC) in the Boston area and Hewlett-Packard (HP) in Palo Alto, California.

The computers these companies were building were general-purpose machines in the Turing–Von Neumann sense, and they were getting more compact, more efficient, and more powerful. Soon, another technological breakthrough would allow even more impressive advances in computer power, efficiency, and miniaturization.

The Breakthrough

Inventing the transistor meant
the fulfillment of a dream.

Ernest Braun and Stuart MacDonald
Revolution in Miniature, 1978

IN THE 1940S, THE SWITCHING UNITS IN COMPUTERS WERE MECHANICAL relays that constantly opened and closed, clattering away like freight trains. In the 1950s, vacuum tubes took the place of mechanical relays. But tubes were a technological dead end. They could be made only just so small, and because they generated heat, they had to be spaced a certain distance apart from one another. As a result, tubes afflicted the early computers with a sort of structural elephantiasis. But by 1960, physicists working on solid-state elements introduced an entirely new component into the mix. The device that consigned the vacuum tube to the back-alley bin was the transistor, a tiny, seemingly inert slice of crystal with interesting electrical properties. The transistor was immediately recognized as a revolutionary development. In fact, John Bardeen, Walter Brattain, and William Shockley shared the 1956 Nobel Prize in physics for their work on the innovation.

The transistor was significant for more than merely making another bit of technology obsolete. Resulting from a series of experiments in the application of quantum physics, transistors changed the computer from a "giant electronic brain" that was the exclusive domain of engineers and scientists to a commodity that could be purchased like a television set. The transistor was the technological breakthrough that made both the minicomputers of the 1960s and the personal computer revolution of the 1970s possible.

Bardeen and Brattain introduced "the major invention of the century" in 1947, two days before Christmas. To understand the real significance of the device that came into existence that winter day in Murray Hill, New Jersey, you have to look back to research done years before.

In the 1940s, Bardeen and Shockley were working in apparently unrelated fields. Experiments in quantum physics resulted in some odd predictions (which were later born out) about the behavior that chemical element crystals, such as germanium and silicon, would display in an electrical field. These crystals could not be classified as either insulators or conductors, so they were simply called *semiconductors*. These semiconductors had one property that particularly fascinated electrical engineers: a semiconductor crystal could be made to conduct electricity in one direction, but not in the other. Engineers put this discovery to practical use. Tiny slivers of such crystals were used to rectify electrical current, that is, to turn alternating current into direct current. Early radios, called *crystal sets,* were the first commercial products to use these crystal rectifiers.

The crystal rectifier was a curious item, a slice of mineral material that did useful work but had no moving parts. The term for such a seemingly inert tool is *solid-state device.* But the rectifier knew only one trick. A different device soon replaced it almost entirely: Lee De Forest's *triode,* the vacuum tube that made radios glow. The triode was more versatile than the crystal rectifier; it could both amplify a current passing through it and use a weak secondary current to alter a strong current passing from one of its poles to the other. This capability to change one current by means of another was essential to the EDVAC-type computer design. At the time, though, some researchers thought the triode's main application lay in telephone switching circuits.

Naturally, people at AT&T, and especially at its research branch Bell Labs, became interested in the triode. William Shockley was working for Bell Labs at the time and was involved, as were other researchers, in a particular area of semiconductor research: the effect impurities had on semiconductor crystals. Trace amounts of other substances could provide the extra electrons needed to carry electrical current.

Shockley convinced Bell Labs to let him put together a team to study this development. He was convinced he could create a solid-state amplifier. His team consisted of experimental scientist Walter Brattain and theoretician John Bardeen. For some time the group's efforts went nowhere. Similar research was underway at Purdue University in Lafayette, Indiana, and the Bell group kept close tabs on the work going on there. Bardeen finally solved the puzzle. An inhibiting effect on the surface of the crystal, he said, was interfering with the flow of current. Brattain conducted the experiment that proved Bardeen right, and on December 23, 1947, the transistor was born. The transistor did everything the vacuum tube did, and it did it better. It was smaller, it didn't generate as much heat, and it didn't burn out. Most important, the functions performed by several transistors could be incorporated into a single semiconductor device. Researchers quickly set about the task of constructing these sophisticated semiconductors. Because these devices integrated a number of transistors into a more complex circuit, they were called *integrated circuits,* or *ICs.* Because they essentially were tiny slivers of silicon, they also came to be called *chips.*

Building ICs was a complicated and expensive process, and an entire industry devoted to making them soon sprang up. The first companies to begin producing chips commercially were the existing electronics companies. One very early start-up company was Shockley Semiconductor, which William Shockley founded in 1955 in his hometown of Palo Alto. Shockley's firm employed many of the world's best semiconductor people around at the time. Some of those folks didn't stay with the company for long. Shockley Semiconductor spawned Fairchild Semiconductor, and Fairchild spawned a number of other companies.

A decade after Fairchild was formed, virtually every semiconductor company in existence could boast a large number of former Fairchild employees. Even the big electronics companies, such as Motorola, that entered the semiconductor industry in the 1960s employed ex-Fairchild engineers. And except for some notable exceptions—Motorola, Texas Instruments, and RCA—most of the semiconductor companies were located within a few miles of Shockley's operation in Palo Alto in the Santa Clara Valley. By this time, nearly all semiconductors were made of silicon, and soon the area came to be known as Silicon Valley. The semiconductor industry grew with amazing speed, and the size and price of its products shrank at the same pace. Competition was fierce. At first, little demand existed for highly complex ICs outside of the military and aerospace industries. Certain kinds of ICs, though, were in common use in large mainframe computers and minicomputers. Of paramount importance were memory chips—ICs that could store data and retain them as long as they were fed power.

Memory chips at the time embodied the functions of hundreds of transistors. Other ICs weren't designed to retain the data that flowed through them, but instead were programmed to change the data in certain ways in order to perform simple arithmetic or logic operations on it. Then, in the early 1970s, the runaway demand for electronic calculators led to the creation of a new and considerably more powerful computer chip.

Critical Mass

*The microprocessor has brought
electronics into a new era. It is altering
the structure of our society.*

ROBERT NOYCE AND MARCIAN HOFF, JR.
**"History of Microprocessor Development
at Intel,"** *IEEE Micro*, **1981**

IN EARLY 1969, INTEL DEVELOPMENT CORPORATION, A SILICON VALLEY
semiconductor manufacturer, received a commission from a Japanese calculator company called Busicom to produce chips for a line of
its calculators. Intel had the credentials: it was a Fairchild spinoff, and
its president, Robert Noyce, had helped invent the integrated circuit.
Although Intel had opened its doors for business only a few months
earlier, the company was growing as fast as the semiconductor industry.

An engineer named Marcian "Ted" Hoff had joined Intel a few
months earlier as its twelfth employee, and when he began working on
the Busicom job, the company already employed 200 people. Hoff was
fresh from academia. After earning a Ph.D., he continued as a
researcher at Stanford University's Electrical Engineering department,
where his research on the design of semiconductor memory chips led
to several patents and to the job at Intel. Noyce felt that Intel should
produce semiconductor memory chips and nothing else, and he had
hired Hoff to dream up applications for these memory chips. But when
Busicom proposed the idea for calculator chips, Noyce allowed that
taking a custom job while the company was building up its memory
business wouldn't hurt.

Hoff was sent to meet with the Japanese engineers who came to discuss what Busicom had envisioned. Because Hoff had a flight to Tahiti scheduled for that evening, the first meeting with the engineers was brief. The trip evidently gave him time for contemplation, because he returned from paradise with some firm ideas about the job. In particular, he was annoyed that the Busicom calculator would cost almost as much as a minicomputer. Minicomputers had become relatively inexpensive, and research laboratories all over the country were buying them. It was not uncommon to find two or three minicomputers in a university's psychology or physics department. Hoff had worked with DEC's new PDP-8 computer, one of the smallest and cheapest of the lot, and found that it had a very simple internal setup. Hoff knew that the PDP-8, a computer, could do everything the proposed Busicom calculator could do and more for almost the same price. To Ted Hoff, this was an affront to common sense.

Hoff asked the Intel bosses why people should pay the price of a computer for something that had a fraction of the capacity. The question revealed his academic bias and his naivete about marketing: *he* would rather have a computer than a calculator, so he figured surely everyone else would, too. The marketing people patiently explained that it was a matter of packaging. If someone wanted to do only calculations, they didn't want to have to fire up a computer to run a calculator program. Besides, most people, even scientists, were intimidated by computers. A calculator was just a calculator from the moment you turned it on. A computer was an instrument from the Twilight Zone. Hoff could follow the reasoning, but nevertheless had a hard time swallowing the idea of building a special-purpose device when a general-purpose one was just as easy—and no more expensive—to build. Besides, he thought, a general-purpose design would make the project more interesting. He proposed to the Japanese engineers a revised design loosely based on the PDP-8.

The design's comparison to the PDP-8 computer was only partly applicable. Hoff was proposing a set of chips, not an entire computer. But one of those chips would be critically important in several ways. First, it would be dense. Chips at the time contained no more than 1000 features—the equivalent of 1000 transistors—but this chip would at least double that number. In addition, this chip would, like any IC, accept input signals and produce output signals. But whereas these signals would represent numbers in a simple arithmetic chip and logical values (true or false) in a logic chip, the signals entering and leaving Hoff's chip would form a set of instructions for the IC.

In short, the chip could run programs. The customers were asking for a calculator chip, but Hoff was designing an IC EDVAC, a true general-purpose computing device on a sliver of silicon. A computer on a chip. Although Hoff's design resembled a very simple computer, it left out some computer essentials, such as memory and peripherals for human input and output. The term that evolved to describe such a device was *microprocessor,* and microprocessors were general-purpose devices specifically because of their programmability.

Because the Intel microprocessor used the stored-program concept, the calculator manufacturers could make the microprocessor act like any kind of calculator they wanted. At any rate, that was what Hoff had in mind. He was sure it was possible, and just as sure that it was the right approach. But the Japanese engineers weren't impressed. Frustrated, Hoff sought out Noyce, who encouraged him to proceed anyway, and when chip designer Stan Mazor left Fairchild to go to Intel, Hoff and Mazor set to work on the design for the chip. At that point, Hoff and Mazor had not actually produced an IC. A semiconductor design specialist would still have to transform the design into a two-dimensional blueprint, and this pattern would have to be etched into a slice of silicon crystal. These later stages in the chip's development cost money, so Intel did not intend to move beyond the logic-design stage without talking further with its customers. In October 1969, skeptical Busicom representatives flew in from Japan to discuss the Intel project. The Japanese engineers presented their requirements, and in turn Hoff presented his and Mazor's design. Despite the fact that the requirements and design did not quite match, after some discussion Busicom decided to accept the Intel design for the chip. The deal gave Busicom an exclusive contract for the chips; not the best deal for Intel, but at least they were going ahead on the project.

Hoff was relieved to have the go-ahead. They called the chip the 4004, which was the approximate number of transistors the single device replaced and an indication of its complexity.

Hoff wasn't the only person ever to have thought of building a computer on a chip, but he was the first to launch a project that actually got carried out. Along the way, he and Mazor solved a number of design problems and fleshed out the idea of the microprocessor more fully. But there was a big distance between planning and execution.

Leslie Vadasz, the head of a chip-design group at Intel, knew who he wanted to implement the design: Federico Faggin. Faggin was a talented chip designer who had worked with Vadasz at Fairchild and had earlier built a computer for Olivetti in Italy. The problem was, Faggin didn't work at Intel. Worse, he *couldn't* work at Intel, at least not right away: in the United States on a work visa, he was constrained in his ability to change jobs and still retain his visa. The earliest he would be available was the following spring.

When Faggin came to Intel in April of 1970, he was immediately assigned to implement the 4004 design. Masatoshi Shima, an engineer for Busicom, was due to arrive to examine and approve the final design, and Faggin would set to work turning it into silicon.

Unfortunately, the design was far from complete. Hoff and Mazor had completed the instruction set for the device and an overall design, but the necessary detailed design was nonexistent. Shima understood immediately that the "design" was little more than a collection of ideas. "This is just idea!" he shouted at Faggin. "This is nothing! I came here to check, but there is nothing to check!"

Faggin confessed that he had only arrived recently, and that he was going to have to complete the design before starting the implementation. With help from Mazor and Shima, who extended his stay to six months, he did the job in a remarkably short time, working 12- to 16-hour days. Since he was doing something no one had ever done before, he found himself having to invent techniques to get the job done.

In February 1971, Faggin delivered working kits to Busicom, including the 4004 microprocessor and eight other chips necessary to make the calculator work. It was a breakthrough, but its value was more in what it signified than in what it actually delivered.

On the one hand, this new thing, the microprocessor, was nothing more than an extension of the IC chips for arithmetic and logic that semiconductor manufacturers had been making for years. The microprocessor merely crammed more functional capability onto one chip. Then again, there were so many functions that the microprocessor could perform, and they were integrated with each other so closely, that using the device required learning a new language, albeit a simple one. The instruction set of the 4004, for all intents and purposes, constituted a programming language.

Today's microprocessors are more complex and powerful than the roomful of circuitry that constituted a computer in 1950. The 4004 chip that Hoff conceived in 1969 was a crude first step toward something that Hoff, Noyce, and Intel management could scarcely anticipate. The 8008 chip that Intel produced two years later was the second step. The 8008 microprocessor was developed for a company then called CTC—Computer Terminal Corporation—and later called Data-Point. CTC had a technically sophisticated computer terminal and wanted some chips designed to give it additional functions.

Once again, Hoff presented a grander vision of how an existing product could be used. He proposed a single-chip implementation of the control circuitry that replaced all of its internal electronics with a single integrated circuit. Hoff and Faggin were interested in the 8008 project partly because the exclusive deal for the 4004 kept that chip tied up. Faggin, who was doing lab work with electronic test equipment, saw the 4004 as an ideal tool for controlling test equipment, but the Busicom deal prevented that.

Because Busicom had exclusive rights to the 4004, Hoff felt that perhaps this new 8008 terminal chip could be marketed and used with testers. The 4004 had drawbacks. It operated on only four binary digits at a time. This significantly limited its computing power because it couldn't even handle a piece of data the size of a single character in one operation. The new 8008 could. Although another engineer was initially assigned to it, Faggin was soon put in charge of making the 8008 a reality, and by March 1972 Intel was producing working 8008 chips.

Before this happened, though, CTC executives lost interest in the project. Intel now found it had invested a great deal of time and effort in two highly complex and expensive products, the 4004 and 8008, with no mass market for either of them. As competition intensified in the calculator business, Busicom asked Intel to drop the price on the 4004 in order to keep its contract. "For God's sake," Hoff urged Noyce, "get us the right to sell these chips to other people." Noyce did. But possession of that right, it turned out, was no guarantee that Intel would ever exercise it.

Intel's marketing department was cool to the idea of releasing the chips to the general engineering public. Intel had been formed to produce memory chips, which were easy to use and were sold in volume like razor blades. Microprocessors, because the customer had to learn how to use them, presented enormous customer support problems for the young company. Hoff countered with ideas for new microprocessor applications that no one had thought of yet. For instance, an elevator controller could be built around a chip. Moreover, he argued, the processor would save money: it could replace a number of simpler chips, as Hoff had done in his design for the 8008. Engineers would make the effort to design the microprocessor into their products. Hoff knew he himself would.

Hoff's persistence finally paid off when Intel hired advertising man Regis McKenna to promote the product in a fall 1971 issue of *Electronic News*. "Announcing a new era in integrated electronics: a microprogrammable computer on a chip," the ad read. A computer on a chip? Technically the claim was puffery, but when visitors to an electronics show that fall read the product specifications for the 4004, they were duly impressed by the chip's programmability. And in one sense McKenna's ad was correct: the 4004 (and the 8008) incorporated the essential decision-making power of a computer.

Meanwhile, Texas Instruments had picked up the CTC contract and also delivered a microprocessor. (TI was pursuing the microprocessor market as aggressively as Intel; Gary Boone of TI had in fact just filed a patent application for something called a single-chip computer.) Three different microprocessors now existed. Intel's marketing department had been right about the amount of customer support the microprocessors demanded. For instance, users needed documentation on the operations the chips performed, the "language" they recognized, the voltage they used, the amount of heat they dissipated, and a host of other things. Someone had to write the information manuals, and at Intel the job was given to an engineer named Adam Osborne, who would later play a very different part in making computers personal.

The microprocessor software formed another kind of essential customer support. A disadvantage with a general-purpose computer or processor is that it does nothing without programs. The chips, as general-purpose processors, needed programs, the instructions that would tell them what to do. To create these programs, Intel first assembled an entire computer around each of its two microprocessor chips. These computers were not commercial products but instead were development systems—tools to help write programs for the processor. They were also, although no one used this term at the time, microcomputers.

One of the first people to begin developing these programs was Gary Kildall, a professor at the Naval Postgraduate School located down the coast from Silicon Valley in Pacific Grove, California. Like Osborne, Kildall would be an important figure in the development of the personal computer. In late 1972, Kildall already had written a simple language for the 4004. It was basically a program that translated cryptic commands into the more cryptic 1s and 0s that formed the internal instruction set of the microprocessor. Although written for the 4004, the program actually ran on a large IBM 360 computer. With this program, one could type commands on an IBM keyboard and generate a file of 4004 instructions that could then be sent to a 4004, if one were somehow connected to the IBM machine. Connecting the 4004 to anything at all was hardly a trivial task. The microprocessor had to be plugged into a specially designed circuit board that was equipped with connections to other chips and to devices such as a Teletype machine. The Intel development systems had been created for just this type of problem solving. Naturally, Kildall was drawn to the microcomputer lab at Intel where the development systems were housed.

Eventually, Kildall contracted with Intel to implement a language for the chip manufacturer. PL/M (Programming Language for Microcomputers) would be a so-called high-level language, in contrast to the low-level machine language that was made up of the instruction set of the microprocessor. With PL/M, one could write a program once and have it run on a 4004 processor, an 8008, or on future processors Intel might produce. This would speed up the programming process.

But writing the language was no simple task. To understand why, you have to think about how computer languages operate. A computer language is a set of commands a computer can recognize. The computer only responds to that fixed set of commands incorporated into its circuitry or etched into its chips. Implementing a language requires creating a program that will translate the sorts of commands a user can understand into commands the machine can use.

The microprocessors not only were physically tiny, but also had a limited logic to work with. They got by with a minimum amount of smarts, and therefore were beastly hard to program. It was difficult to design any language for them, let alone a high-level language like PL/M. A friend and coworker of Kildall's later explained the choice, saying that Gary Kildall wrote PL/M largely because it was a difficult task. Like many important programmers and designers before him and since, Kildall was in it primarily for the intellectual challenge. But the most significant piece of software Kildall developed at that time was much simpler in its design.

Intel's early microcomputers used paper tape to store information. Therefore, programs had to enable a computer to control the paper tape reader or paper punch automatically, accept the data electronically as the information streamed in from the tape, store and locate the data in memory, and feed the data out to the paper tape punch. The computer also had to be able to manipulate data in memory, and keep track of which spots were available for data storage and which were in use at any given moment. Most programmers don't want to have to think about such picayune details every time they write a program. Large computers automatically take care of these tasks through the use of a program called an operating system. For programmers writing in a mainframe language, the operating system is a given; it's a part of the way the machine works and an integral feature of the computing environment. But Kildall was working with a primordial setup. At Intel, Kildall wrote parts of an operating system that was very simple and compact because it had to operate on a microprocessor. Eventually, that operating system evolved into something Kildall called CP/M. When Kildall asked the Intel executives if they had any objections to his marketing CP/M on his own, they simply shrugged and said go ahead. They had no plans to sell it themselves. CP/M made Kildall a fortune.

By building microprocessors, Intel had already ventured beyond its charter of building memory chips. Although the company was not about to retreat from that enterprise, Intel met solid resistance to moving even farther afield. It was true that there'd been talk about designing machines around microprocessors, and even about using a microprocessor as the main component in a small computer. But microprocessor-controlled computers seemed to have marginal sales potential at best.

Wristwatches, now that was where microprocessors would find their chief market, Noyce thought. The Intel executives discussed other possible applications, mostly embedded systems such as microprocessor-controlled ovens, stereos, and automobiles. But it would be up to the customers to build the ovens, stereos, cars; Intel would only sell the chips. There was a virtual mandate at Intel against making products that could be seen as competing against its own customers.

Intel was an exciting place to work in 1972. Its executives felt that Intel was at the center of things and that the microprocessor industry was going to soar. It seemed obvious to Kildall, Mike Markkula, the marketing manager for memory chips, and others that the innovative designers of microprocessors should be working at the semiconductor companies. They decided to stick to putting logic on slivers of silicon and to leave the building (and programming) of computers to the mainframe and minicomputer companies. When the minicomputer companies didn't take up the challenge, Markkula, Kildall, and Osborne thought better of their decision to stick to the chip business. Within the following decade, each of them would create a multimillion-dollar personal computer or personal computer software company of his own.

Breakout

We [Digital Equipment Corporation] could have come out with a personal computer in January 1975. If we had taken that prototype, most of which was proven stuff, the PDP-8A could have been developed and put in production in that seven- or eight-month period.

DAVID AHL
Former DEC employee and founder of pioneer computer magazine *Creative Computing*

BY 1970, THERE EXISTED TWO DISTINCT KINDS OF COMPUTERS AND two kinds of companies selling them. The room-sized mainframe computers were built by IBM, Control Data Corporation, Honeywell, and the other dwarfs. These machines were designed by an entire generation of engineers, cost hundreds of thousands of dollars, and were often custom-built one at a time. Then you had the minicomputers built by such companies as DEC and Hewlett-Packard. Relatively cheap and compact, these machines were built in larger quantities than the mainframes and sold primarily to scientific laboratories and businesses. The typical minicomputer cost one-tenth as much as a mainframe and took up no more space than a bookshelf. Minicomputers incorporated semiconductor devices, which reduced the size of the machine. The mainframes also used semiconductor components, but they generally used them to create even more powerful machines that were no smaller in size.

Semiconductor tools such as the Intel 4004 were also beginning to be used to control peripheral devices including printers and tape drives, but it was obvious to everyone concerned that the chips could also be used to shrink the computer and make it cheaper. The mainframe computer and minicomputer companies had the money, expertise, and unequaled opportunity to place computers in the hands of nearly everyone. It didn't take a visionary to see a personal-sized computer that could fit on a desktop or in a briefcase or in a shirt pocket at the end of the path toward increased miniaturization. In the late 1960s and early 1970s, the major players among mainframe and minicomputer companies seemed the most logical candidates for producing a personal computer. It was obvious that computer development was headed in that direction.

Ever since the 1930s when Benjamin Burack was developing his "logic machine," people had been building desktop and briefcase-sized machines that performed computer-like functions. Computer company engineers and designers at semiconductor companies foresaw a continuing trend of components becoming increasingly cheaper, faster, and smaller year after year. The indicators pointed undoubtedly to the development of a small personal computer by, most likely, a minicomputer company. It was only logical, but it didn't happen that way. Every one of the existing computer companies passed up the chance to bring computers into the home and on top of every work desk. The next generation of computers, the microcomputer, was created entirely by individual entrepreneurs working outside the established corporations. It wasn't that the idea of a personal computer had never occurred to the decision makers at the major computer companies. Eager engineers at some of those firms offered detailed proposals for building microcomputers and even working prototypes, but the proposals were rejected and the prototypes shelved. In some cases, work actually commenced on personal computer projects, but eventually they, too, were allowed to wither and die. The mainframe companies apparently thought that no market existed for low-cost, personal computers, and even if there were such a market, they figured it was the minicomputer companies who would exploit it. They were wrong.

Take Hewlett-Packard, a company that grew up in the Silicon Valley and was producing everything from mainframe computers to pocket calculators. Senior engineers at HP studied and eventually spurned a design offered by one of their employees, an engineer without a degree named Stephen Wozniak. In rejecting his design, the HP engineers acknowledged that Wozniak's computer worked and could be built cheaply, but they told him it was not a product for HP. Wozniak eventually gave up on his employers and built his computers out of a garage in a start-up enterprise called Apple.

Likewise, Robert Albrecht, who worked for Control Data Corporation (CDC) in Minneapolis during the early 1960s, quit in frustration over the company's unwillingness to even consider looking into the personal computer market. After leaving CDC, he moved to the San Francisco Bay Area and established himself as a sort of computer guru. Albrecht was interested in exploring ways computers could be used as educational aids. He produced what could be called the first publication on personal computing and spread information on how individuals could learn about and use computers. The prime example of an established computer company that failed to explore the new technology was Digital Equipment Corporation. With annual sales close to a billion dollars by 1974, DEC was the first and the largest of the minicomputer companies. DEC made some of the most compact computers available at the time. The PDP-8, which had inspired Ted Hoff to design the 4004, was the closest thing to a personal computer one could find.

One version of the PDP-8 was so small that sales reps routinely carried it in the trunks of their cars and set it up at the customer's site. In that sense, it was one of the first portable computers. DEC could have been the company that created the personal computer. The story of its failure to seize that opportunity gives some indication of the mentality in computer company boardrooms during the early 1970s.

For DEC employee David Ahl, the story of DEC's failure to capitalize on an emerging industry began when he was hired as a marketing consultant in 1969. By that time, he had picked up degrees in electrical engineering and business administration and was finishing up his Ph.D. in educational psychology. Ahl came to DEC to develop its educational products line, the first product line at DEC to be defined in terms of its potential users rather than its hardware. Responding to the recession of 1973, DEC cut back on educational product development. Ahl protested the cuts and was fired.

He was rehired into a division of the company dedicated to developing new products, that is, new hardware. He soon became entirely caught up in building a computer that was smaller than any yet built. Ahl's group didn't know what to call the machine, but if it had taken off, it certainly would have qualified as a personal computer. Ahl's interests had grown somewhat incompatible with the DEC mindset. DEC viewed computers as an industrial product. "Like pig iron. DEC was interested in pushing out iron," Ahl later recalled. When he was working in DEC's educational division, Ahl wrote a newsletter that regularly published instructions for playing computer games. After he left and rejoined DEC, Ahl talked the company into publishing a book he had put together, *BASIC Computer Games.* He was beginning to view the computer as an individual educational tool, and games seemed a natural part of the package.

DEC wasn't set up to sell computers to individuals, but Ahl had learned something about the market for personal computers while working in DEC's educational products division. The division would occasionally receive requests from doctors or engineers or other professionals who wanted a computer to manage their practices. Some of DEC's machines were actually cheap enough to sell to professionals, but the company wasn't prepared to handle such requests. A big difference existed between selling to individuals and selling to an organization that could hire engineers and programmers to maintain a computer system and could afford to buy technical support from DEC. The company was not ready to handle customer support for individuals.

The team Ahl was working with intended that this new product bring computers into new markets such as schools. Although its price tag would keep it out of the reach of most households, Ahl saw schools as the wedge to get the machines into the hands of individuals, specifically schoolkids. The machines could be sold in large quantities to schools to be used individually by students. Ahl figured that Heath, a company specializing in electronics hobby equipment, would be willing to build a kit version of the DEC, which would lower the price even more.

The new computer was built into a DEC terminal, inside of which circuit boards thick with semiconductor devices were jammed around the base of the tube. The designers had packed every square inch of the terminal case with electronics. The computer was no larger than a television set, although heavier. Ahl had not designed the device, but he felt as protective of it as if it were his own child.

Ahl presented his plan for marketing personal computers at a meeting of DEC's Operations Committee. Kenneth Olsen, the president of the company and regarded throughout the industry as one of its wisest executives, was there along with some vice presidents and a few outside investors. As Ahl later recalled, the board was polite but not enthusiastic about the project, although the engineers seemed interested. After some tense moments, Olsen said that he could see no reason why anyone would want a home computer.

Ahl's heart sank. Although the board had not actually rejected the plan, he knew that without Olsen's support it would fail.

Ahl was now utterly frustrated. He had been getting calls from executive search firms offering him jobs, and told himself the next time a headhunter called he would accept the offer. Ahl, like Wozniak and Albrecht and many others, had walked out the door and into a revolution.

---◆---

Hackers

*I swore off computers for about a year
and a half—the end of the ninth grade
and all of the tenth. I tried to be
normal, the best I could.*

BILL GATES
Cofounder of Microsoft Corporation

Had the personal computer revolution waited for action from the mainframe computer and minicomputer companies, the PC might still be a thing of the future. But there were those who would not wait patiently for something to happen, and their very impatience led them to take steps toward creating a revolution of their own. Some of those revolutionaries were incredibly young. In the late 1960s, before David Ahl lost all patience with DEC, Paul Allen and his school friends at Seattle's private Lakeside High were working at a company called Computer Center Corporation (or "C Cubed" to Allen and his friends). The boys volunteered their time to help find bugs in the work of DEC system programmers. They learned fast and were getting a little cocky. Soon they were adding touches of their own to make the programs run faster. Bill Gates wasn't shy about criticizing certain DEC programmers, and pointed out those who repeatedly made the same mistakes.

Perhaps Gates got too cocky. Certainly he was exhilarated by the sense of power he got from controlling those giant computers. One day, he began experimenting with the computer security systems. On time-sharing computer systems, such as the DEC TOPS-10 system that Gates knew well, many users shared the same machine and used it

29

simultaneously. Safeguards had to be built into the systems to prevent one user from invading another user's data files or "crashing" a program—thereby causing it to fail and terminate—or worse yet, crashing the operating system and bringing the whole computer system to a halt. Gates learned how to invade the DEC TOPS-10 system and later other systems. He became a *hacker,* an expert in the underground art of subverting computer system security. His baby face and bubbly manner masked a very clever and determined young man who could, by typing just 14 characters on a terminal, bring an entire TOPS-10 operating system to its knees. He grew into a master of electronic mischief. Hacking brought Gates fame in certain circles, but it also brought him grief.

After learning how easily he could crash the DEC operating system, Gates cast about for bigger challenges. The DEC system had no human operator and could be breached without anyone noticing and sounding an alarm. On other systems, human operators continually monitored activity. For instance, Control Data Corporation had a nationwide network of computers called Cybernet, which CDC claimed was completely reliable at all times. For Gates, that claim amounted to a dare. A CDC computer at the University of Washington had connections to Cybernet. Gates set to work studying the CDC machines and software; he studied the specifications for the network as though he were cramming for a final exam. "There are these peripheral processors," he explained to Paul Allen. "The way you fool the system is you get control of one of those peripheral processors and then you use that to get control of the mainframe. You're slowly invading the system."

Gates was invading the CDC hive dressed as a worker bee. The mainframe operator observed the activity of the peripheral processor that Gates was controlling, but only electronically in the form of messages sent to the operator's terminal. Gates then figured out how to gain control of all the messages the peripheral processor sent out. He hoped to trick the operator by maintaining a veneer of normalcy while he cracked the system wide open.

The scheme worked. Gates gained control of a peripheral processor, electronically insinuated himself into the main computer, bypassed the human operator without arousing suspicion, and planted the same "special" program in all the component computers of the system. His tinkering caused them to all crash simultaneously. Gates was amused by his exploits, but CDC was not, and he hadn't covered his tracks as well as he thought he had. CDC caught him and sternly reprimanded him. A humiliated Bill Gates swore off computers for more than a year.

Despite the dangers, hacking was the high art of the technological subculture; all the best talent was doing some hacking. When Gates wanted to establish his credentials a few years later, he didn't display some clever program he had written. He just said, "I crashed the CDC," and everyone knew he was good.

When Intel's 8008 microprocessor came out, Paul Allen was ready to build something with it. He lured Gates back into computing by getting an Intel 8008 manual and telling his friend, "We should write a BASIC for the 8008." BASIC was a simple yet high-level programming language that had become popular on minicomputers over the previous decade. Allen was proposing that they write a BASIC *interpreter*—a translator that would convert statements from BASIC input into sequences of 8008 instructions. That way, anyone could control the microprocessor by programming in the BASIC language. It was an appealing idea because controlling the chip directly via its instruction set was, as Allen could see, a painfully laborious process. Gates was skeptical. The 8008 was the first 8-bit microprocessor, and it had severe limitations. "It was built for calculators," Gates told Allen, although he wasn't quite accurate in his statement. But Gates eventually agreed to lend a hand, and came up with the $360 needed to buy what Gates believed was the first 8008 sold through a distributor. Then, their plan somehow was diverted: they got themselves a third enthusiast, Paul Gilbert, to help with the hardware design, and together built a machine around the 8008.

The machine the youngsters built was not a computer by a long shot, but it was complicated enough to cause them to set aside BASIC for a while. They constructed a machine to generate traffic flow statistics using data collected by a sensor they had installed in a rubber tube strung across a highway. They figured there would be a sizable market for such a device. Allen wrote the development software, which allowed them to simulate the operation of their machine on a computer, and Gates used the development software to write the actual data-logging software that their machine required.

It took Gates, Allen, and Gilbert almost a year to get the traffic analysis machine running. When they finally did, in 1972, they started a company called Traf-O-Data—a name that Allen is quick to point out was Gates's idea—and began pitching their new product to city engineers.

Traf-O-Data was not the brilliant success they had hoped for. Perhaps some of the engineers balked at buying computer equipment from kids. Gates, who did most of the talking, was then 16 and looked younger. At the same time, the state of Washington began to offer no-cost traffic-processing services to all county and city traffic controllers, and Allen and Gates found themselves competing against a free service.

Soon after this early failure, Allen left for college, leaving Gates temporarily at loose ends. TRW, a huge corporation that produced software products in Vancouver, Washington, had heard about the work Gates and Allen did for C Cubed and shortly thereafter offered them jobs in a software development group. At something like $30,000 a year, the offer was too good for the two students to pass up. Allen came back from college, Gates got a leave of absence from high school, and they went to work. For a year and a half, Gates and Allen lived a computer nut's dream. They learned a great deal more than they had by working at C Cubed or as the inventors of Traf-O-Data. Programmers can be protective of their hard-earned knowledge, but Gates knew how to use his youth to win over the older TRW experts. He was, as he put it, "non-threatening." After all, he was just a kid.

Gates and Allen also discovered the financial benefits that such work can bring. Gates bought a speedboat, and the two frequently went water-skiing on nearby lakes. But programming offered other rewards that appealed to Gates and Allen far more than their increasingly fatter bank accounts. Clearly, they had been bitten by the bug. They had worked late nights at C Cubed for no financial gain, and pushed themselves at TRW harder than anyone had asked them to. There was something in the clean precision of computer logic and the sportsmanship in the game of programming that was irresistible. The project they worked on at TRW eventually fizzled out, but it had been a profitable experience for the two hackers. It wasn't until Christmas 1974, after Gates went off to Harvard and Allen took a job with Honeywell, that the bug bit them once more, and this time, the disease proved incurable.

CHAPTER 2

THE VOYAGE TO ALTAIR

You can't deny that Ed Roberts started the industry.

MARK CHAMBERLAIN
An early MITS employee

Uncle Sol's Boys

*Ed Roberts? You gotta give him credit
for doing the first one. But give the guy
[who] published him as much credit:
Les Solomon.*

CHUCK PEDDLE
Computer designer

BILL GATES, PAUL ALLEN, AND OTHER COMPUTER ENTHUSIASTS RELIED on the hobbyist electronics magazines, such as *Popular Electronics* and *Radio Electronics,* to stay up on the latest technological developments. In the early 1970s, what Gates and Allen were seeing in the pages of *PE* and *RE* served to frustrate them as much as excite them. Most of the magazines' readers knew something about computers, and many knew a lot more than that, and every one of them now wanted to own a computer. The computer aficionados who read *PE* and *RE* were an opinionated lot; they knew precisely what they did and didn't want in a computer.

What these enthusiasts wanted most often was more control over the machines they used. They resented having to wait in line to use the very tool of their trade or to engage in their favorite hobby. They wanted immediate access to the files they created on a computer, even if they were off somewhere on a business trip. They wanted to play computer games at their leisure without someone telling them to get back to work. In short, what these enthusiasts wanted was a personal computer. But in the early 1970s, the idea of someone owning his or her own computer was no more than a wild dream.

A giant step toward the realization of the personal-computer dream happened in September 1973, when *Radio Electronics* published an article by Don Lancaster that described a "TV Typewriter." One of the more prolific contributors to electronics magazines, Lancaster later published his groundbreaking idea in book form. His proposed uses for the TV Typewriter were nothing short of visionary:

"Obviously, it's a computer terminal for time-sharing services, schools, and experimental uses. It's a ham radio teletype terminal. Coupled to the right services it can . . . display news, stock quotations, time, and weather. It's a communications aide for the deaf. It's a teaching machine, particularly good for helping preschoolers learn the alphabet and words. It also keeps them busy for hours as an educational toy."

Lancaster's TV Typewriter, for all its visionary appeal, was nevertheless only a terminal: an input/output device that would link to a mainframe computer. It didn't constitute the personal computer that the electronics hobbyists desperately wanted.

At the time Lancaster's article was published, *Popular Electronics* technical editor Leslie (Les) Solomon was actively seeking a computer story for his magazine. Solomon and editorial director Arthur Salsberg wanted to publish a piece on building a computer at home. Neither of them knew if such a thing were even possible, but in their bones they felt that it should be. They didn't realize that their competitor, *Radio Electronics,* was already preparing to publish an article on just such a topic.

If a home-built computer design was possible, Solomon figured that it would most likely come from one of his "boys"—those young, technically sharp *Popular Electronics* contributors, such as Stanford graduate students Harry Garland and Roger Melen (who like Don Lancaster also wrote for *Radio Electronics*), Forrest Mims, and Ed Roberts in Albuquerque.

Designs were being submitted to *PE,* but they weren't from the computer superstars, and Solomon and Salsberg found them unimpressive. Solomon described what he was seeing as "a rat's nest of wires," and Salsberg agreed with his assessment: "They were terrible designs. They were tinker toys. They were kludges."

Solomon wanted to feature a really good design that he could develop into a groundbreaking story. So, he encouraged his guys to send him their best designs, and they took his request seriously. A colorful and ebullient editor with a wry New York wit, Les Solomon was known as "Uncle Sol" to his contributors. He developed a close relationship with them, carrying on lengthy telephone conversations and visiting their labs and workshops whenever he could. Solomon regaled his contributors with far-fetched stories and entertained them with magic tricks, most notably a stunt that involved levitating a stone table. Part of what made Uncle Sol fascinating was in trying to figure out what was for real and what was a complete put-on. But one thing was certain: he was serious about getting the best material for his magazine.

The avuncular Solomon was always willing to give his boys advice. When Garland and Melen submitted one of their designs, Solomon told them that they needed to find a distributor. He put them in touch with Ed Roberts, president of an Albuquerque-based company called MITS.

Solomon had met Roberts some time earlier. The *PE* editor was vacationing with his wife in Albuquerque when he went to visit a contributor of his, the prolific writer Forrest Mims. With Solomon's gift for tall tales and his fascination with gadgets, Mims took an immediate liking to Uncle Sol and brought him to meet his business partner, Ed Roberts. Solomon and Roberts hit it off immediately, and the meeting would prove to be a significant event in the development of the personal computer.

Roberts, like Solomon, enjoyed tinkering with stuff. He had played with electronics since his childhood in Miami and had managed to build a crude relay computer while still in his teens. Although he had originally wanted to become a doctor, Roberts decided to join the Air Force to get training in electronics. In 1968, while stationed in Albuquerque, Roberts, Mims, and two other Air Force officers started a small electronics company out of Roberts's garage. They called their company Micro Instrumentation Telemetry Systems, or MITS, and sold radio transmitters for model airplanes by mail order.

Roberts soon involved MITS in other types of projects. For a time, MITS was building and selling a digital oscilloscope for engineers, but Roberts wanted to take on something more daring and closer to the technological cutting edge. His three partners objected to some of his wilder ideas, but ultimately that didn't matter. By 1969, he had bought them out. Roberts was now alone at the helm, which was how he liked it.

A physically imposing man who became accustomed to giving orders while serving in the Air Force, Roberts ran a tight operation at MITS and would brook no nonsense from his employees. In every sense, MITS was Roberts's company. By 1970, MITS had moved out of the garage and into a former restaurant whose name, "The Enchanted Sandwich Shop," still hung over the door. Roberts began manufacturing calculators.

The calculator market was a dizzying place to be in the early 1970s. In 1969, when Intel got the contract to produce calculator chips for the Japanese firm Busicom, the cost to build and sell a calculator nearly approached the cost to build and sell a low-end minicomputer. By the early 1970s, semiconductor technology had changed the calculator market so radically that Ed Roberts could reasonably consider wrapping some electronics and a case around some chips from Intel and selling the results for a small fraction of the purchase price of a Busicom calculator.

What Roberts actually wanted to do was both more and less ambitious than his plan to combine Intel chips with a case and some additional electronics: MITS was going to produce programmable calculators—more complicated than ordinary business calculators— and sell them unassembled in kit form. A calculator kit was the ideal product to be featured in the hobby electronics magazines, and Roberts made sure to publicize it there. The calculator kits sold well for some time among enthusiasts, and Roberts made the fateful decision to invest the bulk of the MITS capital and development efforts in commercial handheld calculators. The decision turned out to be disastrously ill-timed.

Two trends in semiconductor technology reached critical stages in 1974 and helped to create the climate in which the microcomputer was born. The semiconductor companies began to produce and market applications of their technology—in particular, calculators—directly against Intel president Robert Noyce's dictum that the chip manufacturers shouldn't compete with their own customers. In addition, the early, crude microprocessor chips were being refined with better-thought-out designs and more power. The first trend brought MITS to the brink of bankruptcy; the second yanked it back.

In the early 1970s, the semiconductor houses, racked by fierce technological and price wars, noticed that some of their customers had much healthier profits than they did. One example was Commodore, a Canadian electronics company that had moved into Silicon Valley from Toronto and sold calculators that were assembled around a Texas Instruments (TI) chip. Commodore was raking in money from a product that was little more than a TI chip in a plastic case.

The demand for calculators seemed endless, and great profits were made in meeting the need. By 1972, TI had entered the calculator business on its own, and other semiconductor manufacturers soon followed suit. "They just came in and ripped everybody to shreds," according to semiconductor designer Chuck Peddle. TI's attack on the industry was characteristically aggressive: it burst upon the market and immediately undercut everyone else's prices.

When the semiconductor manufacturers entered the calculator market in force, products became smaller and more powerful, prices dropped dramatically, and profits shrank almost as fast. With a nationwide recession hobbling many businesses, 1974 was not a good year for the calculator industry. Chuck Peddle, who was working on microprocessor design at Motorola, recalled, "The market went to hell that year. Supply started catching up with demand. Everybody that year lost money in the calculator business." Calculators went from being a high-end purchase to a sidewalk giveaway. The average price for a consumer calculator in 1974 was $26.25. A year before it had been $150.00.

One of the firms stricken by the recession and lackluster profits was MITS. In January of 1974, MITS was selling a simple 8-function calculator kit for $99.95, and couldn't bring the price any lower. Texas Instruments was offering a comparable, fully assembled calculator for less than half what MITS was asking. The tiny firm couldn't swim in those competitive waters. Ed Roberts lay awake nights trying to figure out where he had gone wrong.

The other pivotal development in semiconductors happened in April 1974 when the successor to the Intel 8008 microprocessor was completed. Intel had indeed created the brain of a computer in the 8008.

However, the 8008 was, in the words of *Popular Electronic*'s Art Salsberg, "a kludge and a monster." Everything was there, but not in the right places. It handled vital operations in a slow, roundabout way and demanded a contorted, awkward form of programming and design. Engineers at Intel had long argued about whether the 8008 could actually function as the brain of a viable, commercially sold computer. In a sense, their argument provided the answer, and they went ahead to invent its successor, the 8080.

Going for Broke

Why don't you call it Altair? That's
where the Enterprise *is going tonight.*

LAUREN SOLOMON
Daughter of *Popular Electronics* editor,
Les Solomon

E D ROBERTS MADE A DECISION OF HIS OWN THAT SPRING—HE WAS going to build a kit computer. He had been toying with the idea for some time only to find that by early 1974 the chips, so to speak, were down. MITS's calculator business had blown away like desert sand, leaving the company heavily in debt. Faced with the possibility of going under, Roberts decided to go for broke. He would build a product that had essentially no precedent or defined market, a product most people considered fanciful at best. The specter of bankruptcy probably had little to do with his decision. Roberts always cared much more about technological challenges than any business risks they presented. He would have gone ahead with the kit computer under any circumstances.

Roberts studied Intel's chips—the early 4004, the 8008, and a third Intel product called the 4040—and rejected the 4004 and 4040 as too crude. He was considering building a machine around the 8008, until a programmer told him that he had tried to implement the BASIC programming language on the 8008 and had found it to be an excruciating process. The 8008 carried out the BASIC instructions far too slowly to be useful.

Then a new product caught Roberts's eye, the Intel 8080. By this time, Motorola also marketed a microprocessor, the 6800, and Texas Instruments and other companies had similar products. But Roberts figured that the 8080 had the technological edge, making it the best candidate. It had another even more significant advantage. Intel normally charged $360 for an 8080. Roberts was sure he could get the chips much cheaper, and he did. Intel knocked the price down to $75 apiece.

It was an excellent deal, but there was a catch. The contract required him to buy in volume, and each computer needed only one processor. That was fine with Roberts. After the calculator fiasco, which Roberts said was "something you don't want to go through twice in a lifetime," he was geared up to sell plenty of computers to salvage his company. He was now thinking *volume*.

Meanwhile, *Popular Electronics* was narrowing its search for a computer project it could publicize. "We got in a bunch of computers," Art Salsberg recalled. "We wound up with two models and decided it was going to be a choice of one or the other. One amounted to no more than a promise. The promise was, I can get the chips at a lower price and make this whole thing feasible. That was from Ed Roberts. The other choice was a microcomputer trainer by Jerry Ogdin." The model from *PE* contributor Ogdin was actually more a tool for learning about computers than an actual computer.

Roberts offered only a concept, whereas Ogdin's device actually existed and Salsberg and Solomon had seen it. They were both inclined to support a tangible machine over the mere promise of one, even though the machine was built around the 8008 chip, which was about to be phased out. "It looked like it was a go with the microcomputer trainer," Salsberg said of their rationale. Then *Radio Electronics* came out with an article on the Mark-8.

The July 1974 *RE* hit the newsstands with its article by Jonathan Titus on building the Mark-8, an Intel 8008-based computer. The write-up generated a lot of excitement among hobbyists, but not a lot of orders. The article had an effect at *Popular Electronics,* too. The Mark-8 may have been fatally limited by the crude 8008 microprocessor, but its appearance in *RE* made *Popular Electronics* realize that it needed something better to publicize. Salsberg read the article and said, "That kills the trainer." Solomon agreed, noting that Ogdin's trainer was very similar to the 8008 machine that *Radio Electronics* had. *Popular Electronics* had to up the ante with an 8080 machine.

Solomon promptly flew to Albuquerque to meet with Roberts and work out the details. Salsberg wanted the computer packaged like a serious commercial product, and not another "rat's nest." Roberts spent many late nights hashing out the exact components of a desktop computer that could sell for under $500. This presented an enormous challenge. The Mark-8 sold for about twice that price, and when you added up the cost of the components that any computer needed, it was hard to get the price much lower. In the end, Roberts promised to meet the price and to deliver the first machine to *PE* as soon as it was built, and *Popular Electronics* promised to publish a series of articles on it, including a cover story.

When Salsberg agreed to go with Roberts's machine, he staked the reputation of the magazine on a promise and a hunch. No one at MITS had ever built a computer before. Roberts had only two engineers on his staff, and one of them had his degree in aeronautical engineering. Roberts had no prototype and no detailed proposal. But Uncle Sol kept assuring Salsberg that Roberts could pull it off. Salsberg hoped he was right.

Roberts was just as edgy about *Popular Electronics*'s promises. However much he liked and respected Les Solomon, he was wary of Solomon's cheerful assurances. The more he realized how important a cover story in *Popular Electronics* was for MITS, the more nervous he became. His company's future was in the hands of a man who levitated tables for kicks.

The publicity a *Popular Electronics* cover story generated was crucial to any start-up enterprise. The Mark-8 wasn't the first computer built around the Intel 8008, although Roberts had no way of knowing that. That distinction belongs to the Micral computer, built in 1973 by André Thi Truong, a French Vietnamese entrepreneur. Truong sold 500 of the machines, all in France. Later that year, Truong demonstrated an 8080-based computer at a major computing conference in the United States. Whatever impact the demonstration had on the engineers and computer scientists who saw it apparently didn't extend much beyond that conference. The same fate could easily befall Roberts's machine.

Over the summer of 1974, Roberts had sketched out the machine he wanted. As his ideas took shape, he passed them along to the two guys on his engineering team, Jim Bybe and Bill Yates. A quiet and serious man, Yates worked long hours on the layout of the main circuit board for the machine, planning how each electrical signal would get from one point to another in the computer.

Roberts wanted this computer to be expandable, like a minicomputer. He wanted the user to be able to install other circuit boards for particular functions, such as controlling an input/output device or providing extra memory, in addition to installing the main circuit board. Roberts wanted the boards designed to plug easily into the computer, a capability that required not just a socket, but also specific, defined data paths. If different elements of the computer were to reside on physically distinct circuit boards, the boards had to be made to communicate with each other. This communication, in turn, required certain engineering conventions. For instance, one board needed to send information when and where it was expected by another board. Almost by default, a bus structure for the computer evolved.

A bus structure functions something like a highway system. A bus is a channel through which computer data or instructions travel. Typically, a bus is a parallel channel with several different signals passing simultaneously. The MITS computer had 100 separate channels, or paths, and each had to have a stated purpose. Added to that were the physical and electrical constraints that sometimes dictated the design of the layouts. For instance, electrical cross-talk—interference between wires—makes it unwise to place channels for certain kinds of signals too closely together. But Roberts allowed Yates no time to address such niceties of design because the creditors had already begun to bay. Wherever the data channels fell, that's where they stayed. The bus design did the job, but it wasn't pretty.

While Yates laid out the boards, another MITS employee, technical writer David Bunnell, was casting about for a name for the computer. His favorite of all the candidates was "Little Brother," but he wasn't altogether comfortable with the name. Bunnell wasn't really comfortable with the whole notion of computers, Roberts recalled. But Bunnell kept his skepticism in check, given Roberts lack of patience with dissent.

Bunnell had been with MITS since 1972. He and Roberts had coauthored articles for *Popular Electronics,* and their series of tutorials on digital electronics was running in the magazine at the same time they worked long hours in the MITS workshop developing their computer.

Despite their efforts, it was beginning to look as if the computer was destined to die in the workshop. MITS owed around $300,000 to its creditors. With Les Solomon's constant reminders that the article's deadline was imminent, Roberts made a grim trek to the bank. It was mid-September. He was out of money, needed another loan, and fully expected the bank to turn him down. Given his current credit rating and his depleted assets, he doubted anyone would lend him the $65,000 he needed to keep the company's doors open.

The officers of the bank listened patiently. He was going to build a kit computer? And what exactly was that? And who, did he think, would buy such a product? Electronics hobbyists, sight unseen, from ads in magazines? And how many of these kit computers did he think he could sell to these electronics hobbyists through advertisements in magazines in the next year? With a straight face, Roberts told them, "Eight hundred." "You won't sell eight hundred," they said, thinking he was being unrealistic. Roberts was indeed fantasizing. Still, the bank officers saw no advantage in bankrupting companies with outstanding loans. The loan officers figured that if Roberts could sell two hundred of the things it would help MITS to repay the bank something. They agreed to advance him the $65,000.

Roberts did his best to hide his surprise. He was glad he hadn't mentioned the informal market survey that he had just conducted. Trying to get some sense of how the machine would be received, Roberts described it to some engineers he knew and asked if any of them would buy it. They all said no. Although Roberts never considered himself a good businessman, he knew instinctively when it was safe to ignore market research. He took his $65,000 and, with Yates and Bybe, worked feverishly to complete the prototype to send to *Popular Electronics.* It was going to appear on the cover, so they made sure it looked especially attractive.

Because Bill Yates was doing most of the design, he worked with Roberts on the article. While Roberts and Yates were scrambling to finish both the computer and the article, they realized they still didn't have a name for their machine. They figured that Solomon would put a *Popular Electronics* name on it if they didn't, so they beat him to the punch by calling it the PE-8. It was Roberts's last small hedge against *PE*'s scuttling the project. But that wasn't the name by which the machine became famous.

According to Les Solomon, his 12-year-old daughter Lauren was the one who came up with the name that stuck. She was watching an episode of *Star Trek* when her father walked into the room and said, "I need a name for a computer. What's the name of the computer on the Enterprise?" Lauren thought for a moment and said, "Computer." Her father didn't think much of that name, so Lauren suggested, "Why don't you call it Altair? That's where the Enterprise is going tonight."

Some of Solomon's friends told a different story of how the name was arrived at, but Altair it remained. "I don't give a damn what you call it," Roberts told Solomon. "If we don't sell 200, we're finished." Solomon reassured him that things were going well and selling 200 was entirely possible. Solomon wasn't just being polite and trying to soothe the raw nerves of a man who'd been flayed in the calculator market crash. He was confident that the Altair had the potential to far outstrip the Mark-8.

The Mark-8 was an experimenter's toy, a way for the engineering hobbyist to learn about computers firsthand. But the Altair was a real computer. Its bus structure would make it possible to expand the machine's capabilities by allowing the user to plug in new circuit boards. Besides, the 8080 chip was a far better "brain" than the 8008. The Altair had the potential, at least in miniature, of doing everything a large mainframe computer could do.

Solomon was convinced of it and told Roberts as much. But he didn't voice his concern that the message might not get across to the *PE* readers. Art Salsberg told him that *PE* had to offer its readers more than just instructions on building the device. To prove that the Altair was a serious computer, *PE* had to also offer one solid application, a practical purpose for the Altair that could be demonstrated right away. What that application might be, Solomon had no idea.

The deadline arrived for Roberts to deliver the prototype computer to Solomon. Roberts told him that it was coming by Railway Express and to watch for it. Solomon waited. No computer arrived. Roberts reassured him that the computer was in the mail and should be arriving any day. Days later, the prototype was still a no-show. Solomon in turn tried to reassure Art Salsberg at *Popular Electronics* that the machine was on its way, but now everyone was getting nervous. Roberts flew to New York to demonstrate the prototype, confident that it would arrive by the time he did.

But it didn't. Railway Express had apparently lost their computer. This was a catastrophe, both for MITS and for *Popular Electronics*. The magazine had committed to a cover story, and now it had no computer to put on the cover. For weeks, Roberts had lain awake nights, static buzzing away in his brain. Now he felt that his worrying had been justified. His engineers couldn't possibly assemble another computer in time to meet the deadline. They were sunk. Unless, of course, they faked it.

Yates could slap together a box, poke little lights through the holes in the front, and ship it to New York. Les Solomon didn't like the idea. Art Salsberg hated it. Ed Roberts was embarrassed. But when the January 1975 issue of *Popular Electronics* went to press, it featured a flashy cover photo of an empty metal box masquerading as a computer.

By December 1974, Solomon actually had an Altair computer. At first he set it up in his office, but the noise from the Teletype machine he was using as an input/output device made him instantly unpopular in the *Popular Electronics* offices. So he took the system home and set it up in his basement. It was there that Roger Melen first saw it.

The day after Roberts and Yates's piece on the Altair appeared, an article came across Solomon's desk that caught his attention. Harry Garland and Roger Melen, the two Stanford graduate students Solomon had once hooked up with Ed Roberts, sent in a description of a digital camera they had designed. The Cyclops, as Garland and Melen called it, reduced an image to a rectangular grid of light and dark squares and provided a low-cost visual system for a digital computer. In December 1974, coincidentally just before *PE*'s Altair issue came out, Roger Melen decided to fly to New York. His trip ultimately led him to Les Solomon's basement.

Roger Melen reminded Uncle Sol of Ed Roberts in a way. Both were well over six feet tall and heavyset, and both were inveterate engineer-hobbyists, but the Air Force–trained Roberts was older and tougher.

Melen was quiet and soft-spoken, the product of one of the top engineering schools in the world. Nevertheless, the two would see eye-to-eye, Les thought, chuckling to himself at the unintentional joke. Trying to hide his amusement, he led Melen through his basement to a strange-looking apparatus. "What's that?" Melen asked. "That, sir," Solomon told him, "is a computer."

When Solomon told him what the Altair was and how much it cost, Melen politely demurred. There must have been some mistake. Melen knew for a fact that the microprocessor chip alone cost as much as he claimed this whole computer did. Solomon suppressed a smile and assured him that the price was correct. Roberts was actually going to sell this computer for $397. Delighted at Melen's reaction, Solomon picked up the phone, called Roberts in Albuquerque, and checked the price as Melen stood there. Yep, it was still $397.

Melen was stunned. As he and most hobbyists well knew, Intel was at the time charging $360 for the 8080 chip alone. When Melen left New York that day, instead of flying directly back to San Francisco, he took a side trip to New Mexico.

Roberts greeted Melen enthusiastically at the Albuquerque airport that evening and drove him over to MITS. There Melen was in for another surprise: far from being the large company he had expected to see, the MITS office was in a strip mall wedged in between a massage parlor and a laundromat. The MITS headquarters must have looked as odd to Melen as it did to the suburban shoppers who strolled past its doors that winter. "It was obviously the skeleton of what used to be a company, because they had lots of equipment around," Melen later recalled. "But they only had, I think, 10 employees at that time. They had been very successful in producing calculators, but that was a fad that had passed. He [Roberts] saw this as his big chance for success— his second shot to pull him out of his predicament."

Melen recognized a mutual opportunity and proposed attaching his Cyclops camera to the Altair. Roberts was interested, and after a brief tour of MITS, the two men sat down to work. Melen studied the Altair schematics, gathering all the information he thought he would need to design an interface between the two devices. He and Roberts talked about computers in general and the Altair-Cyclops interface in particular until dawn, when Melen hurried back to the airport to catch an 8 A.M. flight to San Francisco.

Soon after the meeting between Melen and Roberts, Solomon wrote to Garland and Melen suggesting a television adapter for the Cyclops. They replied that it would be prohibitively expensive, and instead described their plan to link the Cyclops device to the Altair for use as a security camera. Solomon was gleeful. The security camera was the practical application that Art Salsberg had wanted. He incorporated the idea into Garland and Melen's article on the Cyclops.

The brainstorming session with Melen was not to be Ed Roberts's last sleepless night. His future, his company, *everything* hung on this article in *Popular Electronics,* and on a positive response from *PE* readers. He kept his enthusiasm in check, despite Les Solomon's cheery encouragement. Roberts felt that *PE* could scrap the project even on the eve of publication. If it did, MITS was through. Already hundreds of thousands of dollars in debt, Roberts had borrowed heavily to finance this computer venture. He had purchased enough parts to build several hundred machines—and he still had to pay for advertising. At $397 for one machine, he would need to sell hundreds just to break even. He began to wonder if he had made a terrible mistake.

All Hell Breaks Loose

PROJECT BREAKTHROUGH! World's
First Minicomputer Kit to Rival
Commercial Models . . . ALTAIR 8800

POPULAR ELECTRONICS COVER
January 1975

ED ROBERTS WAS STILL WORRIED ABOUT HIS INVESTMENT EVEN AS THE first orders came rolling in. But within a week, it was clear that whatever problems MITS would face in the immediate future, bank foreclosure would not be one of them. In just a two-week period, Roberts's tiny staff had opened hundreds of envelopes and read with giddy excitement orders for all the computers they had ever hoped to sell. Within a month, MITS had gone from one of their bank's biggest debtors to a fiscal hero. MITS's bank balance went from $400,000 in the red to $250,000 in the black in a few weeks. Just processing the orders seemed to be a full-time job for everyone.

No one had realized just how primed the market was for a personal computer. The January issue of *Popular Electronics* signaled to thousands of electronics hobbyists, programmers, and other technophiles that the era of the personal computer had finally arrived. Even those who didn't send in checks saw the Altair article as a sign that they could now have their own computers. The Altair was the fruit of a technological revolution that dropped straight into the hands of a hungry population. They went crazy for it.

Roberts, who had gambled his company's life on the existence of any market for the machines, was amazed at the magnitude of the response. His experience at selling $99 kit calculators had been of little value in predicting the number of buyers for a $397 computer. In addition to the significant price difference, the calculator had a well-defined and obvious function. By comparison, it wasn't yet clear what the Altair could actually do. Despite Salsberg's artfully vague promise in *Popular Electronics* of "manifold uses we cannot even think of at this time," it was not at all obvious what those "manifold uses" were. That didn't stop Roberts's phone from ringing almost nonstop. People were happy to buy promises.

One of the promises customers bought was delivery in 60 days. Roberts determined that he had to establish priorities or they would never make any deliveries. He issued a no-frills edict: initial production would include only the bare machine. All the bells and whistles, such as extra memory, the clock board, and the interface boards to allow the computer to be connected to a Teletype machine, would have to wait. MITS would ship the box and CPU board with 256 bytes of memory, the front panel, and nothing else until the backlog was cleared. As delivered, the Altair was no more powerful than the Mark-8. Only its possibilities were greater.

A few orders were filled early in 1975. Garland and Melen, working on Cyclops in the guest bedroom of Melen's Mountain View, California, apartment, were MITS's first computer customers. They were not your typical customers. The average order went out only after it inched to the head of the queue, which took time. Garland and Melen received Altair No. 0002 in January. (The first Altair, lost in shipment to New York and never seen again, was unnumbered. Les Solomon got No. 0001.) Garland and Melen immediately set to work on the interface board that would allow the computer to control their Cyclops digital camera.

Despite MITS's promise of 60-day delivery, orders were not filled in any quantity until the summer of 1975. One hobbyist, Michael Shrayer, who went on to write the first personal-computer word processing program, described his experience with MITS: "I sent away my $397. Many phone calls later, the computer finally came. It took forever. At that time, I received a big, empty box with a CPU card and 256 bytes of memory. No terminal, no keyboard, nothing. To put anything in it, one had to play with the switches on the front panel and put in minor programs. A lot of peripherals were being promised but not delivered."

"Minor programs" was a generous description of what you could feed the early Altair. Programs had to be written in 8080 machine language and entered by flipping switches, with one flip of a switch for every binary digit. And once they were entered, the programs could do little except make the lights on the front of the box blink. One of the first programs written for the Altair was a simple game. It caused the lights to blink in a certain pattern, which the player was supposed to mimic by flipping switches.

The Altair buyer faced another problem after delivery. The computer was sold as a kit, and assembling it took many hours. The odds of the computer eventually working depended on the skill of the hobbyist and the quality of the parts. Most of the first machines simply didn't work, despite the skill of the user. Steve Dompier, a young building contractor in Berkeley, California, was surprised to find that some of MITS's advertised equipment didn't even exist. He recalled sending in a check for $4,000 with a succinct request for "one of everything." When half his money came back with an apologetic note from a beleaguered MITS secretary saying that they "didn't have all that stuff yet," Dompier boarded a plane for Albuquerque.

Flying from San Francisco to Albuquerque over a delay in filling an order for hobby equipment might seem overzealous to some, but not to Dompier. "I wanted to see if they were really there. I rented a car and drove past the place about five times. I was looking for a big building with the letters *MITS* on it and a front lawn. It turned out it was in a tiny building next to a laundromat in a shopping center. There were two or three rooms. All they had was a box full of parts." He picked up some of those parts and flew back to San Francisco.

On April 16, 1975, Dompier reported on MITS at a meeting of the Homebrew Computer Club, a pioneering microcomputer club that was formed in Menlo Park, California. Dompier drew an attentive audience. MITS, he told his listeners, had 4000 orders and couldn't even begin to fill them. The thousands of orders, more than anything else, sparked people's interest. What they had been waiting for had happened. They were going to have their own computers.

Maybe all that the Altair could do was blink its lights, but for the Homebrew members, just the fact that it existed was enough for them. They would take it from there.

"They made the business happen," semiconductor designer Chuck Peddle said of these early hobbyists. "They bought computers when they didn't work and when there was no software for them. They created a market, and then they turned around and wrote the programs that brought other people in."

The early purchasers of the Altair had no choice but to write their own programs. MITS initially supplied no significant software with the machine. The typical response of a computer hobbyist to the *Popular Electronics* article was to first send for an Altair, and when it arrived (and had been successfully assembled), begin writing software for it. Two programmers in Boston decided to skip Step one.

Paul Allen was working for Honeywell in Boston. Bill Gates was a freshman at Harvard, where he had customized a curriculum that allowed him to take graduate mathematics courses. On weekends the two would get together to brainstorm about microcomputers. "We were just trying to figure out something we could do with them," Allen recalled. Gates and Allen sent out offers on their old Traf-O-Data stationery to write implementations of the PL/I language for $20,000. (Traf-O-Data was the company that Gates and Allen founded as teenagers after developing an automated device designed to measure traffic flow.) They also considered selling Traf-O-Data machines to a company in Brazil. In the middle of a Boston winter, they were spinning their wheels.

While walking through Harvard Square one day, Allen spotted the *Popular Electronics* cover that featured the Altair. Like many other computer enthusiasts, he realized at once that the Altair was a tremendous breakthrough. But he also saw it as something of personal interest. Allen ran to tell Bill that he thought their big break had finally come. Bill agreed. "So we called this guy Ed Roberts," said Gates. "We had a fairly aggressive posture. We said, 'We have a BASIC. Do you want it?'" In 1975, Allen and Gates were pioneers in the industry practice of preannouncing products that they didn't have yet. In later years, this type of thing would come to be called "vaporware."

Roberts was justly skeptical. He had heard from many programmers who claimed they could write software for his computer. He told Gates and Allen what he told everyone else: he would buy the first BASIC he saw actually running on an Altair.

Unlike the others, Gates and Allen followed through, and about six weeks later Allen flew to Albuquerque to show Roberts their BASIC. The demonstration was a success, even though their BASIC initially did little more than announce its presence. The Traf-O-Data company, newly renamed Micro-Soft (later changed to Microsoft) had made its first sale as a microcomputer software house.

In March, Roberts offered Paul Allen the position of director of software at MITS. Frustrated at Honeywell and eager to work in what he saw as a tremendously promising field, Allen accepted immediately and flew to Albuquerque with all the cash he and Gates could lay their hands on. The title of MITS Software Director, as it turned out, was not quite the illustrious post Allen had imagined. Upon arriving in Albuquerque, he discovered that he *was* the software department.

Putting It Together

*Every good idea was half-executed
at MITS.*

BILL GATES
Cofounder of Microsoft

THE HOBBYIST CUSTOMER NEEDED TO BE PLENTY CREATIVE TO USE THE MITS Altair. By mid-1975, when MITS was delivering product on a regular basis, the assembled machine was no more than a metal box containing a power supply unit bolted next to a large circuit board. This board came to be called the *motherboard* because it was the main piece of circuitry in the machine. It contained 100 strands of gold that connected the motherboard to 18 slots into which other circuit boards could be plugged.

Those 18 slots were a symbol of both the Altair's expandability and an owner's frustration at not being able to use most of them. Regardless of whatever a customer may have ordered, what was shipped was a machine with only two of the slots filled. One slot would have a board containing the CPU (basically, the Intel 8080 chip and supporting circuitry), and the other slot would have a board that contained 256 bytes of memory.

The Altair package also included a front-panel board that controlled the lights and switches on the front of the box. These lights and switches were the I/O, the means by which users communicated with the machine. It was up to the customer to attach the front-panel board to the motherboard by hooking up dozens of wires—a task requiring hours of tedious work. Composed of just a CPU, some memory, and an I/O unit, the early Altair barely met the minimal definition of a computer.

Compared with more fully developed machines, the Altair was seriously deficient in some areas. For instance, it lacked any means of permanent storage. Users could put information into the machine and manipulate it, but once they shut off the power—or left one task to move to another—the information disappeared. Even temporary storage was extremely limited. Although the Altair had a memory board, its 256 bytes of memory wouldn't have allowed enough space to hold this paragraph.

As an I/O system, the front panel setup was awkward to use and required a tedious series of steps. To enter information, users had to flip tiny switches on and off; one flip of a switch equaled one bit of information. To read output, a user had to interpret a series of flashing lights. Entering and verifying a paragraph's worth of information might take several minutes, even with practice. Until paper tape readers and Gates and Allen's BASIC came along, Altair owners had to speak to their machines in *machine language* via this switches-and-lights routine.

Machine language was the native language of the Altair's microprocessor, the Intel 8080. A machine language is a set of commands, in the form of numeric codes, that elicits a response from a computer's CPU. The code causes the CPU to execute one of its elementary functions, for instance, copying the contents of one specified location in memory onto another location or adding the value of 1 to a stored value. Some programmers prefer to work in machine language or something like it because of the intimate and immediate control the language gives them over a CPU's operation. Such programmers are the true hackers. But all programmers agree that programming in a higher-level language is vastly easier than having to work with machine language. Altair BASIC was a higher-level language. Unfortunately, Altair BASIC took up 4096 bytes of memory—remarkably little memory for a high-level language, but 16 times the amount of memory that MITS provided in the Altair.

By filling the Altair's 18 slots with 256-byte memory boards and entering Gates and Allen's BASIC into the system—a tedious process that involved flipping the front-panel switches more than 30,000 times without an error—users could theoretically get a high-level language running. However, the amount of memory left for their own programs would be minuscule. Moreover, the BASIC would have to be reentered every time the machine was turned back on. Two improvements were needed to make the BASIC, and in fact the Altair, useful: higher-density memory boards and a method for entering programs quickly. MITS was at work on developing both of these. When it came right down to it, MITS was at work on a lot of things.

When Paul Allen arrived in Albuquerque, MITS's biggest hardware project was a 4K memory board that Ed Roberts had designed and technician Pat Godding was attempting to build. In computer jargon, the letter *K*, short for *kilo*, represents 1024, the number closest to 1000 with a power of two. Therefore, 4K equals 4096. Because digital computers use a binary number system, in which every number is expressed as a sum of powers of two, exact powers of two are especially easy for a computer to work with. Computer capacities, such as amount of memory or the largest displayable integer, are generally expressed in powers of two. The new MITS memory board could hold over 4000 bytes of information, so Altair BASIC could fit comfortably on it.

Because the 4K memory board would make it possible to run Gates and Allen's BASIC on the Altair, Allen was particularly concerned that the board should work reliably. It didn't. Or rather, it didn't when combined with other boards. The problem wasn't just the board itself, but also the performance of two or more boards together. "It was almost analog circuitry," Allen said. "Things had to be calibrated so exactly."

Bill Yates and the other MITS engineers came to dread Allen's visits to their work area. In order to test the enhancements he was adding to his BASIC, Allen had to try them out on a working Altair with functioning 4K memory boards. Unfortunately, none of the 4K memory boards were working. Allen would bring in his latest modification to a program and key it into the machine, whereupon all the panel lights would turn on, the Altair's way of throwing up its hands in confusion. When technical changes failed to correct the 4K boards, engineers went the redundancy route. At one point, MITS was keeping seven Altairs running constantly just to have three reliable machines at any given time. "That 4K dynamic memory board was atrocious," Roberts later admitted.

The truth was, Allen didn't have to key in all of BASIC every time he wanted to use the machine. The workshop Altair had some secret capabilities that MITS wasn't yet ready to release to customers. For instance, its programs and data could be stored on paper tape and then loaded back into memory later on. When Allen first demonstrated BASIC to Roberts, he brought it to MITS on paper tape. (For a while, paper tape was the major means of distributing the language.) Bill Gates would later curse those paper tapes of his and Allen's because they provided the medium for widespread illegal copying of their BASIC.

Paper tape had some serious drawbacks as a storage medium for microcomputers. Paper tape readers and punches were expensive, considerably more expensive than the Altair computer itself. Paper tape systems were also not terribly fast or efficient.

MITS recognized the need for an inexpensive storage method and was considering using audiocassette recorders. Many computer users already owned cassette tape recorders, and if a recorder could double as an Altair storage device, all the better. But like paper tape, using cassettes was a slow and clumsy way of storing data. By comparison, IBM had long used disk drives for data storage on its large computers. (In disk drives, information is held in tiny magnetized *domains* on the surface of a specially coated, rapidly rotating plastic disk. The disk is read by read/write heads capable of fast, precise positioning over any location on the disk.) Disks, although expensive, solved the main problems of tape storage. They made data storage and retrieval quick and easy.

Roberts was convinced MITS should put disk drives on the Altair. Paul Allen agreed. In 1975, when Bill Gates also made the move to Albuquerque in order to work on MITS programs, Allen asked him to write the software that would allow the Altair to communicate with a disk drive. But Gates was currently occupied with other tasks, and he put off writing the disk code.

MITS had no shortage of either hardware or software projects. The company was working on interfaces to Teletype machines, printers, and cassette recorders, as well as looking for ways to link a simple terminal to the Altair. MITS was also developing programs to control these devices, new versions of BASIC and enhancements to the language, and applications programs. In addition, all these items needed documentation. On top of all this, MITS undertook such public relations projects as a user conference and a newsletter.

One unusual promotional gimmick was the "MITSmobile," also known as the Blue Goose. An outgrowth of Roberts's fondness for recreational vehicles, the Blue Goose was an advertising tool designed to spark interest in microcomputing. Gates recalled touring on the Blue Goose: "It was one of those GM motor homes. We'd drive around the nation, and everywhere we'd go, we'd get somebody to start a computer club. I was part of the song-and-dance for one of the tours." The Blue Goose, like many other MITS innovations, inspired imitators. Utah-based Sphere, one of MITS's first competitors, soon thereafter sent a Spheremobile roving about the land.

The Blue Goose promotion proved effective. One of the clubs it helped initiate was the Southern California Computer Society, which in turn published an influential early microcomputer magazine, the *SCCS Interface*.

Many good reasons existed for starting computer clubs. The equipment in these early days didn't always work or work properly, and software was often unusable or nonexistent. Although buyers were typically engineering hobbyists, few of them had all the skills necessary to fully understand a microcomputer. The clubs encouraged a synergistic sharing of knowledge among the sophisticated but stymied users of the machines. Without this interaction and mutual aid, the industry would not have blossomed as it did.

MITS no longer depended on local initiative. By April, MITS had its own nationwide computer club that held design contests and published a newsletter called *Computer Notes*. David Bunnell started up the publication and Ed Roberts contributed a semiregular column called "Ramblings." Within the year, Bunnell turned the newsletter over to Andrea Lewis, who would later follow Gates and Allen over to their own business venture. Throughout much of the newsletter's published history, Gates and Allen wrote a sizable portion of its contents.

The Altair club offered free membership to Altair owners or those who could pass as owners while they awaited delivery from MITS. Meanwhile, other clubs were springing up that bore no particular allegiance to MITS. The Southern California Computer Society and the Homebrew Computer Club in Northern California, although filled with actual and prospective Altair owners, were also made up of technically sophisticated hobbyists who soon contemplated building computers of their own. The Homebrew Club members were especially interested in this challenge, and from the club's ranks there quickly emerged a true competitor to one of MITS's most important products.

The Competition

*There was no competition until
Processor Tech came out with the
memory cards.*

ED ROBERTS
Founder of MITS

MITS WAS A TRUE CATALYST. PERHAPS MORE BY CHANCE THAN BY merit, the MITS operation inspired the creation of an entire industry. That also meant MITS spawned competitors, and from Roberts's perspective, competitors were poaching on territory he had already claimed. When MITS began delivering its 4K memory boards, it didn't take long for customers to notice what Paul Allen already knew: The boards didn't work. "I don't think I'd trust an Altair memory board to do anything," one MITS executive later admitted.

Although Roberts later admitted the board's design was awful, at the time he brooked no complaints about it, as Bill Gates soon learned. Gates was using a memory-test program he had written to check the boards as they were completed. "Every one that came off the line wouldn't work," Gates said and told Roberts as much. The resulting confrontation between the slight 18-year-old and the burly Air Force veteran permanently damaged their relationship. Roberts considered Gates a teenage smart aleck and simply ignored him. "I think that was a fundamental failing of Ed's," another MITS employee said. "If *he* said the memory boards worked, they worked." Unfortunately, they didn't.

When Californian Bob Marsh, an out-of-work Homebrew Computer Club hobbyist, started a company called Processor Technology in April

1975 and began selling 4K boards that apparently *did* work, Roberts took it as a declaration of war. MITS was making little or no profit on the Altair computers and desperately needed the memory board sales that Processor Technology was cutting in on.

Roberts retaliated by using Gates and Allen's software as a weapon. The BASIC language was a popular item; the MITS 4K board was not. So MITS resorted to a venerable marketing ploy: it tied the price of BASIC to the purchase of the memory board. Customers who bought MITS boards paid $150 for BASIC. Those who didn't buy the boards paid $500 for BASIC—more than the price of the machine.

The tactic backfired, and the effect on the market was dramatic. Hobbyists, seeing the 4K boards as worthless and BASIC as overpriced, made their own paper-tape copies of BASIC and distributed the copies for free. By the end of 1975, most copies of BASIC in use on Altair computers were pirated.

Processor Technology survived the BASIC price ploy and developed more Altair-compatible products. Other companies also began to produce memory boards that could be used in the Altair. A peculiar sort of antagonism developed between Altair and the board manufacturers. Roberts railed at those he regarded as squatters in his territory. The memory board companies responded by crashing David Bunnell's First World Altair Computer Conference. When Roberts denounced certain memory board firms in his newsletter, calling them "parasites," two Oakland, California, hobbyists christened their new memory board company "Parasitic Engineering."

The only board company to win approval from MITS was Garland and Melen's Cromemco, named for Crothers Memorial Hall, their graduate dormitory at Stanford. Garland and Melen had gotten side-tracked from their plan to connect the Cyclops digital camera to the Altair. The interface board that was intended to perform this feat had taken on a life of its own. It had become a video interface board for displaying text and pictures generated by the Altair on a color television monitor. The Dazzler, as they called the board, neatly solved the Altair's I/O problem. Roberts saw it as noncompetitive (MITS had nothing like it), and displayed it prominently with his Altair computers at a conference the following spring.

The First World Altair Computer Conference, held in Albuquerque in March 1976, was the first in a series of microcomputer conventions. Hundreds of people attended this event, but it was strictly a MITS Altair affair. Every one of the dozen or so speakers and presenters were there at MITS's invitation, including one who demonstrated a backgammon game he had written for the Altair. Cromemco was the only hardware company invited. Garland and Melen were there in person, having the show to themselves.

The burly Melen was a match for Roberts in size but far more reticent, while the diminutive Garland was bubbling with enthusiasm. A number of uninvited companies sent out representatives to walk the floor and pass out circulars inviting viewers to see competitive equipment on display in hotel rooms upstairs from the conference center. Among that group were reps from Bob Marsh's Processor Technology, whose memory boards were threatening to eat into Roberts's profits.

The presence of the show-crashers irked MITS management. David Bunnell was so perturbed by the crashers that he ran around tearing down their signs. Lee Felsenstein, who had savaged the Altair in a hobbyist publication before working for Processor Technology, sensed that Roberts was freezing him out.

MITS had more to worry about than the majority of the board companies who were competing against MITS's components. Other firms were springing up that challenged MITS's core product, its computer. Don Lancaster's Southwest Technical Products and Sphere were both working on computers built around Motorola's recently released MC6800 processor.

Roberts had proposed building a 6800 machine, too. But some of his employees, including Paul Allen, opposed this new venture, fearing that the company would spread itself too thin. "No, Ed," Allen objected. "We'll have to rewrite all our software for the 6800. We'll have two instruction sets to support. That just doubles our headaches." Nevertheless, MITS did develop a 6800 machine, starting work on it late in 1975. Named the Altair 680b and attractively priced at $293, that computer was substantially different from the original Altair 8800. Components from the 8800 could not be used in the 680b, nor could the original Altair BASIC.

When the new computer magazine *Byte* unveiled Southwest Tech's 6800 computer in November 1975, the announcement was soon followed by MITS's announcement of its 680b. Additional engineers were hired to work with the new design, and new line employees were added. The struggle to keep up with the orders for the 8800 and the determination to rush out the 680b had swelled the ranks of MITS employees from 12 to more than 100 in just a year.

One of MITS's new employees was Mark Chamberlain, a quiet University of New Mexico student with a knack for understatement and a taste for assembly language programming. Chamberlain had worked on a Digital Equipment Corporation PDP-8 computer, probably the closest thing to a microcomputer that most universities had at the time. "I had done a lot of assembly code . . . and got so turned on to it that they just couldn't keep me out." When a professor mentioned that a small company named MITS was looking for programmers, Chamberlain made an appointment to talk to its software director, Paul Allen.

Allen wasn't sure where MITS was headed and wanted Chamberlain to know the risks involved. Allen had willingly accepted the risks but wasn't about to inflict them on the unaware. He hired Chamberlain but warned him, "If it doesn't work out, well, it doesn't work out." Chamberlain appreciated Allen's candor and commenced writing software for the 680b, a machine that "was not enormously successful," Chamberlain recalled dryly. They had already encountered serious difficulty with the product. "Lots of [the 680b machines] were ordered, but when I came on board at MITS, the whole project was already in trouble. They had to go through a complete redesign." Despite the revamping, the 680b never really took off, but Chamberlain found plenty of other work to do at MITS. Roberts had other machines in mind, and each of them required new software.

Meanwhile, Allen and Gates were putting increased effort into their own company, Microsoft. Throughout 1975, Gates, Allen, and Rick Wyland, who was hired to write 6800 BASIC, were branching out with their versions of BASIC, including developing versions for other companies. The relationship between Microsoft and MITS was becoming less clearly defined as the two companies grew.

The fact that Bill Gates had yet to write the disk code for the Altair 8800 didn't help matters, especially because Gates, on leave from Harvard, was considering returning to school. Paul Allen, in his role as MITS software director, nagged Gates about finishing the code.

According to Microsoft legend, in February 1976 Gates checked into a motel with some pens and a stack of yellow legal pads. When he came out, he had finished writing down the disk code.

By 1976, the switch from dynamic memory to static memory (two means of maintaining information in memory) seemed to have solved the vexing problem with the memory board, but MITS still had to either troubleshoot the dynamic boards already in the field or buy them back. Early in that year, MITS revamped its quality-control procedures in an attempt to increase efficiency in manufacturing. MITS was already shipping the 680b and planned to ship the upgraded 8800 by midyear. A disk operating system written around Gates's disk code was scheduled to be released in July 1976.

Anyone who owned an Altair had probably written a program for it at one time or another. Mark Chamberlain was now maintaining a library of software submitted by Altair users, thereby setting a precedent for the industry. Chamberlain was distributing such programs as widely as possible throughout the community of users, which was a smart move. Sharing of software vastly increased the value of the machine. In particular, he sought software for the new 680b. When Paul Allen announced the price for the 680b BASIC, customers recognized an already familiar tactic. The BASIC cost nothing with the new 16K memory board, but $200 when purchased without it.

By the middle of that year, the competition that Roberts had long feared was becoming a reality. A new company named IMSAI imitated the Altair design and brought out its own computer, the IMSAI 8080. Polymorphic Systems introduced what looked like a serious competitor to the Altair, the Poly-88. And, in July 1976, Processor Technology grabbed the front cover of *Popular Electronics* with its Sol computer, named after Les Solomon. Even MIT's loyal board supplier Cromemco was developing a CPU board designed around the new Zilog Z80 microprocessor as the successor to the Intel 8080 chip that was the heart of the original Altair computer. The Z80 was designed by Federico Faggin, who had left Intel to start his own semiconductor company after his work on the Intel 4004. This new microprocessor was catching a lot of attention among the high-tech cognoscenti.

None of the new microcomputer companies represented an immediate threat to MITS's market share for microcomputers. In that arena,

MITS reigned uncontested. But all of the machines from these start-ups could, in principle, use the same circuit boards as the Altair. They all had the same 100-line bus structure and, as Roberts viewed things, that bus was the key to compatibility in that it allowed competitive boards to be plugged into the Altair. He typically referred to the system as the "Altair bus" and wanted others to do the same. When some didn't comply, David Bunnell suggested sarcastically that they call it the "Roberts bus." The bus-naming story typifies the curious mix of competitiveness and camaraderie in the nascent computer industry. The bus became a major point of contention between MITS and the majority of the microcomputing world.

Roberts's position was simple: he and Yates had designed the bus just as they had designed the Altair. Therefore, it was the Altair bus. His competitors preferred not to share his view. The advertised name for the device grew to absurd lengths in order to credit just about every manufacturer. It was billed as the "MITS-IMSAI-Processor Tech-Polymorphic bus." Garland and Melen talked about the bus name problem on a flight from San Francisco to Atlantic City where PC 76, an early microcomputer conference, was held in August 1976.

Garland and Melen were about to release a CPU board for the Altair bus and were reluctant to refer to it by a lengthy list of competitors' names. They agreed about two things: the name of the bus should not favor any one company, and it should suggest an item that's been engineered. For instance, the name could consist of a letter and some numbers. They liked the name "Standard 100," and in keeping with their theme, shortened it to "S100." That, they thought, sounded sufficiently official.

Their next goal was securing the approval of other hardware vendors. Melen recalled the following: "On the same airplane were the people from Processor Technology, specifically Bob Marsh and Lee Felsenstein. I had a can of beer in my hand, and in the course of our discussing the standard, the airplane hit a little bump, and I spilled my beer on Bob. He agreed [to the new name] very quickly, to get rid of me and my beer can." The name "S100" became the common coin, although MITS and *Popular Electronics* stubbornly clung to the name "Altair bus" for a long while. Seven years later, Ed Roberts was still adamant about it: "The bus was used by MITS for two years before anybody else was producing a computer. It's the Altair bus. Calling the Altair bus the S100 bus is like calling Mona Lisa 'Tom Boy.' I'm the only one in the world who's irritated by that, but I'm irritated."

In addition to the S100 companies, MITS was witnessing disturbing signs of competition from other, even more unnerving sources. MOS Technology, a semiconductor company, was doing well with Chuck Peddle's KIM-1, a low-cost hobbyist computer built around its own bargain-basement 6502 chip. This fact alone may have occasioned no immediate alarm, but two months later, in October 1976, Commodore bought MOS Technology. For the first time, a large and well-established company with extensive channels of distribution for electronics products would be selling a microcomputer. Roberts was justly worried. He remembered how Texas Instruments had stomped all over the calculator business.

An even more ominous threat was looming. Tandy Corporation, having "just gotten through killing off Lafayette [Electronics]," as Peddle put it, was casting about for a computer to sell in its hundreds of Radio Shack stores. "What Radio Shack wanted to do was to come up with a packaged machine," Peddle said, "because they knew their guys couldn't support, and couldn't design, this kind of thing." Radio Shack, with its stores all over the country, could sell thousands of personal computers at rock-bottom prices.

With semiconductor companies and electronics distributors getting into the act, the competition was gearing up.

The Fall

*Q: Did you think it was going
to go under?
A: All the time, all the time.*

BILL GATES
(from an interview)

THE TROUBLED MITS HAD MORE TO WORRY ABOUT THAN ITS COMPETI-
tion. The company had grown too big too fast. "We had too many
irons in the fire," Roberts admitted later. "We had a lot more things
going than a company the size of ours should have had." The faulty
memory boards that were still out there in the field were just one of the
problems. Quality control was not particularly effective, and customers
were complaining. Projects were often launched despite the reservations of many MITS employees. A number of products failed.

"The high-speed paper tape reader is a good example," Mark Chamberlain recalled, "because I know we only sold three of those." The
"spark printer" was another: MITS bought a printer from a manufacturer, rebuilt it and repackaged it, and eventually had to charge considerably more than the supplier's retail price for the original unimproved
item. Naturally, the MITS version didn't take off. Sometimes an entire
major product line was clearly a mistake to everyone at MITS except
Roberts. Paul Allen objected strenuously to the 680b.

MITS's difficulties ran deep. "It really gets into a study of personalities," Mark Chamberlain said. "I don't know if it's possible to understand the situation without understanding all the aspects that were [a
result of] people's different personalities." One thing is clear in retro-

spect. The channels of communication between upper-level employees and the president were not always open. "Ed isolated himself," Gates said. "He didn't have a good rapport with other people in the company, and didn't know how to deal with the growth." Roberts later acknowledged that a problem existed: "I was worried about so many things at the time that I felt like everything was a threat."

A number of changes occurred at MITS toward the end of 1976. By that time, Roberts had brought in his childhood friend Eddie Curry as executive vice president and Bob Tindley from the bank that had financed MITS to help with management. But Roberts was soon to lose an important employee. Paul Allen was restless. Microsoft was becoming a more serious enterprise, and Allen was eager to take control of his own destiny. Convinced that MITS's best days were long past, he and Bill Gates began focusing all their attention on their own company. Mark Chamberlain moved up to replace Allen as MITS's software director.

Chamberlain found that the job bore unexpected challenges. He quickly encountered upper-level dissension over which products to build and which projects to undertake first. Chamberlain, along with his hardware counterpart Pat Godding and others, did not always agree with Roberts on critical decisions. In holding on so tightly to the reins of his company, Roberts may have been trying to shield others from all the uncertainty and vulnerability of the fledgling industry. He took all the responsibility upon himself rather than allowing others to share it. The burden was too much to bear. As Gates acknowledged: "Nobody really knew what was going on. So many things would have obviously needed to be done if you'd had the vision back then. Nobody had the view of the market."

"He did have ideas," Chamberlain said of Roberts. "But we didn't fill out the product line; we didn't provide proper support. I think that the early pioneers who used the Altair in business were up against a hell of a lot of frustration." Among the most frustrated were Chamberlain and Godding. Convinced that their ideas had value and equally certain that Roberts would never accept them, they often went ahead on their projects in secret without his knowledge. One high-level employee spoke with Roberts about a project that he was certain would generate sales immediately with just a little more work. Roberts put his foot down, saying that absolutely no more work would be done on the project. The work progressed anyway. "He didn't know we were doing it," said Chamberlain.

Although MITS grossed $13 million in 1976, the company was losing its edge. Its products were not regarded as anywhere near the best, deliveries were slow, and service was poor. Most other microcomputer companies at the time had similar problems to some degree, but MITS's position in the industry led people to expect more from the firm. Furthermore, MITS had established an exclusive dealership program early on. Retailers who wished to be the only Altair dealers in their area could sell no other brands. But the knife cut both ways, and MITS began to have trouble finding dealers willing to agree to the company's terms.

Retailers and customers alike were dissatisfied. It was not that MITS was in imminent danger of going out of business, as it had been in 1974, but its prospects were not good and the competition was getting serious. By now, more than 50 hardware companies had entered the market. At the first West Coast Computer Faire held in San Francisco in the spring of 1977, Chuck Peddle was showing Commodore's PET, a more serious machine than the MOS/Commodore KIM-1 and a formidable competitor to the Altair machines; also, Apple introduced its Apple II amid fanfare that signaled a change in the market.

On May 22, 1977, Roberts sold MITS to Pertec, a company then specializing in disk and tape drives for minicomputers and mainframe computers. "It was a stock swap," Roberts said. "They bought MITS for essentially six million dollars." Whether Pertec got a bargain or a dud depends on the degree to which Pertec management was responsible for MITS's ensuing slide into oblivion.

Roberts had talked to other companies, especially semiconductor companies, before deciding on a buyer. Pertec had offered him not only personal stock in the company, but his own private research and development lab and the freedom to use it exactly as he pleased. The opportunity to work on new products and to somehow tie his fortunes to MITS undoubtedly meant a lot to Roberts. But he simply wanted to climb down off the nose cone. The bust of the calculator venture still haunted him, and he knew a similar disaster could very well happen with personal computers. "Once you've been there," Roberts said, "staying awake every night wondering whether you're going to make payroll the following day . . . you're pretty gun-shy, and you're making decisions that aren't terribly logical."

The Pertec sale led to acrid fighting over ownership of the software. Gates and Allen had no intention of handing their BASIC over to Pertec. They had written the core of the BASIC before even meeting anyone from MITS, and, unlike Allen, Gates insisted that he had never been a MITS employee. "Pertec thought they were buying the software as part of the whole deal," Gates recalled. "And they weren't. We owned the software. It was all under license."

Suddenly, the whole deal was in jeopardy. Gates later recalled the head of Pertec telling him that if the software were not included in the transaction, Pertec would back out of the deal. If that happened, MITS would fold. The pressure on the boys was tremendous.

"They sent out this big-time lawyer," Gates recalled, and the matter went into arbitration. When it was all over, Gates and Allen had prevailed. The software belonged to Microsoft. Fortunately for MITS, Pertec went ahead with the purchase anyway.

Ed Roberts still believed that the decision was dead wrong. Years later he felt bitter and betrayed. MITS's agreement with Gates and Allen, he insisted, stipulated that they would receive royalties on the software up to a maximum of $200,000 and then the software would belong to MITS. His company had paid them that amount and therefore owned the software. Roberts was convinced that the arbitrator misunderstood clear issues of fact. "It was a fluke," Roberts maintained. "It was just wrong as rain."

Roberts blamed Gates for the outcome. "Our relationship really went to heck," Gates said. "Ed really got his feelings hurt." Having won in the arbitration and with no ties holding them to Albuquerque, Gates and Allen moved Microsoft to their native Bellevue, Washington.

Pertec didn't back out of the MITS acquisition because of the BASIC ruling, but under Pertec, MITS gradually fell apart. Even before the acquisition, the company was losing its dominant role in the very industry it had created. But MITS didn't start its dramatic decline until the Pertec management teams walked onto the scene.

The Pertec people managed to alienate virtually all key MITS personnel. "They kept patting us on the head, saying we didn't understand the business," Roberts recalled. The MITS regulars simply didn't respond well to the Pertec management teams. The standard line on them was that they were "two-bit managers in three-piece suits." The epithet was used so frequently it was shortened to simply "the suits."

Pertec managed MITS as if it were a big business in an established industry. Before agreeing to buy MITS, Pertec executives asked Roberts to show them his five-year marketing forecast. At the time, MITS advance planning "consisted of where things would be on Friday," Roberts said. To please the buyers, Roberts and Eddie Curry invented projections they figured would make the Pertec managers break out the champagne. They told Pertec that sales would double each year and provided a pie-in-the-sky guess of how many machines the company could move. Pertec bought it all. Over the following year, managers came and went at Pertec in extraordinary numbers. "People based their careers on trying to live up to that [bogus forecast]," said Curry.

Mark Chamberlain had no use for the Pertec suits who'd invaded MITS: "They sent in team after team. Each team came in to knock off the previous team. Any given team had about 60 to 90 days to turn the mess into something good, but it wasn't enough time. It was just long enough for the people to come in and switch from a position of trying to understand the problem to becoming a part of the problem. After 60 to 90 days, you were definitely part of the problem. And they'd send in the next guy to fire you." Chamberlain left to go to work for Roberts in his lab. "I wanted out of that Pertec thing like right away," he said. "That thing was crazy." For a while, Chamberlain worked with Roberts on a low-priced computer based on the Zilog Z80 chip, but he soon left to pursue other opportunities.

Others were defecting from Pertec's MITS group. Bunnell departed at the end of 1976 to start *Personal Computing,* an early microcomputer magazine. He published it from Albuquerque throughout 1977 with contributions from Gates and Allen. Andrea Lewis took over as editor of *Computer Notes* and changed it from a company-written newsletter to a slick magazine with outside contributions. Eventually she accepted an invitation from Paul Allen to move to Bellevue and take over Microsoft's documentation department. Sometime after that, Chamberlain also joined Microsoft.

Several engineering people left Pertec to work for a local electronics company. Even Ed Roberts, after five months, became fed up with Pertec. "They told me I didn't understand the market. I don't think they understood it." Roberts bought a farm in Georgia, and told everyone he intended to become a gentleman farmer or go to medical school. Eventually, he did both, with the same concentrated energy he had brought to MITS.

Pertec gradually came to regard the MITS operation as a bad venture and eventually abandoned it. According to Eddie Curry, who stayed on longer than any other MITS principal, Pertec continued making Altairs for about a year after the acquisition, but within two years MITS was gone.

It would be hard to overestimate the importance of MITS and the Altair to the world of microcomputers. The company did more than create an industry. It introduced the first affordable personal computer, and also pioneered the concept of computer shows, computer retailing, computer company magazines, users' groups, software exchanges, and many hardware and software products. Without intending to, MITS made software piracy a widespread phenomenon. Started when microcomputers seemed wildly impractical, MITS pioneered what would eventually become a multibillion-dollar industry.

If MITS was, as writer David Bunnell's ads proclaimed, Number One in the business, the scramble to be Number Two was won by one of the most idiosyncratic of the early microcomputer companies.

CHAPTER 3

THE MIRACLE MAKERS

est killed IMSAI.

ADAM OSBORNE
Industry pioneer commenting on the impact of
the self-help movement on a promising company
in the personal computer industry

After Altair

Everybody wanted to be second.

TED NELSON
Computer visionary, philosopher, critic

Mits may have been the first company to successfully market a microcomputer, but it was not alone for long. MITS (original name, Micro Instrumentation Telemetry Systems) grew from a small electronics firm to become the leading microcomputer company after it introduced the groundbreaking Altair in 1975. MITS even boasted the two future Microsoft founders among its ranks.

During the 2½ years between the January 1975 *Popular Electronics* cover story announcing the Altair 8800 and the May 1977 sale of MITS to Pertec, a disk and tape drive manufacturer, a new industry was on the rise. The Altair announcement triggered both technological and social change. The hobbyists who read the *Popular Electronics* article may not have envisioned the subsequent proliferation of microcomputers, but they did realize they were witness to the start of a radical change in the way people access computers. They had been waiting for it.

Programmers, technicians, and engineers who worked with large computers all had the feeling of being "locked out" of the machine room. In the 1960s, when digital computers became available to scientists and engineers who worked for companies large enough to afford computers, the business of performing complex calculations was greatly speeded up. But there also developed a "computer priest-hood"—a closed club of engineers and technicians through which one had to pass in order to reap the computer's benefits.

Computer time was expensive, and the need to budget each individual's hours on a machine was a continuing annoyance. Users tolerated interruptions at awkward times and submitted programs to bureaucratic layers of intermediaries. Programmers felt the frustration of being skilled workers denied full access to their tools and the source of their livelihood. As a result, it was the rare programmer or engineer who did not dream of owning his or her own machine, even as early as 1975. This desire was the tinder and the *Popular Electronics* article the spark of a revolution.

The Altair from MITS breached the machine room door, and rivals emerged almost all at once from garages all over the country. MITS chief Ed Roberts's price was hard to undercut, and if it had not been for the long delays in delivering the Altair, MITS's early advantage would have been huge. But commercial success was deemed irrelevant to the kindling of the revolution. Those who failed did so openly, with their schematics laid on the table for all to see. Mistakes proved instructive, and failures did little to discourage increased innovation. The revolution was running on its own internal drive, and not according to the external pull of profits. The industry did not take shape according to traditional economic laws.

The MITS competitors were hobbyist enterprises, partly because none of the big corporations wanted to build microcomputers. Only those fanatics who were totally and blindly enthralled by computers and electronics could have endured the tedious detail work required to design and build a computer by hand.

The idea of assembling a computer by hand sounded crazy to most people. It had only recently become possible to attempt such a task at all, and the Altair had yet to prove itself as a computer in anything more than the technical sense. But the hobbyists of 1975 knew that the Altair eventually would make its mark.

Hobbyists were hooked on building computers. For instance, New Mexico fire spotter Don Lancaster had been providing digital know-how to a generation of computer hobbyists through his freelance articles in electronics magazines. Lancaster became involved with a company called Southwest Technical Products in the mid-1970s. Southwest Tech made high-end audio components kits and in 1975 released an Altair-like microcomputer using a new microprocessor from Motorola, the 6800. Many engineers, including Ed Roberts, thought the 6800 was a better chip than the Altair 8080, and Roberts kept a watchful eye on Southwest Tech. Don Lancaster wasn't secretive about his designs, but hardly anyone was then. A spirit of information sharing, unthinkable among most other business competitors, ran throughout the computer hobbyist field. Special-interest magazines had helped create a nationwide community of hobbyists who regularly wrote to one another, argued at length and with passion, and generously shared their knowledge. As a result, they were technically prepared and emotionally geared up to build their own computers. "They wanted it so bad they could taste it," said semiconductor designer Chuck Peddle. At UC Berkeley, computer science professor John Torode examined the Intel 4004 and 8008 chips and decided they were less than ideal for use as central processors. When he got one of the first 8080 chips from his old friend Gary Kildall, who was teaching computer science down the coast in Monterey and consulting at Intel, Torode began to think seriously about building his own microcomputer.

By mid-1974, Torode and Kildall had assembled a microcomputer and a disk operating system of sorts. But they were skeptical about the market for such a device and continued to refine the product strictly as a hobby; Kildall created the software, and Torode fashioned the hardware. They sold only a handful of machines before the Altair burst on the scene, including the two devices they sold to a San Francisco Bay Area computer terminal company called Omron. The two then pursued their interests independently; Torode built computers under the name Digital Systems and later Digital Microsystems, and Kildall wrote software under the name Intergalactic Digital Research (later Digital Research).

Although the Bay Area was recognized as a development hub, the microcomputer phenomenon was spreading nationwide. In Denver, Robert "Dr. Bob" Suding turned his hobby into a business, Digital Group, which soon won the respect of many hobbyist customers. The company initially produced plug-in circuit boards for the Altair and other emerging computer brands. Suding also pioneered an idea that was taken seriously five years later: a machine that could use different types of microprocessors interchangeably. The Altair was an 8080 machine and the Southwest Tech computer a 6800, but either processor would work in a Digital Group computer. This innovation reflected the thinking of the times. An interchangeable microprocessor was a boon to microcomputer designers (that is, hobbyists), but was of little use to ordinary consumers because of the lack of software for the new processors. The hobbyists were designing computers for themselves. Even the appearance of the machines reflected their hobbyist origins. The typical computer resembled a homemade piece of electronic test equipment—a metal box rigged with toggle switches, blinking lights, and wires running out of its back, front, top, or sides—a real "kludge," as computers made up of a hodgepodge of parts came to be called.

No one gave much thought to a machine's visual appeal because designers were creating the computers *they* wanted, regardless of how the end product looked. When the Southern California–based company Vector Graphic rejected a designer's pink circuit board with purple rheostats on the grounds that the components clashed with Vector's green and orange computer, the designer was flabbergasted. Color coordination was seldom a consideration in mid-1970s computer design.

One of the first computer companies to consciously consider aesthetic appeal and economical use of desktop space was Sphere, founded by Mike Wise in Bountiful, Utah. The Sphere computer was *integrated;* that is, the display monitor and keyboard were incorporated into the same case with the microprocessor. The machine was a closed unit, with no mass of wires dangling out of its sides.

The Sphere didn't last. Although a commercial product on the outside, inside it was all hobby machine. The mechanism under the lid wasn't pretty—not even to a hobbyist. It was too much of a handmade item, filled with scores of crisscrossing, hand-soldered wires. The Sphere was not engineered for production, nor was it particularly reliable. Plus, as one hobbyist of the time put it, it had "the world's slowest BASIC."

The names given to the corporate start-ups reflected the informality and tongue-in-cheek humor of the hobbyist movement. Lee Felsenstein started a company called Loving Grace Cybernetics and later another called Golemics Incorporated. Itty Bitty Machine Company (IBM) appeared in Chicago. Chicken Delight Computer Consultants cropped up in New Jersey. Kentucky Fried Computers began in Northern California.

A thin line existed between buyers and manufacturers in those early days. Operating a microcomputer took so much expertise and dedication that to say a skilled user could have become a manufacturer was no exaggeration. There existed a conglomerate subculture of techno-freaks, hobbyists, and hackers untrained in business practices, entrepreneurs who were more interested in exploring the potential of the microcomputer than in making a fortune. One exception was IMSAI Manufacturing in San Leandro, California.

IMSAI became the number two maker of microcomputers and soon thereafter seized the leading sales position from MITS. Started by Bill Millard just months after the January 1975 Altair debut, IMSAI was unique in its origin and philosophy. Practically all the other company presidents were hobbyists who knew each other through club meetings and newsletters. Millard, by comparison, was a former sales representative. He and his associates didn't know the hobbyists and didn't want to know them. They seldom attended the hobbyists' club meetings at which members would swap stories of their experiences with various new (and unreliable) machines, exchange rumors, and share equipment, software, and insights. Millard and company didn't consider themselves part of that crowd.

From the very first, Millard and his team of hard-driving executives saw themselves as serious businesspeople in a field populated by blue-jeaned dilettantes. The IMSAI computer would be *the* desktop tool of the small business, Millard decreed. It would, among other things, replace the typewriter. In the minds of IMSAI executives, the company was building commercial systems for business customers who wanted to do real work. They weren't in the business of making toys for hobbyists. It was prescient on their part to see such potential in those crude early microcomputers. It may have seemed fanciful to build a company on that vision back in 1975, but Millard and his team were not afraid to be seen as overly ambitious. They were operating outside the envelope, and that was how they liked it.

In 1975, when IMSAI began making its 8080 microcomputer, most of the hobbyists thought that Millard was trying to corner the business market a little early. The hard-core hobbyists didn't know just yet what those machines could do, so how could the business community be expected to embrace them? Microcomputers were still experimental and often didn't work right. So what made Millard and his team think that small businesses would buy the machines? "Guesswork," according to cofounder Bruce Van Natta. "We *guessed* that these things were really small business machines, even if the damn things did weight 80 pounds and barely fit on a desk." Technologically, the IMSAI computer was no breakthrough. It was essentially a copy of the Altair with some enhancements—most notably, a better power supply. The Altair's power supply unit, which was supposed to distribute the appropriate DC current and voltages to the various parts of the computer, was regarded by hobbyists as dismal. IMSAI, on the other hand, delivered "a power supply you couldn't lift," as Van Natta later put it. He was exaggerating, of course, although just a few years earlier everyone took it for granted that a computer and its components were almost impossible for one person to lift. Although IMSAI eventually solved other stubborn technical problems, perhaps the company's most significant achievements in hardware design were improving the Altair power supply and eliminating the hand-soldered wires that the Altair required. Those two innovations went a long way toward making the machines truly useful. But IMSAI's most important contribution to the nascent industry was not a technological one; it was the company's pure chutzpah. Millard took a "me-too" design, sold it to a market whose mere existence was dubious, and built a company that became a power to be reckoned with.

Amateurs and Professionals

It was an unusual organization in that it really did believe in high-intensity, enthusiastic amateurs.

BRUCE VAN NATTA
IMSAI cofounder

BILL MILLARD WAS A MAGNETIC ROLE MODEL TO THE IMSAI EXECUtives, and through them he set a singular tone for the company. Millard did not hire hobbyists, but he did hire enthusiastic amateurs. His personality and goals became the corporate personality and the company's goals, so much so that Millard's decision-making style steered IMSAI even when he wasn't around, as happened during some rocky times in the company's history when top-level decisions were critical.

Unlike Ed Roberts at MITS and many others, Millard was not particularly fascinated by hardware. For as long as he maintained an interest in computers, Roberts was a true hobbyist, a computer junkie who really wanted to see what the thing could do. Like a number of microcomputer engineers after him, Roberts built the kind of machine that he wanted to use. If MITS managed to sell just a few hundred computers, enough to keep the company in its little shop next to the laundromat, Roberts wouldn't feel that he had failed. He liked money, but for him a larger part of the thrill was always in the possibilities the machine presented. Bill Millard was different from the other company heads. He burned with a much more acquisitive fire, constantly seeking increased market share, increased capital, and more and more attention. "He was a typical entrepreneur," according to one of his protégés, Bill Lohse, "except maybe a little more careless, a little more gutsy." He was a gambler who liked to take chances.

Millard was also a salesman. He had been a rep for IBM and had done well at it. By the late 1960s, he was manager of data processing for the city and county of San Francisco. In that capacity, he dealt with mainframe and minicomputer companies for five years in the early 1970s. That experience enabled him to identify the potential players who would join him in the biggest gamble of his life. Millard was looking for a loyal and dedicated team to follow him onto the competitive industry playing field. He wanted enthusiastic young men and women who weren't necessarily computer experts but who would take the risks he wanted to take. Every other computer company was run by engineers. Millard created a company run by salespeople. Millard's people all displayed an intense desire to succeed and an unswerving confidence in their sales abilities. They were an odd bunch for the industry at that time. They wore suits. They talked more about money than machines, and more about goals and "miracles" (Millard's oft-used expression) than about money. And, almost without exception, they had "done the training." Doing "the training" for Millard and many other Californians at the time meant going through Erhard Seminars Training, or *est*, one of a spate of self-help movements that sprang up during the late 1960s. Millard had done the training and encouraged his family and friends to do it, too; it became a condition of employment for upper-level executives at IMSAI. One *est* tenet had particular relevance for IMSAI: failure or the admission of its possibility was viewed as evidence of lack of a desire to succeed. Therefore, many *est* graduates were reluctant to admit a task may be impossible or a goal unattainable. Millard liked that tendency in people and actively sought it in his coworkers, which was one of the reasons he hired Joe Killian.

Initially, Millard had no intention of building computers. He started IMS Associates, the IMSAI parent company, to configure computer systems for businesses, which was the sort of work he had once done for San Francisco's city and county governments. IMS determined what hardware and programs companies needed to solve their data processing problems and matched the hardware and software accordingly. Millard needed a good programmer who also knew hardware.

After dropping out of a graduate school physics program, Killian was looking for a job in the Bay Area when a friend introduced him to Bill Millard. Killian had become fascinated with computers in graduate school, and having also gone through *est* training, he formed an immediate bond with Millard. But Killian was not the model IMSAI executive Millard typically sought. Although he was young and enthusiastic, open to new ideas, and attacked technical problems with a hobbyist's zeal, he tended to deliberate before he spoke. He always hesitated a moment before expressing his opinions on a new idea, the moment it took him to reconcile the new idea with his existing knowledge and beliefs.

It took a New Mexico automobile dealer, who was one of Millard and Killian's customers, to steer them in the direction of building microcomputers. Early in 1975, a request from the auto dealer presented both a challenge and a maddening problem for Millard. The dealer had commissioned Millard to find a computer to do his accounting, and Millard thought he knew of an inexpensive way to satisfy him. MITS had just announced the Altair, and Millard planned to buy the rudimentary machine and tack on whatever extras the dealer needed.

Unfortunately, Millard did not fully grasp the MITS situation and what kind of struggles the company was having. Overwhelmed by orders, Roberts's little company was not yet ready to deliver finished Altairs, and Roberts had given no thought to quantity discounts. The idea of selling Altairs at a discount to Millard, who would dress them up as business systems with the appropriate software and attachments, didn't appeal to Roberts. When Millard realized that Roberts couldn't or wouldn't supply him with discount-priced machines, he looked elsewhere.

Had Millard been in tune with the hobbyist community, he might have done business with one of the new hobby firms just popping up. Instead, he drew on his contacts in the minicomputer and peripheral equipment areas. At Omron, a computer terminal company that had coincidentally just bought the first two of John Torode and Gary Kildall's microcomputer systems, Millard chatted with a fellow named Ed Faber. Faber was, in some ways, a kindred spirit. Like Millard, the soft-spoken Faber was an ex-IBM salesman in his mid-40s who was intrigued by risks. Despite connecting with Faber, Millard's immediate goal was to fill the auto dealer's order, and again, nothing acceptable emerged. He was growing frustrated.

Millard realized that a great opportunity had presented itself. It wasn't just a matter of a single auto dealer in New Mexico. Once Millard's people had put together a complete system with all the necessary programs and hardware, they could sell it to auto dealers throughout the country. Millard knew they wouldn't fail. He wasn't about to let this opportunity evaporate. He took the auto dealer's money and with it started a company called IMSAI Manufacturing for the express purpose of building microcomputers.

Millard knew what he wanted. He was convinced that the Altair was the machine for the job, and if Roberts wouldn't sell Altairs to him at a reasonable price, he would build his own. Or Joe Killian would. A friend of Killian's had bought an Altair, and Killian had carefully studied it, but that wasn't enough. External examination was fine, Killian said, but he really needed to get inside the thing and dismantle it. His friend liked his Altair as it was, intact. Millard phoned Paul Terrell, whose nearby Byte Shop was one of the few Altair dealerships in the country. Millard ordered some Altairs for dissection. Over the next few months, Killian would tear the computers apart, figure out how they were made, and replicate them.

Millard's team was beginning to grow. Killian had worked many late nights on another project, and Millard gave him a much-needed vacation in February 1975. In Killian's absence, Millard advertised for a programmer to take his place. The UC Berkeley computer-science grad school dropout who applied for the job was youthful, brash, and willing to take risks; moreover, he knew how to sell himself. In short, Bruce Van Natta impressed Millard immediately. Van Natta in many ways had the typical appearance and manner of an IMSAI executive. He was tall, thin, bright-eyed, and sharply attired, quick with an opinion, succinct and decisive in his speech, and willing to take outrageous risks.

Van Natta fell naturally into the mold of the aggressive IMSAI exec. When Killian returned from his vacation, the three of them sat around a table at Jake's Blue Lion Restaurant in San Leandro talking late into the night about their plans for microcomputers, their new company IMSAI, and making miracles happen. "Make a miracle" was one of Millard's favorite sayings. If Killian or Van Natta complained that Millard was asking the impossible, Millard would tell them, "Make a miracle."

While Killian worked on the IMSAI computer, Bruce Van Natta was promoting the Hypercube, a product idea he had conceived and hashed out during the Blue Lion talks. The Hypercube device was designed to link together several microprocessors in order to produce results similar to those you'd get from a large computer. Van Natta was acclaimed for this concept. He was soon giving lectures around the San Francisco Bay Area, at one point speaking before several hundred electrical and electronics engineers. But he was proudest of his invitation to lecture to the UC Berkeley Computer Science Department, which he had just recently left.

The Hypercube caught the attention of the computer news media, stealing the front page of *Computer World* and the "Product Spotlight" in *Datamation,* two mainframe computer publications. A great deal of attention was being paid to a product that never existed except in Bruce Van Natta's head, but to the computer press editors who were keeping abreast of all the rapid innovations, the linking scheme that Van Natta proposed may have seemed like the only way tiny microcomputers could be made really useful.

In December 1975, with IMSAI's computer in its first production stages, Millard once again met with Omron's Ed Faber. This time he asked Faber to come work for IMSAI. Faber was skeptical. Killian's computer was a kit, like the Altair. Kits were ridiculous, Faber thought. He had never heard of building your own computer, let alone selling it through mail-order ads run in *Popular Electronics.* But the number of calls coming in when he visited IMSAI changed his mind. He soon got swept up in all the excitement and accepted a position as director of sales in January 1976.

Faber did not exactly fit the IMSAI mold. He was seasoned, experienced, and used to giving orders rather than taking them. Most of the other key people were more malleable. Millard, the gambler, had wanted his eager band of executives to follow him anywhere in his high-risk excursions. Would Faber do the same?

In fact, Faber was willing to take risks. He was a veteran IBM employee who had specialized in two fields: sales and start-up operations. Having started a number of new ventures for IBM, Faber found that he relished the exhilaration of the experience. Millard needed someone to organize a sales force, and Faber was willing to do it. Faber's post was a critical one; the sales team was the heart of the company.

Bill Lohse, one of the first salesmen Faber hired, was a vitamin peddler with a degree in philosophy. He, too, seemed to have been poured out of the IMSAI mold. He was tall and thin, a recent and enthusiastic *est* graduate, brash, bright, and fond of wearing the kind of top-quality suits that Van Natta and Millard favored. He knew nothing about computers but was convinced he could sell them to anyone.

Many more employees were hired by IMSAI, including a crew to produce the machines. And some of the new hires, such as ex–rock band roadie Todd Fischer, were out of a different mold than Lohse, Van Natta, and Millard. By the fall of 1976, the production team was turning out Killian's IMSAI 8080 computer in quantity. MITS, which until then had seen competition only in its circuit board market, suddenly had a serious rival.

Building One and Building Two

*Building One was primarily the
administrative building. Building Two was the
production building. There was always this
thing of Building Two versus Building One.*

TODD FISCHER
IMSAI computer repairman

TODD FISCHER LIKED TO FIX THINGS. WHEN HIGH SCHOOL ENDED AND many of his classmates went to college or engineering school, Fischer headed to the Air Force recruitment center to enlist. The Air Force, in turn, taught him to repair electronic equipment. Fischer valued the training, but didn't want to make the Air Force his career. So, when his hitch was up, Fischer went to work for IBM repairing typewriters and keypunch machines. He quit in 1967 after working there only briefly. It wasn't that Fischer didn't like the job. But it was the late 1960s, and to this particular Bay Area boy, IBM symbolized faceless bureaucracies and excessive corporate power.

After leaving IBM, Fischer discovered that he could make money from music—not by playing it, but by fixing band equipment. In the late 1960s, he drifted into the San Francisco rock music scene. This was Fischer's milieu and he loved it. From 1968 to 1971, Fischer worked with dozens of local rock groups. He worked as a roadie for legendary drummer Buddy Miles and for the rock band Uriah Heep. Fischer traveled around the world with stage acts repairing electronic equipment. He was in heaven.

Eventually, Fischer returned to earth. Back in the Bay Area he tried running an electronics repair shop, but couldn't make a go of it. He was doing repair work in a stereo store when a friend invited him to come to work in the service division of a year-old computer company called IMSAI Manufacturing. "Repair computers? Well, why not?" he thought. After touring with the likes of Buddy Miles, the work was a bit of a letdown, but at least Fischer got to fix things.

IMSAI had grown quickly and showed no signs of decelerating. The company already occupied two buildings on Wicks Boulevard in San Leandro; administration, sales, marketing, and engineering were located in one building, and production and support in the other. Millard had assembled a driven organization, a fact nowhere more apparent than among the sales team in Building One. Telephone salespeople such as Bill Lohse came in promptly at 8 A.M. and after a brief meeting got on the phones and stayed there, logging every call until lunch time. Lohse would take an hour off, during which time he compared notes with other sales representatives on how many thousands of dollars of equipment they had sold that morning. Then he'd jump back on the phones again, making calls until the end-of-the-day sales meeting. Lohse learned not to talk in terms of "problems," but instead use the buzzwords "challenges" and "opportunities." Exhortations to "make a miracle" were frequently heard.

Under Millard's encouragement—some say insistence—the IMSAI executives and sales staff did the training, made the miracles happen, and met their goals. IMSAI employees learned to focus on what they wanted to do and then go out and do it. They learned that lesson well, and it intensified their performance in meeting goals and in their relations with coworkers and customers. "Focus on what you want to do and do it" was a powerful message to send to a recent graduate in his or her first serious job. As if things weren't intense enough, the new hires worked for a rapidly expanding company that could either go bankrupt the next week or grow as big as IBM. And, the message was delivered under the leadership of a charismatic entrepreneur, a high-roller who informed each new employee that he or she could perform miracles—and *would* perform miracles.

Millard's exhortations were part of a calculated effort to create an atmosphere that drove his staff to superhuman achievement. Those who could thrive in that atmosphere had to be driven. The intensity created an attitude among IMSAI management of almost manic optimism. They regularly worked well into the night, living and breathing IMSAI, and almost losing sight of the sublunary world. Yet from where Bill Lohse stood, eyebrow-deep in work, it was often difficult to focus on anything but what he was already doing. He saw nothing on the horizon but that week's sales goal.

Meeting sales goals became IMSAI's raison d'être and the sales department the company's heart and soul. No one drove this point home more clearly than Bruce Van Natta. He had held a number of jobs at IMSAI, working in purchasing, programming, engineering, and product planning. One day, to everyone's surprise, Van Natta walked into the sales director's office and announced that he himself wanted to be a sales representative. It seemed an odd thing for a cofounder of the company to request, but before long Van Natta was the company's top agent.

Around that time, Bill Millard set a sales goal of $1 million for the month. Two days before the end of that month, Van Natta checked the sales figures. They totaled $680,000, well short of a million dollars, and no potential customers were left to call on. Van Natta would never say that it was impossible to make the goal; one didn't talk that way at IMSAI. But he thought as much when he headed home that night.

Van Natta's wife, Mary, was IMSAI's sales coordinator, and she, too, knew what the sales figures were. Her birthday was approaching, and she wasn't sure she could enjoy it in the wake of the failure to reach their goal. When Van Natta asked his wife what she wanted for her birthday, she could think of only one thing. "I want the goal," she told him. Van Natta reminded her that with just two sales days left in the month, and their having called on everybody they could possibly contact, they would be lucky to ring up another dime that month. And, $680,000 was a long way from a million bucks.

Mary Van Natta insisted that she still wanted to make the sales goal her birthday present. Bruce Van Natta said okay, and did some mental calculations. He was one of a dozen or so people on the sales team, and he accounted for about 30 to 40 percent of sales. If only he could convince the firm's biggest customer to place a 90-day order instead of a 30-day order, or if only he could renegotiate a few other sales orders. It all just seemed impossible.

For the next two days, Van Natta and the rest of the sales team labored feverishly to close the $320,000 gap. At ten minutes before 5 P.M. on the last day of the month, Van Natta dragged himself over to his wife Mary's desk and added his latest sales to the current total. It came to $990,000. It was amazing—virtually a million dollars, and surely a miracle by any reasonable standard. But it was almost five o'clock and time to quit for the day, Van Natta noted.

What, and fail? Mary Van Natta replied. No way, she said. It's the goal or nothing. There would be no falling short by even $10,000. Bruce Van Natta went back to the phone and called a dealer he knew. He asked the dealer to take $10,000 worth of equipment that Van Natta knew he didn't really want as a personal favor. The dealer reluctantly agreed. They made their goal with literally moments to spare.

Selling a million dollars worth of computers and building a million dollars worth of computers are two different things, and the production people had trouble keeping up with the orders. After one spring month when the company actually shipped a million dollars' worth of machines, the production crew threw a party in Building Two to celebrate. Operations Manager Joe Parsialli brought in the beer, and pizza was ordered for everyone. Nancy Freitas, a production technician, and Todd Fischer, who by then was supervisor of production testing, both got tipsy on just a beer or two.

Freitas noticed that they weren't the only ones feeling the effects of the alcohol. After working long hours for weeks on end, getting drunk on just a couple of beers wasn't surprising. A lot of overtime was expected of everyone. The production team usually arrived to work around 6 A.M. and stayed until at least 8 P.M. They were tired and feeling frazzled, and it wasn't just the hours that were fatiguing them. It was also the constant push and emotional strain. Fischer recalled that after working 12 to 14 hours straight they would sometimes sit in a bar and drink just to stop their hands from shaking.

When things weren't so crazed, the group definitely knew how to have fun together, Fischer discovered. The others shared his interest in music and sometimes, when the pressure eased off a bit, a bunch of them—and not necessarily the same bunch every time—would head out back to throw a Frisbee around. When they went out for lunch, as many as 20 or 30 of them would be seated together.

Fischer valued the camaraderie, and he also noted some other differences between the people in IMSAI's two buildings. Those in Building One were definitely cliquish, whereas those in Building Two were relatively laid back. Building Two employed a few musicians and some dope smokers, but not many *est* graduates. IMSAI was definitely split into two factions, and it seemed that neither could relate to the other. The people in the production department worked together to get the job done, whereas those in Building One competed aggressively against each other.

Millard believed that competitiveness never handicapped a salesperson. In fact, he did all he could to encourage competition. And probably no one at IMSAI, in Building One or Building Two, was more aggressively competitive than the company's director of marketing, Seymour Rubinstein.

Miracles and Mistakes

*What [IMSAI] needed was a way to sell
floppy-disk drives; CP/M is what did it. I
personally consummated the CP/M contract.
[Kildall] got a good deal, considering that
the Navy was supporting him and he didn't
have any other expenses.*

SEYMOUR RUBINSTEIN
Software entrepreneur

WHEN HE FIRST MET BILL MILLARD, SEYMOUR RUBINSTEIN WAS A
programmer for Sanders Associates, a military defense electronics firm in New York. Rubinstein's ambition and self-confidence were
obvious to Millard, as was something else that Millard admired—a willingness, born perhaps of supreme self-confidence, to take on tasks that
others regarded as impossible.

Rubinstein was the quintessential self-made man. Born and raised in
New York City, he put himself through Brooklyn College taking night
classes, including the school's sole computer course. Using his nerve
and innate smarts, Rubinstein turned that one course into a job as a
technical writer, then a job in programming, and finally a position as
chief programmer at Sanders. By the time he left Sanders, he would
tell people later with a chuckle, he had a staff of programmers working
for him.

In 1971, Millard formed his own company, System Dynamics, to sell
an IBM-compatible telecommunications terminal. He recruited
Rubinstein to come and work for him in California on the short-lived

venture. Rubenstein settled in San Rafael, north of San Francisco. When System Dynamics folded the next spring, driven out of business by IBM, Rubinstein and Millard went their separate ways.

Rubinstein remained enthusiastic about the technology. Ed Faber may have been initially skeptical about selling computer kits, but Seymour Rubinstein was not. After System Dynamics took down its tent, he became a consultant. When Rubinstein returned from a consulting trip in Europe in late 1976, he was unaware that an actual microcomputer industry was in its infancy. So, he was surprised to find that a new store called the Byte Shop had opened on a main street of sleepy, suburban San Rafael. The Byte Shop, as its name suggested, sold computer kits. Rubinstein bought a kit, put the device together in a few weeks, and began programming. To his amazement, it was a real computer! Only later did he learn that his computer was manufactured by the same man who had brought him to California, Bill Millard.

In February 1977, Rubinstein joined IMSAI Manufacturing as a software product marketing manager. After Millard persuaded Rubinstein to "do the training," Millard was even more convinced he had done a smart thing by hiring him. Within a few months, Rubenstein moved up to the position that he would have for the rest of his tenure at IMSAI—director of marketing.

As software marketing manager, Rubinstein got to know programmer Rob Barnaby, at least as much as one could get to know the angular, taciturn young man who liked to work alone into the early hours of the morning. Both Barnaby and Rubinstein realized that the IMSAI machine needed more software and more robust software given that the software originally supplied with the machine was scanty and fairly weak.

Barnaby had proposed to write a version of BASIC for the IMSAI, but Millard vetoed the project when he found out how long the task would take. Until that time, Barnaby had been doing miscellaneous programming and helping to hire other programmers such as Diane Hajicek and Glen Ewing, plus negotiating software deals from outside sources. Millard wanted fast results, and buying software was quicker than writing it. When Rubinstein arrived at IMSAI, Barnaby was negotiating two software contracts with individuals from the Naval Postgraduate School in Monterey, where Glen Ewing had studied. Rubinstein soon took over those negotiations from Barnaby.

IMSAI desperately needed a disk operating system. From the start, Millard saw the IMSAI machine as a disk-drive machine, that is, one that would use magnetic disks for permanent information storage. The Altair, by comparison, had initially used slower and less-reliable cassette tapes to store data. Disks were essential for the business applications Millard intended for the machine. But a disk drive was useless without a program that would act as a sort of software "reference librarian" to handle storage of the information on the disks.

IMSAI bought a disk operating system called CP/M from Gary Kildall, a professor at the Naval Postgraduate School in Monterey, California, and the same man who had teamed with John Torode to sell computers to Omron. In 1977, CP/M was brand new. Kildall had given Barnaby the third copy in existence. Rubinstein negotiated with Kildall and his partner and lawyer, Gerry Davis, and closed the deal for a flat $25,000. It was highway robbery, Rubinstein later boasted; if Kildall had had any sense, he would have sold CP/M on a royalty basis, and not for a flat fee. After closing the deal, Rubinstein then chided Kildall that his marketing approach was naive. "If you continue this practice, you are not going to make nearly as much money as you are entitled to," he told him. Kildall shrugged off the warning. This first deal felt good to him.

One of Kildall's students had written a version of the programming language BASIC, and IMSAI picked that up, too. The student, Gordon Eubanks, settled for even less than what Kildall got. Eubanks gave IMSAI his BASIC for the promise of a computer and some technical support. IMSAI in turn supplied him with a computer, disk drives, and printer, and encouraged him to develop the language further, with the understanding that IMSAI would have unlimited distribution rights. Eubanks had also developed CBASIC, which would work with the newly purchased CP/M. It was just what IMSAI wanted. IMSAI got such a good deal on CBASIC that it didn't even consider also buying MBASIC, the BASIC programming language that Bill Gates and Paul Allen were selling under the company name Microsoft.

Later, when IMSAI did begin buying software from Microsoft, Seymour Rubinstein handled the negotiations from start to finish. Rubinstein was a remorseless negotiator and brought all his skills to bear in dealing with Microsoft's young president, Bill Gates. Gates left their meeting thinking that he had done well for Microsoft, but a few days later began to have doubts. Rubinstein, on the other hand, knew at once what kind of deal he had made. "Everything but the kitchen sink," he chuckled, "including the stopper and the faucets." Seymour Rubinstein was making miracles in his own way.

Meanwhile, Building One's glorification of achieving the impossible dream was creating problems for the production and service people in Building Two. According to Todd Fischer, it was easy to think of the buildings as two conflicting individuals because the departments each had such different personalities. The way that the salespeople dictated the production department output levels with no concern as to what production could realistically get done was much too disruptive.

For instance, Fischer said, the sales department would set a production quota of 27 units for an item. Production would then set aside the parts for 27 units and build 27 units. Then, someone from Building One would come running across the parking lot yelling, "I've just sold 30 more of those things! We've got to have 30 more by Friday." Sales seemingly didn't care that production lacked the necessary parts or the available people to build the units. At least that's how it looked from Fischer's point of view in Building Two. Sales had to have the items out by Friday, so production would shift gears and get it done. It was "make a miracle" time.

Fischer didn't like the way the unpredictable work schedules jerked people around. Jarring changes in the work hours threw everybody off, taking a psychological toll on the production crew. They never knew when they would have to work overtime hours or hastily salvage an item in order to obtain some needed parts. This constant uncertainty diminished production's pride in their work because machines often had to be rushed out of the shop without proper testing. One time, Fischer got a call from a customer wondering why his computer had a screwdriver inside of it. Apparently, the computer was sealed up and shipped out before the technician had a chance to retrieve the missing tool.

But even the beleaguered production department was better off than customer support. Nancy Freitas's brother Ed, who worked in inventory, could see that the customer support department got short shrift. When customer support needed a part to repair a customer's machine, supplying that part was low priority. Production got the needed parts first, a practice that failed to charm customers who were waiting for their machines to come back from the repair shop. As a way to fight back, Building Two put an informal (and unauthorized) procedure into effect. If Fischer or Freitas spotted a problem, Freitas would mention it to her brother, who would work his inventory magic. The part that customer support needed would then materialize. Freitas and Fischer often found themselves resorting to this solution. Together they started an underground parts supply network.

Freitas had worked in both inventory and production, so she was able to diagram an operational flowchart that connected all the departments and detailed the route that parts took through the manufacturing and repair phases. She knew exactly what could be done and how long it would take. All that talk of "making miracles" irritated her. Using her chart as proof, she would explain that a certain goal was physically and materially impossible. Management didn't want to hear the word "impossible." Their reply was always the same: make a miracle.

Management's reluctance to acknowledge production limitations also caused friction within Building One, where the engineering department resided. After the release of the IMSAI 8080, engineering's big new project was a computer called the VDP-80. The VDP-80 had a novel design featuring a screen built right into the box, and Killian wanted to see the machine thoroughly tested. The order came down that the machine had to be shipped, and it didn't matter that the whole department, including Joe Killian, said it wasn't ready to go because it needed to be tested first. The prototype seemed to work, the orders were coming in, and the company needed cash.

Engineering threw up its hands. If you want the computer, Killian's group told Millard, it's your baby. Engineering didn't want responsibility for a machine that would soon be clattering with problems, and Millard didn't want to hear about potential problems. Sales was getting more and more orders for the VDP-80 every day. The company needed the money to cover current expenses so it could start shipping product. And that was that.

It seemed to many people in the engineering, production, and customer support departments that the sales group was blindly selling the ground right out from under them. IMSAI cared about success, all right. But management measured success by sales figures first, rather than by the quality of production or level of customer service. IMSAI

▶ *Ada Byron, Lady Lovelace (1815–1852), who studied mathematics; wrote about Charles Babbage's calculating machine, the Analytical Engine; and predicted that such machines would someday have many practical uses, including creating graphics and composing music*

▲ *Charles Babbage, the nineteenth century mathematician who worked on the design for a machine that he claimed would mechanize thought*

Herman Hollerith, inventor of the first
large-scale data-processing equipment
(used to compute the 1890 census) and
founder of the Tabulating Machine Company,
later called Computing-Tabulating-Recording

COURTESY OF IBM ARCHIVES

Thomas J. Watson, Sr., who joined Computing-Tabulating-Recording in
1914 and later turned it into International Business Machines Corporation

COURTESY OF IBM ARCHIVES

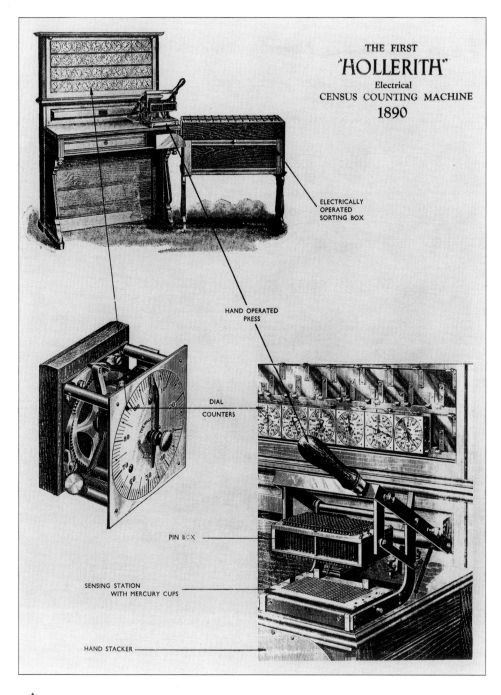

THE FIRST
'HOLLERITH'
Electrical
CENSUS COUNTING MACHINE
1890

ELECTRICALLY
OPERATED
SORTING BOX

HAND OPERATED
PRESS

DIAL
COUNTERS

PIN BOX

SENSING STATION
WITH MERCURY CUPS

HAND STACKER

▲ *The first Hollerith Census Counting Machine, ca. 1890*

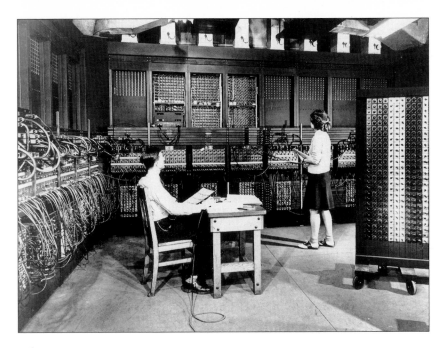

▲ ENIAC, *the first all-electronic digital computer, completed in December 1945*

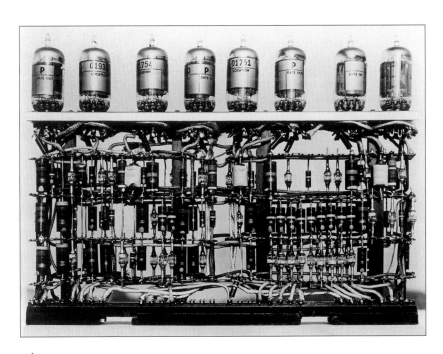

▲ *Vacuum tubes for the IBM 701, ca. 1950*

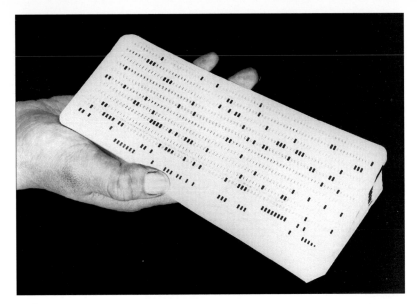

▲ IBM *punch cards, the means of programming for decades before other storage mechanisms were invented*

◀ *John Von Neumann, a brilliant mathematician who created the specifications for the general-purpose computer in 1945*

▲ *Lee Felsenstein with an intercom device at a Philadelphia science fair in 1961*

▲ *William Shockley, who shared the 1956 Nobel Prize in physics with John Bardeen and Walter Brattain for the transistor*

▲ *The first mouse, carved out of wood, which Doug Engelbart invented at SRI in 1964 as part of an experiment to point and click on display workstations*

▲ *Workstation with mouse, ca. 1965, which was custom built for roughly $80,000 (the smaller button device on the left is an early prototype of the keyset input device that was used with the mouse to input command shortcuts)*

▲ *The mouse and companion keyset with keyboard console used by Doug Engelbart at the 1968 Fall Joint Computer Conference demonstration for his "mother of all demos"*

◄ *Gordon Eubanks, whose master's thesis became one of the industry's standard BASIC programming languages*

▲ *Doug Engelbart holding an original mouse next to the modern model, 1984*

▶ *Federico Faggin, semi-conductor pioneer, one of the inventors of the microprocessor at Intel, and founder of Zilog and Synaptics*

Lee Felsenstein with his inventions, clockwise from top left: VDM video circuit board, Pennywhistle modem, Osborne 1 computer, Expander computer, and Sol computer

PHOTO BY LEVI THOMAS

Gordon Moore (left) and Robert Noyce, founders of Intel, which became the computer industry's semiconductor powerhouse

COURTESY OF INTEL CORP.

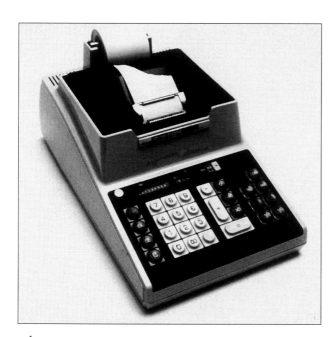

Marcian ("Ted") Hoff of Intel, who led the design effort for Intel's first microprocessor

The Busicom calculator from Japan, for which Intel designed chips, ca. 1972

Stan Mazor, who worked on Intel's first microprocessor project

COURTESY OF INTEL CORP.

Alan Cooper in 1970, cofounder of the early microcomputer software firm Structured Systems Group and later the "father" of Microsoft Visual Basic

COURTESY OF MR. SNOID

▲ *David Ahl visiting Processor Technology in 1977*

COURTESY OF DAVID H. AHL

▲ *Lee Felsenstein in the lab of an optometry professor while a student at UC Berkeley, ca. 1971*

COURTESY OF LEE FELSENSTEIN

▶ *David Ahl's book* Basic Computer Games *(originally titled "101 Basic Computer Games"), which was translated into 8 languages, sold over 1 million copies, and played an important role in the PC sales explosion in the mid to late 1970s*

ISBN 0-916688-07-0
$7.50

Basic Computer Games

Microcomputer Edition

Edited by David H. Ahl

▲ *David Ahl, who left Digital Equipment Corporation and started* Creative Computing *magazine in 1974 to popularize personal computers*

Alan Cooper today and his wife, Sue, who run a software design firm

COURTESY OF KATHY LAFLEUR

David E. Liddle in 1973, manager of Xerox PARC's project to develop the Star computer

COURTESY OF RICHARD SHOUP

▶ *Ed Roberts, founder of MITS and now a physician, standing next to his invention, the Altair microcomputer*

◀ *The MITS Altair 8800 computer system, unassembled*

was a selling machine, and when viewed that way, the company was doing very well.

For Bill Lohse in sales, things were endlessly exciting and challenging. Lohse saw the company as constantly evolving, unafraid to take risks, and scoring some big successes along the way. Millard thrived on change and risky ventures. The sales team was expanding and improving. Salespeople with experience and plenty of IMSAI drive and initiative, such as Fred "Chip" Poode, were being recruited. Then there was the franchise idea.

The computer store was emerging as a serious channel of distribution for microcomputers. Ed Roberts had limited MITS's market reach by demanding that the company's retail outlets sell only Altairs. Bill Millard was not going to make the same mistake, but how could he also ensure loyalty to his product? Millard liked the notion of an independent but friendly franchise, and the idea also interested Ed Faber. Perhaps Faber was chafing in Millard's organization and was seeking more autonomy, or perhaps the initial excitement had worn off since the IMSAI start-up. At any rate, in the summer of 1976, Faber told Millard that he wanted to start a franchise operation. Lohse watched this development with special interest, and when Faber left to start the franchise, Lohse replaced Faber as director of sales.

Lohse immediately had two major challenges to overcome. Chip Poode saw Lohse as a kid fresh out of college and resented being passed over for the director's job, and Seymour Rubinstein, in Lohse's view, thought that the marketing and sales departments should both report to one person, Seymour Rubinstein. Not surprisingly, Lohse and Rubinstein frequently locked horns.

Nevertheless, Lohse thought IMSAI was a great place to be. He enjoyed working in the sales department for Bill Millard and being around his mentor. IMSAI's people sold when nobody else thought they could and hit sales goals that seemed impossible. It was unreal in a way. They did seem to perform miracles.

est and Entrepreneur's Disease

*It was a bunch of people
heavily into* est.

JIM WARREN
Computer publishing pioneer and founder of the
West Coast Computer Faire

MILLARD WAS BUSY THROUGHOUT 1978 CREATING NEW COMPANIES. IMS Associates, the IMSAI parent company, spawned Computer-Land, Faber's franchise operation. Millard also went to Luxembourg for several months to set up IMSAI Europe, a separate corporation that would buy computers from the California operation for resale in Europe. As a result of his frequent absences, Millard failed to notice the dramatic tailspin that IMSAI was in.

IMSAI's high-handed stance regarding customer support was finally starting to hurt the operation, and the company had targeted the wrong market. The prevailing notion was that IMSAI was selling computers to serious business users. However, the quality of the IMSAI machine, like that of every other early microcomputer, was erratic. The individual who bought it for strictly business purposes was likely to be disappointed. The IMSAI 8080 had a distressingly high failure rate, and the instructions that came with the machine, having been written by engineers, were opaque to anyone who tried to use them. Bruce Van Natta's tongue-in-cheek summation of IMSAI's attitude toward documentation was, "You got the schematic? Then what's the problem?"

No software existed for even the simplest business applications when the IMSAI 8080 was first released. The computer was large, unwieldy, and suggestive of nothing so much as a pile of electronic test equipment. It took a huge leap of faith to believe that businesses would rush to install this assemblage in their offices or would entrust their business records to this unproved, unreliable artifact. Therefore, most "business" users were actually hobbyists who only hoped to use the machine in business and tolerated its deficiencies because they were learning how it worked and having fun doing so.

Eventually, IMSAI's inadequate customer support proved too aggravating even for the most tolerant hobbyists. Word spread fast throughout the hobbyist community, whose opinion IMSAI disdained. Sales soon started falling behind projections, and the gambit of funding current expenses with orders for future products began to wear thin.

When Millard was away, Wes Dean was in charge. Dean was IMSAI's president, yet he was beginning to feel despair for the company's future. Looking beyond the day-to-day crises, Dean saw that IMSAI was failing to address critical problems with its support, image, and cash flow that would affect the company in the long term. Dean finally gave up and left and was succeeded by John Carter Scott, who presided over the layoffs that came in early October 1978.

IMSAI's financial problems reached a crisis state in the fall of 1978, and it became clear to Scott that drastic steps were necessary. The company had enough orders for machines and repairs to keep everyone busy, but meeting payroll was impossible. In October, Scott initiated the first in a series of layoffs. Building Two suffered the most. When Todd Fischer, who had moved to a key position in the service department, learned that Nancy Freitas would be cut in the layoffs, he resigned, leaving an unanticipated gap in that already struggling department.

For IMSAI, Fischer's chivalry could not have been more badly timed. The company had started shipping the new and untested VDP-80, and the VDP-80 machines were coming back almost as fast as production could push them out the door. The downsized service department struggled with a variety of defects in the machines, while the sales team sold more and more of the defective products. Because the repairs were done under warranty and were often extensive, the company was making very little, if any, profits on the VDP-80. IMSAI had two options: send the design back to the drawing board and stop selling the computers until the design problems were solved, or continue selling them and repair them all when they came back. IMSAI chose the latter option.

Releasing the VDP-80 prematurely was a bad decision, but not inexplicable. Except for Killian and the engineering department, the folks in Building One did not believe that the VDP-80 had really serious problems. Expressing such a belief would have been tantamount to an admission of failure. Millard had taken pains to surround himself with enthusiastic amateurs, miracle makers, and *est* graduates—people who would never discuss the possibility of failure. Whatever *est* may have meant to others, at IMSAI it became associated with an inability to acknowledge possible failings and an increasingly narrow vision. IMSAI's single-minded focus on "The Goal" eventually caused the company to lose track of who its customers were and the very nature of the market.

The relentless positive thinking that had blinded management contributed to the decision to release the VDP-80 too quickly. Millard and the IMSAI executives had another reason for pushing the defective computers out the door: they needed cash. Even if the machines cost them money in the long run, they brought in cash with every sale. Because IMSAI financed present production with future orders, the company desperately needed ready dollars.

Even with its reduced payroll, IMSAI had severe cash-flow problems. In April 1979, the company took in $20,000 more than it paid out; the following month it took in $12,000 *less* than it paid out. By June 1979, Millard was looking for investors, but by then it was too late. No one was willing to sink money into his struggling company.

Earlier, when IMSAI was more financially healthy, Millard had turned down several investment offers. He was not alone in his reluctance to take on investment capital. Many early microcomputer executives feared that selling even a part of their companies would cause them to lose control of their organizations. They abhorred the prospect. That thinking came to be called "entrepreneur's disease," a company founder's determination to never release any corporate control to anyone for any price. As he neared the end of his reign at IMSAI, Millard began to have regrets and wished he had accepted a little investment money. The $2 million offered by one would-be investor who hoped to turn a profit would have come in handy in 1978.

Charles Tandy, among others, had made a foray into investing in IMSAI. Tandy was head of the nationwide chain of Radio Shack electronic equipment stores. He didn't want his company, essentially an electronics distribution firm, to venture into building microcomputers, but he was interested in carrying them in his stores. Tandy could either buy computers from another company or buy an entire computer company outright. IMSAI was the biggest seller in the field and seemed the logical choice. The day that Bill Lohse observed Tandy walking into Millard's office he knew immediately that the discussion going on inside would be crucial to IMSAI's financial state. It distressed him to learn that Tandy had wasted his time in talking to Millard and that the companies would not do business together.

Millard now thought IMSAI's cash-flow problem was serious enough that it required his presence in San Leandro. Soon, Bill Lohse was packing for Luxembourg to oversee IMSAI Europe.

Death and Rebirth

Rod Smith says that he does want one of my VDP80s and sent a 4.6K check and that's nice. But it feels a little like everything we do is correct and right but nothing produces the result.

BILL LOHSE
IMSAI salesman, in a telex from IMSAI Europe to IMSAI San Leandro

WHEN MILLARD ARRIVED IN SAN LEANDRO, HE FOUND IMSAI IN A terrible cash-flow bind while stuck with a computer on the market that was blackening the company's reputation. To turn things around, he first authorized the redesign of the VDP-80. Millard and the engineering people agreed that it was basically sound and would sell well if it worked—that is, if its reputation had not already been irreversibly damaged.

Another project that held some promise for success was Diane Hajicek's IMNET, a software package that could link several IMSAI machines together. The machines could then share resources, such as disk drives and printers. Together, IMNET and the revised VDP-80 would, Millard hoped, give IMSAI a viable office product to sell. Every step was a gamble now, and time was the opponent. If IMSAI could get the VDP-80 and IMNET earning dollars soon enough, the company could make the miracle it needed. If not, well, Millard didn't engage in negative thinking.

When Millard thought he could safely return to Europe, he left Kathy Matthews in charge. Matthews was Millard's sister and had been an executive in the corporation for some time. But, the money situation didn't improve. Finally, in the spring of 1979, the company filed Chapter 11—a provision of Federal bankruptcy law that keeps a company's creditors at bay while the company cuts expenses back in an attempt to dig itself out of its financial hole. Despite filing for bankruptcy, Kathy Matthews still believed IMSAI could recover and prosper.

Now more than ever, IMSAI needed a miracle. Matthews was doing all she could to generate orders. When Diane Hajicek said IMNET was ready, Matthews went on the road for three days straight to show off the product. With the exception of the presentation at one of Ed Faber's ComputerLand stores that went especially well, many of the demonstrations were embarrassing because IMNET wasn't quite ready to go public. Matthews sent IMNET back to Hajicek for more work, while expressing her wish to the Luxembourg group at IMSAI Europe that they could see "how wonderful and exciting IMNET is."

Layoffs continued, and IMSAI was consolidated into a single building. Company executives who had been living like the big-business officers they dreamed of being now faced seriously reduced circumstances. The interior walls of Building One were rearranged, and the resulting narrow hallways made employees claustrophobic. The functions of the various offices became more generalized, as did those of the company officers. One day, IMSAI vice president Steve Bishop found company president John Carter Scott lying on his back on the floor of the former marketing office assembling machines while chief engineer Joe Killian soldered wires.

IMSAI's European operation wasn't flourishing either. The money just wasn't coming in fast enough. Lohse pronounced the situation grim. Back in San Leandro, at the end of July 1979, Kathy Matthews declared, "We need a great August." Steve Bishop examined the records and found that the company had lost less money than he had feared. IMSAI could at least meet its payroll for another month.

The July issue of *Interface Age* carried a column by industry watchdog Adam Osborne, the former Intel employee who had written the documentation for Intel's first microprocessors, in which Osborne called IMSAI a "financial victim." Matthews felt as if she were reading her own obituary. But they weren't dead yet, she insisted, and wanted "so very much to produce a miracle and create a butterfly from a caterpillar."

Bill Millard decided the San Leandro operation was in need of his personal attention. He booked a flight back and sent telexes on July 31 to Ed Faber, Steve Bishop, and his daughter, Barbara Millard, that said, "I would like to meet with you Wed. 8/2" and named the time and place. Within a week of Millard's return, IMSAI Manufacturing suspended all sales and manufacturing operations. Steve Bishop told Lohse to advise their European dealers of the situation. Meanwhile, Millard was desperately looking for someone with money to keep IMSAI afloat.

On August 7, Steve Bishop telexed Lohse:

"YOU NEED TO CONSIDER YOUR PAY. YOU WERE BEING PAID OUT OF SNLO [IMSAI San Leandro] AND ONLY ONE PERSON IS LEFT ON THE PAYROLL HERE. THE WAY WHM [Bill Millard] IS SAYING IT IS THAT WE CAN STICK AROUND AND MAY GET PAID BUT NO ASSURANCE. ALSO YOU NEED TO CONSIDER YOUR RETURN EXPENSE TO THE U.S. NOT BEING NEGATIVE JUST WANTED YOU TO BE THINKING."

Things weren't working out for Lohse. He had seized the European job in part to escape the problems looming at IMSAI, but there was no avoiding the company's imminent collapse. Lohse had two choices: abandon ship or ride out the storm. Somehow, after all he had experienced, quitting didn't make sense now. But if he stayed, Lohse had to wait for further developments in San Leandro. IMSAI's future was up to Bill Millard. If Millard could find an investor, the sparkle would return to all their lives. Most of the items on Lohse's to-do list said, "Wait for further info." But Lohse wasn't very good at waiting around.

A week later, on August 14, Kathy Matthews and Bill Lohse exchanged terse telex messages:

Lohse: "ANY NEWS?"

Matthews: "NOT A THING."

Lohse: "RATS."

Lohse assessed IMSAI Europe's financial position. It was dismal. No matter how he figured it, the European office could not guarantee payment of its September bills. Lohse would have to sell off essential equipment just to keep a legal minimum balance in the company's bank account.

Lohse informed his staff that there was no money left to pay them.

He had worked closely with these people for six months, and it pained him to give them the news.

Lohse then sent a telex to Matthews: "WE ARE WAITING."

She replied: "WELL, WE HAVE ANOTHER DAY."

Lohse waited a bit, then answered, "WELL, OURS IS ABOUT OVER," perhaps referring to the time difference, or perhaps something else.

On August 21, Lohse put in a request to return home. Bill Millard telexed back his permission, and asked Lohse to bring along the Norelco shaver Millard had left behind on a previous trip.

On September 4, 1979, Millard called a meeting in San Leandro. The building where they met, at one time the base for more than 50 people and several divisions of the company, was now vacant except for that small group of people sitting around a table. There wasn't much to say. The VDP-80 redesign was complete and it was solid, but the machine on which the company pinned its hopes came too late. IMSAI had been dying for a long time, and the final miracle hadn't come through. When the meeting ended, everyone got up and walked out in silence. A short while later, a police officer arrived and padlocked the front door.

But IMSAI wasn't dead yet. Before the lockout, Todd Fischer had arrived to pick up some equipment. He had formed an independent repair company with Nancy Freitas after leaving IMSAI, and they were doing most of the IMSAI repairs when the company filed for Chapter 11 reorganization. Recovery from Chapter 11 almost requires a miracle, and IMSAI hadn't been able to make one.

It was largely due to Fischer and Freitas that a new company was born out of the ashes of the old IMSAI. While IMSAI was foundering, Fischer-Freitas was showing a profit. John Carter Scott didn't want his customers' equipment tied up in judicial wrangling, so he asked Fischer to take all of it, along with whatever tools Fischer needed to keep his operation going. Plenty of IMSAI computers remained in the field, and they would all need service someday. Scott couldn't think of a better person to repair them than Todd Fischer.

After a month, Fischer bought most of the remaining IMSAI inventory at a low-key auction. Later, after he found out the company name was also available, Fischer bought that, too. He and Nancy Freitas, now husband and wife, brought in an old music-industry buddy of Fischer's and incorporated as IMSAI Manufacturing. Operating out of a few hundred square feet in the warehouse district of Oakland, California, they began to build IMSAI computers once more.

The IMSAI that Fischer and Freitas founded was a small company with little resemblance to the frenetic original. The new IMSAI focused more on customer support than on sales and made an effort to get to know its actual customers. (Its one brush with fame came when one of its machines was featured in the early computer-cracker movie *War Games* in 1983.)

The old IMSAI had been remarkably successful with the IMSAI 8080, selling thousands of units over its three-year existence. IMSAI's brief triumph, and no doubt its ultimate failure, stemmed in large part from the managerial philosophy of Bill Millard. His tenure as IMSAI chief was marked by outsize goals, a complete intolerance of failure, an exceptionally aggressive sales force, a stubborn refusal to acknowledge nagging problems, an unwillingness to relinquish any control, and a perhaps fatal scorn for the entire hobbyist community. Many wags in the industry used a term to describe such a business style—*est,* after the movement that Millard so thoroughly embraced. One outspoken computer company president made the pronouncement that "*est* killed IMSAI." As *est* was understood and practiced at IMSAI, many industry insiders would have agreed.

IMSAI's demise may seem like a detour in the growth of the personal computer industry, when in fact IMSAI's rise and fall was a significant forward development. Although the IMSAI decision makers failed to understand the hobbyist culture of their market, they nevertheless fanned the fires of the revolution by giving hobbyists a better Altair. At the same time, IMSAI's attempt to make the industry into something it wasn't helped to define what that newborn industry actually was—a grassroots movement of hobbyists fully conscious that they were ushering in not just a technological revolution, but a social one as well.

CHAPTER 4

HOMEBREW

Are you building your own computer?
Terminal? TV Typewriter? I/O device? Or
some other digital black box? Or are you
buying time on a time-sharing service?
If so, you might like to come to a gathering
of people with like-minded interests.
Exchange information, swap ideas, talk
shop, help work on a project, whatever.

Flyer promoting the Homebrew
Computer Club, 1975

Power to the People

*It had its genetic coding in the
'60s . . . antiestablishment, antiwar, pro-
freedom, antidiscipline attitudes.*

JIM WARREN
Microcomputer industry pioneer

WHY DID THE ALTAIR AND IMSAI COMPUTERS GENERATE SUCH excitement among engineers and electronics enthusiasts? Not because they were technological breakthroughs—they weren't. To understand the wild enthusiasm with which these machines were greeted, you have to get inside the minds of the people who bought them, and who soon thereafter founded computer companies of their own. And you have to remember the social and political milieu into which these first microcomputers emerged. Although the Altair was released in 1975, it was largely a product of the cultural revolution of the 1960s.

Lee Felsenstein had dropped out of engineering school at the end of the 1960s and had gone to work for a company called Ampex as a junior engineer. Ampex didn't require him to work with computers, and that was fine with Felsenstein, who had been cool toward computers ever since an overly ambitious attempt in high school to build one of his own. But while Felsenstein enjoyed the work, as a true child of the 1960s he rebelled at pouring his efforts into projects for the benefit of corporate America. He left Ampex in 1969 to write for the *Berkeley Barb,* a famous and influential counterculture publication, where for a time he was listed on the masthead as "Friday," as in Robinson Crusoe's man Friday.

When internal politics split the *Barb* staff, Felsenstein went to another underground publication, *The Tribe,* where he was employed for his "technical knowledge." That was vague enough to leave his job definition flexible: he functioned as a combination business manager and layout artist. Eventually, coming to see *The Tribe* as "an exercise in applied adolescence," Felsenstein cut back to part-time and returned to Ampex. There, in 1970, he designed an interface for a Data General Nova computer and began to think that maybe computers weren't so bad after all. Felsenstein saved his money and in 1971 reenrolled at UC Berkeley, where he completed his engineering degree. In 1972, he gathered up his engineering degree and counterculture credentials and went to work for Resource One.

Resource One was an attempt to unify—via computer—the switchboards in the San Francisco Bay Area. It was run by people from the San Francisco Switchboard, a volunteer referral agency, along with other computer junkies who had left UC Berkeley in protest of the American invasion of Cambodia. Many of these people lived in an urban commune in a factory building in San Francisco, which was a magnet for counterculture engineers, including Felsenstein.

Resource One had a computer—a large, $120,000 XDS 940, a remnant of Xerox Corporation's abortive attempt to enter the mainframe computer industry. Resource One had inherited it from the Stanford Research Institute, where it had seen service running Shakey, one of the first computer-controlled robots. Felsenstein moved in as part of the second generation at Resource One, signing on as chief engineer to run the computer, a job that paid "$350 a month and all the recrimination you can eat." It was a frustrating job, but he believed in the project, and would later recall being annoyed when two UC Berkeley graduate students, Chuck Grant and Mark Greenberg, refused to get off the system so he could do maintenance on it.

Resource One put Felsenstein in touch with Cal students and faculty, as well as researchers at other sites. He visited Xerox's Palo Alto Research Center (PARC) and saw innovations that dazzled him. However, Felsenstein's sympathies lay less with technological dazzle than with a growing, grass-roots, computer-power-to-the-people movement.

That movement was developing in the San Francisco Bay Area out of the spirit of the times and the frustration of those who, like Felsenstein, knew something of the power of computers. Resenting that such immense power resided in the hands of a few and was so jealously guarded, those technological revolutionaries were actively working to overthrow the computer industry hegemony of IBM and other companies, and to defrock the "computer priesthood" of programmers, engineers, and computer operators who controlled access to these machines.

Ironically, many of those technological revolutionaries had themselves been part of the priesthood. Bob Albrecht had left Control Data Corporation in the 1960s because of its reluctance to consider the idea of a *personal* computer, and had, with friends, started a nonprofit alternative education organization called the Portola Institute. From Portola sprang *The Whole Earth Catalog,* under the orchestration of Stewart Brand, with its emphasis on access to tools. This in turn inspired actress Celeste Holm's son Ted Nelson to write a book similar in spirit, but about access to *computers.* Nelson's *Computer Lib* proclaimed, well before the Altair was announced, "You can and must understand computers now!" Nelson was the Tom Paine and his book the *Common Sense* of this revolution.

The other significant publication at the time that brought information about computers to the Bay Area general public was a tabloid called *People's Computer Company (PCC),* another of Albrecht's projects, which he said was a company in the same sense that Janis Joplin's band Big Brother and the Holding Company was a company.

Albrecht was a passionate promoter of computer power to the people. He wanted to teach children, in particular, about the machines. So, he split off from the Portola Institute to form Dymax, an organization dedicated to informing the general public about computers. Dymax gave rise to a walk-in computer center in Menlo Park and to the thoroughly irreverent *PCC.* Computers had been mainly used *against* people, *PCC* said. Now they were going to be used *for* people. Albrecht was never paid, and others worked for little. The 1960s values that pervaded the company exalted accomplishing something worthwhile beyond attaining money, power, or prestige. If *Computer Lib* had the most revolutionary philosophy and the most brilliantly original ideas,

PCC had solid, practical advice for people who wanted to learn more about computers.

Albrecht and company were not writing about personal computers yet, because personal computers didn't exist. They wrote about personal *access* to computers. In the early 1970s, users typically gained access to computers via time-sharing—that is, by using a terminal connected to a mainframe or minicomputer that was kept in a locked room.

These big machines were getting smaller, though, and cheaper. DEC sold a PDP-8/F minicomputer that could be programmed in BASIC and that featured a 110 Teletype machine for under $6,000, a remarkably low price for a minicomputer. To the most visionary contemporary observer, this may have been a hint of what was to come, but consumers weren't buying the minicomputer and installing it in their dens. At this point, virtually no individual person owned a computer.

Computers like the DEC minicomputer could, nevertheless, be purchased by schools. David Ahl, editor of *EDU,* DEC's newsletter on educational uses of computers, spent a lot of time writing about small computers such as the $6,000 system. He argued that children learning about computers should be able to get their hands on the real machines, not just terminals connected to a remote, impersonal time-sharing system.

Lee Felsenstein was working hard to humanize those time-sharing systems. He helped organize Community Memory, an offshoot of Resource One that installed public terminals in storefronts. The terminals gave anyone who walked in the front door immediate, free access to a public computer network. They were similar to those message boards you see in sandwich shops and other public places. Except that *these* message boards could be updated electronically, had an unlimited number of responses attached to them, and could be read all over town.

There were problems though. People didn't know how to use the Community Memory terminals, and the terminals frequently broke down. To really bring the power of the computer to the people, access wasn't enough: it was necessary to make the thing understandable, and to free users from having to depend on a trained repair person.

Felsenstein approached this challenge in a way characteristic of his approach to technological problems. Instead of merely fixing the terminals, he began looking for the inherent problem in their design. What was the basic shortcoming of the Community Memory terminals? He decided that they weren't "convivial."

Lee's father had once recommended the book *Tools for Conviviality*, by Ivan Illich, author of *Deschooling Society*. Pointing to radio as an example, Illich argued that technologies become useful only when people can teach themselves about those technologies. As a child in Philadelphia, Felsenstein had built his own radio, so he appreciated the comparison. Truly useful tools, Illich said, must be *convivial*. They have to stand up under the abuse people put them through as they're learning how to use and repair them.

Felsenstein took Illich's message to heart. He wanted computer technology to spread like crystal radio technology had done. He began soliciting ideas for a truly convivial terminal, and in true 1960s spirit sought a communal design. He placed notices in the *PCC* and on the Community Memory boards calling for a meeting to discuss the "Tom Swift Terminal," a computer terminal that would appeal to technology-dazzled teenagers who read the ads in the back of science fiction magazines. The terminals would be as easy to build and repair as a crystal radio.

One of those responding to the Community Memory message was Bob Marsh. Marsh and Felsenstein discovered they had already met, but this meeting via computer was the important one.

Bob Marsh had been an engineering student at UC Berkeley. Both he and Felsenstein lived in Oxford Hall, the University Students' Cooperative Association building. With his familiar boyish grin and locks of dark hair falling across his forehead, Bob Marsh looked much the same as he did during his days at Berkeley, but Felsenstein could see that his college chum had done some growing up.

While Felsenstein had not been as serious about school as he was about political events, Marsh never seemed to be serious about anything. Pool playing and beer drinking got more of his attention than did class work, and he had dropped out in 1965 to take a job clerking in a grocery store. Marsh labored there just long enough to save up enough cash for a trip to Europe. When he returned, it was with an altered outlook and the motivation to get a degree. He went to a community college in order to build up a grade point average that would allow him to return to UC Berkeley. He planned to be a biology teacher—but one visit to a teachers' meeting ended that dream. Marsh didn't care for the way principals and administrators treated teachers, and he switched back to an engineering major.

Marsh began working on a series of engineering projects with his friend Gary Ingram. Marsh and Ingram had known each other since 1971, when they collaborated on their first project together. The project was based on a *Popular Electronics* article by Harry Garland and Roger Melen. Marsh had also read the Don Lancaster TV Typewriter article in *Radio Electronics* and had tried to devise an improved version of it, with some success.

Ingram was now working at Dictran International, an importer of dictation equipment, and landed his friend Marsh a job there. When Ingram quit Dictran a month later, Marsh suddenly became chief engineer. Somewhat to his surprise, he found that he liked the position. That job eventually disappeared, but Marsh later said that his stint as a chief engineer had changed his life. Experiencing life as a Berkeley student in the 1960s, being on his own in Europe, seeing what it was like to be a teacher working under others, and getting a shot at being an engineer and manager at Dictran had all contributed to turning Marsh into the prototype for a generation of Silicon Valley entrepreneurs.

But in 1974, Marsh was broke and out of work. As Felsenstein put it, Marsh had worked himself up to the exalted level of an unemployed electronics engineer. With house payments to make, a family to support, and a child on the way, Marsh was looking for a project around which he could build a company. His meeting with Felsenstein about the Tom Swift Terminal led to a discussion about electronic products and launching a corporation. Unlike Marsh, Felsenstein wasn't interested in starting his own company; he was already busy fomenting a revolution.

Marsh decided he needed some work space if he was going to get his company going. He talked Felsenstein into splitting the cost to lease a space. Although Felsenstein still had no plans to start his own venture, he did need to move his home office out of his 276-square-foot apartment. In January 1975, the two rented a 1100-square-foot garage at 2465 Fourth Street in Berkeley for $170 a month. Marsh could barely afford his half of the modest rent, but set up shop nevertheless. Felsenstein laid claim to a workbench and took on freelance engineering projects that came his way. He remained involved in Community Memory while the Tom Swift Terminal project was on hold. Marsh then connected with a friend who had access to cheap walnut planks and with an electronics distributor named Bill Godbout. He planned to use these contacts as part of an effort to build and market digital clocks.

Then the January 1975 issue of *Popular Electronics* announced the introduction of the Altair computer, and although they didn't realize it at the time, it forever changed the lives of Felsenstein, the technological revolutionary, and Marsh, the unemployed engineer. It did so in part because it brought into existence the Homebrew Computer Club, an extraordinary gathering of those with engineering expertise and a revolutionary spirit, from whom would spring dozens of computer companies, and eventually a multibillion-dollar industry.

The Homebrew Computer Club

There was a strong feeling [at the Homebrew Club] that we were subversives. We were subverting the way the giant corporation had run things. We were upsetting the establishment, forcing our mores into the industry. I was amazed that we could continue to meet without people arriving with bayonets to arrest the lot of us.

KEITH BRITTON
Homebrew Computer Club member

EARLY IN 1975, A NUMBER OF COUNTERCULTURE INFORMATION exchanges existed in the San Francisco Bay Area for people interested in computers. Community Memory was one, *PCC* was another, as was the *PCC* spin-off, the Community Computer Center. Peace activist Fred Moore was running a noncomputerized information network out of the Whole Earth Truck Store in Menlo Park, matching people with common interests about anything, not just computers.

Moore became interested in computers when he realized he needed a machine with computing power. He talked to Bob Albrecht at *PCC* about getting both a computer and a base of operations. Soon Moore was teaching children about computers while learning about them himself. At the same time, Albrecht was looking for someone to write some assembly language programs. He found Gordon French, a mechanical engineer and computer hobbyist, who at the time supported himself by building motors for toy slot cars.

After the Altair story appeared in *Popular Electronics,* the need for a more direct information exchange became clear. The *PCC* people took the Altair seriously from the start. Keith Britton, a demolition consultant and *PCC's* treasurer, thought its arrival foretold the eventual demise of the computer "priesthood."

"All of us were champing at the bit to get an Altair," French recalls. So Fred Moore pulled out his list of the computer curious, the revolutionaries, the techies, and the educational innovators, and sent out the call: "Are you building your own computer? Terminal? TV Typewriter? I/O device? Or some other digital black box? Or are you buying time on a time-sharing service?" Moore's flyer asked. "If so, you might like to come to a gathering of people with like-minded interests. Exchange information, swap ideas, talk shop, help work on a project, whatever."

The announcement referred to the gathering as the Amateur Computer Users Group, or alternately the Homebrew Computer Club. The group first met on March 5, 1975, in Gordon French's garage.

Felsenstein read about the upcoming meeting and resolved not to miss it. He collared Bob Marsh, and they drove Felsenstein's pickup truck through the rain across the Bay Bridge to the peninsula that stretches from San Francisco south to Silicon Valley. French's garage was in suburban Menlo Park, a town jogging distance from Stanford University and perched on the edge of Silicon Valley.

At the club's first meeting, Steve Dompier reported on his visit to Albuquerque. It was the headquarters of MITS, the company arguably responsible for the first working microcomputer, the Altair. MITS, he told them, had shipped 1500 Altairs and expected to ship 1100 more that month. The company was staggering under the weight of the orders and couldn't possibly fill all of them. Bob Albrecht displayed the Altair that *PCC* had just received that week. Immediately in front of *PCC* on MITS's waiting list were Harry Garland and Roger Melen, the two Stanford University grad students who had created the Cyclops digital camera and who later founded Cromemco, a company that made computer interface and CPU boards.

Dompier, like Marsh and Felsenstein, had driven down from Berkeley, but most of the 32 attendees at the first meeting were from nearby communities. Albrecht and Gordon French, who chaired the meeting; Fred Moore, who took notes for the club's newsletter; and Bob Reiling, who soon took over editing the newsletter, all lived in Menlo Park. Others came from towns farther south, deep in the heart of Silicon Valley—Mountain View, Sunnyvale, Cupertino, and San Jose—people like Allen Baum, Steve Wozniak, and Tom Pittman, a self-described microcomputer consultant, perhaps the first in the world.

As the meeting concluded, one Homebrewer held up an Intel 8008 chip, asked who could use it, and then gave it away. Many of those there that night sensed the opportunities presented by this community spirit and Dompier's revelations that MITS couldn't build Altairs fast enough to fill its orders.

One person inspired by the meeting was Bob Marsh, who immediately went to see Gary Ingram about forming a business. "I have a garage," Marsh told Ingram. That seemed like enough to get started.

They decided to call themselves Processor Technology, or Proc Tech. Marsh designed three plug-in circuit boards for the Altair: two I/O boards and a memory board. Both Marsh and Ingram thought they looked pretty good. Marsh designed a flyer announcing Proc Tech's products, ran off hundreds of copies on a campus photocopying machine, and distributed 300 of them at the third Homebrew meeting.

By this time, the club was flourishing. Fred Moore was exchanging newsletters with Hal Singer, who put out the *Micro-8 Newsletter* in Southern California and had formed a Micro-8 club shortly after Homebrew started. Other publications were passed around at the meetings. *PCC* and Hal Chamberlin's *Computer Hobbyist* attracted special attention. A Denver organization, identifying itself as a provider of support for Micro-8 and TV Typewriter hobbyists and calling itself The Digital Group, offered subscriptions to its newsletter. It was becoming increasingly difficult to keep up with changes in the movement. Intel introduced its 4004, 8008, and 8080 chips, and at least 15 other semiconductor manufacturers had introduced microprocessors into the market. The newly formed club labored to keep its members informed about them all.

The third Homebrew monthly meeting drew several hundred people, too many for Gordon French's garage. The club moved meetings to the Coleman mansion, a Victorian dwelling that now served as a schoolhouse. There Marsh gave a brief talk, explaining that he was selling memory and I/O boards for the Altair. He hoped to present Proc Tech as a serious company, not just the whim of an unemployed electronics engineer with access to a copying machine. He offered a 20 percent discount for cash prepayment. To his disappointment, no one approached him during or after the meeting.

But, by the following week, the first order arrived. Garland and Melen placed an order written on the stationery of their new company, Cromemco, and requesting 30 days net credit. This was hardly what Marsh had expected. Still, he supposed this meant that Proc Tech was now being treated like a serious enterprise. Proc Tech was a serious company, and Cromemco was a serious company—there just wasn't any serious money being exchanged. It was a start, anyway.

After the Cromemco order, many others followed, and most had cash enclosed. Ingram fronted $360 of his own money for an advertisement in *Byte* magazine, but now with cash streaming in, Marsh and Ingram could afford to advertise in *Popular Electronics*—and they did, spending $1,000 for a one-sixth-page ad. Next, they incorporated, and Ingram was named president. For its corporate headquarters and factory, Processor Technology had half of an 1100-square-foot garage; but it had no products, no schematics for proposed products, no supplies, no employees, and thousands of dollars in cash orders. It was beginning to appear that they had some work ahead of them.

Meanwhile, Lee Felsenstein was getting increasingly involved with Homebrew. He took over the master of ceremonies role from Gordon French but refused to think of himself as a chairman. The meetings were now held in the auditorium at the Stanford Linear Accelerator Center. Over the years, Felsenstein became intimately associated with the club and fostered its anarchic structure. The group had no official membership, no dues, and was open to anyone. Its newsletter, offered free after a nudge from Felsenstein, became a pointer to information sources and a link between hobbyists.

As group toastmaster, Felsenstein performed with a sort of showmanship that was as curious as it was engaging. As one attendee, Chris Espinosa, said, "People call him the Johnny Carson of Homebrew, but he's more than that. He kept order, he kept things moving, he made it fun to go to the meetings. There were 750 people in that room at one time, and he worked it like a rock concert. It's hard to describe, but to see him work a crowd like a Baptist preacher. . . . He was great."

With Felsenstein running them, the meetings didn't follow any conventional rules of order. He gave meetings their own special twist. First came a mapping session, during which Felsenstein recognized people who quickly proffered their interests, questions, rumors, or plans. Felsenstein typically had snappy answers to questions and sharp-witted comments on their plans. A formal presentation followed, generally on someone's latest invention. Finally, there was the Random Access session, in which everyone scrambled around the auditorium to meet others they felt had common interests. The formula worked brilliantly, and numerous companies were formed at the Homebrew meetings. A remarkable amount of information was also exchanged at those meetings. Much information needed to be exchanged; they were all in unfamiliar territory.

Around this time, a branch of Homebrew started at the Lawrence Hall of Science at UC Berkeley. Universities were becoming hotbeds of self-taught microcomputer expertise. Professors with grant money now found it cost-effective to buy minicomputers rather than buy time on the university mainframe computer, which was invariably out of date and overworked. DEC was selling PDP-8 and PDP-11 minicomputers to professors as fast as it could build them. The computers were especially popular in psychology labs, where they were used for experimenting on human subjects, automating animal lab processes, and analyzing data. The invasion of the psych lab by minicomputers created a new kind of expert: someone who may know something about research and data analysis, but who was actually more of a hacker and computer nut—someone to figure out how to run the computer and make it do what the professors wanted.

Howard Fulmer was such a person. Fulmer worked in the Psychology Department at UC Berkeley running PDP-11s, selecting minicomputers for professors to buy, building interfaces, and programming experiments. It all began in early 1975 when one of Fulmer's professors bought an Altair, and Fulmer taught himself how to use it. Soon after, Fulmer left his job to devote more time to microcomputers.

He was not alone: the fever produced by the announcement of the

Altair in *Popular Electronics* spread through UC Berkeley. George Morrow, a graduate student in math, worked with Chuck Grant and Mark Greenberg, two other students at the university's Center for Research in Management Science. They were the same Grant and Greenberg who had refused a few years earlier to get off the Resource One computer to allow Lee Felsenstein to perform maintenance on it. They were attempting to develop a language to use with a microprocessor in computer-controlled research.

Morrow, Grant, and Greenberg found that they worked well together. All three were perfectionists, although in different ways. The thin, prematurely balding Morrow, with the perpetual twinkle in his eye and irrepressible wit, seemed always to be enjoying himself, and especially so when he was hard at work. Grant and Greenberg, on the other hand, tended to be all business. Although Grant and Greenberg often attended Homebrew meetings and profited from the free, open exchange of information, they never considered themselves part of the hobbyist community. But, as far as the technical stuff went, the three formed a good team: Morrow knew hardware, Grant preferred software, and Greenberg was at home with either.

The trio considered making boards for the Altair, or even a computer of their own. They knew that they were a good design team, but they also knew they lacked sophistication when it came to marketing. So Morrow sought the advice of Bill Godbout, a seemingly unlikely choice. Middle-aged, blunt, and opinionated, Godbout freely joked about his expanding paunch and kept an airplane for stunt flying. He was also the electronics distributor who Bob Marsh had tried to interest in his walnut digital clock when he and Felsenstein first moved into the garage at 2465 Fourth Street.

Godbout was at the time selling chips and minicomputer memory boards by mail. Morrow asked him if he intended to sell Altair memory boards. Godbout scoffed. He wouldn't so dignify the product, he said. Morrow wondered if Godbout might be interested in distributing a good computer, one that was the creation of a top-notch design team.

"With you guys?" Godbout sniffed. He gave Morrow the once-over. Godbout felt he was good at sizing people up, and decided Morrow looked all right. They quickly agreed to split the profits down the middle and shook hands on it. No written contract, Godbout insisted.

Written contracts were a sign of mistrust and an invention of lawyers, and if there was anybody Godbout didn't trust, it was a lawyer.

A motley group of engineers and revolutionaries were gathering in Silicon Valley, many attending Homebrew meetings, some actually suspecting the truth: that they were experiencing the birth of something remarkable. They included the irascible Bill Godbout, who hated lawyers; ex–*Berkeley Barb* technical editor and current Homebrew toastmaster Lee Felsenstein; Bob Albrecht, who left a high-paying career to teach children about computers, smoked cheap cigars, and called himself "The Dragon"; Bob Marsh, who was testing his own abilities by turning his love for electronics into a garage corporation; and Keith Britton, who saw himself and the other Homebrewers as pivotal in "an equivalent of the industrial revolution but profoundly more important to the human race."

A surprising number of these early movers and shakers held political views that would have shocked the local Rotary Club, and almost all of them had no love for IBM or the rest of the computer establishment. But they and others like them were pulling off a most startling entrepreneurial achievement. And much of the action took place at Homebrew.

The Homebrew Computer Club was not merely the spawning ground of Silicon Valley microcomputer companies. It was also the intellectual nutrient in which they first swam. Presidents of competing companies and chief engineers would gather there to argue design philosophy and announce new products. Statements made at Homebrew changed the directions of corporations. Homebrew was a respected critic of microcomputer products.

The Homebrewers were sharp, and could spot shoddy merchandise and items that were difficult to maintain. They blew the whistle on faulty equipment and meted out praise for solid engineering and convivial technologies. Homebrewers soon developed the power to make or break new companies. Due in part to Lee Felsenstein, Homebrew encouraged the conviction that computers should be used for and not against people. Homebrew thrived in a kind of joyous anarchy, but the club was also an important step in the development of a multibillion dollar industry.

Processor Technology was one of the children of Homebrew.

Wildfire in Silicon Valley

Processor Technology was a nexus for hobbyists making a transition, trying to be serious about it all and not always succeeding.

LEE FELSENSTEIN
Designer of several microcomputer products

THE FOURTH STREET GARAGE IN BERKELEY WAS A BUSY PLACE IN THE spring of 1975. Lee Felsenstein was making a meager living from odd jobs, including repairing friends' Altairs, while Bob Marsh was tearing open checks, writing ad copy, and doing his best to convince hobbydom that Processor Technology was a million-dollar company when, in fact, it still existed mostly in his head.

Felsenstein had gotten himself in trouble that spring. In getting the word out about the Altair through an article for the industry tabloid *People's Computer Company* (*PCC*), he based his description of the machine's workings and capabilities on information he received from Homebrew and from a telephone interview with MITS president Ed Roberts. Irate letters soon poured into the *PCC* office contending that Felsenstein had not been critical enough of the product. The Altair had serious problems, the letters claimed. Steve Dompier, for one, showed Felsenstein the difficulties he had had with the front panel of his Altair and even got Felsenstein to fix it.

In a *PCC* article he titled "Criticism and Self-Criticism," Felsenstein apologized: "I lied folks; this thing has problems." He detailed the computer's flaws and how to correct them. He also began fixing Altairs for friends and *PCC* readers, working on them in his half of the garage.

Loyal to other hobbyists and feeling guilty about misinforming people, Felsenstein did the work cheaply. In the process, he learned a great deal about those early Altairs.

Meanwhile, Marsh and Ingram were using their half of the garage to create the Altair boards they were getting checks for. But they were stalled early on: they needed a sharp engineer to draw up the schematics for the boards that Marsh had conceived. The engineer had to be willing to work in a cramped and messy garage, and he had to work cheap. Marsh thought he knew someone who might be game.

Felsenstein had made it clear that he did not want to join Processor Technology or any other company. He had better things to do. Although he was working long hours for little pay, he was doing what he wanted and felt beholden to no one. And long hours for little pay was about all Bob Marsh could offer him. Nevertheless, Marsh put forward a new proposal. Would Felsenstein just do the schematic for the first board, as a consultant rather than an employee?

Felsenstein thought it over, agreed, and offered to do the schematic for $50. This price, Marsh thought, was pathetically low. It was a $3,000 job and Felsenstein, the poor goof, was offering to do it for $50. Marsh refused to go below $500. Felsenstein accepted the compromise fee.

It was fast work, and by June they were shipping boards. One of them was first meant to be a 2K memory board for the Altair, an ambitious project given that MITS was shipping only an eighth as much memory. Then, at the last minute, Marsh changed the design, doubling the capacity to 4K. MITS's first real competition came from those 4K memory boards, which definitely cut into MITS's profits. Ed Roberts wasn't pleased.

But MITS's defective memory boards and delivery backlog had already kicked the door open to some real competition. Bruce Seals, a Tennessee hobbyist, flew to Albuquerque in July to discuss an East Coast dealership, and returned to Tennessee with the entire state as his territory and a promise of three-day delivery. When MITS couldn't move the products fast enough, especially the memory boards, Seals saw the same need—and opportunity—that Marsh had, and he, too, designed and began to sell a 4K memory board.

Processor Technology continued to market memory boards while moving on to new designs. The VDM, or video display module, Felsenstein's next contract for Proc Tech, was an interface board that allowed the Altair to display output on a television screen. Chuck Grant and Mark Greenberg, who had left UC Berkeley with George Morrow and were now doing business as G & G Systems, did the software for the module, and Steve Dompier wrote *Target,* a video game that showed off the VDM. Dompier later asserted that it was the VDM that made video games possible.

In the fall of 1975, a local computer show took place at UC Berkeley's Lawrence Hall of Science, where the East Bay spin-off Homebrew Club first got together. MITS was represented by two area Altair dealers, Paul Terrell and Boyd Wilson, who proudly showed Felsenstein and Marsh the hoops their machine could jump through. Marsh was more impressed by the fact that the Altair was filled with Processor Technology memory boards. Harry Garland and Roger Melen were also present, demonstrating how their Cyclops camera could be used with the Altair.

Before the original Homebrew Club had grown large enough to need the auditorium at the Stanford Linear Accelerator Center, *Popular Electronics* technical editor Les Solomon visited the club at the nearby SLAC Orange Room. He was the star of the evening, telling somewhat far-fetched stories of his own experiences. Sometimes he sounded like a counterspy, other times like a vaudeville magician. "It was unclear which country he was working for," joked Lee Felsenstein, who was among Solomon's admirers. At one point, Solomon led the Homebrewers outside, did some hocus-pocus, and instructed them to lift the huge stone table in the yard. They were surprised to find that they could hoist it right up, although Felsenstein noted dryly that the group hadn't tried lifting it without the hocus-pocus.

Some nights at Homebrew, a tall, dapper, charismatic man could be found at the back of the room selling books out of a cardboard box. He was Adam Osborne, a chemical engineer born in Bangkok of British parents, and the same Adam Osborne who had been doing technical writing for Intel. He had self-published a book he wrote called *An Introduction to Microcomputers.* It was, in fact, an introduction to microprocessors, such as the Intel 8080. In the early days, microprocessors were commonly referred to as microcomputers, especially by the public relations departments of semiconductor companies.

Although the people from IMSAI, the leading microcomputer company, almost never attended club meetings, IMSAI cofounder Bruce Van Natta was at Homebrew one night when Osborne was hawking his books and bought a copy. His decision to include a copy of Osborne's book with every IMSAI allowed Osborne to start a publishing company that would eventually be purchased for millions by McGraw-Hill. Ironically, it would be Osborne who would first announce IMSAI's demise in a column in a computer magazine.

After Homebrew meetings, its most fanatical members went to a Menlo Park beer-and-burger place known as the Oasis, which everyone simply called "the O." They sat in wooden booths surrounded by the deeply carved initials of generations of Stanford students, drank beer, and argued computer design. They ignored the fact that they were competitors. There were a lot of things to learn in developing this new kind of product, and they weren't about to let economic issues get in the way. Marsh and Melen regularly traded insights on design, and Grant and Greenberg sometimes joined them at the O.

By the end of 1975, new microcomputer companies were poking up everywhere, with the most furious activity still in the San Francisco Bay Area. IMSAI was located in San Leandro. Bay Area–based Cromemco was designing boards for the Altair. MOS Technology had released its KIM-1 hobby computer, based on its bargain-basement 6502 microprocessor, equipped with a hexadecimal keyboard in place of binary switches. Microcomputer Associates in Los Altos had its Jolt, a 6502 kit.

Southern California was also a center of growing hobbyist activity. In Gardena, Dennis Brown was selling his Wave Mate Jupiter II, a computer based on the Motorola 6800 microprocessor and designed to attract "serious hobbyists," for less than $1,000. Although the Altair had sold for less than half that, a realistic price for an assembled Altair *system,* including some sort of I/O device, adequate memory, and a storage device, was well over $1,000. In San Diego, Electronics Products announced another 6800-based computer, the Micro 68.

On December 31, 1975, Rich Peterson, Brian Wilcox, and John Stephensen quit their jobs to form their own company. Peterson and Wilcox had built an Altair, Stephensen had built his own 8080 machine from scratch, and they found themselves designing boards to make the

Altair run better. Deciding that their hobby could just as well be their vocation, they formed Polymorphic Systems and started working on a computer kit. They first called it the Micro-Altair, and later, under duress, changed the name to Poly-88.

Elsewhere in the West, MITS in Albuquerque was offering a 4K static memory board for its 8080 system and was developing a computer based on what was emerging as the "Southwest chip": Motorola's 6800. Systems Research in Salt Lake City sold a 6800 microcomputer board. Mike Wise's Sphere, operating out of a small factory near Salt Lake City, was offering its 6800 computer with a built-in terminal and plastic case. Southwest Technical Products, run by Dan Meyer in San Antonio, also offered a 6800 system. The Digital Group in Denver was selling a variety of boards.

In the Midwest, Martin Research was offering its Mike CPU boards with 8008 or 8080 chips. Ohio Scientific Instruments in Hudson, Ohio, had 6800 and 6502 kits. Heathkit in Benton Harbor, Michigan, had a computer in the works.

In the East, the hobbyist movement grew up around the Amateur Computer Group of New Jersey. Scelbi, in Milford, Connecticut, put out a popular kit based on the 8008, and Technical Design Labs in Trenton, New Jersey, was developing a computer kit around a new chip, the Zilog Z80. Hal Chamberlain in North Carolina, Bruce Seals in Tennessee, and Georgia Tech student Ron Roberts were active hobbyists working on systems, components, or software.

But the fire burned most strongly in Silicon Valley, with its atmosphere of symbiotic information sharing. New companies that created circuit boards for the Altair popped up almost daily. By the end of 1975, one of these, Processor Technology, was on its way to parlaying its substitute for the defective Altair memory board into financial wealth and, within a curiously anticorporate industry, a kind of corporate respectability.

Nostalgia for the Future

*Bob said he would pay me to design the
video section of the Tom Swift Terminal.
He knew how to manipulate me.*

LEE FELSENSTEIN
Designer of several microcomputer products

IN JUNE 1975, BOB MARSH AND *POPULAR ELECTRONICS* TECHNICAL editor Les Solomon were contemplating an "intelligent terminal" kit. It would consist of a terminal with semiconductor circuitry inside of it that would perform certain display and keyboard decoding functions that another computer attached to it would have otherwise handled. Marsh had some ideas from his own experience and from discussions with Felsenstein about the Tom Swift Terminal. "If you can get me a working model in 30 days, I'll give you a cover story," Solomon said.

Marsh put the proposition to Felsenstein this way: "Do you think it's impossible?" He appreciated Marsh's careful phrasing of the question. To dodge the job, he would have to pronounce it impossible, a distasteful act to any self-respecting engineer.

Marsh said he would pay Felsenstein to design the video portion of his dream machine, the convivial terminal that Felsenstein saw as essential to releasing the power of computers to everyone. Felsenstein liked the idea, and agreed to do it. It soon became apparent that Marsh had a different project in mind. What he wanted was a terminal with a brain—the same Intel 8080 chip that was the brain of the Altair. They argued over the details of the design, with Marsh usually getting the better of the arguments. Neither Felsenstein, Marsh, or Les Solomon

130

realized it then, but the product they were designing would become something more than just a terminal.

Felsenstein had to withdraw from another project when he agreed to design the intelligent terminal. "The roof is falling in again," he told his ex-customer. Up until now, he had paid his share of the rent by consulting for various people. But Proc Tech was expanding to take up the whole garage—all 1100 square feet of it. Felsenstein was gradually being absorbed into Marsh's enterprise.

Marsh had already developed the terminal's architecture and continued to change the design requirements as Felsenstein worked. Felsenstein had enjoyed consulting, in part because he could get some distance between him and the person he was working for and concentrate without interruption on a problem. This advantage evaporated when he began to devote most of his time to the Proc Tech terminal. Marsh insisted on design changes on a daily basis and repeatedly forced Felsenstein to junk much of his careful work and start over. "The situation," Felsenstein later said, "did call heavily on my sense of futility, absurdity, and ultimate irrelevance."

Despite his complaints, Felsenstein was enjoying himself. His grumbling about being manipulated was more of a jab at himself than it was at Marsh, who, for all his entrepreneurial energy, was at least partly involved for the fun of it. At one point in the project, Felsenstein said, "Let's advertise it as having 'the wisdom of Solomon.'" He meant it as a sly reference to Les Solomon, and this whimsical slogan soon inspired them to name the machine "the Sol."

Marsh and Felsenstein argued ceaselessly over the design at Felsenstein's workbench at one end of their garage and at the makeshift Proc Tech offices housed at the other end. They argued about it over meals and while driving across the San Francisco Bay to Homebrew meetings. Despite their continual disagreements over design, they nevertheless got the goods out. On one trip to a Homebrew meeting, they redesigned an entire internal bus.

It eventually dawned on Marsh and Felsenstein that they were designing a real computer. After all, it had an 8080 in it. But clearly it was also a terminal. Until then, computers typically consisted of rectangular boxes with accessory connections to terminals of some kind—Teletypes, cathode ray tubes, typewriters, or printers. But theirs was a screen, a keyboard, and a computer all in one. Could they really pull this thing off?

The question had both technical and political implications. At this point, the Altair dominated the tiny microcomputer industry, and IMSAI had not yet made its entry. And here they were, developing this terminal under the auspices of the Altair's biggest booster outside of Albuquerque—Leslie "Uncle Sol" Solomon. Would he rescind the cover story agreement if they told him they were concocting a computer instead of a terminal?

They decided not to tell him.

And they continued to work. Despite all the arguments, Marsh, Ingram, and Felsenstein were enjoying themselves. "This is a company that's going to have fun," Felsenstein said, "no matter how miserable I have to be." He described his partners as "nostalgic" for the future, like many computer hobbyists of the day, and their discussions were frequently that of visionaries. But the mundane, day-to-day decisions also had to be made. Marsh's friend still had all that cheap walnut originally slated for the digital clock business, and it seemed a shame to let it go to waste, so Marsh incorporated walnut side panels into the Sol's design, giving it the appearance of a 1950s station wagon.

Felsenstein had originally expected to hand the finished schematic to a layout artist. As it turned out, he was the chief layout artist. Because they had long since filled all the available floor space in the garage, a light table for the layout work was installed in a loft above the Proc Tech offices. Felsenstein padded the forehead-level conduit, but couldn't keep from bumping his head on the rafters as he worked with the other layout artist 14 to 17 hours a day, seven days a week. The other artist, pumping himself up with cola, dropped out before the end of the project, and Felsenstein had to finish the job alone, on orange juice.

Marsh kept the pressure on, and within 45 days of his initial discussion with Les Solomon, he had a circuit board. But Solomon had given the team a 30-day deadline, so as they neared completion, Marsh booked a flight to New York and informed a bleary-eyed Lee Felsenstein that he was going, too. They stuffed the Sol into two brown paper bags and carried it with them on the plane.

The demonstration for Solomon at *Popular Electronics* was an utter disaster. The thing just didn't work. They made what excuses they could and, feeling hopeless at this point, flew to an appointment at *Byte,* where the presentation was even more disastrous. Felsenstein, dead on his feet from the grueling work schedule, fell asleep during the *Byte* demonstration.

Well-rested and back in California at his workbench, he quickly located the problem—a short circuit. Marsh promptly put Felsenstein back on a plane to New York to demonstrate a working Sol with strict instructions to not reveal that it was actually a *computer.*

Felsenstein kept his mouth shut, but Solomon was no dummy. When Felsenstein showed him the Sol terminal, he watched it work for a while, and then asked Felsenstein what was to stop him from plugging in a memory board with BASIC on it and running the Sol as a bona fide computer.

"Beats me," Felsenstein deadpanned.

Of course the Sol was a computer. And that meant, Marsh and Ingram realized, that it needed software, particularly BASIC. The two contracted with Chuck Grant and Mark Greenberg to write it. One-time partner George Morrow had a falling out with Grant and Greenberg because he didn't think they were taking their oral agreement with God-bout seriously enough. Morrow decided to deal with Godbout alone, while Grant and Greenberg began doing business as G & G Systems.

As they worked on the BASIC, Grant and Greenberg found they were having the most trouble with the floating-point routines: arithmetic on real numbers, not integers. They simply couldn't process the operation as quickly as they wanted to. They finally decided to build the floating-point math into the hardware, and hired George Millard to help design a floating-point board.

Around this time, the issue of proprietary software reared its ugly head. Conflict arose over ownership of the BASIC computer language. Marsh asserted that the BASIC was being developed for Proc Tech, whereas Grant and Greenberg, with growing ambition, insisted that it was theirs, and began soliciting other customers for BASIC. Proc Tech took Grant and Greenberg to court, and the case lumbered through discovery and delay, doing neither company any good.

Grant and Greenberg had other hot projects going. They developed a cassette-tape interface that would allow microcomputers to save data to tape by using cheap audio tape recorders. But then Shugart, a Silicon Valley minicomputer disk drive manufacturer, announced the introduction of a drive that used 5¼-inch disks—smaller than the 8-inch disks commonly used on big computers—that cost less than any other disk drive. Disk drives were the obvious answer for data storage, if they could be made affordable. So Grant and Greenberg dropped their interest in cassette storage and started designing a controller board to make the Shugart disk drive work with microcomputers.

When they had their disk system together, they gave themselves a new name, North Star, perhaps echoing the name Altair, another bright star in the sky. Simultaneously, as Applied Computer Technology, they contracted to sell IMSAIs bundled with their own BASIC and cassette interface to universities. The market, they discovered, did not want configured systems, but raw computers, so they began selling IMSAIs out of Mark Greenberg's garage. This operation, at Grant's suggestion, was called Kentucky Fried Computers.

Meanwhile, their ex-partner, George Morrow, had bought an Altair, studied it, and decided not to imitate it. He shared Godbout's estimation of the Altair. The computer that he and Godbout planned to build, and that he began to design, would definitely be better. He would base the computer on National Semiconductor's PACE, a microprocessor they hoped to get for $50 from National.

Godbout, however, had reservations about the project. He meditated over Altair's sales figures and decided that memory boards for the Altair may do well after all. Morrow, with some reluctance, put aside the PACE machine and commenced designing a 4K memory board with his own name on it, joining Proc Tech and Seals in the memory market. Godbout sold the board for $189, well under Proc Tech's price, and Morrow suddenly found himself making $1,800 a month in royalties.

Godbout now became intensely interested in selling microcomputer boards. But when he vetoed one of Morrow's ideas, Morrow reevaluated their relationship. Couldn't he sell his boards just as well as Godbout, he asked himself. The only difference, he decided, lay in who placed the magazine ads. Thus was born Morrow's Microstuf.

The market was crazy, according to Morrow. "You could start a com-

pany, announce a product, and people would throw money at you." Bob
Marsh had already learned this lesson with Proc Tech's memory
boards, but was more than willing to take a refresher course. Marsh
and Felsenstein took the Sol to the PC Computer show in Atlantic City,
New Jersey, in June 1976 to unveil it to the world. It went over big.

Back in California again, they continued to enhance and modify the
Sol. While writing tutorial articles on computer design for *PCC*,
Felsenstein added what they called, to use writer Don Lancaster's term,
a "personality module." This tiny circuit board had a ROM chip and
could be plugged into the back of the machine, enabling its "personality" to be changed in a second. Felsenstein wryly imagined employees
popping in game modules for the business modules while the boss was
out of the office.

By late 1976, DEC was selling its LSI-11 bottom-of-the-line minicomputer for slightly over $1,000. In Southern California, Dick Wilcox
gave hard thought to a suggestion in *Dr. Dobb's Journal* about interfacing the LSI-11 with an Altair or IMSAI. What he came up with was the
Alpha Micro, an LSI-like multiuser CPU board, which he demonstrated to Homebrew in December 1976.

New microprocessors continued to arrive. Toshiba released the first
Japanese chip, the T3444. National Semiconductor issued a new
microprocessor and also supplied the development tools hobbyists
needed to start building real computers and writing software.

Scores of new microcomputer companies began to appear. Vector
Graphic in Thousand Oaks, California, introduced an 8K memory
board. Vector consisted of a Stanford engineering school graduate and
two businesswomen. Men had founded almost all the microcomputer
companies, although some had recruited wives or girlfriends as business managers. But Vector's Lore Harp quickly showed she was more
than just a business manager as she guided the company with a shrewd
sense of the market's needs and the possibilities for potential growth.

However, Vector was not doing any better than Proc Tech. During
the winter of 1976–1977, Proc Tech moved to a much larger facility,
14,000 square feet next to a beef-rendering plant in nearby Emeryville.
The atmosphere was uninviting, but the new location was far roomier
than their former digs.

A month after Proc Tech moved out of the Fourth Street garage,

Grant and Greenberg took over two-thirds of the space of the garage, Felsenstein reclaimed the other third, and their three company names were placed on the door: North Star, Applied Computer Technology, and Kentucky Fried Computers. As the latter company, they were now marketing IMSAIs, Polymorphic and Vector Graphic boards, and an Apple I that they were persuaded to take on consignment by a scraggly bearded young man named Steve Jobs. But soon, sales of their North Star disk system soared, and they closed Kentucky Fried Computers to concentrate fully on North Star. A letter from a certain fast-food chain that demanded they cease and desist from using the name Kentucky Fried Computers made the decision easier.

By the end of 1976, Processor Technology, Cromemco, North Star, Vector Graphic, and Godbout were prominent among the Silicon Valley enterprises, building an entire industry where none had existed two years before. And that industry was growing with amazing speed.

Sixers and Seventy-Sixers

I was working on . . . a military project
with $1.5 million to build a display. It
occurred to me maybe I could make a few
concessions and do it for $99 instead.

DON LANCASTER
Early computer hobbyist and writer

BY THE MID- TO LATE 1970S, THE FIRE OF INVENTION BURNED brightly in Silicon Valley, fueled by a unique environment of universities and electronics and semiconductor firms, and the legacy of revolutionary fervor left by the Berkeley Free Speech Movement and 1960s counterculture values. But tinder sparks were igniting in scattered places throughout the country. Some of those figurative sparks were fanned by a man who actually spent his days watching for *real* fires.

Don Lancaster wasn't your typical aerospace engineer. He had gone to work for a defense contractor in the 1960s as a way of avoiding the Vietnam draft, but wasn't too thrilled to find himself working for a company that produced machines designed to kill people. During his tenure there, he began to write articles for *Popular Electronics* and soon found that he could do better on his own. He quit the aerospace job, moved to Arizona, and went to work for the forest service as a fire spotter. Stationed in a lonely ten-foot-square fire tower, he had many hours to think up ideas for electronics projects he could write about.

Lancaster's antiwar sentiments may not have found universal approval in Arizona, but his rugged individualism did. And he looked the part. Many of the California Homebrewers, such as Steve Dompier, were longhairs who rebelled against the "straight" look of the typical engineering student. But not Don Lancaster. Picture Lancaster as a computer-era Chuck Yeager—clean-cut, square-jawed, and tight-lipped, with aviator sunglasses and a cowboy hat planted squarely on his head.

Despite his straight-laced appearance, Lancaster was a genuine revolutionary. His do-it-yourself electronics articles were written by one individualist for other individualists. Those articles put the kind of power formerly reserved for aerospace firms and corporate data-processing departments—in short, the computer priesthood—into the hands of the technically savvy everyman.

Lancaster was prolific. In addition to his freelance articles, he wrote books that electronics enthusiasts devoured, with titles such as *TTL Cookbook, CMOS Cookbook,* and *Cheap Video Cookbook.* An excerpt from his *Cheap Video Cookbook* provides a sense of Lancaster's style and substance, and a glimpse into the kinds of issues that early microcomputer hobbyists had to deal with:

"Cheap video is a brand new collection of hardware and software ideas that dramatically slash the cost and complexity of both alphanumeric and graphics microprocessor-based video displays. A typical cheap video system . . . lets you do things like 12×80 scrolling display using only seven ordinary ICs with a total circuit cost as low as $20, transparently run on a microcomputer system that still has as much as ⅔ of its throughput remaining for other programs."

Lancaster was original, prolific, and generous. *Popular Electronics*'s Les Solomon spoke for all those who had been inspired by Lancaster's books and articles when he said he had been "constantly startled by Don Lancaster's brilliant innovations over the years."

Ed Roberts of MITS was one of those who studied Lancaster's books and articles, and he worried because he thought Lancaster had hitched his wagon to a star brighter than Altair. Soon after *Popular Electronics* featured the MITS Altair on its cover, Lancaster joined up with Southwest Technical Products (SWTPC) in San Antonio. SWTPC had been in the audio component business until late 1975, when it jumped into the business that Ed Roberts regarded as his personal domain: hobby computers. Roberts was convinced that the 6800 microprocessors that SWTPC was getting from Motorola made a better brain for a small computer than the Intel chip that Roberts bought at a clearance to put in his Altair.

Roberts's worries foreshadowed the split in the industry between the supporters of processors from Intel and chips from Motorola and other vendors, an argument that would continue for decades. That dichotomy has echoes in today's industry with the Intel-based or Intel-compatible machines versus Motorola-based machines such as the original Apple Macintosh, although the chip in the Mac is not really a descendant of those early "sixer" chips.

Because the chips in the Intel line usually featured the number 8 prominently in their product names and the Motorola chips usually had a 6 in their names, supporters of the two lines were often called, respectively, "eighters" and "sixers." Roberts was an eighter by default, but wanted to be a sixer. The attendees of the Homebrew Computer Club in Silicon Valley were mostly eighters, with some notable exceptions, such as the young Steve Wozniak, a clearance-sale-shopper sixer who had recently taken a job at Hewlett-Packard. Although the chips weren't all that different in their capacity, the choice of a computer's microprocessor affected myriad hardware and software compatibility issues. A seemingly small decision, it was nevertheless a fateful one. Lancaster was a sixer.

Lancaster's best-known contribution to the technological revolution was one of his earliest: the TV Typewriter. Lancaster published his prescient *Radio Electronics* article that described the groundbreaking TV Typewriter device in 1973, a full two years before Ed Roberts had an Altair up and running. One industry pundit would later crown Lancaster the "father of the personal computer" because of this invention.

The TV Typewriter was just a terminal, but it was a terminal that computer hobbyists could build themselves. The device, and Lancaster's description of its capabilities, got hobbyists thinking about real homebrew computers, and about the kinds of capabilities that the Internet would deliver to a broad market more than two decades later. It is no exaggeration to say that the TV Typewriter influenced a generation of computer hobbyists.

The TV Typewriter impressed Les Solomon. It made it possible for users to enter text on a cheap keyboard and display the characters on a television screen—uniting two inexpensive components that could, in principle, serve as the primary input and output devices for a computer. Bingo. Solomon wanted a way of getting information into and out of the Altair box that was easier and more user-friendly than having to flip switches and read the blinking patterns of the front-panel lights. Inevitably, he thought of Lancaster's TV Typewriter.

The TV Typewriter and the Altair couldn't work together as they were; one or the other would have to be redesigned. But which one? Solomon grabbed the bull by the horns, perhaps a more apt metaphor than he would have liked, and took Lancaster to Albuquerque to meet Ed Roberts. He thought a face-to-face meeting could resolve the issue.

No such luck: Arizona faced off against New Mexico, and neither gave an inch.

The TV Typewriter proved more successful in another context. It was Lancaster's article on the device that got Bob Marsh into computers and had him hook up with Lee Felsenstein, which led to the creation of the Sol. The Sol was the first of the hobby computers to feature a built-in screen and keyboard. So, although the design was not Lancaster's, the germ of the idea was his. The built-in screen and keyboard of the Sol made it, in this regard anyway, the model for computers ever since.

By the spring of 1977, the wildfire had spread around the country and beyond. The most visible signs of the phenomenon were the computer clubs springing up all over. The Philadelphia Area Computer Society tracked developments in its newsletter, *The Data Bus*. The Toronto Region Association of Computer Enthusiasts (TRACE) newsletter already had a rating system for products. In Santa Monica, California, a group of hobbyists had formed an influential club, the *Southern California Computer Society.*

Microcomputer-related companies had already appeared and were doing business in Tempe, Arizona; Englewood, Colorado; Norcross, Georgia; Skokie, Illinois; Olathe, Kansas; Crofton, Maryland; Cambridge, Massachusetts; Saint Louis, Missouri; Peterborough, New Hampshire; New York City, New York; Cleveland, Ohio; Oklahoma City, Oklahoma; Aloha, Oregon; Malmo, Sweden; Provo, Utah; Issaquah, Washington; and Laramie, Wyoming—to cite a few examples. Newman Computer Exchange in Ann Arbor, Michigan, could already boast of its "giant" catalog of microcomputer equipment, bigger than all the other catalogs out there.

Jim Warren, editor of *Dr. Dobb's Journal,* "chairbeing" of the first

West Coast Computer Faire, and strategically placed observer of the rapid spread of this hobby computer movement, in August 1977 estimated that there were "50,000 or more general-purpose digital computers in private ownership for personal use." Whether or not that estimate was accurate, or took into account a few rich enthusiasts who could well afford to house a minicomputer in their basements, it stated with certainty that a wild and unstoppable fire was burning across the land.

If Jim Warren had listed all the microcomputer companies, clubs, magazines, and newsletters he knew about in mid-1977, the list would have bulged with Silicon Valley addresses, and not just because it was Warren's home base. California enterprises in general would have occupied a large share of the list. Other states that were home to mainframe and minicomputer companies, semiconductor companies, and high-tech research schools, including Massachusetts, Minnesota, and Texas, would take another big chunk of the list.

And then you had the New Jersey hackers.

The Garden State was rich with microcomputer companies, such as Technical Design Labs in Princeton and Electronic Control Technology in Union. Roger Amidon and Chris Rutkowski had a "supercomputer," the General, with very good software. There were also the magazines—*Computer Decisions* magazine in Rochelle Park, and the most mainstream, accessible, and entertaining of the lot, David Ahl's *Creative Computing*.

But the clubs were where the ideas were shared, and they were what kept the fire spreading. The Amateur Computer Group of New Jersey (ACGNJ) was one of the most active computer clubs in the country, and one of its fire-starters was a man named Sol Libes.

Like Don Lancaster, Libes wrote books for electronics enthusiasts. But whereas Lancaster was a loner, Libes was a joiner. Or perhaps it was that he could convince others to join *him*. Sol was a little older than some of the hackers, and may have seemed avuncular to a number of them. But he was one of the most active ACGNJ members, always getting involved with projects, including a couple of slick computer magazines.

Magazines were important to the spread of the microcomputer

movement, but they lacked the immediacy that feeds a fast-moving phenomenon. Clubs such as the Homebrew Computer Club and the Amateur Computer Group of New Jersey brought together computer enthusiasts who could share and critique ideas and designs in real time.

Although meeting in real time was critical to the movement, meeting in real space wasn't. It was only a matter of time before some hacker figured out that the best place for computer hobbyists to meet would be on a computer.

Most of the new microcomputers were capable of being hooked up to a modem. That meant with the right software they could be used to allow computer owners to communicate with each other over phone lines, somewhat like ham radio enthusiasts who typed rather than talked.

Despite this capability, that scenario presented certain problems. Even if you had the right software, and even if the right software that both you and your friend had made all the same assumptions, you could talk only when you were both willing and available at the same time. It would be nice if you could leave an electronic message for your friend, but unless your friend's computer and modem happened to be turned on when you sent the message, where would you leave it?

A Chicago computer enthusiast solved these nagging problems. He created a way of transmitting data between microcomputers over phone lines, called XMODEM, that became the communications standard. He also created a place to store messages with the first computer bulletin board system.

This man's name was Ward Christensen, and in 1978 he and Randy Seuss wrote the first software that made it possible to set up CBBSs, computer bulletin board systems. CBBSs, or just BBSs, not only provided a place to store messages for other computer enthusiasts, they also became places where communities of people with common interests—and not just a shared interest in computers—developed.

Over time, communities based not on geography but purely on shared interests developed on BBSs, and later on in Usenet newsgroups, e-mail lists, interactive Web sites, multiuser domains, and virtual worlds. In 1978, most of those developments were still a thing of the future, but the model for every virtual community to come was present in those BBSs.

The virtual electronic communities on BBSs, the computer clubs popping up all over the country, the companies built more for the excitement rather than a desire for big profits—these were all evidence that something was going on that couldn't be understood in terms of economic self-interest. On the other hand, ignoring economic realities is not a good idea in any business, as some of the Silicon Valley firms soon found out.

Home Rule

*The first part of the meeting we were
involved in open combat with Intel.
Intel was out to torpedo any
standardization effort on the S100 bus.*

GEORGE MORROW
**Microcomputer pioneer and founder of
one of the early firms**

ALTHOUGH THE SPIRIT OF SHARING WAS WELL ESTABLISHED IN THE
early days of the microcomputer industry, its participants had a lot
to learn about working together. One thing that accelerated the learning process was fear.

A continuing concern in the developing microcomputing industry
was that "the big boys" would come and spoil all the fun. "The big boys"
sometimes meant IBM and the other mainframe computer and minicomputer companies, but mostly the reference was to such companies
as Commodore and other electronics companies that had waged
Pyrrhic price-cutting wars in the calculator industry. And, most especially, it meant Texas Instruments, known for its ruthless price slashing.
Lee Felsenstein summarized the dread of many hobbyist entrepreneurs: "Anyone but TI!"

Intel and some of the other semiconductor companies, although well
situated to produce microcomputers from their own chips, had
expressed reluctance to do anything that could be construed as competing with their own customers. By this time, the hobbyist-born
microcomputer companies had developed just about enough clout to
be taken seriously as semiconductor customers. Or so it seemed.

Then, in December of 1976, Commodore International, an electronics firm with a lot of market muscle and apparently not burdened with the sort of qualms Intel had, leaked information to *Electronic Engineering Times* about a new product. Commodore, the story went, was ready to release a machine very much like the Sol, but at a lower price. Proc Tech was just shipping the first Sols, and Marsh was thinking about the company's next product, a new version of the Sol with an integrated keyboard and 64K of memory that would be sold for a cheap $1,000. Unfortunately, it was, in essence, the same as the Commodore machine.

Convinced that Commodore actually had their computer product on the launch pad and that Proc Tech could never compete with it, and worried by the news that National Semiconductor was also planning a microcomputer, Marsh scrapped the new-and-improved Sol project. Five years earlier, the rules of battle in the semiconductor wars demanded that companies cut prices to the baseline and push the technology relentlessly, even under threat of corporate extinction. Marsh and Ingram had no illusions about being able to compete with Commodore and National in bloody mortal combat. As it turned out, the Commodore machine would not appear for some time, and the National Semiconductor computer never materialized.

Despite their worries about the big boys, hobbyist-entrepreneurs kept right on launching companies. Many of these new hobbyist-born companies were starting to manufacture microcomputer products, but most of them were turning out boards for the Altair or IMSAI, and practically all were small, start-up companies like Proc Tech.

Howard Fulmer began such a firm in his Oakland basement. After reading an editorial by Ed Roberts in David Bunnell's *Computer Notes* that attacked the Altair-compatible memory board companies as "parasites," he considered calling his own company Symbiotic Engineering, to emphasize his conception of the proper relationship between MITS's products and his own. But a group called the Symbionese Liberation Army was making a name for itself right about then, and he wanted to avoid confusion with the radical political group. Instead, he called his company Parasitic Engineering, sending a rather pointed message to Roberts.

In the spring of 1977, George Morrow and Howard Fulmer, both of whom were designing Altair-compatible products, decided to build a computer together. Morrow would supply the boards he had already designed, and Fulmer would come up with everything else they needed to construct a computer. One of the other things they needed was a name, and Fulmer had one. He called their baby the Equinox 100. It was a solid design for they'd been listening to the ideas advanced by Bill Godbout and Bob Mullen, a founder of the Silicon Valley disk-drive manufacturer Diablo Systems, about improving the S100 bus.

But the timing of the machine's release was unfortunate. The Equinox was an 8080 machine, and the 8080 was no longer the sexy chip; the Z80 was. Technical Design Labs in New Jersey, Garland and Melen's Cromemco in California, and The Digital Group in Colorado were all known to be designing computers based on the new and apparently superior Z80 chip. Cromemco had already produced a Z80 central processor board, and hobbyists were dropping it into the IMSAI chassis to create a mongrel Z80 machine. Faced with that sort of competition, the Equinox did not do well.

Marsh wondered if Proc Tech shouldn't do a Z80 machine as well. But it seemed irrational to dump a successful design in order to achieve a marginal improvement in performance. The Sol was a hit, and he believed the processor mattered much less than the software. The software made the computer work, and that would distinguish one machine from another. It was the software that really mattered.

And that led to the idea that programs—games, business applications, or anything, really—written specifically for the Sol may help sell the machines. But rather than simply commission software to be written for the Sol, Marsh did something subtler: he commissioned the tools to make it easier to write software for the machine. After all, most of Proc Tech's customers were engineers who could write their own software.

Proc Tech called on two programmers, Jerry Kirk and Paul Greenfield of MicroTech in Sunnyvale, who had produced high-level language compilers for minicomputers. They were asked to create a set of programmer's tools, programs that would make it easier to write, edit, and debug other programs on the Sol. Ingram developed their work into Software Package One, which made the Sol the easiest machine to program, giving it a huge advantage.

But software ownership was becoming an inflammatory issue in the Valley and elsewhere. Processor Tech was aggressively pro-sharing, and its hobbyist founders swapped program tapes at Homebrew meetings along with everyone else. Gordon French, who after helping to start Homebrew became Proc Tech's General Factotum (his official title), argued for an open system—that is, free dissemination of software code and internal workings to anyone. He wanted outside programmers and peripheral manufacturers to be able to create compatible products and expand the market.

At the same time, Ed Roberts and the entire mainframe and minicomputer industry held the opposite view, that software should be proprietary. But the hobbyists were bringing their own values to bear in the industry. Most favored openness in hardware and software design. An open architecture—the publicly known, physical design of a machine—was one emerging ideal. An open operating system was another.

At Proc Tech, however, the idea of an open operating system was frowned upon. Marsh and Ingram wanted that particular component to be proprietary. In fact, Proc Tech had its own disk operating system very early on. The company bought PT-DOS from its author, 19-year-old Bill Levy, who developed it at the Lawrence Hall of Science at UC Berkeley. Levy modeled PT-DOS after Unix, a mainframe/minicomputer operating system in use at UC Berkeley. Marsh thought PT-DOS, with its rich set of tools, was much better than the CP/M disk operating system, which did only the bare minimum of what an operating system should do. Unfortunately, PT-DOS was slow to reach the market because of what came to be called "the drive fiasco."

In 1976, when the Sol was released, disk drives posed an alluring challenge. Although they were heavily used on mainframes and minicomputers, mounting disk drives on microcomputers was prohibitively expensive. Drives typically cost $3,500 or more. So Marsh was very intrigued when George Comstock, Bob Mullen's partner at Diablo Systems, announced at a Homebrew meeting one night that he wanted to develop a disk drive for microcomputers. Comstock thought that a drive, complete with a controller board and software, could be sold for around $1,000.

But Diablo was not yet involved in the growing microcomputer industry, and Comstock felt that close consultation with microcomputer companies was crucial. He proposed a joint effort to Marsh. Diablo would develop the drives, the physical mechanisms that read and write information from and to disks, and Processor Technology would write the software and develop an S100 board to control the drives. He also proposed that Proc Tech could market the board on its own.

Disk drives were so clearly destined to be a part of any serious microcomputer system that engineers were already vying to develop a low-cost disk drive system with software and a controller board. Shugart's 5¼-inch disk drives seemed attractive, but they had one drawback. IBM had been using 8-inch disk drives and had established certain standards for the devices. No standards existed for small disk drives, and no one could guarantee that disks written on one brand of machine would be readable on another.

North Star had selected the Shugart disk drive and sold it for under $800. Using an idea borrowed from Eugene Fisher of Lawrence Livermore Labs, both Morrow and San Francisco engineer Ben Cooper had begun developing relatively low-cost 8-inch disk drives. Cooper had perhaps the first commercial 8-inch disk drive controller for microcomputers. Morrow, shortly thereafter, had the first one available for the $1,000 price Comstock was aiming for. He then negotiated with Digital Research and Microsoft for an operating system (CP/M) and BASIC to distribute free with the disk drive system. Both Morrow and Cooper continued to develop disk products, and Cooper created the first *hard disk* controller for microcomputers. Disk storage, including hard disk storage, was coming to microcomputers, a big step in making them truly useful, but as yet there was no standard for disk storage systems.

Meanwhile at Processor Tech, the disk drive plans were crumbling. Diablo encountered trouble with the drives and dropped the project, leaving Proc Tech so far into development of the disk drive controller that it had to continue with the work. Marsh and Ingram raised the price of Proc Tech's disk-drive subsystem for the Sol to $1,700, substituting for the inexpensive Diablo disk drive the more expensive one offered by Perscii. The price was too high, and worse, Proc Tech's disk drive systems didn't always work. Customers could find better deals from Cooper, Morrow, and North Star.

Despite such problems, Proc Tech still seemed to be thriving. The executives were recycling their profits into the company. (Lee Felsenstein was investing his in the Community Memory project.) The Proc Tech staff in Emeryville now numbered 85, not counting nonemployee/consultant Felsenstein, and the company's headquarters was growing crowded. Proc Tech moved south to the bedroom community of Pleasanton. The new offices boasted a spacious executive suite with large windows looking out over the valley.

But the competition was heavy. As 1977 came to an end, Proc Tech found itself part of a more seriously run industry. The open trading of information, the shirt-sleeve management, the flashes of idealism, and the lack of detailed planning that had characterized the industry from the start still existed. But there was a growing belief that professional management may have its advantages; however, scarcely anyone considered it the time to put such a radical idea into practice. The chief users, designers, and company presidents were still hobbyists at heart, and most of the world knew nothing of the revolution that was afoot.

New companies were sprouting like mushrooms overnight. Among the computer and computer-related companies in business at the end of 1977 were Apple Computer (which some insiders thought had great promise), Exidy, IMSAI, Digital Microsystems, Alpha Micro Systems, Commodore, Midwest Scientific, GNAT, Southwest Technical Products, MITS, Technical Design Labs, Vector Graphic, Ithaca Audio, Heathkit, Cromemco, MOS Technology, RCA, TEI, Ohio Scientific, The Digital Group, Micromation, Polymorphic Systems, Parasitic Engineering, Godbout Engineering, Radio Shack, Dynabyte, North Star, Morrow's Microstuf, and, of course, Processor Technology.

The Homebrew influence was still strong. Many of these companies were located in the Bay Area and were associated with the Homebrew Club. The club had grown large and by 1977 tended to assemble in fairly predictable clusters. Up front, performing for everyone, was Lee Felsenstein. Bob Marsh and the Proc Tech group usually assembled along one wall. Steve Wozniak, his boys from Apple, and the other 6502 processor fans sat in the back. Jim Warren of *Dr. Dobb's Journal* sat on the aisle three seats from the back, stage left, ready to rise during the "mapping" session and do his Core Dump, an extemporaneous outpouring of all the news and rumors he had heard. The front row always had Gordon French, who maintained the software library, and Bob Reiling, who wrote the newsletter.

In December 1977, Reiling wrote, "The development of special-interest groups has probably been the biggest change during the past year. At the beginning of the year, the 6800 group was holding regular meetings. At the end of 1977, the groups include not only the 6800 group, but also the P8 Users, North Star Users Group, Sol Users Society, and PET Users." At that time, the Homebrew attendees (the club did not have members) included key people from Apple, Cromemco, Commodore, Computer Faire, *Dr. Dobb's Journal,* Itty Bitty Computers, M&R Enterprises, Mountain Hardware, IBEX, Mullen Computer Boards, North Star, PCC, Proc Tech, and the Bay Area computer stores. The most prominent of them all was Proc Tech. Marsh had, to some extent, realized his dream. The company seemed golden.

Most of these companies were producing machines or boards that used the S100 bus, the interface standard developed at MITS for the Altair. The bus was becoming a problem, though, because no matter how disorganized and unprofessional the companies may have been, they couldn't compare to the anarchy that prevailed among companies using the S100 bus. The bus was the channel over which third-party boards communicated with the 8080 microprocessor in the Altair. Without clear specifications for how the bus worked, all such communication with the brain of the machine was unreliable, to say the least. MITS, which considered the third-party board makers "parasites," wasn't eager to publish such specifications.

In late 1977, Bob Stewart called a meeting to do something about the S100 bus problem. A consultant in optics and electronics and a member of the Institute for Electrical and Electronics Engineers (IEEE), Stewart had bought an Altair and was frustrated with it. He called together some microcomputer company presidents: Harry Garland of Cromemco, Howard Fulmer of Parasitic Engineering, Ben Cooper of Micromation, and George Morrow of what he then called Thinkertoys. *Byte*'s editor, Carl Helmers, was there, too. The idea was to cure the obvious problems of the S100 bus and to establish common standards so that one company's board could work with another's.

Garland explained the virtues of his and Melen's shielded bus, but

Morrow thought he had a better approach. No immediate agreement was forthcoming. Stewart suggested petitioning the IEEE to make the group an official standards body charged with creating an IEEE standard for the bus. The petition won approval, and the group was now official.

Ed Roberts was invited to participate in the microcomputer standards subcommittee, but declined to send a representative or even respond directly. He did say in print that he felt MITS had the sole right to define the bus. The subcommittee ignored him.

At first, the meetings addressed the group's contention with Intel, which fought standardization. Morrow got the impression that Intel wanted no standards unless Intel could set them. But when the subcommittee decided to formulate standards whether Intel liked them or not, the chip manufacturer acquiesced.

This was outrageous cheek. A bunch of hobbyists turned entrepreneurs had simply ignored the biggest microcomputer company of that time and had faced down the leading chip manufacturer—and not been struck by lightning.

Despite its solidarity, the subcommittee had no guarantee that it could really create standards. The subcommittee had 15 assertive, opinionated people disputing an issue about which they held legitimate and conceivably irresolvable differences. Each of the members had a product that would be incompatible with anything likely to be proposed. As the meetings progressed, Roger Melen came in for Cromemco. Alpha Micro was represented. Elwood Douglas appeared for Proc Tech and judged the standard against the memory board he was designing. George Millard spoke for North Star. Someone arrived from IMSAI to read its formal position, which resembled Ed Roberts's. The subcommittee ignored that position, too. Most of its members had written IMSAI off as a place where training in *est* mattered more than training in engineering.

At times, whatever fondness the subcommittee members had for each other wasn't too apparent. They argued for hours, with no one yielding an inch. They would then return to their respective companies and discuss how they might compromise on their own designs to achieve a single standard. At each meeting, they would find themselves inching closer to an agreement. Little by little, these creative, independent people subordinated their egos and any short-term economic gains for the good of the entire microcomputer field.

The committee was attempting a form of "guerrilla" design. In mainframes and minicomputers, the bus was always whatever the bus designer said it was. Independent companies were not about to get together to redesign something as complex as a bus. Timing parameters and other features were dictated by the designers. In fact, IBM and DEC worked this way. But the S100 committee members dug into the Roberts bus, figured out how it worked, and scrapped it in favor of a new, independent bus that was open to all. This was a populist revolt against the tyranny of big business, with MITS, although hardly in the same league as IBM and DEC, held up as a symbol of the Big Company. The revolution was here.

Homebrew Legacy

That's where the source of this industry has been. It hasn't come out of TI, IBM, or Fairchild. It's come from people who are on the edge, who have an alternative vision.

FRED MOORE
Founder of the Homebrew Computer Club

IN 1979, PROC TECH WAS IN DEEP TROUBLE. MARSH AND INGRAM, caught off balance by the Commodore and National Semiconductor threats and worried about competition from the promising Apple Computer company, had become uncertain about where to go with their product line. Their worries clearly showed. Felsenstein made frequent visits to their offices to talk about new products, but Marsh and Ingram seemed unable to decide on any. At last Felsenstein asked, "Look, what the hell do you guys want?" They replied that they wanted to see what Felsenstein could come up with. He finally understood that they really had no product planning.

Proc Tech also lacked the flexibility that more money would have provided the company, but Marsh and Ingram being the green executives that they were suffered, like Bill Millard, from "entrepreneur's disease." Adam Osborne had talked with them about accepting investments, but by now the investors were the ones who were reluctant to talk. Proc Tech was not developing any new products, and the Sol was an aging 8080 machine in a bold new world of computers built around the Z80.

Was the Sol out of date? Not really. But because technology was developing rapidly, and Proc Tech had nothing new in the works, it was

153

hard to see the Sol as the computer of the future. When potential investors asked Felsenstein how much work the Sol needed to keep it technologically advanced, he told the truth: quite a bit. That didn't help.

On May 14, 1979, the wolf came to the Pleasanton factory door and found nobody home. The Proc Tech principals had cashed in their chips and gone on to other ventures.

Theories abounded as to why Processor Technology had problems: too many revisions of the basic product, too much reliance on one product, failure to develop new products, and failure to keep abreast of new technology. Steve Dompier held that the company looked inward too much and tried to deal with all its problems as though they were simply organizational ones. Proc Tech did shuffle people around, however. According to one story, the company had hired a full-time employee merely to relocate phones in the Pleasanton plant. Felsenstein has always contended that Proc Tech's boat sank because it was full of small holes and management tended to puncture even more holes in the vessel.

Maybe it was Gary Ingram's desk. When Proc Tech held its bankruptcy auction, Parasitic Engineering founder Howard Fulmer drove to Pleasanton to check out the defunct enterprise. He walked through the building and passed small, slapped-together cubicles, a sign of a company on the skids. On the top floor of the building, Fulmer found what could only be called the penthouse suite. He'd never been there before and was impressed. There, in the middle of a huge room with large windows, stood Gary Ingram's fine French Provincial desk. Fulmer glanced over his shoulder to check that he was alone in the room, then went over to the desk and sat down behind it. Nice chair, he thought. He settled back, put his feet up on the beautiful desk, looked out across the valley, and sighed contentedly. "I feel rich," he murmured. "Everything must be fine."

Certain fundamental problems at Processor Technology do seem obvious in retrospect. The Sol did not spring from a single mind, and as a result was not designed as cleanly and coherently as it might have been. Despite the talk of the Sol growing out of Felsenstein's Tom Swift Terminal ideas, Felsenstein didn't design the machine to satisfy himself, but to fulfill a contract.

A second problem was a case of "entrepreneur's disease." Ingram refused to surrender any control of Proc Tech, and as a result the company suffered from both his and Marsh's amateurish managerial practices and from undercapitalization. An experienced manager, some investment capital, and greater freedom for the designer might have given the Proc Tech story a happier ending. It might have had no ending.

Nevertheless, Proc Tech and companies like it—ones that operated in ways that baffled seasoned executives—were constructing the microcomputer industry. Soon that industry was shifting its orientation from the hobbyist to the consumer. Market niches were being established. By 1979, Cromemco was known for its square steel boxes full of solidly engineered boards that were sold primarily to engineers and scientists. Vector Graphic was selling business machines that started with the turn of a key and immediately ran a business application program. Apple's computer in its plastic case was the premier game machine. And encroaching on the territory of the minicomputers was Alpha Microsystems, offering microcomputer systems that could support several users simultaneously.

Over the years to come, the Homebrew legacy continued to influence product designs and marketing principles. Homebrew was both a catalyst in the creation of the microcomputer and an active entity that fed its continued development. But because computers were becoming affordable to large numbers of people, another kind of creative effort was needed to make the hardware useful to the average person. Computer power to the people, the dream of computer revolutionaries like Felsenstein, required software. User-friendly, powerful, and affordable programs and the means for producing them were essential to turn the microcomputer into the personal computer.

The newborn microcomputer industry now needed a software industry.

CHAPTER 5

THE GENIE IN THE BOX

I think that most people's real motivation for getting a computer was to learn—they wanted to see what they could do with it.

DAN FYLSTRA
Publisher of VisiCalc

The Altair's
First Recital

*The man with the foolish grin is keeping
perfectly still.*

LENNON/MCCARTNEY

O N THE EVENING OF APRIL 16, 1975, DURING A HOMEBREW COM-
puter Club meeting held at an elementary school in Menlo Park,
California, Steve Dompier put on a show to remember.

Dompier was no showman. A slender, quick moving young man with
straight hair down to the middle of his back, Dompier wore jeans and a
nondescript sport shirt and "spoke quickly in a young person's idiom,"
Lee Felsenstein remembers, "filling in with 'stuff' when he saw no need
to be more precise."

But Dompier had in his possession an actual Altair. Few of the
assembled had ever seen one. Because MITS wasn't delivering Altairs
yet, Dompier had to earn his by flying to Albuquerque to pick it up in
person. It may have seemed fanatical to travel a thousand miles to get
what amounted to a $397 toy, but Dompier made it seem reasonable.
This was an actual computer, he told the Homebrewers. It was real and
it was here now. And all of them could buy it.

Buy their own computers? they thought. It used to be that only a rare
few had the means to own one. Computers were controlled by a priest-

hood of technicians in white coats, who mediated between the machines and ordinary mortals. The technofreaks in the audience that night got caught up in Dompier's excitement and began to imagine what they could do if they had computers of their own, or rather, what they would do *when* they had their own computers.

What Dompier showed them that night made them understand how revolutionary that idea was.

Lee Felsenstein remembers: "He arrived carrying his Altair and other 'stuff' and crouched to set it up in a corner near the door. He unrolled an extension cord out into the hallway where one of the few live electrical outlets could be found, and then hunched over the Altair to enter [his] program through the front panel switches, deflecting all questions with, 'Wait, you'll see.' "

The Homebrewers were interested in the machine, but hardly expected it to do much of anything given that it had no display, no keyboard, and only a teaspoonful of memory. But some of them suspected that Dompier would come up with something interesting. He was a likeable, down-to-earth fellow around whom the computer universe crackled. Lee Felsenstein was curious to see what Dompier could do with the Altair. If some people are accident-prone, Dompier was serendipity-prone, Felsenstein thought.

He wasn't accident-immune, apparently. It took several minutes of painstaking switch flipping for Dompier to enter his program. He knew if he made one mistake, it would all have to be done over. Then, just as he finished, someone tripped over the power cord and erased all his work. He plugged the machine back in and started all over, patiently reentering his program. Finally, he finished it—again.

He straightened up and made a brief announcement to the crowd—little more than an elaboration on "Wait, you'll see." "There was nothing he could have said to prepare us for what happened," Felsenstein recalls. "Noise—sound—*music* began emitting from the speaker of the portable radio he had placed on the Altair's cover. We immediately recognized the melody of the Beatles' 'Fool on the Hill.' "

Dompier didn't wait for applause. "Wait, there's more," he told the crowd. "It just started doing this itself."

And then the tones of "Daisy, Daisy (A Bicycle Built for Two)" came from the speaker. "We were thrilled," Felsenstein recalls, "to hear what many of us recognized as the first song ever 'sung' by a computer—in 1960, at Bell Labs—coming from this completely amateur setup."

The music stopped and the applause began. The crowd gave Dompier a standing ovation.

Technically, what Dompier had done was just a clever but not entirely unfamiliar trick. He had simply exploited a characteristic of small computers that would end up annoying the neighbors of their owners for the next five years. The machines emitted radio frequency interference, the stuff that makes snow in television pictures and static in radio transmissions. When Dompier realized that the Altair made his radio buzz, he decided to play around with the static. He figured out what he had to do with his program to control the frequency and duration of the noise.

Dompier's little "radio interface" program, which on paper would have looked nonsensical to any programmer who didn't know about its accidental side effects, turned the static into recognizable music. Dompier described his accomplishment a year later in an article entitled "Music of a Sort" in *Dr. Dobb's Journal of Computer Calisthenics & Orthodontia,* calling the event "the Altair's first recital."

But the Homebrewers understood the revolutionary implications of Dompier's act. He understood, too, that by claiming this machine for such a trivial, thoroughly unprofessional use, he was planting a flag on newly conquered ground. This thing belongs to *us,* he was saying, and it was this act of rebellion against the spirit of the computer priesthood, more than his technical prowess, that the Homebrewers applauded that night.

Dompier's program was short and simple. The machine did not have the memory to do anything complicated. At the time, hobbyists were more interested in hardware than software. After all, many of them had dreamed of owning a computer for some time, and they couldn't start programming a machine that did not exist. But with the advent of the Altair, software became not only feasible, but essential.

Those early computer enthusiasts had no choice but to write their own software. No one imagined then that anyone would actually *buy* software from someone else. Hobbyists wrote small programs that weren't so much useful applications of the machine as they were demonstrations of its potential.

Before the microcomputer could begin to change the world, software was needed in order to transform a plaything into a useful tool. A few pioneers worked within the tight memory constraints of the first machines and were still able to create some ingenious programs. As more memory became available, it became possible to write more complex and useful programs. The first of the more-complicated programs tended to be frivolous, but soon serious applications and business and accounting software followed.

Programming, which started out as an activity for hobbyists, quickly became an earnest commercial enterprise.

The two kinds of programs the new machines would need very quickly if they were going to be truly useful were *operating systems* and *high-level languages*. The collection of programs that controls input/output (I/O) devices, such as disk drives, and that shunts information into and out of memory and performs all the other operations that the computer user wants done automatically is called an *operating system*. In practice, users typically work with a computer via an operating system. Large mainframe computers had operating systems, and it was clear to many people that microcomputers needed them, too.

Every computer also has what's called a *machine language*, which is simply the set of commands the machine is made to recognize. These commands merely trigger the machine's basic operations, such as moving data between its internal storage registers, storing data in memory, or performing simple arithmetic on data. A computer becomes widely useful only when it is possible to trigger whole groups of these fundamental operations with a single command. Collections of these more powerful and meaningful commands are called *high-level languages*. The intricacies of machine language make it a cumbersome and complex language to use. High-level languages enable a computer user to progress beyond having to plod through the minutiae of machine language, thereby making a computer faster and producing more interesting results.

Beyond the programmer's tools lay the *applications programs*, the software that makes a computer actually accomplish something. But this was 1976, and operating systems and high-level languages weren't yet available, and applications software was even further off. Yet to come were the word processing programs that would turn a computer into a replacement for the typewriter, accounting programs that would keep track of payroll records and print checks, and educational programs that would introduce computer users to new ways of learning. The hobbyists of the day looked at their new machines and asked themselves what they *could* do with them. Play games, they answered.

Pleasure Before
Business

*Man is a game-playing animal, and a
computer is another way to play games.*

Scott Adams
Computer game software pioneer

L ONG BEFORE HIGH-LEVEL LANGUAGES AND OPERATING SYSTEMS SIM-
plified programming, computer enthusiasts created games. They
drew their inspiration mostly from the arcade games that were then
becoming popular. The early microcomputer games were often just
simpler versions of *Missile Command, Asteroid,* and others.

Games provided the early hobbyists justification for having a computer. When friends questioned the utility of having such a machine,
these hobbyists could show off a clever game, perhaps Steve Dompier's
Target or Peter Jennings's *MicroChess,* and listen to the oohs and aahs.

Dompier was among the most creative when it came to programming
games on the Altair. With no I/O except the front-panel switches, it was
a challenge to make the Altair do *anything*. A number of people, Dompier included, wrote variations on the popular *Simon* electronic game,
in which the player chased the 16 blinking lights up and down the front
panel, attempting to press the corresponding buttons to make the lights
flash on and off "real pretty."

Creating games also provided a way to learn how to program. The
availability of a BASIC language provided the essential tool needed to
create simple games for those willing to take the plunge. Several books
were published at the time that listed the programs for loads of differ-

ent games. An Altair, KIM-1, IMSAI, or Sol owner could type in the program and start playing the game in no time. The first such book was David Ahl's *107 BASIC Games,* compiled while Ahl was still at DEC and originally intended for use on minicomputers. Often displaying nothing more graphically sophisticated than patterns of asterisks printed out on a Teletype machine, the early games were primitive compared to today's interactive, multimedia arcade extravaganzas.

Many of the first games jumped over to microcomputers from minicomputers and mainframes. (It can be argued that the earliest ancestor of modern computer games, with all their flashy graphics, was a simple tennis-like game played on an oscilloscope.) Games were nothing new to the early hobbyists who had played them on the big computer systems at their jobs, sometimes even loading games into memory on large time-sharing systems. Of course, if they were caught playing, they faced trouble, but the temptation was too much to resist.

One of the more popular games for large machines was *Star Trek,* which allowed the player to pretend to be Captain Kirk and commandeer the Enterprise through a series of missions against Klingon warships. *Star Trek* was an underground phenomenon, hidden in the recesses of a company or university's computer to be played surreptitiously when the boss wasn't looking. No one paid for copies of the game, and no royalties were ever paid to the writers or creators of the *Star Trek* television show. Scott Adams, an RCA employee working on satellite recognition programs at Ascension Island in the South Atlantic, recalls playing *Star Trek* on the satellite radar screens, an act that did not endear him to government officials.

Because it was everywhere on larger machines, it was only natural that *Star Trek* would become one of the first microcomputer games. Many different versions of it already existed, and many more were soon written for microcomputers, including Dompier's *Trek* for the Sol. When advanced technology made graphics possible on a microcomputer, *Star Trek* programs added visual simulations of "the final frontier."

By late 1976, having graphics capability in a microcomputer was growing increasingly important. Cromemco, with its Dazzler board, and Processor Technology, with its VDM, gave the Altair its first graphics. The VDM video display module, released in 1976, also operated on the IMSAI, Sol, and Polymorphic computers, and any other machine with an S-100 bus structure.

Frequently, graphics software was designed primarily to test or demonstrate the capabilities of a machine. The kaleidoscopic images and changing patterns of John Horton Conway's game of *Life* were popular for that reason. Steve Wozniak's *Breakout* for the Apple and Steve Dompier's *Target* for the Sol were two real games that showcased the computers well. A clever programmer such as Dompier could easily make games to display a computer's hidden talents. One example, *Target*, described by its author as a "shoot-down-the-airplane-type game," became a phenomenon. Employees at Processor Technology regularly played it during lunch, and soon it gained wider exposure.

One evening, Dompier was at home playing *Target* while occasionally glancing at a color television across the room. Suddenly the television screen lit up with video graphics, and there was his game, blazing away in full color on the set. He jerked his hands off the keyboard in amazement. No physical connection existed between the TV and the computer. Was the computer somehow able to broadcast the game to the TV? Even stranger still was that the television screen showed a different stage of the game than what was currently on his terminal, but both screens were certainly displaying *Target*. Suddenly, the game on the TV screen dissolved into Tom Snyder's face, and Dompier realized that the talk show host had been playing *Target* on air, demonstrating the Sol's capabilities from coast to coast.

Another kind of game was generating a lot of publicity at around that time. It also depended on microelectronics, but it wasn't played on a computer. A brilliant engineer and entrepreneur named Nolan Bushnell created an electronic game machine that proved to be the successor to pinball machines. He sold it through his start-up company, Atari. That machine, *Pong*, made Bushnell rich and famous, and eventually spawned millions of arcade and home video game models. Bushnell sold Atari to Warner Communications in 1976 when Atari was doing $39 million in annual sales. Although the game machines that were Atari's specialty were not general-purpose computers, the programmers who wrote games for personal computers took much of their inspiration from the Atari devices. (Atari would later make its own personal computers.)

Although programs such as Dompier's *Target* were receiving mass attention, and the game machines were enjoying great popularity, microcomputer programmers in 1976 generally didn't consider computer software a business, certainly not in the way that computer hardware was a business. At that time, very few programmers sold software to anyone other than a computer company, and in a market that narrow, the software sold cheaply.

A Toronto chess enthusiast named Peter Jennings (no relation to the TV news anchor) foresaw earlier than most people involved with microcomputers that microcomputer owners would gladly buy software from independent companies. Jennings had often toyed with the idea of designing a chess-playing machine. In fact, while still in high school, he built a computer that could make the opening moves in a chess match.

After being introduced to microcomputers, Jennings figured he could program a machine to play the ancient board game. Jennings bought a KIM-1 microcomputer with less than 2K of memory at the PC 76 computer show in Atlantic City, brought it home, and boldly declared to his wife: "That's a computer and I'm going to teach it to play chess."

Writing a chess program compact enough to take up no more than a few hundred bytes of memory is the sort of challenge most people would just as soon avoid. As intricate as the game of chess is, the task could use up a huge chunk of a mainframe's memory. Jennings was undeterred: he welcomed the challenge. Within a month he had written most of the code, after a few more months he had perfected it, and before long he was selling his chess program through the mail.

For $10, Jennings sent a stapled 15-page manual that included the source code for *MicroChess*. His notice for it in the *KIM-1 User Notes* newsletter was one of the first advertisements for microcomputer applications software. When Chuck Peddle, president of MOS Technology, manufacturer of the KIM-1, offered Jennings a thousand dollars for all rights to the program, Jennings declined, saying, "I'm going to make a lot more money selling it by myself."

One day while Jennings waited for the money to roll in, his phone rang and the caller identified himself as Bobby Fischer. The reclusive chess Grand Master wanted to play a match against *MicroChess*. Jennings knew what the outcome would be, but gladly agreed. Later, after Fischer had trounced the program, he graciously told Jennings that the match had been fun.

The experience was fun for Jennings, too, and also lucrative. The orders poured in. Jennings found that people who couldn't play chess, and who weren't even interested in learning chess, nevertheless bought the program. With *MicroChess,* computer owners could show their friends that this thing they possessed was powerful and real. It could play chess. In a sense, *MicroChess* legitimized the microcomputer.

One of the first buyers of *MicroChess* was Dan Fylstra, who ordered the program while an associate editor at *Byte* magazine. Later on, after Fylstra started a company called Personal Software, he called on Jennings and the two struck up a partnership. Soon they were investing money from sales of *MicroChess* into the marketing of a business program called VisiCalc, written by Dan Bricklin and Bob Frankston. The pairing of Fylstra and Jennings created one of the most important software companies in the industry. Bricklin and Frankston's VisiCalc was Personal Software's biggest hit.

The transition from games to business software has occurred a number of times in the microcomputer industry. Several early game companies went on to add business software departments. The games led to profits, and the profits led to business applications.

Adventure was another star of the computer game underground. Originally written by Will Crowther and Don Woods on a mainframe computer at the Massachusetts Institute of Technology, *Adventure* involved a simple form of role playing: the user explored mazes, fought dragons, and ultimately discovered treasure. The game had no graphics whatsoever. Players would type in terse verb-object commands such as "GET GOLD" or "OPEN DOOR," and the program responded by describing whatever was nearby in the imaginary maze.

By storing large dictionaries of verbs and nouns and tying them to certain commands, the programmer was able to create the impression that the *Adventure* program could understand those simple two-word sentences. No one but the programmer knew the program's vocabulary, and figuring out how to communicate with the program was the best part of the game. *Adventure* achieved cult status, and San Francisco Bay Area programmer Greg Yob wrote a limited *Adventure*-type game for microcomputers called *Hunt the Wumpus,* which was played in a maze of tetrahedral rooms.

By 1978, Scott Adams decided that he could launch a company and sell computer games full time. Well-meaning friends warned him that programming *Adventure* on a microcomputer was impossible because storing the data for the maze structure and the library of its commands would require an excessive amount of memory. Nevertheless, Adams did the programming in two weeks and started a company, Adventure International. The company became a microcomputer game empire, and its product attracted huge crowds at computer shows.

Adams became convinced that games like his *Adventure Land* and *Pirate Adventure* were serving to introduce computers to the average person. Other software companies also began selling adventure games. Even Bill Gates and Paul Allen at Microsoft, who until then had shown no professional interest in game software, released a version of *Adventure.* In addition to *Star Trek* and *Adventure,* other games such as *Lunar Lander* made the transition from large to small computers.

When customers walked into computer stores in 1979, they saw racks, wall displays, and glass display cases filled with software, and most of it consisted of games. Games with outer-space themes were especially popular—among them *Space, Space II,* and *Star Trek.* To this day, games still represent a significant percentage of the software titles released each year.

Many games appeared for the Apple II, including Programma's simulation of a video game called *Apple Invaders.* Software companies such as Muse, Sirius, Broderbund, and On-Line Systems reaped great profits from games. Programma amassed a huge and diverse supply of software—not a wise policy, as it later turned out. Programma sold plenty of programs, mostly games, but not all of them were good, and its reputation suffered. When serious competition arrived, Programma's reputation for second-rate wares killed it. Nevertheless, many personal computer programmers got their professional start writing programs for Programma.

Few of those early software companies had the business savvy of the Personal Software people, and fewer still achieved the wide acceptance that Digital Research had earned for its operating system.

The First
Operating System

CP/M was 5K and it gave you no more and no less than what an operating system should do.

ALAN COOPER
Personal computer software pioneer

THE FIRST OPERATING SYSTEM TO QUALIFY AS A STANDARD IN THE developing microcomputer industry actually appeared before the Altair itself. CP/M was not the result of a carefully planned project involving years of research by dozens of software specialists. Like most of the early significant programs, it originated out of one person's initiative.

In mid-1972, Gary Kildall, a computer science professor at the U.S. Naval Postgraduate School in Monterey, California, came across an advertisement on a bulletin board that said "MICROCOMPUTER $25." The item advertised, the Intel 4004, was actually a microprocessor, arguably the first in the world, but it still sounded like a real bargain to Kildall. He decided to buy one.

Although many of the microcomputer company founders didn't fit the typical image of an industry leader, Gary Kildall didn't even act as if he wanted to be in that league. While wrapping up his Ph.D. from the University of Washington, Kildall moved to Pacific Grove, California. He loved the scenic coastal town; its laid-back, fog-draped ambiance seemed to suit him. Kildall was soft-spoken, possessed of a disarming wit, and was most at ease in a sport shirt and jeans. He was an incurable diagram drawer. When he wanted to make a point while speaking, he would frequently fish around for chalk or a pencil. In the early 1970s, Kildall was happy in his job at the Naval Postgraduate School. He enjoyed teaching and the job left him time to program. Kildall had no particular business skills and no real desire to leave academia. He was comfortable just where he was.

Gary Kildall also liked to play with computers, and knew a lot about them, both in an academic and in a practical, hands-on sense. He had been one of two people responsible for keeping the University of Washington's Burroughs B5500 computer up and running. Later, when the university was acquiring its new CDC 6400 computer, Kildall was so well respected for his knowledge of computers that he served as the technical advisor on the purchase.

The other person responsible for keeping the B5500 running was Dick Hamlet. He and three others started a time-sharing company in Seattle that used DEC's PDP-10 computer and some new DEC software. The idea was to allow people to log onto the PDP-10 remotely in order to tap its capabilities. Hamlet's company was called Computer Center Corporation, or C Cubed, and for a time two teenagers named Bill Gates and Paul Allen worked there after hours searching for bugs in the DEC software.

It turned out that the $25 price on the Intel 4004 applied only to volume purchasers, and besides, a microprocessor was useless by itself; it needed to be incorporated into a computer. He did buy the manual for the Intel 4004, wrote a program on the school's mainframe to simulate the 4004, and began to write and test 4004 code to determine what he might eventually do with the "bargain basement" 4004 chip.

Kildall recalled that his father, who owned a navigation school in Seattle, had always wanted a machine that could compute navigational triangles. Kildall wrote some arithmetic programs to run on the 4004, offhandedly thinking that he might come up with something his father could use. He was just fooling around with the 4004, trying to see how far he could go and with what degree of speed and accuracy. He determined that the processor was pretty limited, but he still loved working with it. Soon thereafter, he traded some 4004 programs to Intel for a development system, a small computer built around the 4004, which was in effect one of the first true microcomputers, albeit not a commercial product.

When Kildall visited the microcomputer division at Intel in 1972, he was surprised to see that the pioneering firm had set aside a space no larger than the average kitchen for the entire division. One of the people he met there was a clever programmer named Tom Pittman, a non-employee who like Kildall had been intrigued by the 4004 and was already writing software for it. Kildall and Pittman got along well with the Intel people, and Kildall began working as a consultant for Intel on his one free day a week. In this new role, he tinkered with the 4004 for a few more months until he "nearly went crazy with it." He then realized that he would never go back to working on large computers.

Soon Kildall was dabbling with Intel's first 8-bit microprocessor, the 8008. He was working in the same two-level mode—that is, developing the software for a microprocessor on a minicomputer—that Gates and Allen used. Like Paul Allen, Kildall wrote programs to simulate the microprocessor on a larger machine and then used the simulated microprocessor with its simulated instruction set to write programs to run on the microcomputer. But unlike Gates and Allen, Kildall had the benefit of a development system so that he could check his work as he went along by trying it out on the system.

In just a few months, Kildall created a language called PL/M, inspired by a mainframe language called PL/I that was significantly more elaborate than BASIC. Kildall set up the development system in the back of his classroom, in effect creating the Naval Postgraduate School's first microcomputer lab. Curious students would wander back there after class and tinker with the system for hours. When Intel upgraded the Intellec-8 from an 8008 processor to an 8080 and supplied Kildall with a display monitor and high-speed paper-tape reader, the professor and his students had a system comparable to the early Altair before the Altair was even conceived.

Kildall realized, however, that he was still missing an essential ingredient of a successful computer system—an efficient storage device. Two common storage devices on large computers at the time were paper-tape readers and magnetic disk drives. Considering how slow the microprocessor was, paper-tape storage was simply too cumbersome and expensive. Kildall set out to obtain a disk drive and did a little programming in exchange for a drive from Shugart. There was a catch: in order for the disk drive to work, a special controller was needed—a circuit board to handle the complicated task of making the computer communicate with the disk drive.

Kildall attempted to design such a controller several times. He also tried to create an interface that would allow his system to connect to a cassette recorder. But he found that he needed more than just programming talent to solve the complex engineering problem of interfacing the two machines. The project failed, and Kildall decided he was totally inept at building hardware. Nevertheless, he had demonstrated a lot of vision. It would be years before disk drives came into common use on microcomputers. Finally, at the end of 1973, Kildall approached John Torode, a friend of his from the University of Washington, who would later found his own microcomputer company. "We've got a really good thing going here if we can just get this drive working," Kildall told his friend. Torode got the drive to work.

Meanwhile, Kildall polished the software. At one point in late 1973, during his months of frustration with the disk drive, Kildall had taken a few weeks to write a simple operating system in his PL/M language. He called it CP/M, short for Control Program for Microcomputers. CP/M underwent further development, although it already provided the software needed for storing information on disks.

Some of CP/M's enhancements arose under curious conditions. While he continued teaching, Kildall became involved in a project with Ben Cooper, the hardware designer in San Francisco who had worked with George Morrow on disk systems and had later started his own computer company, Micromation. Cooper thought that he could build a commercially successful machine to chart horoscopes, and he enlisted Kildall's help in the project. The two had no interest or belief in astrology, and in fact considered it patent nonsense, but Cooper had ideas about the hardware and Kildall wanted to do the math that calculated star positions. They also figured that the result might be a commercial success. So Cooper built and Kildall programmed, and they came up with their "astrology machine," which would stand in grocery stores eating quarters like an arcade game and printing out horoscopes. Kildall thought the machine was just beautiful.

Commercially, however, the astrology machine was a failure. Its makers placed machines in various locations around San Francisco, but the fancy knobs and dials that excited the two hobbyists irritated users—and with good reason. Customers would drop their quarters in and the paper would jam up. Kildall and Cooper were stumped on how to fix the problem. "It was a total bust," Kildall later said.

Despite the disappointing results, the astrology machine gave Kildall his first commercial test of portions of his CP/M program. In the process of programming the astrology machine, he rewrote the debugger and the assembler, two tools for creating software, and began work on the editor. These constituted the essential parts of the operating system. In addition, he created a BASIC interpreter that allowed him to write programs for the astrology machine. Some of the tricks he learned in developing the BASIC he would later pass on to his pupil, Gordon Eubanks.

As they worked on interfacing the disk drive, Kildall and Torode exchanged their views about the potential applications of microprocessors without saying much about microcomputers. They continued to believe, along with the designers at Intel, that the microprocessor would wind up in things like kitchen blenders and automotive carburetors. They thought of providing a combined hardware and software development system to encourage alternative uses of microprocessors. Kildall's belief in the future of such "embedded applications" of microprocessors was undoubtedly fostered by his colleagues at Intel. At one point, Kildall and a few other programmers had written a simple game program using the 4004 microprocessor. When they approached Intel chief Robert Noyce with the suggestion that he market the game, Noyce vetoed it. He was convinced that the future of the microprocessor lay elsewhere. "It's in watches," he told them.

So Torode and Kildall, without forming an actual company, sold their hardware and software together—not as a microcomputer, but as a development system. And when Kildall, encouraged by his wife Dorothy, finally incorporated and began to offer CP/M for sale, he had no idea how valuable a program he had written. But how could he know? There were few microcomputer software developers around.

At first, the Kildalls called their company Intergalactic Digital Research. The name was quickly shortened to Digital Research, and Dorothy, who was by this time running the company, began using her maiden name McEwen because she didn't want customers thinking of her as "just Gary's wife." Digital Research's earliest customers grabbed some stunning bargains. For instance, Thomas Lafleur, who helped found an early microcomputer company called GNAT Computers, made one of the first corporate purchases of CP/M. For $90 he gained the right to use CP/M as the operating system for any product his company developed. Within a year, a license for CP/M cost tens of thousands of dollars.

Dorothy later said that a 1977 contract with IMSAI was a turning point. Until then, IMSAI had been purchasing CP/M on a single-copy basis. Its ambitious plans to sell thousands of floppy-disk microcomputer systems prompted marketing director Seymour Rubinstein to negotiate seriously with Gary and Dorothy. He finally purchased CP/M for $25,000. It was a lot more than the $90 that GNAT had paid, but Rubinstein gloated. He thought Gary Kildall was an outstanding programmer but a mere babe in the woods when it came to business.

Rubenstein was convinced that he had virtually stolen the CP/M operating system from its author. The Kildalls's perspective was somewhat different; the IMSAI deal made Digital Research a full-time business. After IMSAI bought CP/M, many other firms followed suit. CP/M was such a useful program that it was not until IBM introduced a microcomputer with a different operating system in 1982 that Digital Research faced any serious competition. The programmers who would provide that competition were still working at MITS in Albuquerque.

Getting Down to BASIC

If anyone had run over Bill Gates, the
microcomputer industry would have
been set back a couple of years.

DICK HEISER
Early computer retailer

WHILE IT'S TRUE THAT THE MICROPROCESSORS AND THE CRUDE microcomputers built by hobbyists/entrepreneurs gave computing power to the people, it was the BASIC programming language that let them harness that power. Two professors at Dartmouth College, seeking a better way of introducing their students to computers, used their grant from the National Science Foundation to give birth to BASIC in 1964. The language John Kemeney and Thomas Kurtz created was an instant success. Compared with the slow, laborious, and complex process of programming in FORTRAN, the comparable computer language in common use at the time, BASIC was a winged delight.

During the following two years, the National Council of Teachers of Mathematics debated over whether to support FORTRAN or BASIC as the standard educational language. FORTRAN, widely used in scientific computing, was considered better for large computational tasks; however, BASIC was far easier to learn. Bob Albrecht was a prominent supporter of BASIC. As a pioneer of computer education for children, he had been frustrated with FORTRAN. The Council's ultimate selection of BASIC was a watershed. The personal computer and the BASIC language would be the two most important products in the effort to convince educators that computers could help students learn.

Bob Albrecht wanted to create software for reasons other than personal ambition. Always interested in turning kids on to computers, when the Altair came out, Albrecht asked himself, "Wouldn't it be nice to have something called Tiny BASIC that resided in 2K and was suitable for kids?" Such a program would fit within the Altair's limited 4K memory and could be used immediately.

Albrecht pestered his friend, computer science professor Dennis Allison, to develop Tiny BASIC. Reports of progress on the program appeared in the *People's Computer Company (PCC)* newsletter and its offshoot, *Dr. Dobb's Journal*. "The Tiny BASIC project at *PCC* represents our attempt to give the hobbyist a more human-oriented language or notation with which to encode his programs," wrote Allison. In an early issue of *PCC*, Allison "& Others" (as the cryptic byline read) explained their goal:

> Pretend you are seven years old and don't care much about floating-point arithmetic (what's that?), logarithms, sines, matrix inversion, nuclear-reactor calculations, and stuff like that. And your home computer is kind of small, not too much memory. Maybe it's a Mark-8 or an Altair 8800 with less than 4K bytes and a TV Typewriter for input and output.
>
> You would like to use it for homework, math recreations, and games like NUMBER, STARS, TRAP, HURKLE, SNARK, BAGELS.
>
> Consider, then, Tiny BASIC.

Many of *Dr. Dobb's* and *PCC's* readers did more than consider Tiny BASIC. They took Allison's program as a starting point and modified it, often creating a more capable language. Some of those early Tiny BASICs allowed large numbers of programmers to start using the microcomputers. Two of the most successful versions came from Tom Pittman and Li-Chen Wang. Pittman, for one, knew microprocessors as well as anyone, including the engineers at Intel, because he had written one of the first programs for the 4004. Pittman and Wang were "successful" in terms of the stated goal for Tiny BASIC—to give users a simpler language. The Tiny BASIC authors were not trying to use it as a path to wealth. Another, more ambitious BASIC was also in the works. In the fall of 1974, Bill Gates had left Washington for Harvard University. Gates's parents had always wanted him to go to law school, and now they felt finally he was on the right track.

But as precocious as he may have been, Gates found himself rooming with a math student who was even sharper than he was, and Gates was shocked when his roommate told him he had no intention of majoring in math but planned to study law. Gates thought, "If this guy's not going to major in math, I'm sure not." Examining his options, he immersed himself in psychology courses, graduate courses in physics and math, and long, extracurricular nightly poker games.

Then the January 1975 issue of *Popular Electronics* appeared featuring a cover article on the MITS Altair. Gates's friend Paul Allen ran through Harvard Square with the article and waved it in front of Gates's face, saying, "Look, it's going to happen! I told you this was going to happen! And we're going to miss it!" Gates had to admit that his friend was right; it sure looked as though the "something" they had been looking for had found them.

Gates phoned MITS immediately, claiming that he and his partner had a BASIC language usable on the Altair. When Ed Roberts, who had heard a lot of such promises, asked Gates when he could come to Albuquerque to demonstrate his BASIC, Gates looked at his childhood friend, took a deep breath, and said, "Oh, in two or three weeks." Gates put down the phone, turned to Paul Allen, and said, "I guess we should go buy a manual." They went straight to an electronics shop and purchased Adam Osborne's manual on the 8080.

For the next few weeks, Gates and Allen worked day and night on the BASIC. As they wrote the program, they tried to determine the minimal features of an acceptable BASIC—the same challenge Albrecht and Allison faced except that Tiny BASIC was to be usable on a variety of machines. Gates and Allen didn't have this restriction. They were free to make their BASIC whatever they wanted. No established industry standard existed for BASIC or for any other software, mostly because there was no industry. By deciding themselves what the BASIC required, Gates and Allen set a pattern for future software development that lasted for about six years. Instead of researching the market, the programmers simply decided, at the outset, what features to put in their software.

Both men threw themselves completely into the project, staying up late every night doing programming. Gates even made the ultimate sacrifice and abandoned some of his nightly poker games. They sometimes worked half-asleep. Paul Allen once observed Gates nod off, head on the keys, wake up suddenly, glance at the screen, and immediately begin typing. Allen decided that his friend must have been programming in his sleep and just kept right on when he woke up.

The two slept at their terminals and talked BASIC between bites of food. One day while in the dining hall at Gates's Harvard dorm, they were discussing some mathematics routines—subprograms to handle noninteger numbers that they felt their BASIC needed. These floating-point routines were not especially difficult to write, but they weren't very interesting either. Gates said he didn't want to write them; neither did Allen. From the other end of the table a voice called out hesitantly, "I've written some floating-point routines." Both of their heads turned in the direction of the strange voice, and that was how Marty Davidoff joined their programming team over lunch in the college cafeteria.

At no time during the project did Gates, Allen, or Davidoff ever see an Altair computer. They wrote their BASIC on a large computer, testing it with a program Allen had written that made the large machine simulate the Altair. At one point when Gates phoned Ed Roberts to ask how the Altair processed characters typed on a keyboard, Roberts must have been surprised that they were actually pursuing the project. He turned the call over to his circuit board specialist, Bill Yates, who told Gates that he was the first to ask this obviously essential question. "Maybe you guys really have something," he told Gates.

After six weeks, Gates and Allen thought the project was nearing an end. When they called Ed Roberts, he invited them out to demonstrate what they had. Paul Allen booked a plane reservation as he and Gates scrambled to finish up the BASIC. On the night before Allen was scheduled to catch a 6 A.M. flight for Albuquerque, they were still working. At about 1 A.M., Gates told his friend to get a few hours of sleep, and when he awoke, the paper tape with the BASIC would be ready. Allen took him up on the offer, and when he did wake up, Gates handed him the tape and said, "Who knows if it works? Good luck." Allen crossed his fingers and left for the airport.

Allen was sure of his and Gates's abilities, but as the plane approached Albuquerque he began wondering if they had forgotten something. Halfway into the landing he realized what it was: they had not written a loader program to read the BASIC off the paper tape. Without that program, Allen couldn't get their BASIC into the Altair. It had never been a problem on their simulated Altair—the simulation had not been that exact. Allen searched for some scrap paper, and as the plane descended, began writing in 8080 machine language. By the time the plane touched down, he had managed to scribble down a loader program. Now when he wasn't worrying about the BASIC, he could fret about this impromptu loader program.

Not that Allen had much of a chance to worry about anything. Roberts was right there at the appointed time to meet him. Allen was surprised at Ed Roberts's informality and by the fact he drove a pickup truck. He had expected someone in a business suit driving a fancy car. Equally surprising to him was the dilapidated appearance of the MITS headquarters. Roberts ushered him into the building and said, "Here it is. Here's the Altair."

On a bench before them sat the microcomputer with the largest memory in the world. It had 7K of memory, on seven 1K boards, and it was running a program that tested memory by writing random information into the computer's memory and reading it back. The memory needed testing, but this program was also the only one they had. As it ran, all the Altair's lights were blinking. They had just gotten it working with 7K that day.

Roberts suggested that they postpone testing the BASIC until the next day and took Allen to "the most expensive hotel in Albuquerque," as Allen recalled. The next day, Roberts had to pay the bill because an embarrassed Paul Allen hadn't brought along enough cash to cover it.

That morning Allen held his breath as the machine chugged away, loading the tape in about five minutes. He threw the switches on the Altair and entered the starting address that invoked the program. As he flipped the computer's run switch he thought, "If we made any mistake anywhere, in the assembler or the interpreter, or if there was something we didn't understand in the 8080, this thing won't work." And he waited.

"It printed 'MEMORY SIZE?' " said Ed Roberts. "What does that mean?"

To Allen, it meant that the program worked. In order to print this message, at least 75 percent of the code had to be accurate. He entered the memory size—7K—and typed "PRINT 2+2." The machine printed "4."

Roberts was convinced and told Allen about some additional features he thought a BASIC needed. A few weeks later, Roberts offered, and Allen accepted, the position of MITS software director.

Gates decided that Harvard was less interesting than Albuquerque and moved there to join his friend. Although never a full-time employee of MITS, Gates spent most of his time there after he and Allen were beginning to realize that a large market for software existed beyond Altair users. The two signed a royalty agreement with Ed Roberts for their BASIC and meanwhile began looking for other customers for their language. Gates and Allen began calling their enterprise Microsoft.

The Other BASIC

Studying computer science was the Navy's idea.

GORDON EUBANKS
Software pioneer

O NLY ONE OPERATING SYSTEM—KILDALL'S CP/M—WOULD DOMINATE the early years of the personal computer industry. By comparison, the relative ease of creating new and different BASIC capabilities led to competition between two higher-level languages. One of those languages was Gates and Allen's. The other was developed by a student of Naval Postgraduate School computer science professor Gary Kildall.

In 1976, a young nuclear engineer named Gordon Eubanks had almost finished his U.S. Navy service. As a civilian, he had logged nine months of experience with IBM as a systems engineer. The Navy offered him a scholarship to take a master's degree in computer science at the Naval Postgraduate School in Pacific Grove, California. Why not? he thought. It sounded like a good deal.

Attending class was a tamer experience than most things that initially sounded enticing to Eubanks. His thick glasses and soft-spoken manner belied a real love of adventure. Eubanks thoroughly enjoyed his work on a nuclear-powered, fast-attack Navy submarine. His friend, software designer Alan Cooper, summed it up: "Gordon thrives on tension."

Gordon also liked to work hard. When he arrived at the Naval Postgraduate School, he soon heard about a professor named Gary Kildall, who was teaching compiler theory. Everybody said Kildall was the toughest instructor, so maybe he'd learn something, Eubanks thought. For Eubanks, the hard work in Kildall's class paid off. He became interested in microcomputers and spent a lot of time in the lab at the back of the classroom, working with the computer Kildall received for his work at Intel. When Eubanks approached his professor for a thesis idea, Kildall suggested that he expand and refine a BASIC interpreter Kildall had begun.

The BASIC that emerged from Eubanks's work, called BASIC-E, differed from the Microsoft BASIC in one important way. Whereas the Microsoft version was an interpreted language, in which statements were translated directly into machine code, the Eubanks BASIC was a pseudocompiled language. This means that programs written in BASIC-E were translated into an intermediate code, which was then translated by another program into machine code. The same general idea was being tried in a BASIC compiler under development at Ohio State University.

Each approach had its merits, but BASIC-E had one critical advantage. Because its programs could be sold in the intermediate code version, which was not human-readable, the purchaser would be able to use the program but could not modify it or steal the programming ideas it incorporated. Therefore, software developers could write programs in BASIC-E and sell them without fearing that their ideas would be lifted. With a pseudocompiled BASIC, it now made sense to start selling software.

As far as Eubanks was concerned, the BASIC-E was solely an academic project. He placed his BASIC-E in the public domain and returned to the Navy for a new assignment. But before he did, he had two important meetings. The first was with two young programmers, Alan Cooper and Keith Parsons, who were interested in starting an applications software company and, as they put it, "making $50,000 a year." They wanted his BASIC-E, so Eubanks gave them a copy of his source code and never expected to see them again.

Goaded on by Glen Ewing, another ex-student of the Naval Postgraduate School, Eubanks visited IMSAI to find out if the young microcomputer company might be interested in his BASIC. IMSAI wasn't (at least not at first), but Eubanks wasn't particularly disappointed. Sometime later, Eubanks received a telegram from IMSAI software director Rob Barnaby requesting a meeting. Soon after that, in early 1977, Eubanks found himself negotiating a contract with IMSAI's director of marketing, Seymour Rubinstein, to develop a BASIC for the company's 8080 microcomputer. Rubinstein gave the young programmer no quarter in the negotiations. Ultimately, Eubanks agreed to develop the BASIC and give IMSAI unlimited distribution rights to it in exchange for an IMSAI computer and some other equipment. The Navy engineer did retain ownership rights to his program.

The trade seemed more than fair to Eubanks. This was his first software deal and he was very green. As Alan Cooper remarked, "Gordon was saying, 'Oh! They're giving me a printer too!' " Eubanks did aspire to earning something more substantial than a printer—he dreamed of making $10,000 on his BASIC so that he could buy a house in Hawaii.

In April 1977, the first West Coast Computer Faire was taking place in San Francisco. Eubanks demonstrated his BASIC-E in a booth he shared with his former professor, Gary Kildall, who had started Digital Research. Alan Cooper and Keith Parsons also showed up and reintroduced themselves to Eubanks. They explained that they had made some modifications in his BASIC and had begun developing some business applications software. Eubanks asked the young programmers if they had suggestions for his IMSAI project. Soon after that, the three of them decided to work together. As Eubanks refined the BASIC and Rob Barnaby, a demanding and meticulous taskmaster, tested it, Cooper and Parsons began writing General Ledger software under the business name Structured System Group, perhaps the first serious business software for a microcomputer.

The development of Eubanks's BASIC was a late-night crash project like the Microsoft BASIC had been. Cooper and Parsons would drive to Cooper's place in Vallejo, California, and sit until 3 A.M. drinking Cokes, poring over lists, and trying to decide which statements to put in the language. Like Gates and Allen had done, Eubanks determined the contents of the BASIC primarily by using his own good judgment. Selections were sometimes less than scientifically based. Sequestered in the Vallejo house, staring at code, Alan Cooper would suddenly suggest, "Why don't you put a WHILE loop in?" referring to a frequently used programming statement. Eubanks would answer, "Sounds good to me," and in the statement would go.

The long nights paid off. The result for Eubanks was CBASIC, which later made it possible for him to found his own company, Compiler Systems. Cooper and Parsons's Structured Systems Group became his first distributor. But Eubanks wasn't sure how much to ask for his BASIC. Cooper and Parsons suggested $150; Kildall suggested $90, the price at which CP/M first sold. Eubanks roughly split the difference and charged $100.

They needed to develop packaging and documentation for the product. Cooper and Eubanks wrote the manual and ordered 500 copies from a printer. They immediately got an order for 400 copies and they had to reprint another batch. They knew they were on their way.

As for Gordon Eubanks, he got his house in Hawaii. In fact, he had underestimated the amount of money he would make on CBASIC, almost to the same degree that he underestimated the cost of houses in Hawaii.

A software industry was just starting to be built, but some of the foundation bricks had already been laid. Another brick was placed independently of either BASIC or CP/M.

Electric Pencil

When I started doing business, I had an
unlisted phone number.

MICHAEL SHRAYER
Ex-camera operator for *Candid Camera*

I N THE FALL OF 1975 AT ONE OF THE EARLY MEETINGS OF THE SOUTH-
ern California Computer Society, a guest at the meeting had a special present for the attendees. Bob Marsh offered up a copy of
Processor Technology's public domain software package called Software Package One. It was a collection of programmers' programs—
tools to make writing and modifying programs easier. Marsh told
everyone, "Here you are, guys, enjoy it."

In the opinion of software developer Michael Shrayer, Software
Package One was the most important product then in existence
because it effectively enabled people to write software. Shrayer, a self-
admitted "laid-back sort," had moved from New York to California several years earlier. He had tired of his hectic life in the commercial film
world where, among other jobs, he worked as a camera operator for
Allen Funt's *Candid Camera*. In the middle of shooting a soft drink
commercial, Shrayer realized that the rat race was no longer worth it.
After moving to California, he hooked up with the Southern California
Computer Society, where he discovered Software Package One.

Shrayer was not fully satisfied with the editor portion of the software
package and thought he could come up with something better. He created Extended Software Package 1 (ESP-1) and the beginnings of a

pioneering software firm. Other computer hobbyists, in numbers that amazed Shrayer, wanted to buy the ESP-1 program. In most cases, he had to reconfigure the program for each customer's particular machine. Almost overnight, the laid-back New Yorker found himself in a brand-new rat race.

Shrayer was soon making enough money to live on. It was a nice hobby, and remunerative, and he found that he liked to program. He gathered with other members of the club and talk endlessly about computers. He filled orders for copies of ESP-1. He was having fun.

Shrayer's next idea proved to have a significant impact on the nascent software industry. Tired of having to type out the documentation for his assembler on a manual typewriter, Shrayer decided to use his Executor software (an upgrade of ESP-1) to get the job done. He asked himself, why not use *the computer* to type a manual? Nothing close to a word processor was available yet. Without having even heard the term *word processor,* Shrayer set about to invent one.

By Christmas 1976, after nearly a year of work, Shrayer's Electric Pencil was ready. Although first written on the Altair, Electric Pencil gained acclaim on Proc Tech's Sol. "The Pencil," as it became known, was soon selling quickly. The former camera jockey called his company Michael Shrayer Software, a decision he later regretted because it publicized his name so widely that it ruined his privacy. Nevertheless, at the outset of his new enterprise, he visited computer clubs to talk about his program and enjoyed the admiration heaped upon him.

The popularity of Electric Pencil was so great that it created a buyer demand that it be on all microcomputers then available. Shrayer spent much of his time rewriting the program for different systems. Not only did each kind of computer require a different version, so did each kind of printer or terminal. Moreover, Shrayer was constantly upgrading the Electric Pencil's capabilities. In all, he wrote about 78 different versions.

Had Shrayer been a more experienced programmer, he might have made the program easier to rework. Had he been a more experienced businessperson, he might have sold it in a more organized fashion. But Shrayer was neither, and the rewriting devoured his time, and sales were often limited to single orders by mail. Shrayer grew tired of Electric Pencil and became irritated that it was growing into a serious business that demanded more of his time. He hired programmers to write some of the new Pencil versions for him.

Shrayer's experience demonstrated that in 1977 hardware manufacturers still didn't recognize the importance of software, perhaps thinking that the marketplace would remain dominated by hobbyists. In any case, no hardware companies were willing to pay Shrayer to adapt The Pencil to their machines, although they certainly wouldn't complain if he did so on his own.

Just as Kildall, Eubanks, Gates, and Allen had done before him, Michael Shrayer proceeded according to his own whims and wishes and wrote programs for whatever machines he wanted to. When he eventually lost his enthusiasm for the whole enterprise, he went back to the quiet life he had found on leaving the film world.

Years later, Electric Pencil seemed to reach immortality. Thousands of personal computer owners continued to use it on machines such as the North Stars and Radio Shack TRS-80s. Shrayer was successful because his program allowed nontechnical people to use personal computers to perform practical tasks.

The Rise of General Software Companies

My unemployment had run out.

ALAN COOPER
Software designer, on why he started a
software company

AFTER HELPING EUBANKS WRITE CBASIC, ALAN COOPER AND KEITH Parsons set out to achieve their personal dream of making $50,000 a year. The two had known each other since high school. Parsons was the person who taught Cooper how to tie a necktie, a skill Cooper shelved at college when he became a self-described "long-haired hippie." Cooper intensely wanted to "get into computers," and asked the older Parsons for advice. "You're overtrained," Parsons told him. "Drop out of school. Get a job." Cooper took the advice. After work, he and Parsons would get together and talk about starting their own company. Nirvana, they thought, is $50,000 a year.

When the Altair came out, Cooper and Parsons drew up their plans. They decided to market business software for microcomputers. They hired a programmer, put him in a tiny room, and told him to write. They were busy writing, too. For a while, the two tried to sell *turn-key* systems—computers with sophisticated software that jumped into action when the machine was turned on. They got nowhere with that idea. What they really needed was an operating system, of which there were none as far as they knew, and maybe a high-level language. A chat with Peter Hollinbeck at the Byte Shop in San Rafael, California, led them to Gary Kildall, CP/M, and Gordon Eubanks.

After months of development on Eubanks's BASIC and their own business software, Cooper and Parsons were ready to start making their $50,000 a year. They placed the first ad for CBASIC in a computer magazine. After much agonizing, they also decided to throw in a mention of their business software. In small print at the bottom of the ad, it read "General Ledger $995." They were prepared for an attack from hobbyists for selling a program that was almost triple the cost of the Altair itself.

It didn't take long to get a response, but it was not the rant they feared. A businessman in the Midwest sent in an order for the General Ledger. Cooper made a copy of the program and inserted it in a zip-lock plastic bag along with a manual, a method of packaging software that became common. Before they knew it, back came a check for $995. Cooper, Parsons, and the whole Structured Systems Group staff went out for pizza.

Meanwhile, they kept working on software. The atmosphere was giddy and the style far from corporate. Parsons paced the office shirtless, while Cooper, hair down to mid-back, guzzled coffee that "would dissolve steel." The two of them, wired on caffeine and the excitement of the $995 check, wrangled about potential markets and dealer terms. Parsons's girlfriend made phone sales while sunbathing nude in the backyard behind their "office."

Three weeks later, another order came in and the staff had another pizza. The pizza ritual continued for two months. People were sending in checks for thousands of dollars. Soon the Structured Systems Group was eating pizza for breakfast, lunch, and dinner.

Another early software company started up soon after the Altair announcement. In suburban Atlanta, far from Silicon Valley, several computer enthusiasts opened an Altair dealership called the Computersystem Center in December 1975. The group, including one Ron Roberts, had met as graduate students at Georgia Tech. They quickly realized that, as much as their customers wanted Altairs, they also wanted software to use with the machines. Business was slow at the outset, and they had lots of time on their hands to program.

The group contacted other Altair computer stores throughout the country and discovered that the need for software existed nationwide.

In 1976, the group approached Ed Roberts with the idea of using the Altair name for their software distribution. Roberts recognized that software could help sell his machine and vice versa, and he agreed. Ron Roberts (no relation to Ed) became president of the Altair Software Distribution Company (ASDC). The idea was to distribute other people's Altair software and to write a little of their own.

The group from Georgia called a meeting of Altair dealers in October 1976, and almost 20 stores (nearly all that existed) sent representatives. MITS representatives also attended the meeting because the dealers wanted to inform the MITS people about how delays in deliveries and mechanical failures were negatively affecting their business. Ron Roberts found that the Altair dealers had a lot in common. They all suffered from lack of software, hardware delivery delays, hardware malfunctions, and the general public's meager awareness of microcomputers. Of all those issues, "software was the biggest item on the agenda," according to Roberts.

Several dealers agreed right away at the meeting to purchase ASDC software. The initial software programs from ASDC were simple business packages: accounting, inventory, and, later on, a text editor. The accounting and inventory programs alone retailed for $2,000. Roberts and his colleagues considered the price reasonable; they'd previously worked in the minicomputer and mainframe industry where prices such as that were considered modest. Given the software vacuum at the time, ASDC was able to find buyers even at that hefty price. "We were making quite a bit of money," Roberts recalled.

Ron Roberts later unhitched his wagon from that star after the sale of MITS to Pertec in 1977 and the subsequent fade-out of the Altair. CP/M was gaining popularity, and Roberts decided to convert the programs to enable them to run on Kildall's operating system. This move allowed for sales on more than one brand of computer because CP/M was no longer machine-specific.

The word *Altair* now seemed inappropriate as part of the ASDC business name, so the company changed it to Peachtree Software after a downtown Atlanta street. "In the Atlanta area, it's a quality name," Roberts said. Peachtree employees were more businesslike than Cooper, Parsons, and the Structured Systems Group crew. Not only did they wear dress shirts instead of T-shirts, they even wore ties. They called their software product Peachtree Accounting and Peachtree Inventory.

In the fall of 1978, Roberts and one of his partners took the software part of the business and merged with Retail Sciences, a small computer consulting firm in Atlanta run by Ben Dyer, who had previously worked for a hardware store chain (of the nuts-and-bolts variety). Following the merger, Peachtree released a general-ledger business package. Sales increased rapidly, as did the number of dealers carrying the Peachtree label, and soon it became one of the best known and respected names in the software field. Eventually Dyer changed the name of the whole company to Peachtree Software.

With SSG on the West Coast and Peachtree in the eastern part of the country, the software industry was establishing itself as an independent entity.

The Bottom Line

*If they have a contest as to who is the best
negotiator in the industry, I'll withdraw
to Seymour's fine abilities. Seymour is a
master. And I was just a poor child.*

BILL GATES
Cofounder of Microsoft

SEYMOUR RUBINSTEIN HAS SAID PUBLICLY THAT HE LEFT IMSAI TO
establish a software firm. But with his sharp business sense, Rubinstein must have seen the financial foundation dissolving under the
house of IMSAI. More important, however, he chose to bring his business skills to a software industry characterized by haphazard marketing.

The lack of business expertise among its executives was holding back
the software industry, Rubinstein felt. He decided that his firm would
not sell to manufacturers, as Gary Kildall, Gordon Eubanks, and Bill
Gates had been doing, nor would it sell by mail to end users, as
Michael Shrayer, Alan Cooper, and Keith Parsons did. The number of
computer stores wasn't large, but it was growing. Rubinstein decided
that his new firm, MicroPro International, would sell only to retailers.

But first he needed some software to sell, and Rubinstein knew
where to turn for that. The day he left IMSAI, he visited another ex-
employee, Rob Barnaby, who had headed IMSAI's software development division. Recalling the exhaustive programs Barnaby wrote to test
Eubanks's CBASIC and other examples of Barnaby's clever and
painstaking programming, Rubinstein knew he wanted Rob Barnaby
for his company. So, he went out and got him. By September, Barnaby

had completed MicroPro's first two products, SuperSort and Word-Master. The first was a data-sorting program, and the second was a text editor that Barnaby had begun working on while still at IMSAI.

Although sales for these two products grew rapidly ($11,000 in September 1978; $14,000 in October; $20,000 in November), Rubinstein felt the market could handle much more; he realized that Shrayer had whetted the appetite of computer owners. MicroPro was inundated with requests for a word processor like Electric Pencil. Not one to shun an opportunity, Rubinstein brought out a similar item. Barnaby's new program, WordStar, was an elaboration of WordMaster into an actual word processor, and it quickly sold more copies than Electric Pencil or any other word processing rival.

WordStar was also superior to Electric Pencil. Shrayer had offered *word wrap,* the feature that allows users to continue typing after the end of a line is reached. But a fast typist could type quickly enough to cause the software to miss one or two characters while the word wrap "carriage" was returning. WordStar overcame that problem and offered another improvement in the form of a what-you-see-is-what-you-get display. In other words, text appeared on the screen in virtually the same form as it did when it was printed.

WordStar soon had rivals. In mid-1979, when MicroPro released WordStar, Bill Radding and Mike Griffin in Houston were almost ready to release their word processor, Magic Wand, a worthy competitor to WordStar.

Rubinstein offered WordStar and his other programs to dealers on a per-copy basis. Michael Shrayer had also investigated that option, but few computer distribution centers or computer stores existed at the time. By late 1978, when MicroPro International commenced sales, the number of computer stores had grown exponentially. Along with two other companies—Personal Software, with its VisiCalc for the Apple, and Peachtree Software, with its General Ledger program—MicroPro established the standards by which applications software developers did business. By selling its product like any other consumer item, the software industry gained self-respect, credibility, and a financial bonanza.

Software is a product like, say, a wristwatch or a stereo is a product; however, software is different in one important respect. Software can be stolen without removing the original item. A thief can simply copy someone else's program—an easier and faster task than audiotaping a phonograph record. From the earliest days of the industry, the ubiquitous problem of unauthorized copying outraged many programmers, who saw the fruits of their ingenuity copied and recopied without the slightest monetary gain.

Bill Gates was the first programmer to call attention to the piracy problem. In January 1976, he wrote an "Open Letter to Hobbyists," which was published, among other places, in the *Homebrew Computer Club Newsletter*. In the letter, Gates lambasted the widespread larceny of paper-tape copies of his BASIC and called the hobbyists who copied the program thieves. "The amount of royalties we have received from sales to hobbyists makes the time spent on Altair BASIC worth less than $2 an hour," Gates wrote. "Why is this? As the majority of hobbyists must be aware, most of you steal your software. Hardware must be paid for, but software is something to share. Who cares if the people who worked on it get paid?"

Gates's diatribe had no effect on hobbyists except to make them even more angry at the $500 MITS charged for Gates's BASIC. Hobbyists could see no justification for the price—which was as much as the computer itself—especially because without BASIC the machine was pretty much useless. They felt it should be included with the machine.

From time to time, software developers tried to protect their programs from being copied by using subtle software tricks that either prevented a disk from being copied or that booby-trapped the copied program. Generally, copy protection has failed for one fundamental reason—if a copy-protected program can be written, it can also be cracked. Most companies began to view piracy as a cost of doing business.

The problem was easier to take given that business was good, very good. Soon software became as good a reason to buy hardware as the computer itself. It was apparent that software was becoming a big business. In fact, it was an easier business to get started in—and possibly get rich in—than hardware. The only cost of making software, as one wag put it, was printing the serial numbers.

The growing software market soon attracted more aggressive entrepreneurs.

Software Empires

*Philippe was frequently absurd and
right at the same time.*

Tim Berry
**Computer consultant who helped write Borland
International's business plan**

THERE'S MONEY TO BE MADE IN THIS BUSINESS. THAT WAS THE MESSAGE
sent out after the success of the early microcomputer software ventures such as Microsoft, Digital Research, Structured System Group,
Peachtree Software, and MicroPro. The message was heard by a group
of high-rollers who were willing to risk everything in a growing market
that seemed to have no rules, no boundaries, and no limit on how
much money might be made. These new entrepreneurs descended on
Silicon Valley from all over the world. Philippe Kahn was visiting from
France on a tourist visa. A saxophone-playing mathematics graduate,
Kahn was big, flamboyant, exuberant, and had a devilish twinkle in his
eye. He had written software for Andre Truong's pioneering Micral
microcomputer, which had hit the French marketplace more than a
year before the Altair made its splash in the United States. Kahn had
also worked under computer science legend Niklaus Wirth on a programming language Wirth had invented called Pascal.

Programming languages were designed for particular audiences.
Programs written in FORTRAN looked something like the math notation you'd see on a classroom blackboard or in an engineer's office; the
language had the style and the capabilities that mathematicians and
engineers wanted. COBOL programs were verbose and more human-

readable, which made them better suited to COBOL's target audience of business programmers. BASIC was simple and forgiving, a good language for students. Wirth's new language, Pascal, was formal, rigid, and precise, a language a pure mathematician would love. Philippe Kahn, by education a mathematician, loved it.

When he came to Silicon Valley in 1982, Kahn rented office space in Cupertino and began doing business as a software consultant, using the name MIT (for Market In Time) and lining up clients, including Hewlett-Packard, Apple, and even a company in Ireland. When the Massachusetts Institute of Technology suggested he stop using the name MIT just about the time the Irish company went out of business before paying Kahn the $15,000 it owed him, he accepted the defunct company's name in lieu of payment. MIT became Borland International.

Borland had one marginally interesting software product called MenuMaster, written by the brilliant Danish programmer Anders Heijlsberg, that worked with the CP/M operating system. By this time, IBM had released its personal computer, and it was obvious that Borland could sell a lot more copies of MenuMaster for the PC than for computers running the CP/M operating system. That, however, would require *porting* the program—rewriting it to work with the PC's operating system. Plus, there were the advertising costs. It was clear that Borland needed an infusion of cash, which meant attracting investors, and for that the company needed a business plan.

Tim Berry was working in the same office complex on Stevens Creek Boulevard in Cupertino where Kahn had his office space. Berry agreed to help Kahn develop a business plan in return for a piece of Borland.

Berry was no entrepreneur; he was a cautious analyst with a family to support. But Kahn was bright, charismatic, and motivated. Berry wanted to sign on to see firsthand what Kahn would do. When the company incorporated in May 1983, Berry found himself on the company's board of directors. He also wrote its earliest advertising, which featured a wildly fictitious story of the company's origin along with a picture of a grizzled character named Frank Borland. Berry was a talented writer and the engaging ad copy helped to personalize the young company.

At the time that Philippe Kahn was writing software for Andre Truong's Micral microcomputer, Lawrence Joseph Ellison, a fast-talking programmer from Chicago, had just landed a job at Ampex, a video and audio equipment manufacturer in Silicon Valley. Four years earlier, Lee Felsenstein had left Ampex to write for the counterculture publication *The Berkeley Barb*. Larry Ellison was no 1960s revolutionary. When Ampex got a contract to develop a tape storage system for the CIA, Ellison was thrilled to be working on the project, which the CIA code-named Oracle.

Ellison was definitely Type-A entrepreneur material: aggressive, bright, fearless, arrogant, and mercenary. In June 1977, Ellison's energy and drive led him to start his own company. Along with two Ampex coworkers, he founded SDL. With the knowledge they gained on project Oracle and some IBM technology, they figured they could put together a salable product.

The IBM technology they used was the *relational model* of databases, invented by Edgar H. Codd. An alternative to the usual *flat-file* model, in which no structure exists that governs the relationship among database entries, the relational model was largely untested. The relational database model required computing horsepower well beyond the capability of the microcomputers of the time. But microcomputers were not yet part of Larry Ellison's world.

Ellison's company, SDL, which soon changed its name to RSI and then again to Oracle, was planning to market a minicomputer database program that would sell "like donuts," Ellison said. He had been telling everyone that he was going to become a billionaire, and to get there he knew he'd have to sell software to everybody. "Everybody" included the CIA, although when he tried to sell agency officials a product called Oracle based on a CIA-financed project by the same name, they told Ellison he "had a lot of nerve." They had no idea.

Ellison was, and remains, a thrill-seeker. He bodysurfed, flew airplanes, sailed boats, and played basketball, pushing himself hard enough to have suffered a few broken bones in the process. Ellison saw to it that his company reflected his gung-ho attitude and pushed the company to double its sales every year. No one in the company, probably not even Ellison, thought this was a sane business model, but somehow, for the first decade of its existence, the company doubled its sales every year.

Ellison insisted that the Oracle program be *portable*—"promiscuous" was his word. Like the Electric Pencil product, Oracle was intended to run on any computer; unlike Electric Pencil, Oracle was engineered to make this task if not easy, at least not extremely difficult.

IBM didn't bring its relational database technology to market in a timely fashion, thereby opening the door for Oracle to get there first with IBM's own technology. Meanwhile, other companies, such as Ingres in Berkeley, were soon also producing relational database products. IBM did Oracle another favor when it embraced an approach to writing database queries called SQL, which Oracle used, rather than a competing approach used by Ingres. IBM then presented Oracle with its biggest opportunity when it released its microcomputer, the IBM PC, in 1982.

In short order, Oracle ported its database program to the IBM PC. Even though simple arithmetic said that the massive program would be unusable on the tiny machine, Ellison didn't care. The Oracle database had to be, to use his term, *promiscuous.*

Microcomputers needed a simpler database tool than the massive Oracle relational database program. What they needed was a simple, programmable, flat-file database program—one that fit within the memory capacity of the machines and that allowed users to build meaningfully complicated databases. That product already existed: it was called dBase II.

In 1980, George Tate and Hal Lashlee founded a company called, oddly enough, Ashton-Tate (there was no partner named Ashton). Tate and Lashlee planned to sell a database program for microcomputers, dBase II, which was written by Wayne Ratliff. dBase II was a novelty for the young microcomputer software industry: it worked well and made computer users more productive. People who were experts in building databases with dBase II, and coding in the simple programming language that it included, were soon making a good living as dBase II specialists. By the early 1980s, when IBM came out with its PC, Ashton-Tate was the database king of microcomputers. When they ported dBase II to the PC, they held onto the title with no problem, untroubled by the existence of Oracle for the PC or any other similar competitor.

By 1985, Ashton-Tate had moved to larger headquarters in Torrance and was buying up other companies and fleshing out its product line, with dBase II remaining its bread and butter. Ed Esber had been brought in as CEO, and as Ashton-Tate acquired companies, Esber bragged, "Every software company is up for grabs." Ashton-Tate's dBase II virtually owned the database market for microcomputers, but that didn't stop others from trying to break in with new and innovative approaches to database software.

In the fast-moving microcomputer software industry of the early 1980s, some of the microcomputing pioneers were embarking on their second or even third careers. Gordon Eubanks was one such example. After developing CBASIC with help from Alan Cooper and Keith Parsons, Gordon Eubanks sold CBASIC for a few years under the business name Compiler Systems. Then in 1981, he sold the company to Digital Research and went to work for his former professor, Gary Kildall, as a Digital Research vice president.

Inspired by an entrepreneurial urge he hadn't really felt when he started Compiler Systems, in 1982 Eubanks left Digital Research to launch C&E Software. Within months, C&E bought another software start-up, Symantec, and assumed its name. Eubanks had helped to develop a simple and easy-to-use flat-file database program with a built-in word processor. It was called Q&A and became Symantec's first product.

If Q&A represented the ease-of-use strategy in tapping a software market, Framework represented a "Swiss army knife" approach to software marketing. Written by first-class programmer Robert Carr, Framework was a remarkably powerful and advanced product—a word processor, spreadsheet, database program, and programming language all in one—and it ran on a PC. Carr hooked up with Martin Mazner, who had written award-winning ad campaigns before getting into the microcomputer software business. In 1982, they founded Forefront Corporation with the specific goal of getting Ashton-Tate, one of the leading microcomputer software companies, to bring Framework to market. Their plan worked.

But dBase remained Ashton-Tate's cash cow, boasting millions of users. By the late 1980s, dBase II was the third best-selling program for the IBM PC, and Ashton-Tate was the world's third-largest personal computer software company, trailing close behind Microsoft (which exploded in size after the release of the IBM PC with its Microsoft-supplied operating system) and Lotus, the spreadsheet king. In 1986, *The Washington Post* called Microsoft, Lotus, and Ashton-Tate "the GM, Ford, and Toyota of the software business." Other successful personal computer database companies were around at the time, but they survived, like Fox Software and its FoxPro did, by touting their compatibility with dBase II. When Philippe Kahn had Tim Berry help him write a business plan for Borland, the initial idea had been to attract some investment capital and port MenuMaster to the PC. But nothing was happening on either front: no investors were lining up and, Berry was alarmed to see, apparently no porting had been developed. Kahn finally admitted that there just wasn't any good development software for PCs for doing the programming the porting job required. So, he put Anders Heijlsberg to the task of writing a Pascal compiler.

Berry was horrified at the thought. Pascal was not a simple language like BASIC. Writing a Pascal *compiler,* a program that would enable someone to program the PC in Pascal, was a huge undertaking, a much bigger job than porting MenuMaster. Now, the porting of MenuMaster would have to wait until the Pascal compiler was finished. In the meantime, everyone around the world was bringing out products for the PC. Borland would miss that window of opportunity for being the first to market with PC software products. This strategy was crazy, Berry thought.

In October 1983, Berry got a call from Kahn to come over to his office right away. Borland had relocated to Scotts Valley, on the other side of Northern California's Santa Cruz mountains, and Berry, an independent consultant, was now working 50 miles away; this was an unexpected two-hour round-trip commute for Berry, but he went.

As Berry and the other Borland directors watched, Kahn demonstrated Turbo Pascal. They were stunned. It was astonishingly fast, and so compact that it easily ran in the limited memory of the PC. This program was better than anything they could remember seeing on a mainframe or minicomputer—a polished, appealing product that was brilliantly coded. Even amateur programmers could use this; one could even learn how to program with it. MenuMaster was never mentioned again.

Kahn dropped another bombshell on the board: they would sell Turbo Pascal for $49.95 by mail order. At the time, Microsoft was selling a Pascal compiler for roughly ten times that price. In theory, the Borland board should have had something to say about these decisions: Kahn was scrapping the business plan, dumping the company's only proven product, and substituting a new product that he proposed to sell at a ridiculously low price. But at Borland International, Philippe Kahn was running the show, and quite a show it was. He was adamant about the $49.95 price; it would cut through the noise in the market, he said, and help them get their message out loud and clear.

Getting the message out would be a challenge. The company had literally no money for advertising. Nevertheless, a full-page ad for Turbo Pascal, with the $49.95 price and a number to call to place an order, appeared in the November 1985 issue of *Byte* magazine. To have made the November issue ad deadline, Berry ruefully observed, Kahn must have placed the ad listing the $49.95 price well before he showed the program to the board. No wonder Kahn was so adamant about the price, Berry thought. He had already committed them to it.

It wasn't just one ad that ran; Kahn had placed $18,000 worth of ads. When the advertising salesperson came to the Borland offices, Kahn had his friends fill the chairs around the offices to create the impression of a more prosperous business in an attempt to bolster his request for credit. He had no choice; Borland had no money to pay for the ads. And, unless they got a lot of orders for Turbo Pascal right away, they had no prospects of getting any money either.

In November, Borland raked in $43,000 in sales, which Kahn immediately spent on more advertising. "He was betting the company every chance he got," Berry said. Within four months, the company was bringing in nearly a quarter-million dollars a month. They were growing too fast to act like a "normal" company, and Spencer Odawa understood that. When a major software distributor offered in late 1985 to carry Turbo Pascal, Odawa turned the distributor down, even though it could have increased Borland's sales significantly. It seemed crazy, but the five-month lag in payments the distributor imposed would have killed them.

Meanwhile, Ashton-Tate and Oracle were on a collision course.

In 1988, Ashton-Tate partnered with Microsoft to bring a relational database product to market, edging in on Oracle's technology industry niche. At the same time, Ashton-Tate filed suit against FoxPro, the competitor in its own backyard, claiming that FoxPro was infringing on Ashton-Tate's copyrights. On the face of it, the claim seemed legitimate: FoxPro's business model basically called for producing something that looked and performed as much like dBase II as possible.

While expanding its market and protecting its flanks, Ashton-Tate was also tending to its current products, bringing out major new versions of dBase and Framework. Then, in late 1988, the boys at Oracle learned that Ashton-Tate was at work on a version of dBase for minicomputers. Now they were moving into Oracle's territory.

Oracle had made a move into Ashton-Tate's territory years earlier with Oracle for the PC, but it wasn't so much a product as a technology demo. Even though nothing much could really be done with Oracle for PCs, given that it was buggy and frequently crashed, one could get an idea of what the software was supposed to do and get a feel for what Oracle on minicomputers was all about. The PC version by and large functioned as advertising for Oracle in a market where it didn't yet have a viable product. When Oracle eventually did have a viable PC version, the company didn't have to educate the market; the demand for the product was already there.

The appeal of the Oracle product was a little difficult to understand. Not only was the PC version inadequate and buggy, the minicomputer versions were often buggy, too. To make matters worse, Oracle had a reputation for delivering products late. However, relational database technology was appealing, and Oracle's sales efforts were formidable. The ad budget was doubling annually by the mid-1980s, along with the sales figures. The slogan of Oracle's ad agency was "God hates cowards." Oracle's could have been "Take no prisoners."

When Ellison learned that Ashton-Tate was planning a version of dBase for minicomputers, Oracle retaliated by pushing its PC version with a vengeance. Ads appeared everywhere showing an Oracle fighter jet shooting down an Ashton-Tate biplane. Oracle began selling its PC version at cost. Because it was making large profits on its minicomputer versions, it could afford to do so. Ashton-Tate, with the bulk of its profits coming from dBase for the PC, had no response.

Unfortunately for Ashton-Tate, its newly released version of dBase was full of bugs. On top of that, the judge in the copyright infringement case Ashton-Tate brought against FoxPro not only decided against Ashton-Tate but also stripped the company of its copyright. The court found that Ashton-Tate had not properly disclosed that its dBase product was based on work done at the government's Jet Propulsion Lab which was in the public domain. The company was soon bleeding red ink. CEO Ed Esber was shown the door.

While Ashton-Tate suffered, Borland prospered. It had gone public in 1986, and by the end of the 1980s, with a half-billion dollars in revenues, it was one of the biggest software empires. In 1991, Borland bought Ashton-Tate.

Next, Microsoft launched an assault against Borland's market niche. In 1986, Microsoft released a major new release of QuickBasic, turning the latest version of the language Microsoft had been rewriting and redefining since 1975 into what it hoped would be a Turbo Pascal killer. This was an important development: Microsoft had built its reputation on programming languages, and Borland's fast, compact, and cheap language had hurt Microsoft's sales in computer languages and made Microsoft look old and stodgy. QuickBasic was to change that perception, and Microsoft did what it came to do best: it staged a killer press event to promote the product.

Technical journalists were invited to the Microsoft "campus" in Redmond, Washington, to see the latest technology. Those invited were editors and writers for technical magazines, and many of them were programmers in their own right. Microsoft treated the journalists to a fine meal and then issued them a challenge: each would compose a programming task that could be achieved in a few hours of work. A description of each task would then be pulled at random out of a hat, and from those descriptions the journalist/programmers would begin to write code. Whoever was the first to run a program that successfully completed a task would win a prize. The journalists were free to use their own computers and any programming software they liked. Microsoft's new QuickBasic would be represented, and the programmer using it would be Bill Gates.

It had been nearly four years since Gates had written code. The last time was when he completed the software for the Tandy TRS-80, a book-sized portable computer much prized by journalists. Gates was nervous and had stayed up late the night before familiarizing himself with QuickBasic. One of the journalists, a sharp programmer named Jeff Duntemann, would be using Turbo Pascal, and Duntemann knew Turbo Pascal inside and out.

When the contest was over, Bill Gates and QuickBasic had won. It was a crazy thing, an outrageous PR gamble, but it had paid off. The message was clear: Microsoft was run by a sharp, highly competitive businessman who also happened to have helped start the industry. Plus, he was profoundly knowledgeable about the technology, and no slouch as a programmer, either. QuickBasic ended up selling well against Turbo Pascal.

Borland soon found itself in trouble in a now ruthlessly competitive market. But Borland was out for blood, too: when one of its executives left to work for Gordon Eubanks at Symantec, Borland sued the former executive. It wasn't Borland's first major lawsuit. Lawsuits were becoming more and more common. The stakes were high, and competition was getting brutal.

Getting Connected

The strange thing is that all of this took
so long and then happened so suddenly.

TED NELSON
Author of the influential book, *Computer Lib*

ANOTHER, LESS MERCENARY STRAND WAS EVOLVING FROM THE DNA OF personal computer software developers. As the kitchen-table entrepreneurs, electronics hobbyists, and 1960s cultural revolutionaries turned 1970s technological innovators labored to bring the personal computer into existence, forces were also at work to turn the devices into *interpersonal* computers. Along with the desire to wrest power from the computer "priesthood" (that exclusive cadre that ran or had access to the big machines) and share it among others for their personal use was also the desire to use the computer itself as a tool for exchanging ideas with other people.

In the late 1970s, when Ward Christensen dreamed up his data-transmission standard and the concept of a computer bulletin board system (BBS), he was not the first person to think of hooking computers together to facilitate the sharing of information. It's not that computers weren't already being hooked together, or that ordinary people couldn't get access to computers. As far back as the early 1970s, some managers of minicomputer systems were providing public access to a limited number of their machines' capabilities via time-sharing systems. Anyone with a terminal and a modem could pay for access to one of these time-share systems.

But time-share systems were remote from users and impersonal. Lee Felsenstein tried to personalize the time-share concept in his work with the Community Memory project. The Community Memory terminals were installed in public places and free to use. The terminals implemented a bulletin board model that, while not as powerful as Ward Christensen's, required virtually no instruction: one could walk up to the terminal and start using it within minutes. The concept lives on today in freestanding information kiosks, the difference being the Community Memory system also allowed users to add their own information.

Another significant development in connecting people via computers began much earlier. Back in 1960, Harvard student Ted Nelson came up with an idea for solving a problem that had long nagged at him: how to organize his notes. Nelson, a peripatetic thinker, was looking for a way to interconnect the thousands of ideas he'd scribbled down on countless note cards. What he came up with was a plan for storing information on computers. He called the technique *hypertext*.

The system he conceived in order to implement hypertext was something he called Xanadu. Depending on the level of financial support it got, Xanadu waxed and waned over the following decades, but it was the most ambitious and well-articulated vision of the future of computer interconnectivity at the time. Xanadu was to be no less than a universal information repository, the future intellectual home of humankind. More prosaically, Xanadu, like BBSs and Community Memory, was an approach to connecting computers that would enable large numbers of people to share ideas with one another quickly.

At Stanford Research Institute, Douglas Engelbart was thinking along similar lines as Ted Nelson. In the 1970s, Engelbart put together a system called NLS, short for oNLine System, that was in fact the first hypertext system. Even earlier, he invented the first integrated two-way computer/video teleconference system. He demonstrated how individuals in different locations could exchange data instantaneously and watch one another in live video, all under the control of a computer. Engelbart is justly credited with the invention of the computer mouse, hypermedia, multiple-window screens, groupware, online publishing, and electronic mail.

Stanford Research Institute had been deeply involved in connecting computers for some time. In 1969, the institute was part of a project sponsored by the U.S. Department of Defense. Participants in the project were working to create a computer communications system that would stay operational even if some of its constituent parts were disabled due to nuclear war or some other crisis. The first remote terminal connection was tested between the Stanford Research Institute and UCLA. This experiment grew into a wide-area network called ARPAnet, which interconnected computers at Defense Department research and academic sites and also provided computer users with services such as remote log-in and file transfer, and later on as an afterthought, electronic mail.

By 1981, approximately 200 sites were on ARPAnet. In 1993, the entire network switched over to a new protocol that involved a new way of transferring bits of data, and whole new networks of computers were able to connect to one another. ARPAnet evolved into a network of networks. By 1986, some 3000 sites were on the network, and three years later the number was up to around 150,000. This network of networks came to be called the Internet.

In the early 1980s, an innovation called Ethernet, developed by Robert Metcalfe at Xerox PARC (Palo Alto Research Center), made possible the local area network, or LAN. It was an entirely different model from Christensen's BBS. A local area network is made up of physical computers spread over a relatively limited area. LANs weren't designed to build or serve a community of computer users as the Community Memory terminals were meant to do. The LAN was designed from the outset to be a tool used primarily for business collaboration. It linked individual personal computers in businesses so that data and resources could be shared.

Ethernet was based on technology similar to that underlying the Internet. As such, it also had an unforeseen benefit: through LANs, individual personal computers could have access to the Internet, even though they didn't have the capability to actually be on the Net.

Much of the drive to connect people to each other by connecting their computers was happening in academia, either at universities or at university-connected research facilities. Another phenomenon rising out of the academic computing culture, and most visibly at MIT in the

1960s, was the free software movement. Thanks to the efforts of student Richard Stallman, the idea that software should be freely distributed became a shared value of the growing programming community.

Stallman founded the Free Software Foundation (FSF) to promote the idea. *Free* in this context meant *open*, rather than at no cost. The FSF people weren't against anyone making money from programming; they were programmers themselves. They just hated the idea of worthwhile information being locked up. Everyone should be able to make use of the ideas that are out there, they thought. It was once again a case of rebellion against the exclusivity of the computer priesthood, just in another form.

The variety of approaches to the single problem of hooking computers together was impressive. Christensen invented an electronic version of the community bulletin board in which people could leave each other messages, and did it all in software, so that anyone with a computer, a modem, and a telephone line could use his code to create a community of computer users. Felsenstein's Community Memory, on the other hand, didn't assume that the user had a computer, a modem, or even a telephone: his low-tech, convivial terminals were situated in public places, for everyone's free use, and they were tough enough to survive untutored users with grimy fingers pounding away at the keyboards.

The original designers of that entity that eventually became the Internet were working to build a defense-research communication channel robust enough to survive a nuclear attack. Those Xerox PARC designers were inspired by the remarkable Douglas Engelbart, whose lifelong goal has been the continued enrichment of the human intellect. The problem the Xerox PARC designers were trying to solve when they created Ethernet was how to better facilitate collaboration among coworkers in an office.

Ted Nelson's vision, the one he'd imagined nearly two decades before, was perhaps the most ambitious. His concept encompassed a vast, richly structured network of human knowledge. In his vision of the future, information could be dispensed through franchise sites on every busy street corner, a sort of McDonald's for the mind.

The various approaches to connecting people via computers fared differently and evolved in ways sometimes unimagined by their creators. BBSs flourished. Community Memory faltered but struggled on, barely. Ethernet and the local area network caught on in a big way. And the Internet grew, slowly at first, remaining chiefly the province of academics and the military, and then grew explosively, doubling its number of users each year. Not even the visionaries Doug Engelbart and Ted Nelson imagined the overwhelming influence and scope the Internet would have by the end of the century.

The visions Engelbart and Nelson had of a community of computer users has yet to be fully realized, but the Web continues to evolve, if not always in the direction those visionaries foresaw.

CHAPTER 6

RETAILING THE REVOLUTION

*Computer magazines built the real
enthusiast's marketplace.*

DAVID BUNNELL
Founder of several computer magazines

Spreading the Word:
The Magazines

*The [computer] magazines basically
defined a nationwide small town.*

CARL HELMERS
The first editor of *Byte* magazine

T HE MEANINGS OF WORDS CAN CHANGE OVER TIME, COMPLICATING THE
job of the historian.

It's perfectly accurate to say that computer magazines, user groups,
shows, and stores were crucial to the development of the personal computer. But saying this creates a misleading impression unless one
explains that the magazines, shows, and stores of the early days of the
personal computer revolution were very different from magazines,
shows, and stores today. The essence of the difference is that, whatever
the motives of the editors, organizers, or storekeepers, the magazines,
shows, and stores were primarily about community building. They all
helped to create a culture in which computers for individuals could be
imagined, built, understood, and, almost incidentally, bought and sold.

Before there were microcomputer magazines, the electronics magazines helped ease the pain of mail-order buying. In those days, buying
microcomputers by mail required a healthy measure of blind faith.
Customers mailed checks to companies they had never heard of to
acquire products they couldn't be sure existed. In essence, they were
playing "micro roulette." All they knew was that they wanted a computer, so they mailed their money and waited. And waited. And waited.
It was considered a novel way to market computers. Fortunately for the

213

manufacturers, the earliest buyers of microcomputers rarely demanded customer service. They were hobbyists who would tolerate almost anything—including the mirage world of mail order—to get their own computers. That the machines were affordable was service enough.

Products were commonly announced before they were even designed, let alone built. *Popular Electronics* had passed off an empty box as the original Altair and a mock-up as the Processor Technology Sol in a couple of its cover stories. The journalistic excesses were probably harmless, but ads also used the same technique. *Byte*'s Carl Helmers said, "I'm not saying [the technique was] legitimate, but it's certainly one that's used all over the place in technology. A product may be there to show in so-called functional simulation form, and that functional simulation is one step toward making the thing actually happen."

The "functional simulation" was the least misleading of the ads because it at least gave the buyer some idea of what the machine could do. Other ads were more fantastic than factual. "A guy who is in love with writing copy about computers can dream up any kind of system," said Helmers. "And there were people who did that."

The computer magazines of the time played dual, almost schizoid roles in this frenzy. Editors encouraged the frenzy by reporting advances, printing ads, and sometimes failing to alert readers to substandard items. Carl Helmers, for instance, rationalized his refusal to assess product quality on the grounds that "products that don't fulfill [their promises] over the long haul will sort themselves out and die." But some publications did actively sift the good from the bad. Adam Osborne, who had been selling books out of a cardboard box at Homebrew meetings, started a muckraking column that appeared in *Interface Age,* and later in *InfoWorld,* that alerted buyers to the shortcomings of certain products. *Dr. Dobb's Journal,* the offshoot of the *People's Computer Company* (PCC) newsletter, took a strong consumerist stance, steering readers away from purchases that they'd later regret.

Byte was one of the great success stories among microcomputer magazines, but the success grew out of conflict and, perhaps, betrayal. *Byte* was launched in mid-1975, the brainchild of Wayne Green, who had published 73, a magazine for ham radio enthusiasts. The Peterborough, New Hampshire, resident was part hobbyist and part huckster. Green enjoyed promoting those things he believed in: ham radio, microcomputers, and himself. Some viewed Green as a front-porch philosopher who was fond of contemplative argument and prone to thinking out loud. But others saw a complex individual who could be difficult to work for. His busy, impatient mind would flit from the latest software developments to psychic phenomena, but it always came back to the bottom line. Wayne liked to make money.

By 1975, Green was looking to computerize 73's circulation department. He called the major computer firms, each of whom sent a representative. Every rep warned him of the dangers inherent in buying a rival's machine. Green found all their warnings convincing. The computer investment was beginning to feel like a leap into darkness. Before paying $100,000 for a computer, Green decided he should learn something about the players in the field.

Green discovered that the computer books and magazines that were available seemed to be written in a foreign language. Only computer club newsletters were understandable. They also were the only good sources of information about these new microcomputers. The more Green thought about it, the more he realized that he was not alone. The country was full of people who needed an introduction to computers written in plain English.

Green saw his opportunity and decided to create a magazine to ease beginners into microcomputing. He needed a name for his publication, one that was short, catchy, and evocative of the machines themselves. He decided on *Byte*.

Green recruited Carl Helmers as editor. Helmers had been issuing a periodical called *ECS* (*Experimenters Computer Systems*) solo in Boston. Since January 1975, just after the *Popular Electronics* announcement of the Altair, Helmers had been writing 20 to 25 pages each month on his ideas for building and programming microcomputers. He then shepherded the pages through editing and photo-offset printing and had them distributed to some 300 readers. Helmers accepted Green's offer and moved to New Hampshire. Green drew his *Byte* contributors and readership from the early newsletters such as *ECS* and from his own ham radio enthusiast subscribers, believing the latter to be a natural audience for *Byte*. When the first edition of *Byte* appeared on August 1, 1975, its 15,000 copies sold out immediately. A new magazine genre had been born.

With Wayne's ex-wife, Virginia Green, as office manager, Helmers installed as editor, and much of the 73 staff filling in the personnel ranks, Green set about compiling a second issue. He estimated that 20 percent of *Byte*'s readership came from the 73 mailing list. To beef up the subscription list, Green took the first issue around to manufacturers, including MITS in Albuquerque, Sphere in Salt Lake City, and Southwest Tech in San Antonio. Green was greeted with enthusiasm, and the manufacturers supplied him with customer address lists. Those lists, he guessed, gave *Byte* another 20 to 25 percent of its subscriptions.

Byte was immediate, chatty, enthusiastic. It caught the flavor of the computer and electronics hobbyist newsletters, and spoke directly to the people building and buying and lusting for their own microcomputers. It was the right formula, and it was wildly successful.

Wayne Green had struck a mother lode and was exhilarated. But he had one problem. He didn't own the company. It belonged to Virginia, from whom he had been divorced for 10 years. This unusual arrangement was a result of Green's legal difficulties: he had been convicted of tax evasion and had other pending legal issues. "The lawyers said we should set up the new magazine as a different corporation and have somebody keep the stock separate from other assets until the suits were resolved," Green explained. He entrusted *Byte* to Virginia.

The trouble started almost immediately. Helmers had a good sense of what the computer hobbyists wanted, but Green had been publishing successful magazines for years and was convinced that he had the formula. Anyone should be able to pick up two or three issues and get up to speed, he was convinced. Helmers had put together something far more technical, a kind of bulletin board for a highly technical community.

Green was pushing Helmers to simplify the content to reach a broader audience, and Helmers pushed back. After the first issue hit the stands, he and Virginia forced Wayne out and took over the publication. By January 1977, *Byte* had a readership of 50,000 and was the premier magazine in the field. In its field it had the stature of *Scientific*

American, the in-crowd feel of *The Village Voice* in the beat era, and the style of a Homebrew Club meeting. Helmers remained as editor and part owner of the company, which he and Virginia eventually sold to publishing giant McGraw-Hill in April 1979. Helmers stayed with the publication until September 1980.

Wayne Green did not sit still for long. In August 1976, he circulated among the computer manufacturers to find out if they would support a new magazine with himself at the helm. The response, he said, was unequivocally positive. Green wanted to call the publication *KiloByte,* but *Byte* claimed it would infringe on its name. Because Green was telling people that the publication's mission would be to "kill *Byte,*" that was probably not an unreasonable claim; so Green christened his magazine *Kilobaud.*

Kilobaud was an expansion of a regular feature on computers called "I/O" that Green had run in the pages of *73*. The new publication strove to achieve the Wayne Green ideal: anyone should be able to pick up the publication and after reading two or three issues understand its contents. Green lamented that *Kilobaud* never overtook *Byte* in circulation or advertising, but it was clearly a success nonetheless.

Green kept an eye on how his market developed. When he started *Kilobaud,* almost all his readers were hobbyists, people who had no qualms about building their own accessories or using a soldering iron to modify the apparatus. Around 1980, Green recognized a new kind of hobbyist, one who liked to use the equipment but shunned all that tinkering. Responding to this change, Green renamed the magazine to give it broader appeal. He called it *Microcomputing.* Around the same time, he started another journal, *80 Microcomputing* (later called *80 Micro*), aimed at users of the Radio Shack TRS-80 computer line. Green later launched other, even more consumer-oriented publications. Helmers and his successors at *Byte* held *Byte* to a high technical level for years.

Carl Helmers saw the early periodicals as having a threefold purpose: economic, educational, and social. The magazines defined a market, spread important news, and helped bring hobbyists together. These publications created a nationwide community of computer users. "Peterborough, where I live, is a small town, but it's geographically constrained," Helmers said. Like a small town where everyone knows everyone else and news of events is spread almost as soon as they happen, everyone and every event was known among the small village of microcomputer hobbyists, wherever they really lived. And, no publication had more of a small-town flavor than Wayne Green's early *Kilobaud,* with its chatty editorials, industry gossip, and calendar of events.

To Carl Helmers's threefold statement of purpose, Jim Warren would have added two more elements: social consciousness and a cheerful antiestablishment attitude straight out of the 1960s.

California born, Warren was raised in Texas, where he taught mathematics for five years. He then moved to the San Francisco Bay Area, where he worked another five years as chair of the math department at the College of Notre Dame, a Catholic women's academy in Belmont, just north of Silicon Valley. At the time, Warren liked to throw huge get-togethers at his home, with most of the revelers partying in the nude. "The parties were rather sedate by any common standards, except that people didn't have any clothes on," he recalled.

The media descended on Warren's home. *Playboy* photographed these affairs; the BBC filmed them; and *Time* did an article on them. All the publicity forced officials of the College of Notre Dame to take action. Warren was told that his conduct struck a sour note at the Catholic school, and the college officials asked him to leave. Warren shrugged it off. In this enormous world, there had to be more interesting jobs than this one, he thought.

Warren was looking for something new when a friend suggested that he go into programming. "You'll pick it up," the friend assured him. So Warren went to work doing programming at the Stanford Medical Center and ended up loving it. Just for the sheer fun of it, he became an avid follower of state-of-the-art developments in the field. He had become an enthusiast.

In the early 1970s, the Stanford Medical Center was also home to the Stanford Free University, which offered an alternative, noninstitutional approach to higher education that was much to Warren's liking. He soon became the Free University's executive secretary and newsletter editor, while taking on a variety of consulting jobs. And it was there that he met Bob Albrecht and Dennis Allison.

Then the Altair appeared, followed by Gates and Allen's BASIC. Bob

Albrecht, getting pudgy on beer and pizza when not playing tennis or encouraging kids to use computers, and Dennis Allison, a computer science professor at Stanford, began seeking ways to bring their expertise to the cause of spreading the word about computers. *Byte* had debuted in September 1975 and was publishing information on hardware design, but no software magazine existed yet. Hobbyists turned to the *People's Computer Company* newsletter to provide one. Dick Whipple and John Arnold of Tyler, Texas, sent *PCC* a long list of code that constituted a "Tiny BASIC," a 2K version of the full-blown BASIC, designed for machines with limited memory. Allison decided to publish a limited edition, three-issue magazine to get this code into hobbyists' hands.

The response to the magazine was overwhelming. In January 1976, the publication became an ongoing project called *Dr. Dobb's Journal of Tiny BASIC Calisthenics and Orthodontia*. "Dobb's" was a contraction of "Dennis" and "Bob," Allison and Albrecht's first names. The rest of the title was an in-joke about "running light without overbyte." Jim Warren was hired to run the publication. Warren thought the name was too specific and soon changed it to *Dr. Dobb's Journal of Computer Calisthenics and Orthodontia*.

The magazine published, among other material, classic Tiny BASIC implementations by Li-Chen Wang, Tom Pittman (the consultant who had programmed Intel chips before Gary Kildall), and others, along with all the micro news, rumors, and scuttlebutt Warren could unearth. *Dr. Dobb's* adopted an irreverent, folksy tone that reflected the influence that the 1960s had on its editor. Warren believed in contributing one's efforts to the good of all humanity; in fact, in the early 1970s he wondered whether he should continue working with computers at all. He thought of the machines as mostly gadgets; they were playthings as stimulating as chess but by and large devoid of social utility. As he later put it, "Somewhere back there I'd been raised with a Puritan work ethic (if not all the Puritan values), a make-a-contribution-to-society ethic, which was certainly illustrated in my 10 years of teaching at destitute wages, over which I have no regrets at all."

Nor did he have any regrets about editing *Dr. Dobb's* at $350 a month when he could have been earning far more consulting. Money wasn't of paramount importance as long as he was making a contribution to society. He liked to quote Dennis Allison's slogan: "Let's stand on each other's shoulders and not on each other's toes."

Warren was enjoying himself and believed that others should, too. He infused *Dr. Dobb's* with a sense of merriment that became one of the publication's hallmarks. Idleness might ultimately ruffle his conscience, but pleasure was still one of the great rewards of existence. "Let's not worry about conformity and tradition. Let's just do whatever works and let's have fun doing it," he said. He was attracted to *PCC* partly because it was the first newsletter to treat computers as objects suited to intellectual forms of recreation.

A large variety of other computer-enthusiast magazines quickly appeared, some of which spun off from existing publications. For instance, *PCC* spun off *Recreational Computing*, which addressed a broader and less technically inclined audience. Corporations produced other publications. *Computer Notes* came straight from MITS and focused on the company's Altair line. Its editor, David Bunnell, later quit to run the slick-looking *Personal Computing* magazine, with articles geared to beginners.

Still other magazines grew out of informal newsletters exchanged by hobbyists, while many others seemed to appear spontaneously. Hal Singer and John Craig started the *Mark 8 Newsletter* to provide information for fellow users of the Mark 8. (Craig later became the editor of *Kilobaud*.) The Southern California Computer Society produced a newsletter called *Interface*. After David Ahl left DEC, he started *Creative Computing*, which had the bright and mirthful air of its somewhat rumpled and clever editor. *ROM* offered regular contributions from iconoclasts such as Lee Felsenstein and Ted Nelson, and "chipcake" centerfolds, including the droid R2D2 from *Star Wars*. *ROM* lasted less than a year.

This crop of magazines spread the word about microcomputing and enabled hobbyists in the most far-flung parts of the country to stay current on personal computing trends. As personal computers matured into a big business in the 1980s, explaining them became a great satellite industry. The demand for information about computers seemed to grow faster than the demand for the equipment itself.

Computer books were now hot. Computer technology sections

appeared in both the chain stores and mom-and-pop bookstores, and began to eat up shelf space. At least a few writers and several publishing houses were making a lot of money on books that explained how to use software, the very same task that a user manual was designed to accomplish. In one legendary deal, a publisher paid a $1.1 million advance for *The Whole Earth Software Catalog,* a book that offered reviews of software products. The huge advance was paid even though many of the reviews were already out of date before the book was published, recalled Stewart Brand, who coordinated the project.

Industry magazines were evolving right along with the products they featured. The more technically geared magazines like *Byte* spanned platforms (such as computers running the CP/M operating system, IBM PCs, and Macintosh computers) in their coverage and addressed readers interested in all kinds of computers. As the computer became more of a consumer product and the computer market settled into one of two camps, IBM-compatible or Macintosh, magazines became more platform-specific in their coverage. The change was inevitable, because an IBM owner had absolutely no use for an article about Macintosh software, and vice versa. These new publications offered elaborate product reviews that helped customers to assess the relative merits of both hardware and software. Good reviews were invaluable to vendors. "Product reviews made all the difference," said Seymour Rubinstein, founder of MicroPro International, which sold the popular WordStar software.

Among the more prolific computer publishers was David Bunnell of MITS, who launched an array of successful computer magazines, including *PC Magazine, PC World, MacWorld, Publish,* and *New Media,* and in 1996 became publisher of the computer business magazine *Upside.*

Bunnell had founded *PC Magazine* right after the IBM PC debuted and published it out of his San Francisco home. The first issue in January 1982 included a review of John Draper's EasyWriter word processor that was entitled "Not So Easy Writer." The product never fully recovered from the review.

The first issue of *PC Magazine* was 100 pages and chock-full of ads, including one from IBM. The second issue went to 400 pages. A year later Bunnell was looking for an outside investor or even a buyer. Both publishing giants Bill Ziff of Ziff-Davis and Pat McGovern of IDG coveted the magazine. Bunnell thought he had an agreement with McGovern, but his initial investor struck a separate deal with Ziff. Bunnell and his staff were furious and resigned en masse to start the rival *PC World* for IDG. Bunnell thus has the distinction of having started both the leading magazines for PC users.

Despite its staff's departure, *PC Magazine* became a fabulous success. Ziff, too, had a formula. He invested a large initial sum to stake out his territory, then let the paid circulation, product-oriented text, and flashy look and feel do the rest. The formula usually worked well, although he had some conspicuous failures, such as *Corporate Computing* in 1992. Eventually, Ziff grew tired of managing the company and in 1994 sold it to an investment bank that turned it over two years later to a Japanese entrepreneur for $2.1 billion.

Bunnell's *PC World* also thrived, and by the late 1990s both *PC World* and *PC Magazine* boasted million-plus circulations that brought in a great tide of ad revenues. Both magazines routinely published issues as thick as phone books. "Getting ads was so easy," said Bunnell. "All you had to do was answer the phone."

The computer magazines single-handedly resurrected mail-order computer sales. As customers became more product savvy, they no longer shied away from buying products sight unseen, especially if a magazine had covered the gear in one of its articles. "Mail-order advertising occurred overnight," said Bunnell. This trend contributed to the rise of Dell Computer and other firms whose businesses are based on direct sales to customers. Mail order also contributed to the downfall of some retail chains. In retrospect, mail order was a harbinger of events to come with the explosive growth of the Internet.

As the Internet laced the globe and entered people's homes, the major publishers started grappling with the questions of how, when, and how much to migrate to online publishing. One early change was in the content. When a magazine established an online presence, the news usually moved increasingly "Netward" to reach the world more quickly. Once it was aired on the Web, however, the news quickly grew stale, and magazines felt silly repeating in print what they'd already published online. So most of them were trending toward more interpretation in the print publications. But it was still experimental. No one seemed to really know how online publishing fit into the big picture. And little proof existed at the time that Internet advertising could yield significant profits. Nevertheless, everyone tried to create a presence on the Web.

In 1998, CMP, a major technology publisher, purchased *Byte* from McGraw-Hill and turned it into an online publication, then was itself acquired by Miller Freeman Publications, which had acquired *Dr. Dobb's Journal* several years earlier. Almost 25 years after these pioneering computer magazines were launched, programmers could read articles from both magazines at the same Web site.

Computer magazines were changing, but remained an important vehicle for promoting and communicating new products and ideas. Another effective method over the years for getting the message across was the computer show.

Word of Mouth: The Clubs and Shows

The First [West Coast] Computer Faire was definitely a torn T-shirt, computer-junkie crowd. It was a gas. We didn't know what the hell we were doing. The exhibitors didn't know what they were doing. The attendees didn't know what to expect. But we pulled it off.

JIM WARREN
Computer industry pioneer

COMPUTER CLUBS AND SHOWS WERE THE PUBLIC FORUMS OF THE early micro world. They offered hobbyists not only an entree into an interesting social club, but also supplied otherwise unobtainable news about product releases and industry innovations. The clubs provided ongoing support for hobbyists and featured free and wide-ranging discussions about products, which often led to the publication of another newsletter. The fairs were technology spectacles, and their carnival atmosphere ignited each attendee's enthusiasm for the growing field. These fairs gave hobbyists the opportunity to try out the latest novelties with their own hands.

Homebrew Computer Club, with Lee Felsenstein presiding and other microcomputer pioneers in attendance, served as the prototype of the computer enthusiast club. The group's candid assessments of market offerings had an impact that reached far beyond the four walls of the club's meeting room. Its influence reached user groups all over the country. When the magazines emerged, they sent reporters to cover the Homebrew meetings, spreading the club's influence even farther.

The Homebrew club's opinion could be critical to a company's success. Processor Technology, Apple, and Cromemco all profited from Homebrew endorsements. Many other corporations received less flattering appraisals, which were felt in their sales figures.

The first Homebrewers realized early on that they could affect the image and the future of the computer industry itself. Prior to 1975, computers were associated with technicians in lab coats—the "high priests" of the big machines—who would retire to an air-conditioned environment with a problem to solve and emerge sometime later with a printout. The Homebrew Computer Club helped replace that vision with one of rugged, if not ragged, individualism in which solo mental efforts could lead to multimillion-dollar companies. The Homebrewers felt that they had a duty to chart a road map of the future. The first edition of the club's newsletter, issued in March 1975, predicted that home computers would perform tasks ranging from editing text and storing information, to controlling household appliances and doing the housework (robotically), to instructing users and providing pleasant diversions.

Like Homebrew, the Amateur Computer Group of New Jersey (ACGNJ) became an arbiter and conduit for the new technology. For instance, the founders of Technical Design Labs of Trenton, New Jersey, started their company by selling used computer terminals at the ACGNJ meetings.

One early club that was run more like a professional organization than an informal group of hobbyists was the Boston Computer Society (BCS), even though its founder, Jonathan Rotenberg, was 13 when he started it. Rotenberg eventually developed BCS into a 7000-member organization with 22 different committees, a resource center, and a lengthy list of industry and corporate sponsors. Rotenberg would later insist that BCS was a "users' group, not a club." BCS and the other users' groups were computer clubs that had developed into something more. They served as informal think tanks, social groups, and arenas for the exchange of information. The clubs fostered a spirit of voluntarism and adherence to consumer advocacy that was carried over into the users' groups. These groups worked to protect computer buyers to an extent that was unprecedented for any American industry. Committees worked diligently against shoddiness in manufacturing and deception in advertising. The clubs were responsible for directing the efforts of the free-spirited microcomputer manufacturers of the day. Without the feedback from the clubs, the early hobbyist-oriented microcomputers might never have developed into the useful personal computer of today.

For the hobbyist shopping for hardware, nothing substituted for a hands-on demonstration of a new product. For that reason, and for that taste of "the future is now" that sends the imagination into orbit, hobbyists flocked to the computer shows.

The first microcomputer fair to attract a sizable crowd was actually a single-company event. Early in 1976, David Bunnell of MITS began promoting the World Altair Computer Conference in Albuquerque in the MITS news organ *Computer Notes*. By the time the event took place in March, several hundred people turned out.

Among the speakers was *Computer Lib* author Ted Nelson, who delivered a scandalous and wildly entertaining speech on what he called "psycho-acoustic dildonics." Lee Felsenstein (of Homebrew Computer Club, Community Memory project, and Processor Technology fame) was surprised some audience members didn't drag Nelson off the stage during his carefully detailed explication of computer technology's potential contribution to sex toys. After this off-the-wall presentation, Nelson talked to several people about setting up a computer store in the Chicago area. He wanted to call it the Itty-Bitty Machine Company (in a sly reference to IBM). Among those showing interest was Ray Borrill, who was then building his own small network of computer stores in the Midwest.

MITS chief Ed Roberts had planned the conference as a showcase for MITS and only MITS. He refused to give booth space to competitors such as Processor Technology. Proc Tech's Lee Felsenstein and Bob Marsh were undaunted. Felsenstein suggested to Marsh that the two of them set up shop in a hotel room during the conference. "Great idea," Marsh answered. They nabbed the penthouse suite and posted signs around the conference floor inviting people to drop by. They demonstrated Steve Dompier's *Target* by using as their video display monitor the television set. Because the Sol wasn't ready yet, they had an Altair on hand. When Ed Roberts stopped by, it was the first time that he and Felsenstein had spoken since Lee had criticized the Altair in *Dr. Dobb's Journal*. Meanwhile, David Bunnell was busy tearing down all the signs that Marsh and Felsenstein had posted.

More shows soon followed in other places around the country. In May 1976, Sol Libes of ACGNJ put together the Trenton (New Jersey) Computer Festival, something of a hardware swap meet and discussion session. The fair pioneered the idea of an open computer conference that wasn't tied to a single manufacturer. It also showed Californians that the microcomputer revolution was not confined to the West Coast. Featured speakers included premier hobbyist Hal Chamberlin from North Carolina, and David Ahl and Dr. Bob Suding of Denver. Ahl and Suding's Digital Group had just received advance copies of the Z80 chip from Federico Faggin's new semiconductor company, Zilog, and were raving about what could be done with this hot chip.

What started on the coasts soon spread across the country. In June 1976, a loosely organized group of hobbyists staged the first Midwest Area Computer Club conference. The inaugural event drew nearly 4000 people. Midwest dealer Ray Borrill shared a booth with Processor Technology, which displayed its new Sol-20 computer. Borrill and Proc Tech sold thousands of dollars worth of parts and supplies, and because they hadn't thought to bring along a cash box, money was stacked in piles on the table. By the end of the show, people were snapping up whatever was left in the booth, just to buy *something*. The computer hobbyist fever was running high.

Then in August 1976, in Atlantic City, New Jersey, hobbyist John Dilkes staged the Personal Computing Festival. This show was significant for being the first national computer show. This event helped popularize the term *personal computing*. Before that festival most people spoke in terms of *hobby computing* or *microcomputing*. Wayne Green's *Kilobaud* magazine booth at the Festival took in more than a thousand subscriptions to the start-up publication. Peter Jennings bought the KIM-1 computer that he would later use to write *MicroChess*. Other such shows were held in 1976, including events in Denver and Detroit.

But not in California. *Dr. Dobb's Journal* editor Jim Warren had both an appreciation of these festive get-togethers and a gnawing sense that something was out of whack. "My myopic contention was that all of this good stuff was happening on the wrong coast," he said. About a week or two before the Atlantic City show, Warren commenced planning a show for the San Francisco Bay Area. He decided to call it a computer *faire* after the medieval summer spectacles in Elizabethan England. It was an apt name, he thought. A Renaissance faire celebrates the past; the computer faire would celebrate the future. In April 1977, Jim Warren staged the first West Coast Computer Faire.

When David Bunnell got wind of Warren's plans, he contacted him on behalf of MITS. Bunnell said MITS was also planning a West Coast show, and suggested that the two merge their efforts and stage a conference sponsored by *Personal Computing* magazine. Warren would get 10 percent of the gate and profit further from his partner's greater experience and professional acumen. Warren wasn't at all comfortable with this proposal. He didn't consider it appropriate that he, as editor of *Dr. Dobb's,* be involved in a show sponsored by *Personal Computing* or any other magazine. He was also uneasy about the emphasis on money. "I wasn't thinking about doing a big-bucks thing at all," he recalled. "I just wanted to stage this event. I'd done the be-ins in the '60s. I just wanted this [computer fair] stuff happening out here."

Warren tried to reserve some space at Stanford University for his event but couldn't get the dates he wanted. He then looked into the San Francisco Civic Auditorium. It would be a great spot for the event, he thought. It had excellent conference facilities and a splendid exhibition room. He asked how much it would cost. Rental was $1200 per day. He was stunned.

Later that day, Warren got a bite to eat with Bob Albrecht at a restaurant called Pete's Harbor. They did some figuring on a table napkin. If they could get at least 60 exhibitors, charge them around $300 each, and draw maybe six or seven thousand people, they could break even. What the hell, Warren thought, they could actually make money on the event. That's the precise moment when he founded his company Computer Faire.

As it turned out, Warren greatly underestimated the attendance figures. He had hoped to draw 7000 to 10,000 people between Saturday and Sunday. Instead, almost 13,000 showed up. For several hours on Saturday morning, two lines of attendees stretched around one side of the auditorium and three lines stretched around the other side to the back of the building. It was a clear and windy day, and fairgoers stood in line chatting with each other. It took an hour to get through the door, but no one seemed to care. The fair had begun outside during the discussions among individuals who were equally rabid about computers.

Once inside, attendees found themselves in computer heaven. Rows and rows of festively decorated booths touted the latest advances in personal computing. An inquiring hobbyist could find him- or herself chatting up the very person who had designed some innovative product. Company presidents in T-shirts and blue jeans staffed a number of booths. The Apple II was unveiled in a large and rather attractive booth staffed by Steve Jobs, Mike Scott, and other Apple executives. Gordon Eubanks demonstrated his BASIC-E in a booth he shared with Gary Kildall. The Commodore PET was also introduced at the event.

Sphere had failed to rent booth space, but still made its presence known. The Sphere folks parked the Spheremobile, a 20-foot motor home modeled after MITS's Blue Goose, out front and sent an employee to walk through the fair wearing a placard saying, "Come see the Sphere." The excitement could be felt everywhere. "It was like a toy store at Christmas. It was mobbed," said attendee Lyall Morrill. Among the many cosponsors were the Homebrew Computer Club, the Southern California Computer Society, *PCC,* and the Stanford Electrical Engineering Department. Science fiction writer Frederick Pohl spoke, as did Ted Nelson, Lee Felsenstein, Carl Helmers, and David Ahl. Everyone agreed it was a gas.

Jim Warren spent most of the weekend in a whirlwind, racing around to smooth out little snafus. At subsequent Faires, he saved time by dashing around the convention halls on roller skates. Even while attending to the administrative duties, Warren was as thrilled to be there as everyone else. "It was the excitement of turning all those people on," he recalled. He felt proud of his accomplishment. The first West Coast Computer Faire was three to four times larger than any previous computer show. It also led to the first published proceedings of a personal computer conference. Warren had made his contribution to the industry by staging this watershed event.

Before the first West Coast Computer Faire even opened, Warren had decided to stage a second one. It took place in March 1978, in San Jose, California. Exhibit space was sold out a month in advance. Lyall Morrill once again was on hand, but this time he represented his own software company, Computer Headware. "Either by the luck of the draw or the strange humor of Jim Warren, my booth was positioned next to the IBM booth," he noted. The contrast between the two booths was striking. IBM had mounted a slick chrome booth staffed by men in business suits and polished dress shoes. The booth featured the IBM 5110, a relatively expensive desktop minicomputer that didn't particularly impress the attendees.

Morrill, wearing a propeller-topped beanie, was showing off his software package, a simple database management program called WHATSIT, a loose acronym for Wow! How'd All That Stuff get In There? He had created his signs the night before with a felt-tip pen. Jim Warren enjoyed the IBM–Computer Headware juxtaposition so much that he had photos taken of Morrill socializing with the IBM staff.

IBM and Computer Headware's sales results by the close of the fair were as far apart as their corporate style. IBM got just a few orders, whereas Morrill was besieged with them. Customers cued up at his booth, credit cards in hand, to buy his program.

The second West Coast Computer Faire was such a great success that Warren decided to do one every year. If, as Carl Helmers said, the magazines defined the microcomputer community, shows such as Warren's gave the community a meeting place.

Hand-Holding:
The First Retailers

We didn't want to sell Altairs.
We wanted to solve problems.

DICK HEISER
Computer retailer

O N JUNE 15, 1975, 125 HOBBYISTS AND COMPUTER NOVICES GATHERED in the recreation room of the Laurel Tree Apartments in Miraleste, California. Digital engineer Don Tarbell and computer neophyte Judge Pearce Young had brought them together to form the Southern California Computer Society. The participants engaged in a lively debate over the structure and purpose of the club. At one point, someone asked for a showing of hands of those who either owned or had ordered an Altair. A forest of raised arms popped up from the crowd.

Dick Heiser, a systems analyst who was among the assembled, was struck by the response. He realized that these Altair customers were going to have a lot of questions about assembling their kits. He thought that maybe he could be of help. Heiser had recently spent $14,000 building a video word processor for a low-cost minicomputer. With the introduction of the Altair, he realized that he could write a similar program for the Altair for about $4,000. He was familiar with the innards of a computer and was eager to work on an Altair.

Heiser then had a brainstorm: why not set up a small storefront to market the Altair kits and provide advice and support for buyers? Heiser had little business experience and never imagined working as a salesman, but he knew that he'd have fun putting his technical skills to use. He wondered whether it could be profitable. He sat down and devised a cash-flow plan. If he paid $200 in rent per month and sold around 10 to 20 assembled computers at $439 each, he could stay in the black. It seemed to be worth a try.

In June 1975, Heiser flew to Albuquerque to talk to the people at MITS. The MITS execs weren't sure what to make of Dick Heiser. Ed Roberts thought he was a "nice guy" but lacked the aggressiveness that marked a born entrepreneur. Roberts also worried about Heiser's profit margin. MITS was selling the Altair kits for $395 ($439 assembled), which left skimpy profits. MITS couldn't afford to discount its prices for anyone. Roberts hadn't built any room for discounts into the Altair's asking price. Heiser could buy the kits, assemble them, and sell them at the assembled price, for a pitiful 10 percent margin. Despite all this, Roberts took Heiser seriously. Others had approached MITS with the retailing idea, but Heiser was the first to come with a spreadsheet. "They thought I was a little weird," Heiser recalled, "but they told me it sounded like a good idea, and we signed a contract."

Heiser leased a small space for $225 a month in a low-rent area of West Los Angeles and launched the world's first computer store. In mid-July, he opened for business. In large letters across the front of his store he advertised the outlet's official name, Arrow Head Computer Company. In smaller letters, below the name, he added the tag line "The Computer Store" because he thought it sounded "funky" and interesting. Soon everyone was calling the outlet The Computer Store.

It was a strange kind of store. Heiser, an imposing figure with his beard and cowboy hat, would be engaged in a serious technical discussion with a hobbyist one minute, and the next minute be assuring a skeptic that the Altair, despite its low price, was truly a computer. When not attending to customers, he'd hole up in the back room where he repaired equipment and worked on his own computer, which he was still in the process of soldering together.

Heiser quickly discovered that his spreadsheet was seriously in error. He had anticipated getting a small but steady stream of individual computer purchases at $439 each, the price of an assembled Altair. Instead, he found that someone who was buying a computer could easily spend another $4,000 on accessories—extra memory, video terminals, disk drives, and such. It was his first small excursion into retailing and Heiser was amazed that so many people were willing to spend real money on these machines. In his first month, he took in between $5,000 and $10,000, and in his first five months in excess of $100,000. By the end of 1975, he was ringing up more than $30,000 in sales per month.

Heiser did little advertising other than posting flyers at large engineering firms such as System Development Corporation, Rand, and TRW. As a result, most of his early customers were engineers, who were typically computer enthusiasts who had moved to California to work in high technology. This being Southern California, he also got his share of celebrities: Herbie Hancock, Bob Newhart, and Carl Sagan visited The Computer Store. But the clientele consisted mainly of hobbyists.

A customer base consisting exclusively of hobbyists was probably just as well, because the process of assembling an Altair generated each and every problem Heiser anticipated. "It was really tough in those days," he recalled. "You had to know electronics as well as software. You had to bring up the raw machine, and you had to use the toggle switches to put in the bootstrap loader," he said, describing the various steps required to get an Altair up and working. Buyers who stumbled at various points en route to setting up their Altairs came running back to Heiser, who patiently instructed them about careful assembly, repaired any malfunctions, and lent a sympathetic ear to complaints about the MITS memory boards.

Although Heiser was selling enough computers to make a healthy profit, a careful accounting of his and his employees' time would have shown that most of their time was spent explaining the technology, repairing machines, setting up systems, and reassuring customers. Hand-holding, community building, proselytizing. It worked, but it sure wasn't the business school model of retail sales.

The Computer Store was not without some local competition. In late November 1975, John French opened his Computer Mart in a small rented office suite. French offered the IMSAI, which was simply a better piece of computer hardware than the Altair. On the other hand, Heiser, with Gates and Allen's BASIC computer language, had the superior software offering. Software was the more important ingredient of the two, but because BASIC could run on French's machines, French thrived along with Heiser. Eventually, French sold his interest in Computer Mart and invested in his friend Dick Wilcox's computer company Alpha Micro.

Heiser also faced competition from a group of devout Indian Sikhs in Pasadena. Although American by birth and upbringing, they embraced the culture of their Indian ancestors. They also embraced cutting-edge technology. "For them, it wasn't, 'Let's sit by the river and meditate,'" Heiser observed. Dressed in their turbans and white coats, the Sikhs sold computers manufactured by Processor Technology, and later sold Apple products. Heiser respected them immensely. Like himself, they cared more about solving a customer's problems than moving more inventory.

In May 1976, Heiser moved The Computer Store to Santa Monica to a facility four times the size of the one in West Los Angeles. He now had several employees and was making $50,000 to $60,000 a month. He installed carpets and desks that made the store look like the offices of a bank executive. Customers would sit across the desk from a salesperson to discuss system requirements and how best to meet them. Heiser saw himself as more of a counselor than an entrepreneur. The problem-solving approach also gave him personal satisfaction. "I'm a computer enthusiast and a compulsive explainer," he said.

One problem nagged at Heiser that he simply couldn't solve. MITS was pressuring him into making questionable deals with his customers. MITS bound the purchase of Gates and Allen's BASIC to the purchase of the notoriously defective MITS memory boards. Heiser understood the value of the BASIC, but he realized that no one wanted to buy memory boards that didn't work and he simply didn't want to carry them.

"We went through a lot of grief trying to make a viable computer system and a viable computer business when we didn't have any memory devices," he said. Then MITS decreed that Altair outlets would sell only its products and no one else's. MITS was worried that if its retailers also offered competitors' wares, customers would buy the MITS software but reject its hardware. As it turned out, the company's worries were unfounded given that most of the early computer stores quickly sold out of whatever they got their hands on. Heiser complained to Ed Roberts, but Roberts was adamant and, according to Heiser, threatened to shut down dealers who disobeyed his edict. This policy of exclusivity cost MITS many dealers, but Heiser remained loyal and reluctantly abided by the rules until Roberts sold MITS to Pertec.

Heiser concluded that if MITS was out of touch, Pertec must be roaming the ether. Thinking it could inject MITS with much-needed capital and a proper business orientation, Pertec called a meeting of MITS's 40 dealers. Heiser listened to the Pertec representatives' marketing ideas but didn't think much of them. Pertec figured that if it could sell one computer to General Motors, for instance, the automotive giant would return to Pertec for its next 600 computers. Retailers would soon be filling 600-item orders left and right. The company would rocket into the Fortune 500.

Heiser was amazed at Pertec's naiveté. It was clear to him that the company was oblivious to the problems it had acquired with MITS. At the end of the meeting, Heiser stood up and said that Pertec would have to deal with the immediate problems if it ever hoped to succeed financially with MITS. At that point, Heiser began making plans to go his own way and started stocking other computers, including the Apple II and the PET.

Dick Heiser watched the computer retailing scene change dramatically over the coming years. Discounters entered the market. They employed salespeople with no technical backgrounds who sold machines "with the staples still in the box," Heiser said. "They may as well have been selling canned peaches." It was becoming increasingly difficult for Heiser to maintain his standards of excellence. In March 1982, he left the store for good.

Like many of the personal computer pioneers, Heiser had broken new ground through his unflagging enthusiasm for the technology. Even in retailing, the hobbyist ideal led the way. But unlike computer design, which can be done for love *or* for money, retailing is necessarily a commercial venture. Computer retailing quickly attracted individuals more aggressive than Heiser, including Paul Terrell.

Paul Terrell's friends warned him that retailing computers would never work. Some people, Terrell mused, also said it never snowed in Silicon Valley. Terrell recalled his friends' warnings as he watched snow drifting down on December 8, 1975—the day he opened his Mountain View Altair dealership, the Byte Shop, in the heart of Silicon Valley.

Like all the other Altair dealers, Terrell soon ran headlong into the

MITS exclusivity policy, except that Terrell chose to ignore it. He was selling all the Altairs he could get, between 10 to 50 a month, plus anything else he could get from IMSAI and Proc Tech. The MITS edict, Terrell concluded, was not only pointless but, if he followed it, financially harmful as well.

It wasn't long before David Bunnell, then MITS vice president of marketing, called to cancel the Byte Shop's Altair dealership. Terrell argued that MITS should regard the Byte Shop as something like a stereo store that carried many different brands and could turn a profit for them all. Bunnell waffled. It was Roberts's decision, he said. At the World Altair Computer Conference in March 1976, Terrell approached Roberts directly about his being dropped from the roster of MITS dealers. Roberts stood firm. Terrell was out.

At the time, Terrell was selling twice as many IMSAIs as Altairs, and he consoled himself with the fact that MITS's policy of excommunicating the unfaithful would ultimately hurt Roberts more than his dealers. Terrell was still selling whatever he could stock. As Terrell saw it, he and John French, Dick Heiser's Computer Mart competitor in Orange County, were responsible for most of IMSAI's early business. They used to do battle for the product. Terrell would rent a van and drive to the loading dock at IMSAI's manufacturing site in Hayward to collect his and French's orders. Check in hand, Terrell would ask, "You want cash on the barrelhead, boys?" It was hardware war.

Terrell had opened the Byte Shop in December 1975. By January, people who wanted to open their own stores were approaching him. He signed dealership agreements with them in which he would take a percentage of their profits in exchange for the name and business guidance. Other Byte Shops soon appeared in Santa Clara, San Jose, Palo Alto, and Portland. In March 1976, Terrell incorporated as Byte, Inc.

Terrell was part of the hobbyist community. He took the name of his store from the leading hobbyist magazine, and he insisted that Byte Shop managers in the Northern California area attend meetings of the Homebrew Club.

A single Homebrew meeting might have a half-dozen Byte Shop managers in attendance. "If I had a store manager that didn't attend the club meetings, he wasn't going to be my store manager for long. It was that important," Terrell said. At one Homebrew meeting, a long-haired youth approached him and asked Terrell if he might be interested in a computer that a friend named Steve Wozniak had designed while working out of a garage. Steve Jobs was trying to convince Terrell to carry the Apple I. Terrell told Steve Jobs he had a deal.

Terrell discovered, as Dick Heiser had before him, that customers needed help assembling the machines and obtaining the proper accessories. He got the idea to offer his customers "kit insurance." For an extra $50, he would guarantee to solve any problems that arose in the course of putting the computers together. Terrell understood that he was doing true specialty retailing and so he had to provide essential information and a certain amount of hand-holding. Terrell likened computer stores to the stereo stores of a decade or two earlier, when clerks routinely had to explain woofers, tweeters, and watts of power to puzzled customers.

The Byte Shop cachet soared after the July 1976 issue of *Business Week* described the chain of stores and suggested that it offered significant opportunity to investors. "We had something like five thousand inquiries come in," Terrell said. He found himself talking to people such as the president of the Federal Reserve Bank. The chairman of Telex Corporation called to ask if Oklahoma was available for franchising. "The credentials [of the callers] were staggering," Terrell said.

The chain was adding eight stores a month, and Terrell had negotiated a price for an 8080 chip below what IBM was paying. (IBM was not yet building a microcomputer.) By the time Terrell sold the Byte Shop operation in November 1977, he had 74 stores operating in 15 states and Japan. He valued the chain at $4 million.

Other computer stores were popping up in many parts of the country, many starting out as Altair dealers, then defecting to carry other brands. Dick Brown opened a shop also called The Computer Store on Route 128 in Burlington, Massachusetts. On Long Island, Stan Veit didn't like the MITS deal from the start and launched his store selling anything he could get his hands on.

In the Midwest, Ray Borrill opened Data Domain in early 1976, with the aim of "out-Terrelling" Paul Terrell. Borrill quickly spun off nearly a dozen affiliated stores from his first outlet in Bloomington, Indiana.

He also helped start the Chicago-based Itty-Bitty Machine Company, an ill-fated venture that was conceived during conversations with Ted Nelson at the World Altair Computer Conference.

With computer stores opening across the country, countertop sales had clearly started to elbow aside mail order. At computer club meetings, Terrell reminded the assembled over and over again, "You don't have to buy through mail order any more." Relief from the potential hazards of buying through mail order was one of the best selling points the new retailers could offer.

While running the Byte Shop, Terrell began marketing his own brand of computer. Called the Byte 8, it was a private-label product with a profit margin close to 50 percent, twice the average retailer's 25 percent margin. It proved to be an easy commercial success. "All of a sudden, I realized the power of distribution that Tandy/Radio Shack had. Guaranteed sales." Tandy, a huge electronics distributor, much bigger than Terrell's chain, had not yet ventured into computers, although some microcomputer retailers feared Tandy in the way that microcomputer makers feared Texas Instruments. Neither group had cause to worry—for the moment.

The Sales Representative

*My most ambitious hopes were that we'd
have some store somewhere that might
be able to do $50,000 a month. Well,
the average ComputerLand store does
$130,000 a month.*

ED FABER
First CEO of ComputerLand, in a 1983 interview

IMSAI WAS A MANUFACTURING COMPANY RUN BY A SALES FORCE. THE San Leandro, California, manufacturer of the 8080 microcomputer cared little if its products featured the latest technological breakthroughs. IMSAI thrived for a time on its vigorous sales effort and ultimately failed through sheer neglect of its production and customer service side. It is fitting that IMSAI's most lasting contribution to the personal computer field was a sales enterprise—a chain of retail stores, a computer franchise—ComputerLand, started by Ed Faber in 1976.

Faber was an old hand at start-up operations. In 1957, after graduating from Cornell University and serving in the Marine Corps, he joined IBM as a sales representative. In 1964, IBM sent Faber to Holland to set up a European Education Center for the corporation. He was working at a distance from direct management and found that he liked it. In 1966, IBM assigned him to a project he enjoyed even more.

Faber was tapped to help develop a department called New Business Marketing, which was designed to ease IBM into the small-business area. Faber helped create a business plan that would include a newly assembled sales force and a fresh marketing concept for the company. This was his first start-up operation, and he relished the challenge. He identified problems, devised solutions for them, and then, as corporate start-up strategies inevitably go, he had to deal with a set of new problems created by the solutions. By 1967, Faber decided to steer his career development toward start-ups rather than line sales management, the more common path to advancement at IBM at the time.

In 1969, after 12 years with IBM, Faber left to join Memorex. At Memorex, and later at a minicomputer company, Faber was hired to build the internal marketing organization. A pattern was developing, but Faber didn't mind it. After he had created and launched a program, running it became merely routine. He liked to work closer to the edge and he was open to bold new ideas.

In 1975, Bill Millard invited Faber to join him at IMSAI. At the time, Faber was working for Omron, a small San Francisco subsidiary of a Japanese electronics firm. Millard described the IMSAI opportunity in lavish terms, which Faber automatically suspected was overstatement. The idea of selling kit computers through the mail for buyers to assemble at home seemed preposterous to Faber, the quintessential IBM man. But Faber couldn't argue with the market's response to kit computers. IMSAI was knee-deep in orders. At the end of December 1975, he joined IMSAI as its director of sales.

Almost immediately, Faber was in contact with John French, Dick Heiser's competitor in Southern California. French had approached IMSAI with the idea of buying kits in quantity and retailing them through a computer store. Again, Faber was dumbfounded. Sell computers to customers right off the street? The idea was ludicrous, he thought. On the other hand, Heiser's retail operation was more than solvent, and IMSAI had little to lose. Faber sold French 10 computer kits at a 10 percent discount, not much for a retailer to work with. French quickly moved the 10 units out the door and was asking for another 15. More orders followed. Other retailers were contacting Faber seeking similar deals. By March 1976, IMSAI had raised its price in order to give retailers a 25 percent margin.

Faber had an excellent reason for courting the dealers. Selling computers to retailers in batches of 10 or 15 was much easier than selling single units to individuals over the telephone. Furthermore, the retail market was wide open. The MITS exclusivity policy was forcing dealers over to IMSAI. Not only were Altair dealers required to carry the MITS line and nothing else, but late arrivals were geographically subservient to early ones, who had established "territory." Enterprising dealers such as Paul Terrell chafed at the restrictions and ended up bolting to freedom.

The MITS retailing strategy amazed Faber. Ed Roberts sought to dominate his dealers and compel their loyalty. Given the entrepreneurial spirit of the time, Faber predicted that dealers would eventually balk at attempts to control them, and Roberts's marketing tactics would backfire on him. Defiantly, Faber took a stance in complete opposition to Roberts's. He encouraged nonexclusivity in the kinds of products dealers could sell, and the freedom to open outlets wherever they pleased. If two dealers wanted to open stores a block away from each other, it was fine with Faber if they competed for sales. IMSAI products would vie with any others on the dealers' shelves. By the end of June 1976, some 235 independent stores in the United States and Canada were carrying IMSAI products.

Faber kept an eye on the competing dealers, making note of their relative strengths and weaknesses. Most of them, he realized, were hobbyists with scant experience running a business. Their inexperience was reason enough to fail, he thought; however, they weren't failing. They were buying more and more merchandise from IMSAI and selling it almost as soon as it came in. In addition, the number of retailers was growing steadily.

Bill Millard got together with Ed Faber to discuss the phenomenon. They wondered what would happen if someone with a well-recognized name started providing comprehensive services including product purchasing, continuing education, and accounting systems for a network of small, retail storeowners. They were both thinking *franchise*. They couldn't find one reason not to start a franchise operation. Faber talked to John Martin, a former associate of Dick Brown's who was knowledgeable about that kind of business, and attended a seminar on franchising offered through Pepperdine University. When Faber sat down with Millard to talk about launching the operation, Millard asked Faber what he would choose to do. Faber sensed the *est* in this question and replied that he wanted to be in charge of the franchising operation.

ComputerLand incorporated on September 21, 1976, with Faber as president and Millard as board chairman, and opened its pilot store in Hayward, California, on November 10 of that year. This store served not only as a retail outlet, but also as a training facility for franchise owners. Gordon French, who had helped start the Homebrew computer club, worked for ComputerLand early on, helping to evaluate products and establish the pilot store before moving on to do consulting work. ComputerLand eventually sold the flagship outlet and became a pure franchise operation owning no stores at all. The first ComputerLand franchise store opened on February 18, 1977, in Morristown, New Jersey. The second store appeared soon thereafter in West Los Angeles. The stores initially offered products manufactured by IMSAI, Proc Tech, Polymorphic, Southwest Tech, and Cromemco, the last being one of the first manufacturers to support the new enterprise. Cromemco's Roger Melen and Harry Garland told Faber they thought the franchise was a terrific idea and gave him one of the best discounts then available.

Faber later developed a strong relationship with Apple Computer, partly because of the marketing tactics of Apple's chief rival in the nascent consumer marketplace, Commodore. Commodore had recently come out with its PET computer, which was sold mainly in Europe. When Commodore introduced the PET in the United States, the company demanded a large deposit each month. ComputerLand found this demand unreasonable and became interested in stocking Apple's computers instead. Apple, in turn, proved to be extremely cooperative, to the point of placing advertising that linked the two company names together. Apple products became a ComputerLand staple.

Even with Faber running daily operations, ComputerLand, like IMSAI, was essentially Bill Millard's enterprise. He founded it and poured the initial working capital into it. He chaired its board of directors. As further proof, in 1983 close to 25 percent of ComputerLand employees were *est* graduates.

When IMSAI began to falter in 1978, it created a problem for ComputerLand. Its customers had the impression that the corporations were tied together. The franchising business had descended from IMSAI, Bill Millard was at the helm running both companies, and ex-IMSAI sales director Ed Faber was ComputerLand's president. People wanted to know, would ComputerLand be dragged down into a hole with IMSAI?

Faber spent much of his time assuring customers that the companies were legally separate entities. ComputerLand did have a buyer-vendor relationship with IMSAI, purchasing products from IMSAI and paying its bills, but IMSAI imposed no formal quotas on ComputerLand. When IMSAI went bankrupt, Faber was proven correct. The gap between IMSAI and ComputerLand was enough that IMSAI creditors were unable to get at ComputerLand's assets.

ComputerLand went on to achieve spectacular success as the nation's largest chain of computer stores. At the close of 1977, it had 24 stores. By September 1978, it had 50, and its growth continued rapidly. By November 1979, there were 100 ComputerLand franchises in existence; by December 1981, there were 241; by December 1982, there were 382; and by June 1983, 458 stores were operating. ComputerLand outdistanced the Byte Shop chain, and its fiercely competitive practices helped bury the Data Domain chain in the Midwest. In the early 1980s, Faber could reasonably claim that, as far as the general public was concerned, the place to buy computers was ComputerLand.

In 1982, the chain launched plans for a string of software stores called ComputerLand Satellites. ComputerLand intended to license the new software stores to existing franchise owners in its chain. By 1983, Ed Faber had planned to be semiretired and living in some bucolic setting within five years. He loved to fish and hunt game fowl and was looking forward to a little relaxation. But for the moment, he was busy squelching the competition. To spur the performance of his franchise, whenever he could he opened a ComputerLand outlet near a store belonging to his biggest rival, the new Radio Shack Computer Centers chain.

The McDonald's of Electronics

*Not a kit, the TRS-80 comes completely
wired and tested, ready to plug in and use.*

A Tandy Corporation press release

Ed Roberts had seen the well-heeled established electronics companies come crashing into the calculator business, cutting margins to the bone and driving out the little guys. He and the other "little guys" who had created this nascent microcomputer industry dreaded the day when the big guys would enter their world.

In 1977, it looked like it was about to happen, and the company that was going to change the nature of the game was a retailer, the leading electronics distributor, with stores in nearly every town in the country. Tandy/Radio Shack was going to make and sell its own microcomputer.

Computer retailing at the time, even when it was profitable, was still more about building community than pushing products. Ray Borrill's store in Bloomington, Indiana, was typical: in 1977 the store employed repair technicians and programmers, but no salespeople. Borrill himself was the closest thing the store had to a salesperson, but his conversations with customers ranged from broad discussions of the power of microcomputers to risky promises of what Borrill's team could put together for the customer, promises based mostly on how much "fun" Borrill thought the project would be: that is, how challenging it was.

The specter of Radio Shack loomed over Borrill and the other retailers as much as over the computer companies. None of them could compete with this powerhouse. Or so it seemed.

The Tandy Corporation began as a wholesale leather business. In 1927, Dave Tandy and his friend Norton Hinckley founded the Hinckley-Tandy Leather Company, which soon established a solid reputation around Fort Worth. In 1950, Tandy's son Charles, a graduate of Harvard Business School, conceived of expanding the business into a chain of leathercraft stores that would sell goods partly by retail and partly by mail order. Cofounder Hinckley balked at the idea and left the Tandy Leather Company.

Charles Tandy had an engaging, magnetic personality and a dry sense of humor, and he seemed to have an influence on everyone around him. He was an inveterate instructor who was engrossed in the daily operations of the company. When he had nothing else to do on a Friday afternoon, he would phone his retail outlets to ask how business was doing.

Tandy quickly set about building a national retail chain. By 1961, he had 125 stores in 105 cities in the United States and Canada. In 1962, Tandy bought a company that fundamentally changed the nature of the corporation. Tandy got wind of a small, nearly bankrupt chain of nine mail-order electronics stores called Radio Shack. He took control of the Boston-based company in 1963 and at once began reconstructing it, adding hundreds of retail stores throughout the country. Before Tandy took over, Radio Shack had been losing $4 million annually. Within two years after Tandy bought the chain, it was turning a profit. By 1973, when Radio Shack purchased its closest competitor, Allied Radio of Chicago, Radio Shack so dominated the market that the Justice Department brought an antitrust suit against it and compelled Tandy to divest itself of the corporation.

Tandy had begun manufacturing some of its own wares in 1966, but resisted making microcomputers when they arrived on the scene, even though some Tandy employees were caught up in the computer hobbyist movement. The behemoth chain was pushed into microcomputer manufacturing chiefly by one man: Don French.

French was a buyer for Radio Shack in 1975 when the Altair was released. He bought one as soon as he could and thoroughly studied it.

Concluding that microcomputing had potential, French began to concoct his own machine. Although forbidden to develop his computer on company time, French eventually managed to convince John Roach, then vice president of marketing at Radio Shack, to take a look at his project. As French recalls, Roach was not particularly impressed with French's efforts. Nonetheless, Radio Shack offered Steve Leininger of National Semiconductor payment to examine French's design. Leininger needed no arm-twisting, and by June 1976 he and French were working together on the project, using equipment and software of their own design.

French and Leininger received the official go-ahead to develop a Radio Shack computer in December 1976, even though the firm was only casually committed to their project. Radio Shack told French to "get it done as cheaply as possible." This was a more encouraging statement than the one he had heard a few months earlier when a Radio Shack executive had telexed French saying, "Don't waste my time. We can't sell computers."

Tandy was, however, protecting its turf. When Bill Millard and Ed Faber launched ComputerLand in 1976, it was under the name "Computer Shack." That was too close for Tandy's comfort, and the company notified Faber that it intended to protect its trademark. Faber stood firm, seeking a court judgment in California. Tandy immediately sued in New Jersey. Faber got the message: Tandy was going to sue him state-by-state, keeping him tied up in court forever. He quietly changed the name of his franchise to ComputerLand.

In January 1977, just a month after they began work on the project, French and Leininger had a working model. They demonstrated their new machine for Charles Tandy in the Radio Shack conference room. The keyboard and display sat on the table, but the computer itself lay hidden beneath it. The two engineers had devised a simple tax accounting program, H & R Shack, and asked the magnate to try it out. Tandy typed in a salary of $150,000 for himself and promptly crashed the program. After French and Leininger explained the limits of integer arithmetic in BASIC, Tandy gracefully entered a much smaller figure, but French made a mental note that the machine needed better math capabilities.

Serious work began on the machine a few months later. The company assigned it a target retail price of $199 and projected sales of

1000 units per year. French thought that the 1000-unit figure was absurd. MITS had sold more than 10,000 Altairs in a year without the overwhelming advantage of Radio Shack's retail network. French wasn't too sure the $199 price was right, either.

Soon after that, Tandy and Roach met with computer division personnel to discuss what to do with the little computer if it failed to sell. Could they at least use it for internal Radio Shack accounting? After all, French was doing some simple record keeping on his handmade version. If nothing else, the company's own stores could serve as a backup customer base and absorb the first year's projected production.

Radio Shack announced its new TRS-80 in August at New York City's Warwick Hotel. The $199 price hadn't survived; the machine would retail for $399 and come complete and ready to use in a black-and-gray plastic case. By September 1977, with projected sales at 3000 units annually, Radio Shack stores had already sold 10,000 TRS-80s.

Back in June 1977, Radio Shack had assigned French the task of establishing retail outlets for the TRS-80. The computer was the orphan of the Radio Shack family. The company wasn't sure how successful it would be, and didn't take it that seriously. When the TRS-80 was introduced, Radio Shack outlets didn't even stock it. Their customers were forced to special order the company's own product.

Tandy management's hesitation about selling computers was in part based on the very accurate assessment that selling computers wasn't like selling calculators or answering machines. There was a reason why the existing computer stores operated the way they did: their customers needed a lot of support and hand-holding. Computer retailing really was still about community building and support more than about moving products. This was not the Radio Shack model.

Tandy/Radio Shack ventured out a bit into the computer retailing business when it opened its first all-computer store in Fort Worth in October 1977. The outlet carried not only the TRS-80, but also IMSAIs and other companies' products. It was regarded as an experiment. But that venture succeeded, too, and resistance to microcomputers began fading away within the Tandy Corporation ranks. Radio Shack outlets began stocking the TRS-80s, and Radio Shack Computer Centers were appearing all over the country, staffed by individuals who knew more about computers than the average electronics salesperson.

The backlog of orders was tremendous: in June 1978, Radio Shack president Lewis Kornfeld admitted that only about one-third of the stores had TRS-80s in stock, though over half had sold some.

Charles Tandy celebrated his sixtieth birthday in style, making an entrance to his birthday party astride an elephant. A few months later, on a Saturday afternoon in November 1978, Tandy died in his sleep. The following Monday, the value of the Tandy Corporation stock dropped 10 percent on Wall Street. But the Tandy Corporation was not a one-man show. Charles Tandy had surrounded himself with capable executives, and after his death the company retained a solid financial footing.

The original TRS-80 was fairly limited in what it could do. It had only 4K of memory, a Z80 processor running at slightly under half its rated speed, a sketchy BASIC, and very slow tape cassettes for data storage. Most of these limitations stemmed from the company's cut-rate approach to manufacturing. The first TRS-80 lacked the capability to type lowercase letters. This was not an oversight. French and Leininger had deliberately omitted them to save $1.50 on parts, which translated to $5 on the purchase price.

Tandy quickly supplemented the TRS-80 with a better BASIC and add-on memory kits, and soon after that offered a combination disk drive and printer. These enhancements were a prelude to Tandy's announcement, on May 30, 1979, of the TRS-80 Model II, a respectable business system that overcame many of the drawbacks of the original model. The Model II showed that Tandy had learned from its mistakes with the first TRS-80 and was capable of creating a state-of-the-art business machine. This surprised some, given Tandy's underpowered entry into the personal computer field.

Between 1978 and 1980, personal computers and related equipment rose from 1.8 to 12.7 percent of Radio Shack's North American sales. In 1980, Radio Shack introduced a spate of new machines. Its Pocket Computer, slightly larger than an advanced calculator with four times the memory of the original Altair, sold for $229. Its Color Computer, at $399, offered graphics in eight colors and up to 16K of memory. And the TRS-80 Model II was an upgrade of the Model I.

The TRS-80 Model I had introduced a price breakthrough, and people who knew nothing about computers began buying Model Is.

The result, far from driving the little guys out of the market, actually expanded the market and helped to legitimize microcomputers in the eyes of the general public. Tandy's toylike machine and reputation as a hobbyist's company didn't do much for the idea of the microcomputer as a business tool, although some businesses did experiment with TRS-80s. But the home/hobby computer market began to expand rapidly.

Tandy was not the only company driving prices down, thereby opening the market for home computers. Nolan Bushnell's Atari, which initially produced only video game machines, began putting out low-priced devices that could legitimately be called computers. Commodore, with its strong distribution channels for its electronics equipment, was doing well with its PET computer and had added more sophisticated machines to its product line that were geared less to hobbyists and more to the average consumer. Texas Instruments, the company that so many microcomputer manufacturers feared would announce a bargain-basement computer, did just that with its TI-99/4. And in Britain, a daring and brilliant entrepreneur named Clive Sinclair introduced a tiny computer called the ZX-80, later replaced by the ZX-81, which was distributed by Timex and sold for under $50.

In 1981, when 42-year-old John Roach took over the reins at Tandy, he seemed like a youth to those who were used to seeing Charles Tandy in the boss's seat. But Roach's relative youth began to look like an advantage after the TRS-80 faced serious competition from the most youthful company of all. The stiffest competition Tandy faced during the early 1980s came from a Silicon Valley firm financed by the sale of two calculators and a Volkswagen bus.

CHAPTER 7

AMERICAN PIE

I try to get people to see what I see. . . .
When you run a company, you have to
get people to buy into your dreams.

STEVE JOBS
Cofounder of Apple Computer

The Prankster

*The world of computer design had Steve
Wozniak for a golden moment.*

CHRIS ESPINOSA
Early Apple employee

IN 1962, AN EIGHTH-GRADE BOY IN SUNNYVALE, CALIFORNIA, BUILT AN addition-subtraction machine out of a few transistors and some parts. He did all the work himself, soldering wires in the backyard of his suburban home in the heart of what is now known as Silicon Valley. And when he entered the machine in a local science fair, no one who knew him was surprised that he won the top award given for electronics. After all, he had designed a tic-tac-toe machine two years earlier, and, with a little help from his engineer dad, he had assembled a crystal radio in the second grade.

The boy, born Stephen Gary Wozniak, but called Woz or The Woz by his friends, was bright, and when a problem caught his interest, he worked relentlessly to solve it. When he enrolled in Homestead High School in 1964, The Woz quickly became one of the top math students there, although electronics remained his true passion. Unfortunately, that wasn't his only passion. If it were, Wozniak would have caused the teachers and administrators of Homestead High much less trouble.

The Woz was a prankster, and he applied the same ingenuity and determination to carrying out his pranks as he did to building electronics. He spent hours at school concocting the perfect prank. His jokes were clever and well executed, and he usually emerged from them unscathed.

But not always. Once, Woz got the bright idea to wire up an electronic metronome and plant it inside a friend's locker, its bomblike ticking audible to anyone standing nearby. But before Woz's friend could discover the "bomb," the high school principal found it. Falling for the trick, the principal bravely snatched the metronome from the locker and ran out of the building with it. Wozniak thought the whole incident was hilarious. "Just the ticking would have sufficed, but I taped together some battery cylinders with the labeling removed. I also had a switch that sped up the ticking when the locker was opened," said Woz. The principal showed his appreciation of the joke by suspending Woz for two days.

Soon after, Steve Wozniak's electronics teacher, John McCullum, decided to take him in tow. The Woz clearly found high school less than stimulating, and McCullum saw that his pupil needed a genuine challenge. Although The Woz loved electronics, the class McCullum taught was nowhere near demanding enough. McCullum worked out an arrangement with Sylvania Electronics whereby Wozniak could visit the company's nearby facilities during school hours to use their computers.

Woz was enthralled. For the first time, he saw the capabilities of a real computer. One of the machines he played with was a Digital Equipment Corporation (DEC) minicomputer called the PDP-8. "Play" for Wozniak was an intense and engrossing activity. He read the PDP-8 manual from cover to cover, soaking up the information about instruction sets, registers, bits, and Boolean algebra. The teenager read the microchip manuals as well. Confident of his newfound expertise, within weeks Woz began drawing up plans for his own version of the PDP-8.

"I designed most of the PDP-8 on paper just for the heck of it. Then I started looking for other computer manuals. I would redesign each [computer] over and over, trying to reduce my chip count, and using newer and newer TTL chips in my designs. I never had a way to get the chips to build one of these designs as my own."

He knew that he was going to design computers himself one day—he hadn't the slightest doubt of that. Only one thing bothered him: he wanted to design them now.

During the years Steve Wozniak attended Homestead High, semi-conductor technology advances made possible the creation of smaller computers, dubbed *minicomputers*. The PDP-8 was one of the most popular minicomputers, while the Nova, produced by Data General in 1969, was one of the most elegant. Woz was enchanted by the Nova. He loved the way its programmers had packed so much power into a few simple instructions. Writing a flabby program capable of doing this and that is one thing, but the Data General software was not only powerful, it was beautiful. The computer's chassis also appealed to him. While his buddies were plastering posters of rock stars on their bedroom walls, Woz covered his with photos of the Nova and brochures from Data General. He then decided—and it became the biggest goal in his life—that he would one day own his own computer.

The Woz was not the only student in Silicon Valley with such a dream. Actually, in some ways he was fairly typical. Many students at Homestead High had parents in the electronics industry. Having grown up with new technology around them, these kids were not intimidated by it. They were accustomed to watching their parents mess around with oscilloscopes and soldering irons. Homestead High also had teachers who encouraged their students' interests in technology. Woz may have followed his dream more single-mindedly than the others, but the dream was not his alone.

The dream was, however, highly unrealistic. In 1969, it was almost unthinkable that individuals could own their own computers; the cost to buy one was astronomical. Even minicomputers such as the Nova and the PDP-8 were priced to sell to research laboratories. Nevertheless, Woz went on dreaming. He did well on his college entrance exams but hadn't given much thought to which college to attend. When he eventually made his choice, it had nothing to do with academics. On a visit to the University of Colorado with some friends, the California boy saw snow for the first time and was enchanted. He concluded that Colorado would suffice. His father agreed he could go there for a year, at least.

At the University of Colorado, Woz played bridge intensely, designed more computers on paper, and engineered pranks. After creating a device to jam the television in his college dorm, he told trusting hall-mates that the television was badly grounded, and they would have to move the outside antenna around until they got a clear picture. When he had one of them on the roof in a sufficiently awkward position, he quietly turned off his jammer and restored the television reception. His hallmate remained contorted on the roof, for the public good, until the prank was revealed.

Woz took a graduate computer class and got an A+. But he also wrote so many programs (to calculate chemistry and physics tables) that he ran his class many times over its budget for computer time. His professor instructed the computer center to bill him. Woz was so scared to tell his parents that he never returned to school there.

It became obvious that academics were not Wozniak's main priority. After his first year, he returned home and attended a local college. In the summer of 1971, he found a job with a small computer company called Tenet Incorporated that built a medium-scale computer. The company made a quality product but didn't succeed due to a recession. "It was a sad learning experience that a successful product could still fail," said Woz. Nevertheless, he enjoyed it enough to stay on into the fall, rather than returning to school.

The same summer he started work, Woz and his old high school friend Bill Fernandez built a computer (Wozniak's first) out of parts rejected by local manufacturers because of cosmetic defects. Woz and Fernandez stayed up late cataloging the parts on the Fernandez family's living room carpet. Within a week, Woz showed up at his friend's house with a cryptic penciled diagram. "This is a computer," Woz told Fernandez. "Let's build it." They worked far into the night, soldering connections and drinking cream soda. When finished, they named their creation the Cream Soda Computer; it had lights and switches just as the Altair would more than three years later.

Woz and Fernandez telephoned the local newspaper to boast about their computer. A reporter and a photographer arrived at the Fernandez house, sniffing out a possible "local prodigy" feature. But when Woz and Fernandez plugged in the Cream Soda Computer and began to run a program, the power supply overheated. The computer literally went up in smoke, and with it Woz's chance for fame, at least for the moment. Woz laughed the incident off and went back to his paper designs.

Besides assisting with the Cream Soda Computer, Bill Fernandez did something that would profoundly change the life of his friend. He introduced Woz to another electronics hobbyist, an old friend of his from junior high school. Although a good number of Silicon Valley students were interested in electronics because their parents were engineers, this friend, a couple of years behind Fernandez in school, was an anomaly in that respect. His foster parents were blue-collar workers, unconnected to the computer industry. This friend, a quiet, intense, long-haired boy, was named Steven Paul Jobs.

Although Jobs was five years younger than Woz, the two hit it off immediately. Both were fascinated with electronics. In Woz's case, this led to the concentrated study of schematics and manuals and lengthy sessions designing electronic gadgets. Jobs was as intense as Woz, but his passion showed itself in different ways, and it sometimes got him into trouble.

Jobs confessed to being a terror as a child. He's claimed that he would have "ended up in jail" if it hadn't been for a teacher, Mrs. Hill, who moved him ahead a year to separate him from a boisterous buddy. Mrs. Hill also bribed Jobs to study. "In just two weeks, she had figured me out," Jobs recalled. "She told me she'd give me five dollars to finish a workbook." Later, she bought him a camera kit. He learned a lot that year.

Even as an adolescent, Jobs had an unshakable self-confidence. When he ran out of parts for an electronics project he was working on, he simply picked up the phone and called William Hewlett, cofounder of Hewlett-Packard, to ask for help in obtaining them. "I'm Steve Jobs," he explained to Hewlett, "and I was wondering if you had any spare parts I could use to build a frequency counter." Hewlett was understandably taken aback by the call, but Jobs got his parts. The 12-year-old was not only very convincing but also surprisingly enterprising. He made money at Homestead High by buying, selling, and trading electrical equipment; he would buy a stereo, fix it, and sell it at a profit.

But for Woz, it was a mutual love of practical jokes that cemented his relationship with the gutsy teen. Jobs, he discovered, was another born prankster. This shared inclination led the two to engage in a rather shady early business enterprise.

Blue Boxes, Buddhism, and *Breakout*

*I didn't know what I wanted to do with
my life. I knew there was this spirit, but
I didn't know the form of it. I thought,
I really want to go to India.*

STEVE JOBS
Apple Computer cofounder

WOZ RETURNED TO SCHOOL, THIS TIME TO THE UNIVERSITY OF CALIfornia at Berkeley to study engineering. He had resolved to take school more seriously and even enrolled in several graduate courses. He did well, even though by the end of the school year he was spending most of his time with Steve Jobs building notorious little items called *blue boxes*.

Woz first learned about blue boxes—devices that enabled people to make long-distance phone calls free of charge—in a piece in *Esquire* magazine. The story described a colorful character who used such a device as he crisscrossed the country in his van, the FBI panting in pursuit. Although the story was a blend of fiction and truth, the descriptions of the blue box sounded very plausible to the budding engineer. Before Woz even finished the piece, he was on the phone to Steve Jobs, reading him the juicy parts.

It turns out the *Esquire* story was drawn from the extraordinary real-life experiences of John Draper, a.k.a. Captain Crunch. He owes his nickname to his discovery that a whistle stuffed inside boxes of Cap'n Crunch cereal had an interesting capability. When the whistle was

▲ *The MITS Altair 8800, assembled*

Created by Man.

The Affordable Computer.

Not too long ago, computers were practical only when it came to handling large quantities of data.

In more recent times, computers have been engineered to be smaller and less expensive without loss of power or speed. Computer uses have multiplied. And most importantly, computers have become easier to understand and to use.

The engineers who designed the Altair Computer understood this trend perhaps better than anyone else in the computer industry. They designed the Altair to be a powerful, general purpose computer that sells for $439.00 in kit form and $621.00 assembled.

They did it without sacrificing performance or quality. 78 basic machine instructions, a cycle time of 2 microseconds, and buss orientation make the Altair Computer ideal for thousands of existing and new applications.

The Altair Computer can directly address up to 65,000 words of memory and 256 input/output devices. It can be connected to a growing number of Altair Computer Options such as memory boards, parallel and serial interface boards, floppy disc storage, audio tape interface, alpha-numeric displays and keyboards, computer terminals, line-printers, etc.

You can order the Altair Computer by simply filling out the coupon in this Ad or by calling us at 505/265-7553. Or you can ask for free technical consultation or for one of our free Altair System Catalogues.

PRICES: Altair Computer Kit with complete assembly
Instructions $439.00
Assembled Altair Computer $621.00

1,000 word static memory cards $176.00 kit
                                  & $254.00 assembled.
4,000 word dynamic memory card $264.00 kit
                                  & $338.00 assembled.

MITS/6328 Linn, NE, Albuquerque, New Mexico 87108

NOTE: Altair Computers come with complete documentation and operating instructions. Altair customers receive software and general computer information through free membership to the Altair User's Club. Software now available includes a resident assembler, system monitor and text editor. Basic language soon to be available.
Prices and specifications subject to change without notice. Warranty: 90 days on parts for kits and 90 days on parts and labor for assembled units.

MAIL THIS COUPON TODAY!
☐ Enclosed is check for $ _____
☐ BankAmericard # _____ ☐ or Master Charge # _____
☐ Credit Card Expiration Date _____
☐ ALTAIR 8800 ☐ Kit ☐ Assembled
☐ Options (list on separate sheet)
Include $8.00 for postage and handling.
        ☐ PLEASE SEND FREE ALTAIR SYSTEM CATALOGUE

Name _____
ADDRESS _____
CITY _____ STATE & ZIP _____
MITS/6328 Linn NE, Albuquerque, NM, 87106 505/265-7553

▶ *An early MITS Altair ad written by David Bunnell in 1975, which ran in various magazines such as* Popular Electronics, Radio Electronics, *and* Scientific American

▲ *Cromemco's Cyclops camera, which was designed to work with the Altair, 1974*

◀ *Steve Dompier, an early Homebrew Computer Club member, who made the Altair play music in 1975*

▲ Steve Dompier, an early Homebrewer, visiting the microcomputer company
Processor Technology in 1976

▲ Les Solomon's basement with a collection of computers designed by
various microcomputer pioneers

▲Art Salsberg and Les Solomon, editorial director and technical editor of Popular Electronics, with historic 1975 Altair cover

▶The Xerox PARC Alto computer, built in 1973, which used bit-mapped graphics, a mouse, menus, icons, and other features that later became common for computers

▶ *Andrew Fluegelman, originator of the term "freeware," distributed his PC Talk program freely, asking only for a donation from those who found it useful*

◀ *Clive Sinclair, the British inventor who brought the price of computers below $100 with his tiny ZX-80 computer in 1980*

George Morrow posing for an early advertisement for circuit boards, ca. 1976

COURTESY OF GEORGE MORROW

Harry Garland (left) and Roger Melen of Cromemco

COURTESY OF ROGER MELEN

▲ *Roger Melen at the Great Wall of China. The computers of his firm, Cromemco, were selected in 1979 to teach a new generation of elite programmers throughout China. Cromemco subsequently sold many thousands of computers to Chinese universities.*

▲ *Chuck Grant (left) and Mark Greenberg, founders of Kentucky Fried Computers and North Star Computers, next to a North Star Horizon computer*

Chuck Grant, cofounder of Kentucky Fried Computers and North Star Computers, at a computer expo

COURTESY OF DAVID H. AHL

Gary Kildall, creator of the first programming language for the Intel 4004 micro-processor, founder of Digital Research, and lover of fast cars

COURTESY OF TOM G. O'NEAL

▲ *Tom Rolander (front center), Gary Kildall (front right),*
Dorothy McEwen, and other Digital Research employees in front of
their headquarters in Pacific Grove, California, ca. 1977

▲ *Digital Research's later office in Pacific Grove*

▲ *The Digital Research booth at an early West Coast Computer Faire trade show in San Francisco*

◄ *Ted Nelson, author of* Computer Lib *in 1974, in which he wrote, "You can and must understand computers now!"*

$13.95
First Edition.
ISBN 0-89347-002-3

Front and back cover of Ted Nelson's
Computer Lib

An Open Letter to Hobbyists

To me, the most critical thing in the hobby market right now is the lack of good software courses, books and software itself. Without good software and an owner who understands programming, a hobby computer is wasted. Will quality software be written for the hobby market?

Almost a year ago, Paul Allen and myself, expecting the hobby market to expand, hired Monte Davidoff and developed Altair BASIC. Though the initial work took only two months, the three of us have spent most of the last year documenting, improving and adding features to BASIC. Now we have 4K, 8K, EXTENDED, ROM and DISK BASIC. The value of the computer time we have used exceeds $40,000.

The feedback we have gotten from the hundreds of people who say they are using BASIC has all been positive. Two surprising things are apparent, however. 1) Most of these "users" never bought BASIC (less than 10% of all Altair owners have bought BASIC), and 2) The amount of royalties we have received from sales to hobbyists makes the time spent of Altair BASIC worth less than $2 an hour.

Why is this? As the majority of hobbyists must be aware, most of you steal your software. Hardware must be paid for, but software is something to share. Who cares if the people who worked on it get paid?

Is this fair? One thing you don't do by stealing software is get back at MITS for some problem you may have had. MITS doesn't make money selling software. The royalty paid to us, the manual, the tape and the overhead make it a break-even operation. One thing you do do is prevent good software from being written. Who can afford to do professional work for nothing? What hobbyist can put 3-man years into programming, finding all bugs, documenting his product and distribute for free? The fact is, no one besides us has invested a lot of money in hobby software. We have written 6800 BASIC, and are writing 8080 APL and 6800 APL, but there is very little incentive to make this software available to hobbyists. Most directly, the thing you do is theft.

What about the guys who re-sell Altair BASIC, aren't they making money on hobby software? Yes, but those who have been reported to us may lose in the end. They are the ones who give hobbyists a bad name, and should be kicked out of any club meeting they show up at.

I would appreciate letters from any one who wants to pay up, or has a suggestion or comment. Just write me at 1180 Alvarado SE, #114, Albuquerque, New Mexico, 87108. Nothing would please me more than being able to hire ten programmers and deluge the hobby market with good software.

Bill Gates

Bill Gates
General Partner, Micro-Soft

▲ *Bill Gates's attack on software piracy published in the Homebrew Computer Club newsletter, 1976 (note the "Micro-Soft" spelling)*

Bill Godbout, who started building S100 microcomputers in 1976, early in the industry's development

Michael Shrayer with his pioneering word processor, Electric Pencil, in 1976

▲ *Scott Adams, who created some of the first games for personal computers in the mid-1970s*

▶ *Wayne Green, founder of Byte, Kilobaud, and other personal computer publications*

Seymour Rubinstein, an early IMSAI employee, who founded MicroPro International, published WordStar, *and is now CEO of Prompt Software*

COURTESY OF SEYMOUR I. RUBINSTEIN

William Lohse, who ran IMSAI's European office during the company's last days and later became president of Ziff-Davis Publications

COURTESY OF DAVID H. AHL

Ed Faber, who left IMSAI to found ComputerLand

COURTESY OF COMPUTERLAND

▲ *Paul Terrell in his Byte Shop, which he opened in 1975 in Mountain View, California*

▲ *The original Byte Shop from the outside*

blown directly into a telephone receiver, the whistle exactly mimicked the tones that caused the central telephone circuitry to release a long-distance trunk line. This made it possible to make long-distance calls for free with very little chance of getting traced.

John Draper was the world's premier *phone phreak,* someone who uses electronic gadgets or other devices to "outwit" central telephone circuitry in order to make free calls or otherwise exploit the phone system. Draper virtually invented phone phreaking and was for many years its leading practitioner, the legendary "phirst phreaker." True phreaking, purists say, is motivated solely by the intellectual challenge of getting past a complex network of circuits and switches. The telephone company, however, took a dim view of the enterprise and prosecuted phreaks whenever it could catch them.

A blue box, so called because it was actually a blue-colored box, enabled its user to gain control of telephone trunk lines. Draper, an itinerant champion of the device, traveled around the country showing people how to build and operate them.

Woz didn't know the full extent of the Draper saga at the time he read the *Esquire* article, but he was intrigued by it and began researching the "phone phreak" technology. Around the same time, he came across some information in a book by Yippie leader Abbie Hoffman on how to construct a device that prevented incoming phone calls from being billed. With his customary thoroughness, Wozniak collected articles on phone phreaking devices of all kinds. In a few months, he had become a phone phreaking expert himself, known to insiders by the nickname Berkeley Blue. Perhaps it was inevitable that Woz's newfound infamy would get back to the man who had inspired him. One night a van pulled up outside Woz's dorm.

Wozniak was thrilled to meet John Draper, even though Captain Crunch's famous van, which Woz had expected to look like something out of *Mission Impossible,* was disappointingly conventional. Woz and Draper quickly became good friends, and together they used phone phreak techniques to tap information from computers all over the United States. At least once they listened in on an FBI phone conversation, according to Wozniak.

It was Jobs, however, who made this pastime turn a profit. Jobs got into phone phreaking, too, later claiming that he and Woz had called around the world several times and once woke the Pope with a blue-box call. Soon Wozniak and Jobs had a neat little business marketing phone-phreaking boxes. "We sold a ton of 'em," Woz would later confess. When Jobs was still in high school, Woz made most of the sales to students in the Berkeley dorms. In the fall of 1972, when Jobs entered Reed College in Oregon, they were able to broaden their market.

Jobs had considered going to Stanford, where he had attended some classes during high school. "But everyone there knew what they wanted to do with their lives," he said. "And I didn't know what I wanted to do with my life at all." On a trip to Reed, he had fallen in love with the school, seeing it as a place where "*nobody* knew what they were going to do. They were trying to find out about life." Jobs was visiting Woz at Cal Berkeley when his father called to say that Reed had accepted him. He was ecstatic.

Even at a place as seemingly hospitable as Reed, Jobs remained a recluse. As the son of working-class parents, he may have felt out of place in a school populated largely by upper-class youths.

At Reed, Jobs began investigating Eastern religions. More and more often, he stayed up late at night with his friend Dan Kottke to discuss Buddhism. They devoured dozens of books on philosophy and religion, and at one point Jobs became interested in primal therapy. Jobs was at home philosophically, if not socially.

In the year Jobs spent at Reed, he seldom attended class. After six months, he dropped out but managed to remain in the dorm. "The school sort of gave me an unofficial scholarship. They let me live on campus and looked the other way." He remained for over a year, attending classes when he felt like it, spending much of his time studying philosophy and meditating. He converted to vegetarianism and lived on Roman Meal cereal, partly because a box costing less than 50 cents would feed him for a week. At parties he tended to sit quietly in a corner. Jobs seemed to be clearing things out of his life, searching for some simplicity.

Although Woz had little interest in Jobs's nonscientific pursuits, his friendship with Jobs remained strong. Woz frequently drove up to Oregon to visit Jobs on weekends.

Woz took a summer job in 1973 at Hewlett-Packard, joining Bill Fernandez, who was already working there. Woz had only just finished his junior year, but the lure of Silicon Valley's most prestigious electronics company was hard to resist. College would have to wait once again as Woz continued his education in the firm's calculator division. At the time, HP was manufacturing the HP-35 programmable calculator, and Wozniak realized just how much the device resembled a computer. "It had this little chip, serial registers, and an instruction set," he thought. "Except for its I/O, it's a computer." He studied the calculator design with the same energy that he applied to the minicomputers of his high school days.

After his year at Reed College, Jobs returned to Silicon Valley and took a job with a young video game company called Atari. He stayed until he had saved enough money for a trip to India that he and Dan Kottke had planned. The two had long discussions about the Kainchi Ashram and its famous inhabitant, Neem Karoli Baba, a holy man described in the popular book *Be Here Now.* Jobs rendezvoused with Kottke in India, and together they searched for the ashram. When they learned that Neem Karoli Baba had died, they drifted around India, reading and talking about philosophy.

When Kottke ran out of money, Jobs gave him several hundred dollars. Kottke went on a meditation retreat for a month. Jobs didn't go with him, but instead wandered the subcontinent for a few months before returning to California. On his return, Jobs went back to work for Atari and reconnected with his friend The Woz, who was still at HP.

Jobs himself had worked at Hewlett-Packard years before, right after making his brazen phone call to William Hewlett asking for spare parts, a call that netted him a summer job at HP. Now he was at Atari, and though he was still just as brash and just as convinced that he could get anything he wanted, he had been changed in subtle ways by his year at Reed and his experiences in India.

Woz was still a jokester at heart. Every morning before he left for work he would change the outgoing message on his telephone answering machine. In a gravelly voice and thick accent, he would recite his Polish joke for the day. Woz's Dial-A-Joke phone number became the most frequently called phone number in the San Francisco Bay Area, and he had to argue more than once with the telephone company to keep it going. The nature of his jokes also caused trouble. The Polish American Congress sent him a letter asking him to cease and desist with the jokes, even though Woz himself was of Polish extraction. So Wozniak simply made Italians the butt of his jokes instead. When the attention faded, he went back to Polish jokes.

In the early 1970s, computer arcade games were becoming popular. When Woz spotted one of those games, *Pong,* in a bowling alley, he was inspired. "I can make one of those," he thought, and immediately went home and designed a video game. Even though its marketability was questionable (when a player missed the moving blip, "OH SHIT" flashed on the screen), the programming on the game was tops. When Woz demonstrated his game for Atari, the company offered him a job on the spot. Being comfortable with his position at HP, Woz turned them down. But he was devoting much of his time to Atari technology, nonetheless. Woz had already dropped a small fortune in quarters into arcade games when Jobs, who often worked nights, began sneaking Woz into the Atari factory. Woz could play the games for free, sometimes for eight hours at a stretch. It worked out well for Jobs, too. "If I had a problem, I'd say, 'Hey, Woz,' and he'd come and help me."

At the time, Atari wanted to produce a new game, and company founder Nolan Bushnell gave Jobs his ideas for what came to be called *Breakout,* a fast-paced game in which the player controls a paddle to hit a ball that breaks through a wall, piece by piece. Jobs boasted he could design the game in four days, secretly planning to enlist Woz's help. Jobs was always very persuasive, but in this case he didn't have to bring out the thumbscrews to get his friend to help him. Woz stayed up for four straight nights designing the game, and still managed to put in his regular hours at Hewlett-Packard. In the daytime, Jobs would work at putting the device together, and at night Woz would examine what he'd done and perfect the design. They finished it in four days. The experience taught them something: they could work well together on a tough project with a tight deadline and succeed. Woz also learned something else, but not until much later. The $350 Jobs gave Woz as his share of the amount Bushnell had paid was considerably less than the $6,650 cut that Jobs kept for himself. With Jobs, friendship only went so far.

Starting Apple

*I met the two Steves. They showed
me the Apple I. I thought they
were really right on.*

MIKE MARKKULA
Ex-chairman, ex-president, and ex–vice president
of marketing at Apple

*B*REAKOUT WASN'T WOZ'S ONLY EXTRACURRICULAR PROJECT AT HP.
He also designed and built a computer terminal. Jobs had heard
that a local company that rented computer time needed an inexpensive
home terminal to access the company's large computer. Jobs told Woz
about it, and Woz designed a small device that used a television set for
a display, a kind of TV Typewriter. Around that time, Woz began attending the Homebrew Computer Club meetings.

Homebrew was a revelation for Steve Wozniak. For the first time, he
found himself surrounded by people who shared his love for computers, and who were more knowledgeable about computers than any of
his friends, or even himself. At the time, Woz hadn't even heard of the
Altair. He attended the Homebrew meeting only because a friend of his
at HP told him that a new club was forming for people interested in
computer terminals. When he arrived at Gordon French's suburban
garage, he felt a little out of place. Club members were talking about
the latest chips, the 8008 and the 8080, and Woz was unfamiliar with
them. Club members were interested in the video terminal he
designed, however, and that encouraged Woz. He went home and studied up on the latest microprocessor chips. He bought the first issue of

Byte and made it a point to attend the biweekly Homebrew Computer Club meetings.

"It changed my life," Woz would later recall. "My interest in computers was renewed. Every two weeks the club meeting was the biggest thing in my life." And Woz's enthusiasm, in turn, invigorated the club. His technical expertise and innocent, friendly manner attracted people to him. For two younger club members—Randy Wigginton and Chris Espinosa—Woz became the prime source of technical information, as well as their ride to meetings. (The two budding computer pioneers didn't have their driver's licenses yet.)

Woz couldn't afford an Altair, but he watched with fascination as others brought theirs to the gatherings. He was impressed by the smooth tact with which Lee Felsenstein chaired the meetings. He realized that many of the home-built machines shown at the club resembled his Cream Soda Computer, and he began to feel that he could improve on their basic designs. What he needed was a low-cost chip.

MOS Technology had advertised that it would sell its new 6502 microprocessor chip at the upcoming Wescon electronics show in San Francisco for only $20. At the time, microprocessors were generally sold only to companies that had established accounts with the semiconductor houses, and they cost hundreds of dollars apiece. The Wescon show did not permit sales on the exhibit floor, so Chuck Peddle, of MOS Technology, rented a hotel room from which to make the sales. Woz walked in, gave his 20 bucks to Chuck Peddle's wife, who was handling the transactions, and went to work.

Before designing the computer, Woz wrote a programming language for it. BASIC was the hit of the Homebrew Computer Club, and he knew he could impress his friends if he could get BASIC to work on his machine. "I'm going to be the first one to have BASIC for the 6502," he thought. "I can whip it out in a few weeks and I'll zap the world with it." He did wrap it up in a few weeks, and when he finished, he set to work making something for it to run on. That was the easy part, because he already had experience building a computer.

Woz designed a board that included the 6502 processor and interfaces connecting the processor to a keyboard and video monitor. This was no mean feat. The Intel 8008, which *Popular Electronics* had ignored in publishing the groundbreaking Altair story, was arguably far more suited to be used as the brain of a computer than the 6502 processor. Nevertheless, Woz finished the computer within a few weeks. Woz took his computer to Homebrew and passed out photocopies of his design. The design was so simple that he could describe it in just one page and anyone who read the description could duplicate his design. The consummate hobbyist, Woz believed in sharing information. The other hobbyists were duly impressed. Some questioned his choice of processor, but no one argued with the processor's $20 price tag. He called his machine an Apple.

The Apple name was actually Jobs's idea. He later insisted that he picked the name at random, but it may have been inspired by either the Beatles' record label or by Jobs's experience working in apple orchards in an Oregon commune.

Whatever the origin of its name, the Apple I had only the bare essentials. It lacked a case, a keyboard, and a power supply. The hobbyist owner had to connect a transformer to it in order to get it to work. The Apple I also required laborious assembly by hand. Woz spent a lot of time helping friends implement his design.

Steve Jobs saw a great financial opportunity in this skeletal machine, and urged Woz to start a company with him. Woz reluctantly agreed. The idea of turning his hobby into a business bothered him, but Jobs, as usual, was persistent. "Look, there's a lot of interest at the club in what you've done," he insisted. Woz conceded the point with the understanding that he wouldn't have to leave his job at Hewlett-Packard, which he loved.

They founded the company on April Fool's Day, 1976 (an appropriate date for two pranksters), together with a third partner, Ron Wayne. An Atari field service engineer, Wayne agreed to help found the company for a 10 percent stake. Wayne immediately started work on a company logo, a drawing of Isaac Newton seated under an apple tree.

Jobs sold his Volkswagen microbus and Wozniak sold his two prized HP calculators to pay someone to create a printed circuit board. The PC board would save them the trouble of assembling and wiring each computer—a task that was forcing them to clock 60-hour workweeks. Jobs figured they would be able to sell the boards at Homebrew.

But Jobs wasn't content to sell boards merely to hobbyists. He also began trying to interest retailers in the Apple. At a Homebrew meeting in July 1976, Woz gave a demonstration of the Apple I. Paul Terrell, one of the industry's earliest retailers, was in attendance. Jobs gave Terrell a personal demonstration of the machine. "Take a look at this," Jobs told Terrell. "You're going to like what you see."

Jobs was right. Terrell did like the machine, but he didn't immediately place an order. When Terrell told Jobs the machine showed promise and that Jobs should keep in touch, Terrell meant what he said. The machine was interesting, but there were a lot of sharp engineers at Homebrew. This computer could be a winner, or some other machine might be better. If Jobs and Wozniak really had something, Terrell figured they'd keep in touch with him.

The next day, Jobs appeared, barefoot, at the Byte Shop. "I'm keeping in touch," he said. Terrell, impressed by his confidence and perseverance, ordered 50 Apple I computers. Visions of instant wealth flashed before Jobs's eyes. But Terrell added a condition: he wanted the computers fully assembled. Woz and Jobs were back to their 60-hour workweeks.

The two Steves had no parts and no money to buy them, but with a purchase order from Terrell for 50 Apple I computers, Jobs and Woz were able to obtain net 30-days credit from suppliers. Jobs didn't even know what net 30-days credit meant. Terrell later received several calls from parts suppliers who wondered whether Jobs and Woz really had the guarantee from Terrell that they claimed they did.

Jobs and Woz were now in business. But even though they had successfully worked together under time pressure in the past, they knew they couldn't do this task alone. The parts had to be paid for in 30 days, and that meant they had to build 50 computers and deliver them to Paul Terrell within the same time period. Jobs paid his stepsister to plug chips into the Apple I board. He also hired Dan Kottke, who was on summer break from college. "You've got to come out here this summer," Jobs told Kottke. "I'll give you a job. We've got this amazing thing called 30-days net."

Terrell got his 50 Apple I machines on the 29th day, and Apple Computer was off and running. Jobs ran the business. All of the 200 or so Apple I computers eventually built were sold either through a handful of computer stores in the Bay Area or by a parcel service out of Jobs's "home office" (initially his bedroom, and later his parents' garage). The Apple I was priced at $666 (the so-called Number of the Beast from the Book of Revelation)—evidence that the prankster spirit was alive and well at Apple.

Unfortunately, the Apple Computer partnership wasn't faring as well. Ron Wayne, overwhelmed by Jobs's intensity and ambition, wanted out, and submitted his formal resignation. Jobs accepted the resignation and bought him out for $500.

By the end of the summer, Wozniak had begun work on another computer. The Apple II would have several advantages over the Apple I. Like Processor Technology's Sol, which had not yet appeared, the Apple II would be an integrated computer, featuring a keyboard and power supply, BASIC, and color graphics, all within an attractive case. For output, the user could hook the computer up to a television set. Jobs and Woz made provisions to sell just the circuit board to hobbyists who wanted to customize the machine. They were both sure the Apple II would be the hit of Homebrew, and Jobs hoped it would have a much broader appeal.

After deciding on the features to include in the Apple II, Woz and Jobs argued over its price. Jobs wanted to sell the board alone for $1,200. Woz said that if the price were that high, he wanted nothing to do with it. They finally decided to charge $1,200 for the board and the case.

Now they had at least the outline of a real commercial product, and Jobs's ambition flowered. "Steve was the hustler, the entrepreneurial type," said Woz. Jobs wanted to build a large company, and once again he went straight to the top for help, seeking advice from Atari founder Nolan Bushnell. Figuring that Apple needed a money guy in their corner, Bushnell introduced Jobs to Don Valentine, a successful venture capitalist in Silicon Valley. Valentine suggested that Jobs talk to a friend of his named Mike Markkula. Although he had just retired, this former Intel executive would be interested in Jobs and Wozniak's machine, Valentine was sure.

It was an inspired connection.

In the busy two years after the introduction of the Altair, the microcomputer industry had reached a critical turning point. Dozens of companies had come and gone. MITS, the industry pioneer, was foundering; IMSAI, Processor Technology, and a few other companies were jockeying for control of the market even as they faltered. Before long, all these companies failed.

In some cases, the failure of these early companies stemmed from technical problems with the computers, but more often it was a lack of expertise in marketing, distributing, and selling the products that did in these companies. Their corporate leaders were primarily engineers, not managers; they weren't versed in the ways of business, and therefore alienated their customers and dealers. MITS drove retailers away by forbidding them to sell other companies' products; IMSAI ignored dealer and customer complaints about defects in its machines; and Processor Technology responded to design problems with a bewildering series of slightly different versions, failed to keep pace with advances in the technology, and boxed itself in by refusing the venture capital needed for growth. Computer dealers eventually grew tired of these practices.

At the same time, the market was changing. Hobbyists had organized into clubs and users' groups that met regularly in garages, basements, and school auditoriums around the country. The number of people who wanted to own computers was growing, as were the ranks of knowledgeable hobbyists who wanted "a better computer." Unfortunately, would-be manufacturers of that "better computer" all faced one seemingly insurmountable problem: they didn't have the money to develop such a device.

The manufacturers, usually garage enterprises, needed investment capital, but there were strong arguments against giving it to them: the high failure rate among microcomputer companies, the lack of managerial experience among their leaders, and—the ultimate puzzle—the absence of IBM from the field. Investors had to wonder, if this area of computer technology had any promise, why hadn't IBM preempted it? In addition, some of the founders of the early companies looked unfavorably on the notion of taking money from an outside source, as that could mean losing some control of their companies.

For the microcomputer industry to continue advancing, an individual with a special perspective was needed—someone who could see beyond the basic risks to the potential rewards, right the bad management and poor dealer relations, and address the sometimes slipshod workmanship in order to capitalize on the enormous potential of these garage entrepreneurships.

In 1976, Armas Clifford "Mike" Markkula, Jr., had been out of work for over a year. His unemployment was self-imposed and rather pleasant. Markkula had done well for himself during his tenure with two of the most successful chip manufacturers in the country, Fairchild and Intel, largely because he was uniquely suited to the work. Although a trained electrical engineer who understood the possibilities of the microprocessor, at Intel he worked in the marketing department where he was considered a wizard at the job. Beyond the excitement of being around emerging technology, Markkula enjoyed forging ahead with a large company in a competitive environment.

Outside the hobbyist community, few people understood the potential of microprocessor-based technology as well as Mike Markkula did. With his rare combination of business savvy and engineering background, Markkula was just the person microcomputer companies needed to promote their technology, if any could afford him.

In 1975, Mike Markkula retired from Intel. Although Markkula was only in his early thirties, Intel stock options had made him a millionaire, and financially he didn't need to work any longer. He was a dedicated family man and wanted to spend more time at home. He planned a leisurely existence, and he convinced himself that after the breakneck pace of life in the semiconductor industry, he could be happy learning to play the guitar and going skiing at his cabin near Lake Tahoe. Friends may have observed that his investments in wildcat oil wells did not bespeak a full commitment to the idle life, but Markkula was adamant about being out of the rat race for good.

In October 1976, at Don Valentine's suggestion, Markkula visited Jobs's garage, and he liked what he saw. It made sense to provide computing power to individuals in the home and workplace. When Markkula offered to help the pair draw up a business plan, he told himself he wasn't violating his resolve to stay retired—he was just giving advice to two sharp kids. He was doing it more for pleasure than business, he rationalized, as Jobs and Woz couldn't afford to pay him what a consultant with his experience would normally get.

Within a few months, Markkula, abandoning his determination to stay retired, decided to throw in with these two kids. He assessed Jobs and Woz's equity in the company at about $5,000. He put up a considerably larger chunk of money himself, promising Apple up to $250,000 of his own money, and then investing $92,000 to buy himself a one-third interest in the company. Jobs and Woz were stunned by Markkula's assurance that they each owned a third of a nearly $300,000 company.

Why did this 34-year-old retired executive throw in his lot with two long-haired novices who had no collateral except their ingenuity, ambition, and creative ideas? Even Markkula couldn't answer the question completely, but by this time he had become convinced that Apple could make the Fortune 500 list in less than five years, a feat never before accomplished. He was hooked on the notion that this could happen.

The first decision Markkula made was to keep the name Apple. From a marketing standpoint, he recognized the simple advantage of being first in the phone book. He also believed that the word *apple,* unlike the word *computer,* had a positive connotation. "Very few people don't like apples," he said. Furthermore, he liked the incongruous pairing of the words *apple* and *computer,* and believed it would be good for name recognition.

Thereafter, Markkula set out to turn Apple into a real company. He helped Jobs with the business plan and obtained a line of credit for Apple at the Bank of America. He told Woz and Jobs frankly that neither of them had the experience to run a company and hired a president. Michael Scott, nicknamed Scotty, was a seasoned executive who had worked for Markkula in product marketing at Fairchild. He was accustomed to a traditional business environment, and for this reason would later have problems with what he perceived as Woz's lack of professionalism. He had no problem with Woz's ability, however.

The Evangelist

*Woz was fortunate to hook up
with an evangelist.*

REGIS MCKENNA
Head of Apple's first advertising agency

B Y THE FALL OF 1976, WOZ HAD ALREADY MADE PROGRESS ON THE design of his new computer. The Apple II would embody all the engineering savvy he could bring to it. The Apple II would be the embodiment of Steve Wozniak's dream computer, one he would like to own himself. He had made it considerably faster than the Apple I. There was a clever trick he wanted to try that would give the machine a color display, too.

Wozniak was skittish about forming a company from the start, and now he was worried about working full time for it. He had always enjoyed his job at Hewlett-Packard. HP was legendary among engineers for its commitment to quality design. It seemed crazy to give up a job at HP. Woz had even shown his Apple I design to the managers at Hewlett-Packard with the hope that he could convince the company to build it. But they told him that the Apple was not a viable product for HP. HP eventually gave Woz a release that permitted him to build the machine on his own. In addition, Wozniak made two attempts to join computer development projects at HP—the project that eventually developed into the HP 75 computer and a handheld BASIC machine— and, lacking the experience and the academic credentials of many HP employees, was turned down for both.

Wozniak was unarguably an outstanding engineer, but he could only work on projects that interested him, and then only for as long as they interested him. Jobs understood his friend's genius better than anyone. He constantly urged Woz on, and the pressure sometimes led to arguments.

Woz had no interest in designing the connector for hooking the computer up to the television set, nor did he want to design the power supply. Both devices required skill in analog electronics, which differed from the relatively clean digital electronics that Woz and Jobs were used to working with. The internal circuitry of a computer basically comes down to its being on or off, at 1 or 0. To computer engineers, you either have power or you don't. To design a power supply or send a signal to a television set, an engineer has to consider voltage levels and interference effects, among other things. Woz didn't know or care about these things.

Jobs turned to Al Alcorn, one of his former superiors at Atari, for help. Alcorn suggested that Jobs talk to Rod Holt, a sharp analog engineer at Atari. When Jobs phoned Holt in the fall of 1976, Holt was feeling dissatisfied with his position at Atari. "I was a second-string quarterback," he later said. Holt thought he had been hired just in case his manager, whose hobby was racing motorcycles, got hurt. Holt was notably different from Wozniak and Jobs, except for his love of electronics. For one thing, he had a daughter older than Steve Jobs. And he had trouble understanding the West Coast culture that shaped Apple's founders.

Holt told Jobs that as an Atari engineer, he felt helping Apple represented an obvious conflict of interest. Besides, he added, he was expensive. His services ran at least $200 a day. But that didn't worry Jobs. "We can afford you," Jobs said. "Absolutely." Holt liked the brash young entrepreneur at once. Regarding the conflict of interest, Jobs told him to check with his boss to see if it would be all right. "Steve is a nice guy. Help the kids out," Holt recalled his boss Al Alcorn telling him.

Holt started working evenings at Atari on the television interface and the power supply, concentrating especially on the latter. He also persuaded Jobs not to challenge FCC regulations by trying to build an interface for a television set. Holt knew that the FCC would hassle them over the interface issue. Jobs was frustrated at first, but then hit on a clever way out of the problem. He made it a simple task for others to design the modulators to link the computer to a television set. If laws were broken or regulations bent, the malefactor wouldn't be Apple—at least not technically—it would be the consumer.

All his life, it seemed that Jobs had gotten what he wanted. He had landed himself a job at HP—from one of the founders—when he was 13, had lived at Reed College for free, and had pulled in Markkula. Jobs could be extremely persuasive and had a gift for making people believe in his dreams. Rod Holt could have named his job back in the Midwest, and he was also building a reputation in the Valley. But instead, he went to work for Apple.

After a few months, Holt came on full time. He handled all kinds of tasks at Apple. When no one else had the technical or managerial expertise to solve a problem, Holt took care of it. "I was the everything-else guy," he said. As the company began growing faster than even Markkula had hoped, Holt found that he was overseeing the quality control department, the service department, the production engineering department, and the documentation department. Things got so stressful that Holt threatened to resign several times. But Apple was just too interesting to leave.

Rod Holt was not the first employee Woz and Jobs hired. That honor went to Bill Fernandez, the friend who had introduced them to each other several years earlier. As a formality, Jobs tested Fernandez with a series of questions about digital electronics before officially hiring him to manufacture Apple I computers. Fernandez practiced the Bahai faith and he and Jobs spent many hours discussing religion in Jobs's garage that doubled as their workshop.

Other early employees included high-school students Chris Espinosa and Randy Wigginton, Woz's friends from the Homebrew meetings. After the meetings, the trio routinely headed to Woz's house to continue discussing ways to improve the capabilities of the Apple I to turn it into something more powerful.

Espinosa and Wigginton were hobbyists, but of a different sort than either Jobs or Woz. They had no special expertise in designing machines. Instead, they enjoyed writing programs. Whenever Woz brought the Apple I to the Homebrew meetings, Espinosa and Wiggin-ton would knock off some programs on the spot in order to demon-strate the machine to club members. Woz had built a working prototype of the Apple II by August of 1976, and loaned one to Espinosa, who began developing games and demonstration software for the computer. By actually using the new computer, the self-confident teenager was able to suggest ways to better its design.

Espinosa also spent a lot of time at Paul Terrell's Byte Shop. He recalled that a "tall, scraggly looking guy would come in every day and say, 'We got a new version of the BASIC!'" That was how Espinosa met Steve Jobs. Later, at one of the few Homebrew meetings that he attended, Jobs noticed a demo program running on the Apple I. He asked Espinosa, "Did you do that?" Shortly thereafter, Espinosa was working for Apple.

Espinosa spent Christmas vacation of his sophomore year in high school in Jobs's garage, helping debug the BASIC that would be sold with the Apple II. Jobs took him under his wing, although Espinosa's early impression of Jobs was as something other than a paternal figure. "I thought he seemed dangerous," Espinosa said about Jobs. "Quiet, enigmatic, almost sullen, a fierce look in his eyes. His powers of per-suasion are something to be reckoned with. I always had this feeling that he was shaping me."

Jobs then faced the biggest obstacle thus far to his legendary powers of persuasion. By this time, Markkula had agreed to join Jobs and Woz. The final hurdle was convincing Woz to leave his job at Hewlett-Packard to work full time for Apple. Markkula would have it no other way.

Woz wasn't sure he wanted to make the move. Jobs was panicking. All of his carefully wrought plans depended on Woz. Then, one day in October 1976, Woz said that he would not leave his great job at HP, and that his decision was final. "Steve went into fits and started cry-ing," said Woz. Moments later, Jobs pulled himself together and began lobbying with Woz's friends, having them call Woz to persuade him to change his mind.

Woz was afraid that designing computers full time would be drudgery, unlike the efforts he put into designing the Apple I and II.

Somehow his friends convinced him otherwise, and he left his job at HP to join Apple full time. It was a brave move given that Woz imagined that they would, at best, sell no more than a thousand Apple II computers. But Jobs had an entirely different vision and aggressively set out to get people who could help him achieve it—people such as Regis McKenna, owner of one of the most successful public relations and advertising firms in Silicon Valley.

Jobs had placed an ad in the computer magazine *Interface Age*. He'd also seen the Intel ads in various electronics magazines and was impressed enough to call the semiconductor company and ask who had done them. He was given McKenna's name. Jobs wanted the best for Apple, and, deciding that McKenna was the best, set about getting his firm to handle Apple's PR.

McKenna's ads had been very good for Intel, as well as for McKenna himself, whose office decor spelled success. Customarily dressed in a natty suit, McKenna sat behind a large desk backed by photographs of his favorite Intel ads. He spoke softly and reflectively, in sharp contrast to the unkempt and pushy kid who walked into his office one afternoon in cutoffs, sandals, and what McKenna called a "Ho Chi Minh beard," after the former Vietnamese leader. McKenna was accustomed to taking start-up companies as clients, so Jobs's garb didn't put him off. "Inventions come from individuals," he reminded himself, "not from companies," and this Jobs was certainly an individual.

At first, McKenna turned the offer down. But Jobs was remarkably convincing. "I don't deny that Woz designed a good machine," said McKenna. "But that machine would be sitting in hobby shops today were it not for Steve Jobs. Woz was fortunate to hook up with an evangelist."

McKenna eventually succumbed to Jobs's persistence, and his agency became Apple's PR firm. The agency immediately made two major moves.

The first was its logo—a rainbow-striped apple with a bite taken out of it. The logo was designed by Rob Janov and has served as the company's trademark ever since. From a printing standpoint, there was some initial fear that the multiple colors would run together. Jobs vetoed the addition of lines to separate the colors, making the cost of printing the logo very high. Apple president Michael Scott called it "the most expensive bloody logo ever designed." But when the first foil labels arrived for the Apple II, everyone loved the look of the design. Jobs made one change: he rearranged the order of the colors to put the darker shades at the bottom. A later president of Apple products, Jean-Louis Gassée, would say that the logo was perfect for Apple: "It is the symbol of lust and knowledge, bitten into, all crossed with the colors of the rainbow in the wrong order . . . lust, knowledge, hope, and anarchy."

McKenna also decided to run a full-color ad in *Playboy* magazine. It was a bold, expensive grab for publicity. A cheaper ad in *Byte* would have reached virtually all the microcomputer buyers of that time, and *Playboy* seemed an off-the-wall choice given that there were no demographic studies to support it. "It was done to get national attention," said McKenna, "and to popularize the idea of low-cost computers." Other companies had been selling microcomputers for two years, but no one had yet tried to capture the public's imagination in this way. Apple's publicity campaign resulted in follow-up articles in national magazines, and not just about Apple, but about small computers in general.

Jobs's persistence persuaded McKenna to buy into the Apple dream as it had with Woz, Markkula, and Holt. Woz invented the machine, Markkula had the business sense, McKenna provided the marketing talent, Scotty ran the shop, and Holt was the everything-else guy, but the pushy kid with the scraggly beard was the driving force behind it all.

By February 1977, Apple Computer had established its first office in two large rooms a few miles from Homestead High School in Cupertino. Desks were hauled in and work benches were trundled over from Jobs's garage. The night before they were to begin working in their new suite, Woz, Jobs, Wigginton, and Espinosa scattered around the 2000-square-foot office playing telephone games, with each trying to buzz one of the other extensions first. It all felt like play. It was hard to imagine that they were starting a real business. "We never thought that we'd grow up to be battling one-on-one with IBM," said Espinosa.

The young company faced a more modest challenge than tackling IBM: to finish the Apple II design in time for Jim Warren's first West Coast Computer Faire in April and get it ready for production shortly thereafter. Markkula was already signing up distributors nationwide, many of whom were eager to work with a company that would give them greater freedom than microcomputer manufacturer MITS had, as well as provide functional products.

Steve Wozniak is justly credited with the technical design of the Apple I and Apple II. Nevertheless, an essential contribution to making the Apple II a commercial success came from Jobs. Most early microcomputers were far from being attractive consumer fare. They were typically drab and ugly metal boxes. Steve Jobs decided to spruce up the look of the product. He covered the device with a lightweight beige plastic case that melded the keyboard and computer together in a modular design. Woz could design an efficient computer, but he cheerfully admitted that he didn't care whether or not wires were left dangling out of it. Jobs realized that the Apple had to look presentable to better the competition.

It took a gargantuan effort to ready the Apple II for the West Coast Computer Faire. Woz worked day and night, as was his modus operandi, until it was done. Jobs made sure that nobody would miss it. He arranged to have the biggest and most elegant booth at the show. He brought in a large projection screen to demonstrate programs and placed Apple II computers on either side of the booth. Jobs, Mike Scott, Chris Espinosa, and Randy Wigginton manned the booth while Mike Markkula toured the auditorium signing up dealers for the company. Woz walked around checking out other machines. All in all, the Computer Faire was a big success for Apple. Everyone seemed to like the Apple II, although *Computer Lib* author Ted Nelson complained that it displayed only uppercase letters.

Woz couldn't resist playing one of his practical jokes. He decided to advertise a product that did not exist. To avoid being called on it, he had to fake a product from a company that wasn't at the show. Conveniently, MITS was absent. With the help of Randy Wigginton, Woz whipped up a brochure on the "Zaltair," supposedly an enhanced Altair computer.

"Imagine a dream machine. Imagine the computer surprise of the century, here today. Imagine BAZIC in ROM, the most complete and powerful language ever developed," the fake advertisement purred. Woz was satirizing the marketing hype that he'd learned from Jobs. The brochure gushed on, "A computer engineer's dream, all electronics are on a single PC card, even the 18-slot motherboard. And what a motherboard. . . ." On the back of the brochure was a mock performance chart comparing the Zaltair to other microcomputers—including the Apple I. Jobs, who knew nothing of the joke, picked up one of the brochures and read it in dismay. But after a quick, nervous scan of the performance chart, he looked relieved. "Hey," he said, "We came out okay on this."

Magic Times

*After the West Coast Computer Faire,
we had a sense of exhilaration for
having pulled off something so well, not
just for Apple, but for the whole
computer movement.*

CHRIS ESPINOSA
Apple Employee No. 8

IN 1977, APPLE COULD DO NO WRONG. IT WAS AN ENCHANTED TIME FOR the tiny company, whose principals radiated an innocent confidence. Hobbyists praised Woz's design, dealers clambered for the new computer, and investors were itching to sink money into the company.

Right away, Woz and Jobs offered work to their friends in the Valley. Chris Espinosa and Randy Wigginton frequently came by the Apple offices after school to help develop software for the new machine. They were paid a modest hourly wage, which was fine with them because they mostly did it for fun. They enjoyed working with Woz because he was their technical mentor, an "extremely brilliant" computer genius, according to Wigginton.

In May, Woz reviewed Wigginton's performance to see if he deserved a raise. His work was fine, but Woz—ever the stern taskmaster—demanded more. Woz was irritated that he had to walk around the block to get to a nearby 7-Eleven because a large fence blocked direct access to the store. If Wigginton would remove a large board from beneath a section of the fence, Woz could pass under it and Wigginton would get his raise. The next day Woz found the board on his desk, and Wigginton started earning $3.50 an hour.

Apple employee Chris Espinosa was in his first semester at Homestead High. Every Tuesday and Thursday he drove to the Apple offices on his moped, purchased with Apple earnings, and because he wasn't old enough to drive a car without a license. There he supervised the twice-weekly public demonstrations of the Apple II. Once when representatives of the Bank of America dropped by, Espinosa acted quickly to remove "OH SHIT" from Woz's implementation of the *Breakout* game and replace it with "THAT'S TERRIBLE." The scholarly Espinosa had an air of responsibility that impressed everyone given his youth. Jobs and Markkula were thankful that he kept the visitors engaged so that they could attend to the more important task of signing up new dealers. "For about six months, I was the sole means by which people off the street in the Bay Area would learn about Apple Computer," Espinosa said.

There were indications that the youthful Apple staff was trying to grow up. Markkula and Scott were growing tired of the crowd that frequently dropped in to check out Woz's progress. Sometimes they did more than watch: Allen Baum, a close friend of Wozniak's from Hewlett-Packard, contributed important design ideas. But if they could contribute ideas, they could just as easily swipe them. Mike Scott finally decreed that some confidentiality was necessary. He felt it was his job to instill a professional attitude at Apple. Baum visited less and less frequently as the year progressed. Scotty recognized some young talent, however, and he convinced young Randy Wigginton to stay involved by offering to have Apple pay for his college education.

Mike Scott was a complex individual who was vital to Apple's success. Unlike the smooth, dapper Mike Markkula, he was down-to-earth, boisterous, frank, and not one to hide his feelings, whether positive or negative. He liked to stroll through the company and chat with employees, often using maritime metaphors. He saw himself as a captain of a ship, wheel in hand at the helm. "Welcome aboard," he would say to a new employee. When Scotty was happy, those around him were happy. According to Rod Holt, Scotty had a slush fund for special expenses, part of which paid for an enormous hot air balloon and a sail for Holt's yacht, each sporting the Apple logo. One Christmas, he walked around the company handing out presents dressed in a Santa Claus suit. Then again, if Scott was displeased with your performance, he let you know it.

Scott quickly grew impatient when projects were delayed. And at least once, Woz's generosity to his friends caused friction with Scotty, who was less tolerant than Markkula of eccentricity in the corporate environment. He couldn't understand Wozniak's irregular work habits, which swung from total dedication to headstrong avoidance, depending on his interest in the task at hand. Scotty also objected to some of Woz's friends—John Draper, for example (a.k.a., the notorious "phone phreak" Captain Crunch).

In the fall of 1977, Draper was visiting Woz at Apple and expressed interest in helping design a digital telephone card for the Apple II. No one understood telephone technology better than Captain Crunch. Scott had granted Woz a separate office in which to work, hoping that it might encourage his creativity, and soon John Draper was working there, too. But many of the other employees disliked Draper. He was an awkward young man with strange interests, and he made them feel uncomfortable.

Draper and Woz constructed a device that could, among other things, dial numbers automatically and function much like a telephone answering machine. But Draper also built a blue-box capability into the card. The cards were dangerously powerful. According to Espinosa, a network of a dozen Apples equipped with Draper's cards could bring down the nation's entire phone system. When Scott learned that the device could be used illegally, he stalked the Apple offices in a rage.

The phone card didn't last long after that, although, without Draper's knowledge, modifications were being designed into the card by other engineers to nullify most of its phone phreak capabilities. According to one Apple board member, Scott considered firing Woz after that. It wasn't inconceivable that Scott would have made one of the company's founders walk the plank. "Scotty is the only guy that would dare fire me," said Woz. "That guy could do anything." Rod Holt agreed: "Scotty could fire anybody. All he needed was a single excuse. When John Draper was later arrested for phone phreaking, he had an Apple computer with him. The machine was confiscated, and Scotty again cursed Woz.

At the same time Woz hired Draper, Scotty recruited two other key employees. In August 1977, Gene Carter became Apple's sales manager and Wendell Sander came on board to work under Rod Holt.

An electrical engineer with a Ph.D. from Iowa State University, Sander had years of experience in the semiconductor field. But it wasn't his high-technology experience that convinced Apple to hire him.

Sander had bought an Apple I a year earlier and was working on a version of a *Star Trek* game for his teenage children to play. In the course of writing the program, he had met Steve Jobs while chasing down updated versions of the integer BASIC programming language. Jobs supplied him with the updates and in the process learned about the *Star Trek* program. When Jobs was getting ready to ship the first Apple IIs, he invited Sander to the company's office and asked him to rework the program to run on the new machine. Sander met with Mike Markkula and decided that he wanted to work for the young company. After he was hired, he took a loan on his San Jose home in order to buy Apple stock. Woz, Rod Holt, and Sander made up the core of Apple's engineering department for the remainder of 1977.

During 1977 and 1978, Woz worked on a number of accessory products that were necessary to keep Apple on stable ground during its formative years. To make the Apple II appealing to customers outside the hobbyist realm, add-on peripherals were needed. These add-on devices enabled the machine to work with different kinds of printers and connect with modems used to transfer information from one machine to another over a telephone line.

Thanks to its small size and well-oiled internal mechanism, the company could choose and build new products more easily than many other firms. Among the most important of these items were *peripheral cards:* printer cards, serial cards, communications cards, and ROM cards. Woz worked on developing most of these, with Wendell Sander and Rod Holt contributing their share of the development duties.

Business was promising. More and more dealers signed on, and Apple began manufacturing the Apple II. By the end of 1977, the company was making a profit and doubling production every three to four months. An article in *Byte* helped to further popularize the Apple II. Mike Markkula had also attracted investment capital from the successful New York–based firm of Venrock Associates, which was formed by the Rockefeller family to invest in high-tech enterprises. Venrock's Arthur Rock became a member of Apple's board of directors.

By year's end, the company moved into a larger office on nearby Bandley Drive in Cupertino. The structure felt huge, and gave the Apple employees a feeling that the firm was going to become something big. They were right. Apple soon outgrew the building and added another on the same street. Perhaps the most significant accomplishment of this period occurred during Woz's 1977 Christmas vacation.

The Disk

It was a brilliant execution by Woz.

ROD HOLT
Early Apple employee

BEFORE THE END OF 1977, WOZ HAD STARTED WORKING ON HIS NEXT big project. The idea arose from a December executive board meeting attended by Markkula, Scott, Holt, Jobs, and Woz. At the meeting, Markkula stepped forward and wrote on a board a list of goals for the company. At the top of the list, Woz saw the words *floppy disk.* "I don't know how floppy disks work," Woz thought.

Woz knew Markkula was right in his priorities. Cassette tape storage of data was utterly unreliable and dealers were constantly complaining about it. Markkula had decided that disk drives were essential about the time he and Randy Wigginton were writing a checkbook program that Markkula thought the Apple needed. Markkula was fed up with the laborious task of reading data off cassette tapes and realized how much a floppy disk drive would facilitate the use of his program. He told Woz that he wanted the disk drive ready for the Consumer Electronics Show that Apple was scheduled to attend in January.

Markkula knew that by issuing the edict he was in essence taking away Woz's Christmas vacation. It was unreasonable to expect anyone to devise a functioning disk drive in a month. But this was the kind of challenge Woz thrived on. No one had to tell him to work long hours over the vacation. Woz wasn't ignorant about disk drives, even though he'd never read a book on the subject or worked on disk drives professionally. While at Hewlett-Packard, he had perused a manual from Shugart, the Silicon Valley disk drive manufacturer. Just for fun, Woz designed a circuit that would do much of what the Shugart manual said was needed to control a disk drive. Woz didn't know how computers actually controlled drives, but his method seemed to him to be reasonably simple and clever.

When Markkula challenged Woz to put a disk drive on the Apple, he remembered that disk drive circuit and began seriously considering its feasibility. He examined how other computers—including those from IBM—controlled drives. He also dissected disk drives—particularly the ones produced by North Star. After reading the North Star manual, Woz knew just how clever his design was—his circuit could do what theirs did, and more.

But Wozniak's coming up with a circuit solved only part of the disk control problem. The puzzle had other pieces—such as how to handle synchronization. A disk drive presents tricky problems with timing. Somehow the software has to keep track of where the data is while the disk is spinning. IBM's technique for dealing with timing involved complex circuitry, which Woz studied until he fully understood it. The circuitry was unnecessary, he figured, if he could alter the way in which the data were written to the disk. For the Apple disk drive, he decided to eliminate the synchronization circuitry completely. The drive would synchronize itself automatically with no hardware circuitry at all.

This "self-sync" technique scored a point against IBM: Woz gloated over the fact that the mammoth corporation lacked the flexibility to come up with such an unlikely solution. He also knew that no matter what economies of scale IBM built into its product, *no* circuitry is still less expensive than some.

Wozniak could now write the software to *read from* and *write to* the floppy disk. At this point, he called in Randy Wigginton to help. Woz needed a *formatter,* a program that could write a form of "nondata" to the disk, essentially wiping it clean to set it up for reuse. Woz gave Wigginton just the essential instructions, such as how to make the drive motor move via software. Wigginton took it from there.

Woz and Wigginton worked day and night throughout December, including a 10-hour day on Christmas. They knew they couldn't get a complete disk-operating system running for the show, so they spent time developing a demo operating system. They wanted to be able to type in single-letter filenames and read files stored in fixed locations on the disk. When they left for the Consumer Electronics Show in Las Vegas, they weren't even able to do something that simple.

The Consumer Electronics Show was not a hobby computer show. Many of the exhibitors were established consumer electronics firms that manufactured stereo equipment and calculators. The buyers of such items were general consumers, not electronics hobbyists. But Markkula wanted Apple to pursue a broader market, and he regarded this show as vital for Apple's growth. For Woz and Wigginton, it was an adventure outside time.

Wigginton and Woz arrived in Las Vegas the evening before the event. They helped set up the booth that night and went back to work on the drive and the demo program. They planned to have it done when the show opened in the morning even if they had to go without sleep. Staying up all night is no novelty in Las Vegas, and that's what they did, taking periodic breaks from programming to inspect the craps tables. Wigginton, 17, was elated when he won $35 at craps, but a little later back in the room, his spirits were dashed when he accidentally erased a disk they had been working on. Woz patiently helped him reconstruct all the information. They tried to take a nap at 7:30 that morning, but both were too keyed up.

Despite the snafus, the demo went well. After the show, Woz, together with Rod Holt, completed work on the disk drive so that it met Woz's expectations as to what it could realistically accomplish. Normally the layout work was sent to a contracting firm, but the contractor was busy and Woz wasn't. So, Woz himself laid out the circuit board that was to control the drive. He worked on it every night until 2 A.M. for two weeks.

When Woz was finished, he saw a way to cut down on *feed-throughs*—signal lines crossing on the board—by moving a connector. The improvement meant redoing the entire layout, but this time he completed the task in less than 24 hours. He then saw a way to eliminate one more feed-through by reversing the order of the bits of data transmitted by the board. So he laid out the board again. The final design was generally recognized as brilliant by computer engineers and beautiful by engineering aesthetics. Woz later said, "It's something you can only do if you're the engineer and the PC board layout person yourself. That was an artistic layout. The board has virtually no feedthroughs."

The disk drive, which Apple began shipping in June 1978, was vital to the company's success, second only to the computer itself in importance. The drive made possible the development of robust software such as word processors and database packages. Like most early successes at Apple, it represented an enormous amount of unconstrained individual effort, as did the early achievements of the Altair and the Sol. But at Apple, the hobbyist spirit was being channeled by a few sharp executives who understood how to build a company.

The Apple II desperately needed a good technical reference manual. When the company started shipping the computer in 1977, the instruction manual wasn't much better than any other documentation in the industry, that is, it was unspeakably bad. Documentation was the last thing a microcomputer company worried about in 1977. Customers were still mostly hobbyists and would tolerate abominable documentation because they welcomed the challenge of assembling and troubleshooting their machines. But Apple couldn't afford to neglect documentation if it wanted to bring a broader spectrum of consumers into personal computing.

Apple lured Jef Raskin from a writing job at *Dr. Dobb's Journal* to run the company's documentation effort. Raskin encouraged Chris Espinosa, who had planned on attending college full time in the fall, to write something that would explain the Apple computer to its users.

The manual's genesis is a true hobbyist's story. Espinosa had left his high-school job at Apple to go to college and was a freshman living in the dorms at Cal Berkeley—Lee Felsenstein and Bob Marsh's alma mater—when he began work on a manual that would explain, in a clear and organized fashion, the technical details of the Apple II. Espinosa wasn't quite finished with it when he had to leave his dorm at the end of the term. For a week, he slept in parks and in the campus computer rooms, living out of his backpack and working 18-hour days to complete the manual. He typeset it on university equipment and turned it in to Apple.

The Red Book, as the manual came to be known, provided the kind of information that mattered to people who wanted to develop software or add-on products for the Apple II; it was a great success and unquestionably aided in Apple's growth. It would be hard to overestimate the contribution made to Apple by outsiders and such third-party developers as Espinosa, who wasn't employed by Apple when he wrote the Red Book.

Apple was definitely on to something, but if it was going to continue to grow, it had to create a perceived need for personal computers within the buying public. People had to believe that the machines served a practical purpose. Gary Kildall's CP/M operating system and the subsequent development of business applications software helped some companies, such as Vector Graphic, sell machines in quantity. But Apple's operating system was different from CP/M, and the Apple machines needed their own software.

Several programmers started writing games and business applications for the Apple. And although some of them were impressive, none were good enough to induce people to buy the computer just to use the program. That is, not until VisiCalc.

VisiCalc

*Without VisiCalc, things would have
been tougher for Apple. But without
Apple, things would have been tougher
for VisiCalc.*

DANIEL FYLSTRA
Coinventor of VisiCalc

DANIEL FYLSTRA WAS A CALIFORNIAN WHO HAD GONE EAST TO STUDY
computers and electronics at MIT. As an associate editor for *Byte*
magazine in its early days, he had been impressed with the chess program designed by Peter Jennings. Soon after reviewing the program in
Byte, Fylstra left for Europe to work as an engineer in the European
Space Agency. He quickly grew frustrated with management problems
in the intragovernmental bureaucracy and decided to return to the
States to get an MBA degree from Harvard Business School. (Also on
the Harvard campus at the time was a freshman from Washington
State named Bill Gates.)

By the time Fylstra received his MBA in 1978, he had already started
a small software marketing company, called Personal Software, whose
chief product was Jennings's *MicroChess.* By this time, Tandy Corporation had entered the microcomputer field, and the first version of the
program Fylstra sold ran on the TRS-80 Model I. Fylstra liked the way
graphics programming worked on the Apple II, and soon he was also
offering *MicroChess* for the Apple II.

Meanwhile, another Harvard MBA candidate, a quiet and unassum-
ing student named Dan Bricklin, conceived an idea for a computer program to do financial forecasting. He thought it would be especially

useful in real estate transactions. Bricklin had been a software engineer with DEC and had worked on its first word processing system. He thought he could sell his program to users of DEC minicomputers, or perhaps even sell it in the new microcomputer market.

Bricklin approached a Harvard finance professor with the idea. The academician ridiculed Bricklin. Another financial forecasting program? He better not expect to be carried down Wall Street on the shoulders of business financiers. The professor added that Bricklin may want to talk to an ex-student of his, Dan Fylstra, who had researched the market for personal computer software. The professor also gave Bricklin the same warning he'd once given to Fylstra: because of the availability of time-sharing systems, microcomputer software would never sell, and the venture was a complete waste of time.

Fylstra ended up liking Bricklin's idea for the financial forecasting program. The only machine he had available at the time was an Apple. He loaned it to Bricklin, who began designing the program with a friend of his, Bob Frankston. Something of a mathematics genius, Frankston had been involved with computers since he was 13. And he had done some programming for Fylstra's company, converting a bridge game program to run on the Apple II.

Shortly thereafter, Bricklin and Frankston founded a company, Software Arts, and started in on coding the financial analysis program. Throughout the winter, Frankston worked on the program at night in an attic office, and during the day consulted with his partner on his progress. Occasionally the two would get together with Dan Fylstra to dream of the lucrative future that would soon be theirs.

A prototype of the program was ready by the spring of 1979. Bricklin and Frankston called it VisiCalc, shorthand for "visible calculations." VisiCalc was a novelty in computer software. Nothing like it existed on any computer, large or small, and in fact there were reasons why such a program had not been developed for mainframe computers. In many ways, VisiCalc was a purely personal computer program. It kept track of tabular data, such as financial spreadsheets, using the computer's screen like a window through which a large table of data was viewed. The "window" could slide across a table, displaying different parts of it.

The VisiCalc program simulated paper-and-pencil operations very well, but also went dramatically beyond that. Data entered in rows and columns in a table could be interrelated so that changing one value in the table caused other values to change correspondingly. This "what-if" capability made VisiCalc very appealing: one could enter budget figures, for instance, and see at once what would happen to the other values if one particular value were changed by a certain amount.

When Bricklin and Fylstra began showing the product around, not everyone responded as enthusiastically as they had expected. Fylstra recalls demonstrating VisiCalc to Apple chairman Mike Markkula, who was unimpressed and proceeded to show Fylstra his own checkbook-balancing program. But when VisiCalc was released through Personal Software in October of 1979, it was an immediate success. By this time, Fylstra had moved his company to Silicon Valley.

Another early application program for the Apple was a simple word processor called EasyWriter, a program similar to Electric Pencil, written by John Draper. Eventually Draper marketed his program through Information Unlimited Software of Berkeley, California, the same company that was selling the early database management program, WHAT-SIT.

But VisiCalc was far more significant.

Fylstra asked his dealers to estimate a competitive price for VisiCalc, and he was told between $35 and $100. Initially Fylstra offered the package for $100, but it sold so fast that he quickly raised the price to $150. Serious business software for personal computers was rare, and no one was sure how to price it. Plus, VisiCalc had capabilities other business software didn't. Year after year, even as VisiCalc increased in price, the volume of sales rose dramatically. In its first release in 1979, Personal Software shipped 500 copies of VisiCalc per month. By 1981, the company was shipping 12,000 copies per month.

Not only did VisiCalc sell, but the popularity of the program also helped to sell Apple computers. During its first year, VisiCalc was available only for the Apple, and it provided a compelling reason to buy an Apple. In fact, the Apple II and VisiCalc had an impressive symbiotic relationship, and it's difficult to say which contributed more to the other. Together they did much to legitimize both the hardware and the software industries.

The Apple III
Fiasco

Committee marketing decisions—
that was the major source of all
the problems.

DAN KOTTKE
Early Apple employee

DURING APPLE'S THIRD FISCAL YEAR, WHICH ENDED ON SEPTEMBER 30, 1979, sales of the Apple II increased to 35,100 units, more than quadruple the number of the previous year. Nevertheless, the company recognized a need to develop another product soon. No one believed that the Apple II could remain a best-seller for more than another year or two.

In 1978, Apple took several steps to gear up for the challenge. Chuck Peddle was hired in the summer, although his responsibilities were as yet undefined. As the designer of both the 6502 microprocessor and the Commodore PET computer (the latter of which competed with the Apple II), he seemed like a good person to have around. Before Apple had emerged from the garage, Peddle had tried to convince Commodore to purchase the small operation, but Apple and Commodore were unable to come to terms.

Peddle's PET computer (said to stand for either Personal Electronic Transactor or Peddle's Ego Trip, but actually named after the pet rock fad of the day) was introduced at the first West Coast Computer Faire in 1977, as was the Apple II. As it turned out, the PET did not greatly influence the development of the American personal computer industry, largely because Commodore president Jack Tramiel opted to concentrate on European sales and Commodore delayed in providing a disk drive for its computer. Eventually, Apple executives failed to agree with Peddle on what role he would play at the company, and he returned to Commodore at the end of 1978.

By that time, Tom Whitney, Woz's old boss at Hewlett-Packard, was hired to supervise and enlarge the engineering department in order to begin designing new products.

In late 1978, several new computer projects were started. The first, an enhanced version of the Apple II with custom chips, was code-named Annie. Woz worked with another engineer on it but didn't complete the project. Moreover, he didn't pursue it with the intensity he had given to his previous computer designs or to the disk drive project. But Wozniak wasn't twiddling his thumbs either.

Apple executives discussed having Woz design a supercomputer that utilized something called *bit-sliced architecture,* which would spread the capabilities of the microprocessor over several identical chips. The chief advantages of such an architecture were speed and variable precision—that is, high-precision arithmetic scientific data and low-precision arithmetic other data. An engineering staff was put together to create this computer, code-named Lisa. The Lisa project started slowly and passed through many incarnations over several years. Eventually John Couch, a former Hewlett-Packard engineer hired by Tom Whitney, took over as project director.

Meanwhile, Wendell Sander took charge of designing the next Apple computer, the Apple III. Sander, one of Apple's most trusted employees, was asked to design a machine that would equal the success of all the other Apple products. When he commenced work on the Apple III, company executives told him that they hoped he could finish it within a year.

When Wozniak had designed the Apple II, he was free to create a machine that encompassed everything he wanted in a computer. Sander, on the other hand, had constraints from the outset that stemmed from a meeting of the executive staff, which still included Chuck Peddle. The executive staff compiled a general and somewhat vague list of guidelines, mentioning such desired items as enhanced graphics and additional memory. The few detailed concepts added to the list seemed cosmetic by comparison. For instance, executives wanted the machine to be capable of displaying 80 columns, rather than 40, and upper- and lowercase characters onscreen.

Sander was told that the new machine should be able to run software designed for the Apple II. Although this compatibility was desirable considering the large pool of software being developed for the Apple II by outside programmers, it posed a problem. Designing a computer with such "backward-compatible" capabilities is not an easy task. The hardware itself determines what the software must and should do. For instance, the microprocessor chip determines the possible machine language operations, and the disk drive determines the features of the operating system software.

When hardware differs between two computers, those computers can run the same applications software only through an intermediate layer of software built into one of the machines. This added layer permits an *emulation mode*. The layer intercepts commands from the application program and translates them into corresponding commands or sequences of commands for the underlying hardware. The process is inherently inefficient, and the inefficiency is most evident in programs where timing is vital. The most critical hardware feature for emulation is the microprocessor, and Apple decided to simplify this aspect of the emulation problem by using the same processor found in the Apple II, the venerable and underpowered 6502.

The emulation layer edict that came down from the Apple executive offices was not without controversy. Apple engineers and programmers felt that emulation would limit the capabilities of the breakthrough machine they were supposed to create. They themselves wouldn't want this kind of machine. But the marketing staff saw emulation as a stimulus to sales: an existing body of software could run on the Apple III immediately, and Apple could claim it was designing a family of computers. The edict was not rescinded.

In a sense, emulation boxed Sander in by limiting his creativity. The most important decision in the design of a computer—selection of a microprocessor—had been made by others. When Chuck Peddle designed the 6502, he hadn't even intended it to be used as the central processor in a computer. Apple considered adding an additional processor, with some capacity to switch from one to the other, but a dual-processor machine would have been too expensive. Sander wasn't one to protest. He liked designing computers, and he uncomplainingly set out to implement the guidelines given to him.

Dan Kottke worked as Sander's technician on the project. Each day, Sander would hand Kottke a drawing of a new part of the computer. Kottke would then copy over the schematic to make it more legible, slap on his stereo headphones, and wire-wrap the computer to music. Within a few months, they had a working prototype of the main board.

Around that time, Apple assembled a software team to design an operating system and a few applications for the new computer. Management wanted the Apple III to have a better operating system than the simple one Woz had created for the Apple II. Indeed, the Apple III required a more complex system to handle its extra memory.

Although the 6502 microprocessor could normally handle only 64 kilobytes (K) of memory, Sander was sidestepping that limitation by a technique known as *bank switching*. The computer would have several banks of 64K, and the operating system would keep track of which bank was currently active and what information was in each bank. The operating system could then move from bank to bank as necessary. The microprocessor would behave as though the machine had only 64K, but the applications software would run as though the machine were handling 128K or 256K directly.

Sander labored on the Apple III throughout 1979, and discovered that the emulation requirement also limited the extent to which he could improve the new computer's graphics. In the Apple II, a chunk of memory was reserved for the bits and bytes representing the colors of pixels on the screen. Apple II software accessed this graphics screen map whenever it needed to update the screen with new colored lines and pictures. The Apple III needed to have the same map, in the same size, at the same location in memory, and with the same means of access. This need precluded many possibilities for enhancing graphics on the Apple III.

Woz occasionally checked in with Sander on the project, but he trusted his colleague who he called "an incredible engineer" to get the job done without his interference. Nevertheless, Woz later complained about the emulation software. It didn't adequately emulate the II, he felt. "Apple claims they've got it and they don't," he said.

Because no project had completely captured his attention, Woz was in a joking mood. One day Woz sneaked into a programmer's cubicle and placed a mouse inside his computer. When the programmer returned, it took him more than a few minutes to figure out why his Apple was squeaking.

Delays in the Apple III were soon causing concern in the marketing department. The young company was beginning to feel growing pains at last. When Apple was formed, the Apple II was already near completion. The Apple III was the first computer that Apple—as a company—had built from scratch. The Apple III was also the first Apple not built by Steve Wozniak in pursuit of his personal dream machine. Instead the Apple III was a bit of a hodgepodge, pasted together by many hands and designed by committee. And, as is typical of anything created by committee, the various members weren't completely happy with the results.

Moreover, the pressure put on the Apple III project group for a swift completion probably wasn't even necessary. Although new companies were entering the personal computer market, Apple had overtaken Radio Shack to become the leading personal computer company. In 1980, Apple II sales doubled to more than 78,000 units. Nevertheless, the marketing people were worried and pushed for the release of the Apple III.

Although he felt the curtain was being raised on the Apple III a bit prematurely, Sander consented to introduce the new machine at the National Computer Conference in Anaheim, California, in May 1980. With a few functioning prototypes and the operating system software somewhat in working order, Sander thought they may be able to pull it off.

For a time, it seemed the saga of glamour and riches would continue to unfold at Apple. At the computer conference, the Apple III was well received by both the industry and the press. In addition to unveiling its new computer, Apple also announced the new software it intended to have ready by the time the machine shipped a few months later—a word processor, a spreadsheet program, an enhanced BASIC, and a sophisticated operating system. The marketing plan called for the Apple III to be portrayed as a serious computer that could be used in professional offices. The machine seemed likely to succeed.

A few months later, continuing to ride the tide of acclaim, Apple announced its first public stock offering. *The Wall Street Journal* wrote, "Not since Eve has an apple posed such temptation."

When Apple was first formed, Mike Markkula dreamed of building the largest privately held company in the nation, a company fully owned by its employees. What he didn't foresee at the time was the explosive growth of the personal computer industry. To keep pace with advances in personal computing, investment in research and development, as well as advertising and marketing, was essential. On November 7, 1980, when the company registered with the Securities and Exchange Commission for an initial public stock offering, Apple revealed that its advertising budget alone for the year had doubled to $4.5 million.

Jobs and Woz were now millionaires many times over. But the young moguls, and their cohorts at Apple, were about to pay for their hastily rushing a product to market.

After shipments of the Apple III commenced in the fall of 1980, it quickly became apparent that the machine had defects. Users brought the computers back to their dealers in droves, complaining that programs were crashing inexplicably. The dealers, in turn, started complaining to Apple.

The Apple III staff now attempted to isolate the problem, carrying out the diagnostic tests they should have done before the computer was announced, or at least before it was released. As problems with the Apple III became public knowledge, Apple slowed its promotion of the new computer and called a temporary halt to production. The staff isolated one problem: a loose connector. While working on the Apple III, Dan Kottke had noticed that on occasion the machine would die. When he lifted it a half inch off the table and let it drop, it would turn back on again. Kottke suspected a faulty connector, but he had hesitated, as a lowly technician, to voice his doubts to his superiors. Wendell Sander, the engineer, was not involved with mechanical details like connectors. It was a problem that had literally fallen through the cracks.

Another shortcoming owed to a bad break rather than faulty design. Sander had counted on having a special National Semiconductor chip to use as an internal electronic clock. National informed him late into the project that the chip would not be available. Apple considered other chips, but finally scrapped the entire idea. However, because the Apple III had been advertised as having an internal electronic clock, the price of the computer had to be lowered due to its lacking a promised feature.

The problems were identified by January 1981, but selling a defective computer for several months had hurt Apple's reputation. Until then, the company could do no wrong, and a certain amount of overconfidence led Jobs, Markkula, and Scott to release the Apple III without properly testing it first.

Black Wednesday

*I have always loved and cared for
those at Apple. That responsibility
will never end.*

MIKE SCOTT
Apple Computer's first president

O N FEBRUARY 7, 1981, WOZ CRASHED HIS FOUR-SEAT, SINGLE-ENGINE
airplane at the Scotts Valley Airport, just a short drive from Apple.
He had been practicing touch-and-go landings with two friends and his
fiancée Candi on board. Woz and his sweetheart were injured and his
friends escaped unscathed. Fortunately, he didn't smash into a crowded
skating rink that was just 200 feet away.

Candi recovered quickly. Woz suffered cuts on his face, but was otherwise thought to be in remarkably good condition. No one realized,
not even Woz, what the accident had actually done to him. At the time,
Woz's family and friends thought he seemed a bit slow, mentally. They
didn't know that while he could remember everything up to the day
before the accident, his memory of events just prior to the crash, and
for a period afterward, had been wiped out.

"I didn't know I had been in a plane crash," said Woz. "I didn't know
I had been in the hospital. I didn't know I had played games on my
computer in the hospital. I thought I was just resting on a weekend and
after the weekend I would go back to work at Apple." He had what doctors call anterograde amnesia, a condition not uncommon in plane
crash survivors.

A month passed, during which time Woz still had no knowledge of his condition. After watching the movie *Ordinary People,* he became troubled by the *idea* of being in a plane crash. "Was I in a plane crash," he asked his fiancée, "or did I dream it?"

"Oh, you dreamed it," Candi said, thinking he must be kidding.

But the thought continued to nag at Wozniak, and he began to dwell on it. He brought back the events leading up to the flight, every detail he could force himself to remember, right up to putting his hand on the throttle. Then—nothing.

This was exciting. The explanation was amnesia! He had a gap in his memory. He found hundreds of get-well cards next to the bed, some dated weeks before, which he couldn't remember ever seeing. Now he knew the gap was weeks long.

It took Woz more than a month to "talk himself" out of his amnesia, as he put it. Even after his memory returned, Woz didn't want to go back to Apple right away. He had already phased himself out of the major decision making there. He simply wasn't interested in the business end of the company. He was an engineer, and he had continued to work on the engineering projects assigned to him. "I'm not a manager type. I just love instruction sets," he said.

One of Wozniak's last projects before the crash involved creating math routines for a new software program that Randy Wigginton was developing. The program itself was Mike Scott's idea. Frustrated with the long project delays at Apple, Scott had ignored the company bureaucracy and assigned the young Wigginton a major role in developing a spreadsheet program similar to VisiCalc.

Wigginton worked faster than Woz had anticipated and was ready for the routines almost before Woz had begun creating them. Mike Scott, angered by Woz's inconsistent work habits and by delays in shipping of the Apple III, began pressuring him. Woz worked night and day, suffering Scotty's daily complaints about his slow progress.

At one point, in order to get Scott off his back, Woz dreamed up yet another practical joke. Woz knew that Scotty was a fan of movie director George Lucas, and Scotty had told Woz that he hoped the director might join Apple's board of directors. So Woz had a friend phone Scott's secretary saying that he was George Lucas and that he would call again. Scott, anxiously anticipating Lucas's call, left Woz alone for the next few days.

Woz wasn't sure even a year later, but he believed that he may have had the final spreadsheet routines with him when he crashed the plane. However, subsequent events at Apple had a more devastating effect on the company than the loss of that code.

Just three weeks after Woz's accident, Mike Scott decided that Apple needed a healthy shakeup. The ship he was steering had listed a bit, in his estimation, and he decided it was time to jettison some of the dead-weight. On a day referred to as Black Wednesday, Scott fired 40 Apple employees and terminated several hardware projects that he believed were taking too long to complete. The move stunned the company at every level.

Mike Scott had never hidden his volatile personality. He had had a number of arguments with both Woz and Jobs. "I've never yelled at anybody more in my life," Jobs recalled. Sometimes Jobs would leave the president's office in tears after a long altercation. Scott was also known for his flamboyant behavior. He was a familiar figure around the company, visiting line employees regularly to keep in touch with what was happening. Scott also knew how to boost the company's morale, as evidenced by his suggestion that the company pay for a trip to Hawaii for the entire staff. But the Apple III exhausted Scotty's limited patience.

Because the necessity of the firings was questionable, the young company was shocked. At first, remaining employees wondered who would be next. Simultaneously, they mounted an effort to hire back some of the people Scotty had fired. Even those who agreed that a shakeup was necessary felt that Scott had fired some good employees unfairly.

Chris Espinosa visited Jobs in his office the day after the firings and told him flat out, "This is a helluva way to run a company." Although Jobs defended the mass ejection, he seemed to be as demoralized as everyone else. Scotty had acted too arbitrarily for the taste of either Jobs or Markkula.

A month later, Jobs and Markkula demoted Scotty to a lesser rank. Scott was no longer at the helm, and by July he decided the current state of affairs was intolerable. In a bitter letter of resignation dated July 17, he announced that he was fed up with "hypocrisy, yes-men, foolhardy plans, a 'cover your ass' attitude, and empire builders." Perhaps his most significant allegation, one that epitomized his approach to management, was that "A company's quality of life is not and cannot be set by a committee." The next day he flew to Germany to attend the Bayreuth opera festival, something he had wanted to do all his life.

Despite the problems with the Apple III, Woz's amnesia, Black Wednesday and its aftermath, and Scotty's resignation, Apple continued to prosper. As always, Woz's labor of love, the Apple II, carried the company. Net sales of Apple IIs had more than doubled during fiscal 1980 and continued to climb through the first half of 1981. By April 1981, Apple employed more than 1500 people. The company had opened domestic manufacturing facilities in San Jose, Los Angeles, and Dallas, in addition to Cupertino. To meet the growing demand in Europe, a facility was opened in Cork, Ireland. Worldwide sales of Apple products were increasing at a pace of 186 percent above the previous year, and now totaled more than $300 million. The number of Apple dealers had risen to 3000. Mike Markkula took over from Scotty as president of Apple, a position he believed to be a temporary one, and at age 26, Steve Jobs became chairman of the board.

Apple was now investing millions of dollars in research and development to create a product that would stun the world. It wanted to prove that it had learned the lessons of the Apple III, that Apple could indeed introduce a new product successfully. By the fall of 1981, rumors abounded in the trade journals about new products Apple was developing.

The rumors were wrong, though not even Apple realized it at the time. Apple would indeed unveil a computer that stunned the world, but its roots lay elsewhere, with the work of a brilliant engineer a few miles up the road and a technology over a decade old and still unknown to most of the world.

The Mother of All Demos

What I really wanted to do was dream.

DOUG ENGELBART
Computer technology visionary

IT WAS, BY ALL ACCOUNTS, ONE OF THE MOST IMPRESSIVE TECHNOLOGY demonstrations since the atomic bomb test at Alamogordo.

In December 1968, the Fall Joint Computer Conference (FJCC) took place in San Francisco, and it included a presentation by Douglas Engelbart and his colleagues from what was then called the Stanford Research Institute in Menlo Park, a few miles up the peninsula from Cupertino.

Engelbart, an angular man who spoke quietly and efficiently, took the stage decked out in microphone and headphones, and seated himself in front of a bizarre device that featured a keyboard and odder implements. Behind him was a screen, on which much of the demonstration would play out.

The demo showed how a computer could deal with everyday chores such as planning one's tasks for the day. Engelbart kept all this information in an electronic document he could organize and examine in many different ways.

At a time when a clanking Teletype was a common way of getting information out of a computer, Engelbart took the FJCC audience into a new world. He showed them lines of text that expanded into hierarchical lists and then collapsed back down; text that could be "frozen" at the top of the screen while the prose below changed, much like frames in Web documents today; and the mixing of text, graphics, and video on a split-screen display.

And Engelbart controlled it all with an extraordinary device called a "mouse" that had an apparently telepathic link with a dot (they called it a "bug") that moved around the screen, specifying where instructions would take effect. For instance, by using the mouse, Engelbart could click on a word and jump to another location in the document or to another document.

The demonstration got even more interesting when Engelbart introduced one of his team members via a video/audio link. This man also sat in front of a device like Engelbart's, and wore a microphone and headphones. Both he and Engelbart were in front of television cameras, so they could speak to each other. And both, it soon became clear, could also work on the documents on Engelbart's screen, taking turns controlling that telepathic bug, manipulating the document collaboratively in real time while talking and seeing one another in half of the split-screen display.

The demo anticipated many breakthroughs that wouldn't reach computers for a generation. It included collapsible and expandable outline lists, text with embedded links to other documents as in Web browsers today, a mouse, a one-handed chording keyboard that left one hand free for the mouse, and live video- and audio-conferencing with a user in another city. And this was in 1968, before personal computers even existed.

Engelbart presented more innovation that day than most acknowledged greats of the field achieved in a lifetime, and he was still a young man. When he finished, the audience gave him a standing ovation. It was later called "The Mother of All Demos," and the Smithsonian Museum of American History has preserved elements of it. That's appropriate. It was historic.

Computer scientist Alan Kay had seen Engelbart's technology before the demo. "I knew everything that they were going to show. I had seen it. And yet it was one of the greatest experiences of my life. It was the totality of the vision, the breadth of the vision, the depth of the vision. The standing ovation there came from that instant recognition that something important had happened and we didn't have to be the same thereafter. That happens in Texas tent meetings when you get converted, and most Baptist preachers will tell you it doesn't last long. But for the few who realized what Doug was trying to do, it made an enormous difference."

Writer and industry prognosticator Paul Saffo later said, "This demo set a brush fire burning that swept across the computing landscape that inspired one researcher after another to head off in their own direction. It quite literally branched the course of computing off the course it had been going for the previous 10 years, and things have never quite been the same again."

For Engelbart, the journey to that moment began in 1951. As an engineer just out of college, he landed a plum job at what later became NASA Ames Research Center in Mountain View, California. It was a dream come true. He met a woman, fell in love, got engaged: another dream come true. And then he realized with a shock that he had achieved all his life goals.

"How did I get to be 26 and these are all my goals?" he asked himself. He decided he'd better set himself a more ambitious aim.

He thought he would try to solve the problem of complexity.

The complexity of many problems surpassed humans' ability to deal with them, Engelbart knew, and he believed that the new giant brains, the electronic digital computers that had stumbled into existence in the 1940s, were the solution. He began to puzzle out just how this new technology could bring complexity down to human scale.

Throughout the 1950s, he had continued to wrestle with this problem. By 1962, he had transferred to the Stanford Research Institute, later called just SRI, and in that year he produced a report entitled "The Augmentation of Human Intellect." It was quite a document. Its framework would underlie all his professional work for the next 30 years and breed seminal ideas and basic inventions.

The Department of Defense agency DARPA supplied research funds, and Engelbart launched the Augmentation Research Center (ARC, later the Augmented Human Intellect Research Center, or AHI) within SRI. Out of ARC came a 13-year-long computer system project called NLS (oNLine System), which introduced an amazing collection of new ideas and technologies, including e-mail and the mouse. Engelbart also helped create DARPA's ARPAnet, which evolved into the Internet.

Engelbart developed a "bootstrap" philosophy: build tools that let you build better tools (that let you build better tools . . .). His researchers thoroughly imbibed this philosophy. They invented shared-screen tele-conferencing to hold more efficient meetings in which to plan new tools, and they introduced online "journals," which merged researchers' notes into a collective information structure. This approach was radical, powerful, and visionary, and it led to some amazing breakthroughs, but it also greatly stretched the distance to implementation.

Most of Engelbart's ideas came together in that presentation at the Fall Joint Computer Conference in 1968.

The demo should have opened all the doors. In another era, investors would have been throwing money at Engelbart. But in 1968, few of them recognized high tech as a promising area for funds. So Engelbart and his crew continued to work on the technologies that they had pre-viewed at the demo. Yet the experience was such a high for the team that going back to work seemed an anticlimax. Members began to leave for other jobs. They didn't see any closure on the horizon. Just as they were achieving some goal, Engelbart would move the goal line.

Then in 1977, when NLS seemed almost ready to bring its ideas to a broader public, Engelbart's funding was cut and SRI dropped the pro-gram. It was the end of his dream, at least until he could start it all up again.

Engelbart went to a company called Tymshare, and many of his for-mer staff ended up at a new research center in Palo Alto called Xerox PARC.

At PARC, Xerox did its most advanced research, extending the bourne of new office technology. Among its achievements was Small-talk, a computer language that was more than a language, really a new way of thinking about how to map real problems to computer solutions. PARC also developed key technology for connecting an office full of computers in a local network. With the addition of Engelbart's innova-tions, PARC held the greatest treasure trove in the history of comput-ing. It was the future, yet the only parts of that future that ever seemed to dribble out of the PARC lab were those that meshed well with Xerox's copier business.

The Big Leagues

*When you have nothing to lose, you can
shoot for the moon. So we shot for the
moon, and we knew if we were successful
that it would come down to Apple and IBM.
And that's exactly what's going to happen.*

STEVE JOBS
Apple cofounder, in a 1983 interview

APPLE WAS NOW TAKING THE FINAL STEPS TO CORRECT THE DAMAGE
from the Apple III snafu. In late 1981, Apple officially reintroduced the Apple III. Now the machine included increased memory
storage in the form of a hard disk and improved software. But two other
important computer projects were also underway at the time.

The Lisa was originally conceived of as a multi-CPU computer, and
Woz was going to design it. That plan had changed over time, and now
the Lisa was going to use a single very powerful CPU, the Motorola
68000. And programming whiz Bill Atkinson, instrumental in getting
the Pascal language on the Apple II, was spearheading the software
development team. Lisa was to be a potent machine with novel features. Atkinson envisioned a "paper" paradigm—the screen background
would be white, and text and graphics would mix freely, as on a printed
page. The Lisa would address the market the Apple III failed to reach.
It would be a wedge in the corporate door, a personal computer for
business.

If the Lisa was the high-end, costly business machine, the Apple
Macintosh was to be in many ways the opposite: small, inexpensive,
easy to use, and simple. That was the plan, anyway, of Jef Raskin, who
led the Macintosh project. It was Raskin who as head of documenta-

tion for Apple had induced Chris Espinosa to write the Red Book, which helped popularize the Apple II. Now Raskin was making better use of his computer science degree running an actual computer project. The Macintosh Raskin foresaw would be a low-cost, portable device, with none of the dazzle of the Lisa. It bore little resemblance to the Macintosh Apple eventually shipped.

At the time, few personal computer entrepreneurs were aware of the work at PARC. It was primarily a research facility, and a different world. PARC was closer to the world of academia than to the industrial sector.

Jef Raskin was the rare individual with a foot in both worlds. He was an academic computer scientist who was also working for the hottest personal computer company. He knew what was up at PARC and was convinced that Steve Jobs should know about it, too.

But Raskin had no illusions about his relationship with Jobs. He thought Jobs was quick to judge people, and was binary about it. Individuals were either ones or zeros—on his good list or his bad list. Raskin didn't believe he was on Jobs's list of ones, but he didn't particularly care. The feeling was mutual.

Raskin knew he was not the man to convince Jobs to look at the wonderland at PARC. But Bill Atkinson, whom Raskin had hired, did have Jobs's respect. Raskin encouraged Atkinson to get Jobs to take a tour of PARC. Xerox PARC was a fairly open place in the 1970s. So Atkinson brought PARC to Jobs's attention and piqued his interest.

The ploy worked. According to Jobs, he also negotiated a better than average demo with Xerox.

"I went down to Xerox Development Corporation," Jobs said, "which made all of Xerox's venture investments, and I said, 'Look. I will let you invest a million dollars in Apple if you will sort of open the kimono at Xerox PARC.'"

PARC researcher Adele Goldberg was furious at the exchange of money for privileged information. She felt that Xerox would be giving away all its secrets. Others had gotten tours of PARC and seen demonstrations of the technology, but now for the first time Xerox was opening its doors to a computer company executive in a position to bring the technology to market. But Xerox Development Corporation overruled her.

Jobs made two trips to PARC in November and December of 1979, with Bill Atkinson, Mike Scott, and others. There, Larry Tesler showed them around and gave them "look-but-don't-touch" demos of the innovations. For the first time they saw a *graphical user interface*: documents appeared in overlapping frames on a white screen, and software programs were made tangible through icons and direct manipulation of on-screen elements. Supplementing the keyboard was Engelbart's mouse, now part of a fully functioning system, which let one click on items and drag them around the screen. It all astounded Jobs.

Although he and his colleagues paid close heed to the demos, they really learned nothing about how the PARC engineers had done their magic; they saw only the results. But that was enough to alter Apple's plans fundamentally, and the change took place right then and there when Steve Jobs decided that Apple would implement these marvels. PARC didn't really give Apple folks the technology so much as the vision.

Some time later, Apple took more from PARC when it hired Larry Tesler to work on the Lisa. Soon, several more PARC engineers moved over to Apple, recognizing that it offered them their chance to bring their graphical user interface vision to market.

Jobs insisted that the Lisa project was to change direction and embody the PARC revelations. Jobs was fired up and was driving everyone hard, insinuating himself into the project at many levels. He was, by many accounts, driving everyone nuts. If this had happened only a few months later, he might have gone unchallenged, but at the time Apple still had a president who could intercede. Scotty pulled Jobs off the Lisa project. Former Hewlett-Packard engineer John Couch, who had been hired in 1978, was placed in charge of Lisa.

Unwilling either to accept the decision or to challenge it, Jobs reacted by moving in on the Macintosh project. He had Raskin pushed aside, and he completely redefined the Macintosh to be something very similar to the Lisa—the major difference being that Jobs wanted his team to make the Mac better than the Lisa. He moved the Mac team offsite, pulled in top-notch engineers and programmers, drove them to work long hours, criticized them as much as he praised them, and told them that they were the future of the company and everyone else at Apple was the past.

In 1981, Apple spent $21 million on new product research and development, three times what it had spent the year before. Jobs toured the world's leading automated factories and then commissioned a new factory for Apple in Fremont, California, to build the Macintosh. "We have designed the machine to build the machine," Jobs said. "The manufacturing of the Macintosh has been designed from day one to be highly automated."

Jobs and others at Apple wanted to see the company's rapid growth continue and establish Apple as the technology leader, for a number of reasons—the main one being the likelihood of a late-1981 entry into the personal computer market by a company called International Business Machines Corporation.

Apple was not surprised by rumors that IBM planned to produce a personal computer. The company had considered the possibility for several years. Jobs described the situation as being like a gate that's been inching down slowly, and Apple had been running at top speed for four years to get through the gate before it finally shut. Apple made this concern public knowledge in December 1980 in the prospectus for its initial stock offering. Apple also expected competition soon from Hewlett-Packard and various Japanese firms. But the greatest challenge by far was IBM, the chrome colossus whose name meant "real" computers to most people, a multinational corporation richer than many small countries. Whatever IBM had to offer, Apple would be meeting it with its Lisa and Macintosh.

There was no looking back.

CHAPTER 8

THE GATE COMES DOWN

We got creamed.

DON MASSARO
President of Xerox's office products division

Osborne's Portable Computer

*Early personal computer companies
were managed by amateurs who deluded
themselves into believing that their
transient success had something to do
with good management or foresight.*

ADAM OSBORNE
Personal computer pioneer

IN THE YEARS SINCE THEY HAD LEFT ALBUQUERQUE FOR THEIR NATIVE
Bellevue, Washington, Bill Gates and Paul Allen had established a
successful software business specializing in programming languages
for personal computers. The BASIC they had originally written for the
MITS Altair was still their most popular product, a standard in an
industry with few standards. In addition, Gates and Allen had introduced other programming languages, such as mainframe-originated
FORTRAN and COBOL, to personal computers.

Gates, 24, and Allen, 27, were pleased with their accomplishments.
Microsoft was racking up $8 million in annual sales and it employed 32
people, most of them programmers. Nothing shabby about that, but in
July 1980 they became involved in a project that would jolt and transform their company and the entire personal computer industry.

By 1980, dozens of personal computer hardware and software companies were running businesses that were fundamentally sound, if not
earth-shattering success stories. It was the success of Apple Computer
that notified the world that personal computers were serious business.

The growth of this garage operation into a large company, Apple's enormous annual sales increases, and the proliferation of smaller companies writing software and making add-on hardware for the Apple II convinced skeptics that the personal computer was not another hula hoop.

The biggest skeptics were the large minicomputer and mainframe corporations. Some of them, such as Digital Equipment Corporation and Hewlett-Packard, had rejected employee proposals to build personal computers in the early 1970s.

There were many reasons why they were slow to convert to the new technology. Prior to Apple's success, they could still question the existence of a market for personal computers. Besides, for non-IBM companies, the established markets already offered sufficient risks. Launching an unproven product is perilous, and while a start-up company has relatively little to lose, an established firm can damage its reputation badly by plunging into untested waters. The expense was higher for the established companies, too. Their engineers' salaries for assessing the feasibility of a personal computer alone could cost a big company more than MITS and Proc Tech ever spent on research and development. The company would also need prototypes and market research, which cost more money. Finally, there was the seemingly intractable problem of the sales force. Engineers who understood their inner workings sold large computers one at a time. The transaction often involved several visits, long phone calls, and many hours of a highly trained professional's time. In this system, the cost to a company of selling a mainframe would easily exceed the total price of a personal computer. This method was clearly inappropriate for personal computers, but no large computer company was eager to explore new approaches and perhaps alienate its valuable sales force in pursuit of a chimerical market.

But Apple proved that the "niche" personal computer market was very real indeed. It no longer took much vision to see that a company with a well-designed machine, some marketing savvy, and the funds for promotion could reasonably expect to sell personal computers at a profit.

This fact was not lost on Adam Osborne. In 1980, Osborne, who had started in the industry by selling his books at Homebrew Computer Club meetings, hatched a plan.

As one of the most quotable figures in microcomputing, Osborne had a tongue as glib as his pen. His commanding, distinctive voice, highlighted by a precise British accent, seemed to find the right word at all times, and his delivery convinced his listeners that he had stated the matter in its finality. Osborne had gained a good deal of notoriety in the field from his writing—first books on microprocessors and then columns in *Interface Age* and *InfoWorld*.

His columns began as straightforward analyses of Silicon Valley chip technology. But Osborne quickly gravitated to other issues, and soon wrote muckraking indictments of computer companies. He was particularly critical of the common practice of preannouncing items and then bankrolling their development with money from the ensuing orders. Silicon Valley was the source of his information, and he called his column "From the Fountainhead." Osborne had never been accused of toe-scraping humility, and many readers innocently assumed he meant the title to refer to himself.

Osborne felt comfortable writing exposés about the industry because he was not directly involved in it. The Berkeley-based computer book publishing company he founded as an offshoot of his microprocessor consulting business attracted the attention of McGraw-Hill. After he sold the book company, now called Osborne/McGraw-Hill, he began looking for something else to do.

For a long time, Osborne believed that computers should be portable—a pipe dream in those days. Portability would be the next product innovation, he felt, a fact that companies did not yet understand. During visits to computer shows, Osborne met industry pioneers such as Bill Gates and Seymour Rubinstein and sought their reaction to this idea. "At first he was saying, 'Why doesn't someone do this?'" recalled Gates. "And the next thing I knew it was, 'It'll be called the Osborne 1.'"

But Osborne wasn't going to design it himself.

On a hot day in June 1979, Lee Felsenstein was on the auditorium floor of the National Computer Conference in New York City. No one had told him that Processor Technology, the company for which he was consulting, had folded. He waited, patient but sweating, with the prototype of his latest Proc Tech board in hand until it sank in that Bob Marsh and Gary Ingram were never going to show up.

Felsenstein returned to Berkeley, where he tried to drum up business to offset his lost royalties. He tried selling the design of the last Proc Tech board, an enhanced version of his VDM video board, to other companies, but had no luck. He undertook various freelance projects. The jobs offered him a bare subsistence—he was particular about the kinds of work he would accept. "I was running into the ground," he said. "I was just waiting for the opportunity to do what I wanted to do and closing my eyes to the monetary considerations."

Felsenstein recalled an evening later that year when he sat wire-wrapping video boards late into the night while listening to the Berkeley alternative radio station KPFA. The disc jockey played the romantic ballad "The Very Thought of You" six times in a row. As it ended the first time, Felsenstein continued his work and wondered what song would be next. Up it came again and again and again. "That was the low point," he says. "It was as if I was trapped; the sun was never going to rise; I was just going to have to keep going and going and going. The rest of the world didn't exist, and all I would do was listen to this song and keep working."

Things didn't improve much for Felsenstein in 1980. In February, he moved into the Berkeley barn that housed the Community Memory project he had helped start before hooking up with Marsh. The "barn" was a big room with a black ceiling, white walls, and many sandblasted wood beams, evidence of the "earthquake proof" architecture of the early 1900s. As Community Memory's founder, he expected that he wouldn't have to pay rent. Unfortunately, Community Memory was teetering financially and Felsenstein found his living situation growing more and more precarious.

His luck finally took a turn for the better at the West Coast Computer Faire in March when Adam Osborne approached him with a bold assertion: he was going to start a hardware company and he was "going to do it right." Felsenstein told Osborne: "You took the words right out of my mouth."

Osborne and Felsenstein knew each other through Osborne's publishing company, for which Felsenstein reviewed books and consulted on technical projects. Felsenstein showed Osborne a batch of his unsold designs, including a controller that "would have been able to control a room full of joysticks and run a group space war game."

Osborne summarily rejected those ideas. He knew what he wanted. He was going to sell a personal computer and offer bundled software— that is, applications software included with the machine. Until then, hardware and software companies served the same consumers but did not work together on purchases. Osborne knew that novice computer buyers often were confused about what software they needed. By offering the most common applications—word processing and spreadsheet programs—packaged with the computer, Osborne thought he could attract buyers. Of course, the device would be portable.

Osborne didn't want state-of-the-art hardware for its own sake; he wanted only those innovations necessary to make the computer easy to carry. Thinking portable, he asked for a 40-column display. The Sol had 64. Felsenstein split the difference and gave him 52. Osborne wanted the computer to fit under an airplane seat. Felsenstein obliged by minimizing the number of characters on the screen so that the screen would be tiny enough—only five inches—to leave room inside for cushioning the tube. Because people would tote the machine around, they would inevitably drop it. Felsenstein designed it to survive a drop test, and that meant adding cushions. He also met the small screen requirement by storing a larger screen's worth of information in memory and giving the user keys with which to scroll the information on that screen across the display. The user saw what seemed to be a sheet of paper sliding behind the glass.

Serious microcomputers at that time had two disk drives, so Felsenstein put two in the Osborne 1 as well. Unsure whether high-density drives could tolerate rough handling, he used relatively primitive drives that gave the machine adequate but unimpressive storage. "Adequacy," Osborne pronounced, "is sufficient." The machine had a Z80 microprocessor, 64K of memory, and standard interfaces to devices—typical fare for the time. But it was designed, from its overall dimensions down to the disk pockets Osborne insisted on, for portability. Osborne then set out to get the software for it. He needed some simple programs, tools that would facilitate software development. He called Richard "The Surfer" Frank, a sandy-haired Silicon Valley software developer. Frank made a variety of contributions to the company and even provided space to work in his plant before Osborne built a building of his own.

For the operating system, Osborne turned to the industry leader: Gary Kildall's CP/M. For the programming language, BASIC was the obvious choice. Osborne had two widely used versions to choose from. Because the two BASICs had complementary virtues, he decided to offer them both and made deals with Gordon Eubanks for CBASIC and Bill Gates for Microsoft BASIC.

Osborne also needed a word processor. In 1980, the man with the leading word processor was Seymour Rubinstein, president of Micro-Pro. Osborne gave Rubinstein a part of his company in exchange for WordStar at a bargain price. Osborne had also offered Gates, Kildall, and Eubanks stock in the company. Only Kildall refused, on principle, to avoid the appearance of favoring one customer over another. Gates turned down a position on Osborne Computer's board of directors but accepted the stock in exchange for a special deal on Microsoft BASIC. Osborne offered Rubinstein more—the presidency of the new company. Rubinstein turned it down and instead took the position of board chair. He thought Osborne's idea was so good, though, that he invested $20,000 of his own money in the company.

Unable to make an acceptable deal with Personal Software for the spreadsheet program he needed, Osborne turned to Richard Frank and his company Sorcim to develop a spreadsheet program, which Frank called SuperCalc. The per-copy market value of Osborne's software now totaled almost $2,000, and he planned to include it all in the basic price of the machine.

Until January 1981, when Osborne Computer filed for incorporation and obtained office space in Hayward, California, most of the design work was done in the Community Memory building.

Osborne introduced his Osborne 1 at the West Coast Computer Faire in April, where it was the hit of the show. People jammed his booth. Osborne towered over the others and seemed to be gloating. The machine was no technological marvel, but it was a bold step forward. It was the first commercially successful portable computer that came with all the software an average buyer needed. Even better, the price—$1,795—was unheard of. Many people said he was selling software and had thrown in the computer for free.

There were sardonic comments from those—including the irascible Bill Godbout—who remembered Osborne's tirades against manufacturers who took customers' money before making the products, and who now saw Osborne doing the same thing himself. But in September 1981, Osborne Computer Corporation (OCC) had its first million dollar sales month. New companies quickly sprang up trying to duplicate or improve on his design, and others seized on his ideas of portability and of including software in their system packages.

The $1,795 price became a target. The Kaypro portable contained software similar to that of the Osborne 1 and had the same look and the identical price. George Morrow's Morrow Designs also brought out a machine for $1,795, and Harry Garland and Roger Melen of Cromemco introduced one for five dollars less. But whatever their merits, none of the portables, none of the machines with software included, and none of the other $1,795 wonders had the impact of Adam Osborne's first venture into computer manufacturing. One of the industry's early participants had further advanced the development of the personal computer, and the Osborne 1 quickly became one of the new industry's top-selling personal computers, reaching a peak sales rate of about 10,000 a month. Since Osborne's initial business plan called for selling 10,000 total, OCC had certainly skyrocketed to success. Staying there was another matter.

The HP Way and
the Xerox Worm

*One of the things [Hewlett-Packard]
learned is that closed architectures
aren't going to work, that you really
have to depend on third-party suppliers.*

NELSON MILLS
Project manager, Hewlett-Packard

OSBORNE WAS AMONG THE LAST PIONEERS TO OPEN NEW TERRITORY
before civilization arrived. After the Osborne 1 appeared in 1981,
the big companies began to enter and transform the market. Soon
IBM, DEC, NEC, Xerox, AT&T, and even Exxon and Montgomery
Ward were thinking about producing a personal computer. Some companies, such as Hewlett-Packard, had started much earlier, though.

Hewlett-Packard hadn't rejected Steve Wozniak's Apple I design
because it didn't believe in the idea of a personal computer. It did. HP
built both large computers as well as calculators, so it understood how
to sell relatively inexpensive, *personal* technology products. There are
many reasons why HP may have turned Wozniak down. One was that
his machine did not lend itself to mass production. As Jobs later
acknowledged, "It was designed to be built in a garage." It was also true
that the Apple I was not a machine for the engineers and scientists who
made up HP's primary market. Woz was clearly told that the Apple I
was more appropriate for a start-up company than for HP. He may also
have even been turned down because he had no university degree,
which would not have been surprising at any established computer
company at that time. Woz did return to school for his bachelor's
degree as soon as he finished propelling Apple into the Fortune 500.

320

Those reasons aside, HP had another reason to reject a personal computer design in 1976: it was already working on one of its own.

In early 1976, a crew of engineers at HP's Cupertino, California, facility began to coalesce around a project with roots in its calculator technology. Chung Tung, the engineer in charge of Project Capricorn, brought in engineer Ernst Ernie along with Kent Stockwell to direct the hardware design and George Fichter to oversee software. There was no shortage of talent at HP, and Capricorn was a significant project.

Initially, Capricorn was intended to be a computer-like calculator but more elaborate than any of HP's small machines. HP already made highly specialized calculators. The calculator market war that had driven Ed Roberts to create the Altair had not hurt HP as much as it had other calculator manufacturers because HP had concentrated on scientific calculators that did more and sold for more than the less-expensive commercial versions. Capricorn was at first intended to have a liquid crystal display, like a calculator, but with several lines instead of one. It would be a desktop, BASIC-language calculator. By summer, the project had redefined itself, and Capricorn was ornamented with a cathode ray tube, a significant change both in terms of manufacturing costs and the potential market for the machine. Capricorn was slowly turning into a computer.

HP was perhaps better suited to develop a personal computer than any other established computer company—with the possible exception of Xerox. HP was headquartered in Silicon Valley, near most of the semiconductor companies and in the midst of the growing micro mania. Some of the Capricorn engineers were actually hobbyists like Woz, working on their own homebred systems. HP also had far more resources to devote to creating such computers than the garage start-ups. By the time they finally designed a machine, the Capricorn staff had grown to over a dozen engineers and programmers.

This computer was becoming quite distinctive. It was to have a small built-in printer and a cassette tape recorder for data storage, a keyboard, and a display, all in one desktop package that was smaller than the Sol (which had not appeared yet and would not include an integrated display or data storage when it did). Its chip was also ahead of its time—but this was not necessarily an advantage. In 1976, the only microprocessor that looked feasible was the Intel 8080, the Altair's chip, but the Capricorn team wanted one better adapted to its purposes, and turned the problem over to another HP division. Hence, Capricorn got its own HP-designed proprietary microprocessor. It was a decision some members of the team later regretted.

Another problem soon emerged. In the fall of 1976, in a corporate-level decision, the project was moved out of Silicon Valley to HP's offices in sleepy Corvallis, Oregon, a shift that played havoc with the schedule and damaged morale. Woz, who more than anything else wanted to design computers at HP, seriously considered joining the Capricorn team and moving to Corvallis. He thought he would like living in Oregon, and he wanted to get in on the project. But HP turned him down. Then in October, Mike Markkula made his first visit to Steve Jobs's garage, and Woz began being pulled into Jobs's plan to start a company. Unlike Woz, many other Capricorn engineers felt that Corvallis was exile, that they were being asked to leave the center of the universe and move into the void. Some elected not to move and dropped out of the project. When others did make the move, they found the plant wasn't ready for them. At first, programmers had to commute 70 miles to do software development on the nearest mainframe computer.

For all the delay, however, the Capricorn team was progressing. By November, they had developed a prototype. It had no tape drive, printer, or display yet, and the CPU chip and certain other microprocessors the engineers wanted for controlling peripherals were still in the layout stage. In 1977, they solved the tricky problems of mixed technologies that were posed by building a printer into the computer. Finally, the chips began to appear. During a visit of the corporate brass, one executive vice president told the engineers that the machine needed more I/O ports on the back to connect it with other HP devices or to allow future capabilities to be added. It was a little late to suggest significant design modifications, but the changes were made. The move and the modifications helped Capricorn slip a year behind schedule.

When project became product in January 1980, it was an attractive, solidly engineered machine, but relatively expensive—even given its capabilities—at $3,250. It was called the HP-85 and had a 32-character display, almost as wide as the 40 characters on Wozniak's Apple II.

Although the HP-85 sold well enough for HP's purposes and led to a series of related machines, it did not set cash registers ringing as the Apple II did. Then again, it wasn't designed to—HP sold it not as a business machine but as a scientific and professional one. Nevertheless, HP's sluggish pace in completing and marketing the product unquestionably hurt sales. By the time this machine with its built-in cassette tape drive came out, the field was moving toward using floppy disks, which were more reliable than tape cassettes and stored much more information. Moreover, the HP-85 cost more than some of these floppy disk–based systems.

In the long run, however, the HP-85's greatest flaw may have been its closed system design that required HP software and HP peripherals. When the Apple II was released in 1977, the Capricorn team believed its machine would compete with it. But by the time the HP-85 appeared three years later, some Capricorn programmers were privately conceding the general and business market to Apple. There was real irony here because the Apple II's 40-column, lowercase display was clearly inappropriate for basic applications such as word processing and report generation, and its 6502 processor was no number cruncher. Apple machines eventually got 80-column upper- and lowercase display capabilities, but only because Wozniak had left the architecture open and other people created the necessary boards and software. Third parties were continually improving the Apple II, whereas they were shut out of the HP-85. HP soon concluded that the closed architecture had been a mistake.

Still, HP had beaten the other established computer companies into the market by over a year, and the HP-85 and its successors carved out a solid market niche for themselves. The next big manufacturer to introduce a personal computer fared less well.

Falling Star

*Xerox was aiming a little too high and
trying to do something very difficult
and didn't see the opportunity.*

BILL GATES
Cofounder of Microsoft

XEROX HAD MADE ITS NAME IN PHOTOCOPYING MACHINES, BUT THE company had flirted with computers as well, and maintained close ties with Silicon Valley. After acquiring Scientific Data Systems (SDS), a computer company in El Segundo, California, and renaming it Xerox Data Systems (XDS), Xerox became one of the dwarfs—the seven mainframe computer companies living in IBM's shadow. XDS, however, was a financial millstone, and Xerox finally sold it, although it retained the El Segundo facility itself for some integrated circuit and electronics design and systems programming.

Xerox purchased Shugart, the disk drive manufacturer, in the winter of 1977–1978. Don Massaro, president of Shugart through the early 1970s, recalled that in the days before Apple soared to its zenith, young Steve Jobs was in his office nearly every week nagging him to devise a disk drive that personal computer users could afford. Massaro and his colleague James Atkinson did just that, helping make Apple and Shugart leaders in their fields. When Xerox bought Shugart, it acquired that wedge in the personal computer market, and it also got Massaro, who proved instrumental in Xerox's foray into the market some years later.

Xerox made its greatest contribution to the personal computer through PARC, the research center it opened in 1970. Xerox had separated the often-linked research and development functions, and PARC was strictly a cutting-edge research institute with no commitment to develop commercial products. PARC was chartered to explore technological frontiers, which it did. One Silicon Valley observer called PARC a national resource because of PARC's open sharing of technical knowledge with the outside world, an openness more akin to an academic institution or to the computer hobbyist movement than to the research wing of a large corporation. With both the freedom of a university and the financial backing of a large corporation, PARC was an exciting place for any computer engineer or programmer to work.

That combination attracted some talented people. Hungarian-born Charles Simonyi, who had learned programming on a Russian vacuum tube computer and had degrees from Berkeley and Stanford, worked there. Also working at PARC was John Shoch, who finished his Ph.D. at Stanford while helping get PARC started, and the fiercely independent but farsighted Alan Kay, who adorned his desk with a cardboard model of his dream computer—a machine that Kay called Dynabook, powerful and yet small enough to fit in a bookbag. Larry Tesler brought the newest programming techniques to his PARC software. Bob Metcalfe was involved in a technique for networking computers.

Over several years these engineers and programmers created an impressive workstation computer called the Alto. The Alto boasted an advanced language called Smalltalk, an input device borrowed from SRI called the mouse, and that networking technique called Ethernet for connecting individual Altos for communication and cumulation of effort, as if they were one big computer. Xerox referred to the whole arrangement as the "office of the future," and it was both visionary and technically sound. Xerox marketed Altos to government agencies, placing them in the White House, the Executive Office Building, the National Bureau of Standards, the Senate, and the House of Representatives, where they were used to print the Congressional Record.

The Alto was 20 times more computer than the original Altair. Not only did it have impressive speed and display graphics, but the Smalltalk language was a generational leap beyond BASIC. Because work on it was completed in 1974, some people, particularly those at Xerox, claim it as the first personal computer ever. But the Alto was never a commercial product. No more than 2000 were ever built, and its cost removed it from the category of a personal computer, even if it was a self-contained machine for one individual's use. It was priced as a minicomputer.

The Alto took two years to develop—from 1972 to 1974—and was used for three more years before Xerox decided to develop it further into a marketable product. In January 1977, David Liddle was put in charge of this task, and Charles Simonyi came to work for him. Liddle had joined PARC in 1972 after having worked on computer display systems in a project funded by DARPA. But the project proceeded slowly. Many researchers at PARC, attracted by the freedom to design technologically dazzling innovations, were growing frustrated that their creations remained sequestered in the lab. They could see things happening in quickstep around them, particularly at Apple, while Xerox dawdled. Before Xerox got a personal computer product to market, several key people left, with others departing soon after. Tesler went to Apple, Kay to Atari, and Simonyi to Microsoft.

Meanwhile, Xerox released its Ethernet network and began linking personal computers. In 1981, four years after it started, Xerox announced the 8010 Star Information System. It was an impressive machine, using much of the advanced Alto technology that Jobs had seen in 1979. But at $16,595 the Star was not really a personal computer either. Nor did Xerox try to convince people it was. For example, the company did not try to sell the machine in computer stores. If HP's laggardly development of the HP-85 had caused it to miss its commercial window by offering a tape-based machine in a disk-based world, the Xerox Star missed the whole market altogether.

A month later, though, Xerox introduced a true personal computer. The Xerox 820, announced in July 1981, was code-named The Worm during development, perhaps because Xerox had dreamed it would eat into Apple's market. Like many existing personal computers, the Xerox 820 used the Z80 chip. Xerox also offered Kildall's CP/M and the two BASIC languages written by Gates and Allen and by Eubanks.

Don Massaro led the 820 project. The 820s would be inexpensive, individual workstations on Ethernet systems in Fortune 500 corporations, the same market the Star sought. Development took only four months, and the machine quickly went into manufacture. "All we wanted to do was reserve those desks for Stars later on," Massaro said. Given that target market, Xerox's next move didn't make much sense.

"It was designed to go after the end-user market through our direct sales organization," Massaro explained. "Xerox has always sold through its own sales organization. Xerox had 15,000 salespeople worldwide, and that was one of the real strengths of Xerox." But ComputerLand waved huge purchase orders before Xerox corporate eyes, and "in a moment of weakness, we went to that channel."

Mass marketing was a mistake. Xerox fared poorly in the developing shelf-space war in ComputerLand stores. Perhaps it was the paucity of technological innovation in the 820, or Xerox's failure to learn from the lesson of open architecture. Or perhaps the competition was simply getting too heavy even for Xerox by that point. In Bill Gates's view, the company misunderstood the market. "Xerox was aiming a little too high and trying to do something very difficult and didn't see the opportunity," said Gates. "When they did, they threw something together in a couple of months, and it was too little too late."

"We got creamed," Massaro admits. And it was IBM that did it.

IBM

IBM is a big company.

BILL GATES
Cofounder of Microsoft

HEWLETT-PACKARD AND XEROX HAD MADE LESS-THAN-IMPRESSIVE entries into the personal computer market, and there was intense curiosity within that industry about how IBM would fare. The mega-firm was considered successful in almost everything it had tried. Its reputation had held up at least since the mid-1960s, when IBM owned two-thirds of the computer market. And when IBM chief Tom Watson, Jr., had bet the company on a new semiconductor-based computer line that instantly made IBM's most profitable machines obsolete—and the bet paid off—IBM only appeared all the more infallible. T. Vincent Learson, who had directed development of that computer, the 360, succeeded Watson as CEO in 1971. Two years later, Frank Cary, a man willing to risk if not the company, at least some of its pristine reputa-tion on a very un-IBM venture, succeeded him.

Size alone did not define success in the personal computer business, however. In Bellevue, Washington, Microsoft was a little company compared with Apple, and nonexistent next to the multinational IBM. Although it had only a few dozen employees—mostly programmers who came to work in T-shirts if they wanted to—Microsoft was clearly doing very well. It had even made money selling hardware.

The hardware story began on a tailgate. Paul Allen and Bill Gates were sitting in the back of a pickup truck in the Microsoft parking lot discussing the "Apple problem." None of Microsoft's programs would run on the single leading personal computer at that time. Gates shook his head at the thought of converting all his firm's software to work with the 6502 microprocessor that was the brain of Apple's computers. Allen suggested, "Maybe there's a way to do it in hardware."

They brought in Tim Paterson of Seattle Computer Products, located across Lake Washington, to try to build a card for the Apple that would let it run Microsoft's 8080 and Z80 software. They called it the SoftCard. Paterson did a series of prototypes before Don Burdis took over the project. Of course, to run the application software the card also had to run the operating system that the software was written for: CP/M. Gates signed an agreement licensing CP/M for the Soft-Card from Digital Research.

One afternoon Allen and Gates sat discussing SoftCard's potential. They agreed that if Burdis could make the SoftCard work, they might sell about 5000 of them. Burdis did make it work, and they sold that many in three months—and many more thereafter.

The SoftCard solved the specific problem of the 6502, but what would happen when the next hot microprocessor came along? Microsoft would have to come up with another SoftCard or translate all its software. In the summer of 1980, Microsoft decided to end its translation nemesis for good. Microsoft approached it by first rewriting all its software into a "neutral" language on a large DEC minicomputer and then writing the chip-specific translator programs that would automatically convert their "neutral" software to the form needed by the 6502 or any other particular processor. The task was massive, but cost-effective if the company intended to supply software to all microcomputer manufacturers and to establish its products as industry standards. That was the idea.

In June, Paul Allen was working on enhancements to a BASIC for machines built around Intel's new 8088 and 8086 chips. The 8086 was one of a fresh generation of microprocessors created explicitly for small computers. It had a more logically designed instruction set and more capabilities for the systems programmer to use. It also possessed a 16-bit architecture; that is, the 8086 could handle information in chunks twice as large as the chunks that the 8080, the Z80, the 6502, or any other common 8-bit microprocessor on the market could handle. This difference affected a machine's performance exponentially so that its memory capacity jumped by a factor of thousands. The 8088 was a compromise version of the 8086 with some old 8-bit characteristics but the same instruction set as the newer 8086.

That July, Bill Gates, busily developing a BASIC for Atari, received a phone call from a representative of IBM. He was surprised, but not greatly so. IBM had called once before about buying a Microsoft product, but the deal had fallen through. However, this communication was more tantalizing. IBM wanted to send some researchers from its Boca Raton, Florida, facility to chat with Gates about Microsoft. Gates agreed without hesitation. "How about next week?" he asked. "We'll be on a plane in two hours," said the IBM man.

Gates proceeded to cancel his next day's appointment with Atari chairman Ray Kassar. "IBM is a pretty big company," he explained sheepishly.

Because IBM was indeed a pretty big company, he decided to turn to Steve Ballmer, his advisor in business matters and a former assistant product manager at Procter and Gamble. Gates had known Ballmer when he attended Harvard in 1974. In 1979, when Gates decided that Microsoft was getting difficult to manage, he hired Ballmer. Ballmer was brash and ambitious. After Harvard, he had entered Stanford University's MBA program but had dropped out to start making money sooner.

Ballmer had been glad to join Microsoft. He was enthusiastic about the little software company, and he liked Bill Gates. He reminded Gates how, at Harvard, he had convinced Gates to join his men's club. As an initiation rite, he dressed his friend in a tuxedo, blindfolded him, brought him to the student cafeteria, and made him talk to other students about computers. Gates's dealings with IBM would remind him of this experience.

Gates liked Ballmer, too. Gates had played poker during the evenings in the Harvard dorms, and after being cleaned out, he often went to Ballmer to describe the game. As they started working together at Microsoft in 1980, Gates found he still enjoyed discussing things with his friend, who quickly became one of his closest business confidants, and he naturally turned to him after IBM's call.

"Look, Steve," Gates said, "IBM is coming tomorrow and IBM is a *big* company. We better show those guys a little depth. Why don't we both sit in on the meeting?"

Neither of them could be sure that the call was anything special, but Gates couldn't help getting worked up over it. "Bill was superexcited," Allen later recalled. "He hoped they'd use our BASIC." Thus, Ballmer said, he and Gates "did the thing up right," meaning suit and tie, which was unusual attire at Microsoft.

Before the meeting began, IBM asked Gates and Ballmer to sign an agreement promising not to tell IBM anything confidential. Big Blue used this device to protect itself from future lawsuits. Hence, if Gates revealed a valuable idea to the company, he could not sue later on if IBM exploited the concept. IBM was familiar with lawsuits; adroit use of the legal system had played an important part in its long control of the mainframe computer business. It all seemed rather pointless to Gates, but he agreed.

The meeting seemed to be little more than an introductory social session. Two of the IBM representatives asked Gates and Ballmer "a lot of crazy questions," Gates recalls, about what Microsoft did and about what features mattered in a home computer. The next day Ballmer typed up a letter to the IBM visitors thanking them for the visit and had Gates sign it.

Nothing happened for a month. In late August, IBM phoned again to schedule a second meeting. "What you said was really interesting," the IBM representative told Gates. This time IBM would send five people including a lawyer. Not to be outdone, Gates and Ballmer decided to front five people themselves. They asked their own counsel—a Seattle attorney whose services Microsoft had used before—to attend the meeting along with two other Microsoft employees. Allen, as usual, stayed in the background. "We got five people in the room," said Ballmer. "That was a key thing."

At the outset, IBM's head of corporate relations explained why he had come along. It was because "this is the most unusual thing the corporation has ever done." Gates thought it was about the weirdest thing Microsoft had ever been through, too. Once again, Gates, Ballmer, and the other Microsoft attendees had to sign a legal document, this time stipulating that they would protect in confidence anything they viewed at the meeting. Then they saw the plans for Project Chess. IBM was going to build a personal computer.

Gates looked at the design and questioned the IBM people across the table. It bothered him that the plans made no mention of using a 16-bit processor. He explained that a 16-bit design would enable him to give them superior software—assuming they wanted Microsoft's. He was emphatic and enthusiastic and probably didn't express himself with the reserve they were used to. But IBM listened.

IBM did want Microsoft's languages. On that August day in 1980, Gates signed a consulting agreement with IBM to write a report explaining how Microsoft could work with IBM. The report was also to suggest hardware and Gates's proposed use of it.

The IBM representatives added that they had heard about a popular operating system called CP/M. Could Gates sell that to them as well? Gates patiently explained that he didn't own CP/M, but that he would be happy to phone Gary Kildall and help arrange a meeting. Gates later said that he called Kildall and told him that these were "important customers" and to "treat them right." He handed the phone over to the IBM representative, who made an appointment to visit Digital Research that week.

What ensued has become the material of personal computer legend. Instead of landing a contract with IBM, "Gary went flying," Gates recounted, a story that became well known in the industry. Kildall disputed Gates's recollection. He denied that he was out flying for fun while the IBM representatives cooled their heels. "I was out doing business. I used to fly a lot for pleasure, but after a while you get tired of boring holes in the sky." He was back in time for his scheduled meeting with IBM.

That morning, however, while Kildall was airborne, IBM met with Kildall's wife Dorothy McEwen. Dorothy handled Digital Research's accounts with hardware distributors. The nondisclosure agreement that the IBM visitors asked her to sign troubled her. She felt that it jeopardized Digital Research's control of its software. According to Gary, she stalled until she could get hold of Gerry Davis, the company's lawyer. That afternoon Gary arrived on schedule, and along with Dorothy and Gerry Davis, he met with IBM's representatives. Kildall signed the nondisclosure agreement (NDA) and heard IBM's plans.

When it came to the operating system, though, they had an impasse. IBM wanted to buy CP/M outright for $250,000; Kildall was willing to license it to them at the usual $10 per copy rate. IBM left with promises to talk further, but without having signed an agreement for CP/M.

They immediately turned to Microsoft. Gates required no prodding. Once IBM agreed to use a 16-bit processor, Gates realized that CP/M was not critical for their new machine because applications written for CP/M were not designed to take advantage of the power of 16 bits. Kildall had seen the new Intel processors, too, and was planning to enhance CP/M to do just that. But it made just as much sense, Gates told IBM, to use a different operating system instead.

Where that operating system would come from was a good question, until Paul Allen thought of Tim Paterson at Seattle Computer Products. Paterson's company had already developed an operating system, SCP-DOS, for the 8086, and Allen told him that Microsoft wanted it.

At the end of September, Gates, Ballmer, and a colleague took a red-eye flight to deliver the report. They assumed it would determine whether they got the IBM personal computer project. They nervously finished collating, proofreading, and revising the document on the plane. Kay Nishi, a globetrotting Japanese entrepreneur and computer magazine publisher who also worked for Microsoft, had written part of the report in "Nishi English," which, according to Ballmer, "always needs editing." The report proposed that Microsoft convert SCP-DOS to run on IBM's machine. After the sleepless flight, Gates and Ballmer were running on adrenaline and ambition alone. As they drove from the Miami airport to Boca Raton, Gates suddenly panicked. He had forgotten a tie. Already late, they swung their rental car into the parking lot of a department store and waited for it to open. Gates rushed in and bought a tie.

When they finally met with the IBM representatives, they learned that IBM wanted to finish the personal computer project in a hurry—within a year. It had created a team of 12 to avoid the kind of corporate bottlenecks that can drag a project on for years—three and one-half for the Xerox Star, four for the HP-85. IBM president Frank Cary dealt roughly with all internal politics that could cause delays. Throughout the morning, Gates answered dozens of queries from members of

IBM's project team. "They pelted us with questions," said Ballmer. "Bill was on the firing line."

By lunchtime, Gates was fairly confident Microsoft would get the contract. Philip Estridge, who was the project head, an IBM vice president, and an owner of an Apple II, told Gates that when John Opel, IBM's new chairperson, heard that Microsoft might be involved in the effort he said, "Oh, is that Mary Gates's boy's company?" Opel had served with Gates's mother on the board of directors of the United Way. Gates believed that connection helped him get the contract with IBM, which was finally signed in November 1980.

Microsoft first had to set up a workplace for the project, a more difficult task than might be imagined. IBM wasn't just any company. It treasured secrecy and imposed the strictest security requirements. Gates and Ballmer decided on a small room in the middle of their offices in the old National Bank building in downtown Seattle. IBM sent its own file locks, and when Gates had trouble installing them, IBM sent its own locksmith. The room had no windows and no ventilation, and IBM required that the door be kept constantly closed. Sometimes the temperature inside exceeded 100 degrees. IBM conducted several security checks to make sure Microsoft followed orders. Once Microsoft was caught taking a breath, and the IBM operative found the secret room wide open and a chassis from a prototype machine standing outside it. Microsoft wasn't used to dealing with this kind of strictness.

But Microsoft learned. To speed communication between Microsoft and IBM, a sophisticated (for those times) electronic mail system was set up, which sent messages instantly back and forth between a computer in Boca Raton and one in Seattle. Gates also made frequent trips to Boca Raton.

The schedule was grueling. The software had to be completed by March 1981. IBM's project managers showed Gates timetables and more timetables, all of which "basically proved we were three months behind schedule before we started," Gates said.

The first order of business was the operating system. Paterson's SCP-DOS operating system was a close but crude imitation of CP/M. It needed a lot of work to make it fill the bill for the IBM job. Gates brought Paterson in to work on adapting his operating system. The operating system APIs, in particular, had to be completed as soon as possible.

APIs are application program interfaces. They specify how application programs, such as word processors, interface with the operating system. Despite the generally tight security surrounding the PC, developers writing application programs for the IBM machine had to have the APIs to do their work. That provided a crack in the security through which Gary Kildall managed to see, before the machine was released, what Microsoft's operating system was like.

When he saw the APIs, Kildall realized just how close to his CP/M the new IBM/Microsoft operating system was. He threatened to sue. "I told them that they wouldn't have proceeded down that path if they knew [the IBM operating system] was that closely patterned after mine. They didn't realize that CP/M was something owned by people." IBM met with him and agreed to offer the 16-bit version of CP/M as well as Microsoft's operating system for their PC. Kildall, in return, agreed not to sue. IBM said that it couldn't set a price, though, because that would be a violation of antitrust laws.

When Gates heard about IBM's dealing with Digital Research, he complained, but IBM reassured him that Microsoft's DOS was its "strategic operating system." It would turn out that Gates had nothing to worry about. Kildall's operating system would never be given a chance to compete with Microsoft's.

Meanwhile Gates took charge of converting Microsoft BASIC, the warhorse originally written for the old Altair, to the IBM computer. He worked on it with Paul Allen and Neil Konzen, another Microsoft employee. Six years before, Allen, as MITS software director, had nagged Gates to do the Altair disk code and teenaged Gates had procrastinated. Ironically, Gates was doing the supervising this time and Allen did most of the work. Other Microsoft programmers labored on the various language conversion projects.

Gates was feeling the pressure from IBM, and he passed it on to his employees. Some of them were used to spending winter weekends as ski instructors—but not that winter. "Nobody went skiing," said Gates. When some of them wanted to fly to Florida to watch the launch of the space shuttle, Gates was unsympathetic. But when they insisted, he said that they could go if they completed a set amount of work beforehand. The programmers spent five days straight at Microsoft, even sleeping there, in order to meet his demands. Allen remembers programming until 4 A.M. when Charles Simonyi, formerly of Xerox PARC, walked in and declared that they were flying down to Florida for the launch that morning. Allen protested. He wanted to continue his work. Simonyi dissuaded the exhausted programmer, and they were on the plane a few hours later.

Gates discussed the design of the new machine with IBM continually, usually with Estridge. He pointed out that the open architecture of the Apple computer had contributed immeasurably to its success. Gates had reason to appreciate openness because the SoftCard, Microsoft's only hardware product, was a cornerstone of the corporation. Because Estridge owned an Apple II, he had leaned toward an open architecture at the outset. With Gates's encouragement, IBM defied its tradition of secret design specifications and turned its first personal computer into an open system.

This was an extraordinary move for IBM, the most aloof and proprietary of all computer companies. It was deliberately inviting the "parasites" that Ed Roberts had condemned. IBM would use standard parts and design considerations created by kids in garages, and it would encourage more contributions from them. It was shrugging off the tailored tux to don the ready-to-wear clothes of the hobbyists and hackers.

Gates understood the open-system issue from MITS's experience. Ed Roberts had accidentally created an open system in 1974 by making the Altair a bus-based machine. Other manufacturers could, and did, produce circuit boards for the Altair, and an entire S100 industry developed, to Roberts's dismay. When Roberts tried to hide the bus's details, the industry effectively took the bus away from him, redefining it to standard specifications.

Gates was intent on making Microsoft's operating system, now called MS-DOS, the industry's standard operating system. He abandoned the symbiotic relationship he had once enjoyed with Digital Research whereby DR was the operating system firm and Microsoft did languages. Gates made a strong and convincing case to IBM for an open operating system, too. The IBM people in charge of the PC were receptive, but openness was not an IBM hallmark. The benefits took some explaining. If people knew the details of the operating system, they could develop software for it more easily, and VisiCalc had shown that good third-party software can help sell a machine. He may have had more practical considerations in mind, however. Having broken into mainframe operating systems when he was 14, having seen his original Altair BASIC become an industry standard through theft, Gates may simply have found it wiser to give away what would otherwise be preempted.

The operating system was also open in another way. Gates managed to get IBM to agree to let Microsoft sell its operating system to other hardware manufacturers. IBM apparently did not understand the riches they were handing to Microsoft.

Although pressure to finish the software was extreme, Gates was confident in his ability and the capability of his company, which was glittering with programming talent. But he had one fear that he could not overcome. It concerned him even more than the deadline, and it haunted him right up to the announcement of the IBM computer: would IBM cancel the project?

They were not really working with IBM, after all. They were working with a division of IBM, a maverick division on a short tether. There was no telling when IBM might pull in the rope. IBM was a Goliath with many, many projects. Only a small percentage of the research and development work done at IBM ever appeared as finished projects. What other secret IBM personal computer projects might be proceeding in parallel with Chess he didn't know and would probably never know. "They seriously talked about canceling the project up until the last minute," said Gates, "and we had put so many of the company's resources into the thing."

Gates was under strain, and any talk of cancellation upset him. He worried about stories appearing in the press about an IBM personal computer. Some were quite precise. Would IBM question his company's compliance with its security requirements? When an article in the June 8, 1981, issue of *InfoWorld* accurately described four months early the details of the IBM machine, including the decision to develop a new operating system, Gates panicked. He called the magazine's editor to protest the publication of "rumors."

When IBM came out with its personal computer, fortunes would be won and lost. Bill Gates wanted to be sure nothing prevented Microsoft from being among the winners.

The Accidental
Entrepreneur

I didn't have a direction. I was drifting.
I was kind of an intellectual gypsy.

MITCH KAPOR
Coinventor of Lotus 1-2-3

THE INDUSTRY THAT **IBM** WAS PREPARING TO ENTER IN 1981 WAS A curious environment, with its own set of values, its own culture, even a kind of mythology.

The story of VisiCalc was a legend in the personal computer industry. Indeed, VisiCalc's success was one of the chief arguments for it being an industry, rather than merely a market for hobby equipment.

By 1981, it seemed that anyone who had any connection with personal computers could tell you how Dan Bricklin had come up with the idea for the first spreadsheet program while studying business in graduate school at Harvard; how he had recruited old MIT computer science classmate Bob Frankston to develop the program; how they had formed Software Arts; and how in April 1979, Software Arts had contracted with Personal Software (which was a respected personal computer software firm at the time, even if it was just Dan Fylstra and his fiancée selling software out of an apartment) to market their program VisiCalc. And how VisiCalc, developed initially for the Apple II, was a runaway success and became Personal Software's top seller, running up 100,000 unit sales in two years, truly impressive for the time. What Bricklin had invented was a thing of beauty. Not the VisiCalc program itself, but the spreadsheet paradigm. That was the *invention*, that sliding window on an infinitely large blackboard. The grid of cells whose values can be dependent on one another. The whole idea of doing math in two dimensions. The things left out, or worked out, of the design. The truly uncluttered simplicity of the concept.

And *invention* was, in those days, what sold.

David Reed, who worked for Software Arts later on, summarized the basic fact of market position back then: "The first generation of product was what succeeded. If something new came along, you could just find gobs of new people to try the thing."

Reed put it in terms of products and markets, but products can create markets, and in the early days of the PC industry that was more often than not the case with successful products. The success of the first product in a market wasn't always just a matter of somebody filling an existing niche first. It was sometimes a matter of creating the niche, of inventing a new kind of thing in the world.

When the early personal computer customers were snapping up these new things, they were buying inventions, and rewarding inventors. There was, in those giddy days, often a close conversation between the inventor and the market.

And the spreadsheet was indeed an invention, more so than many software gadgets that have subsequently been granted patent protection. Which made Bricklin's deliberate decision not to try to patent the spreadsheet concept all the more significant. It left the door open for enhancements to the concept and for the kind of iterative collaboration that in those days fueled software development.

Or it can be put this way: Bricklin's decision opened the door for Mitch Kapor. The Kapor story, though, starts much earlier—in the 1960s.

The kid, as anyone could see, had promise. There was that computer he built as a science fair project in junior high. All right, so it was really just an adding machine with a rotary phone dial for input. Still, how many kids would even have thought of building a computer in 1964?

He was given every encouragement to live up to that promise. His dad, a successful small business owner, discouraged Mitch from thinking about business as a career. A college professor—that was a worthwhile goal for the bright young kid from Boston. His school gave him every encouragement, too; it offered a course in computer programming, which was highly unusual for a high school in the 1960s. Add to that the National Science Foundation–sponsored enrichment courses in the summer, classes at Columbia University on weekends. . . .

Then, in 1967, came graduation. And along with it a few other things.

It was the Summer of Love, the flowering of Haight-Ashbury in San Francisco, the release of the Beatles' *Sgt. Pepper* album. Mitch was going to Yale in the fall, but that summer his mind was 3000 miles away, his event horizon a week out, and his priorities more or less sex, drugs, and rock 'n' roll.

His parents were not happy.

Oh, Mitch *was* the good son; he did the Yale thing, got the degree. And he had some further encounters with computers along the way, which both intrigued and frustrated him. He went on to graduate school. But the culture of the 1960s had gotten inside Mitch Kapor.

In the 1960s, dropping out was a viable option. You could live on the fringe, not being a visible blip on the economic radar screen but not starving either. Kapor may have made $12,000 one of those years, but generally it was less. He was drifting, directionless, an "intellectual gypsy" as he later characterized that period of his life. He drifted into teaching transcendental meditation, into a stint as a disc jockey, into work as a counselor in a mental hospital, and into and out of a marriage.

Closing in on 30 years old, low on cash, and without direction, he seized on an old fascination. Pawning his stereo, he bought an Apple II computer and started programming. He became a BASIC hacker.

It was at this point that the random walk of Mitch Kapor's life intersected the vector of VisiCalc's success.

Kapor's relationship with programming was schizoid: he was fascinated with the cleanness and the orderliness of what computers could be made to do, but he was also exasperated whenever he tried to make them do it. He didn't think he was a very good programmer. He persevered, though, and got good enough that he was able to complete a program that worked with VisiCalc spreadsheets to plot and analyze spreadsheet data.

He had done a good enough job, in fact, that he was able to interest Personal Software. Dan Fylstra, who was flush with cash from sales of the very successful VisiCalc, was looking for new products, and Mitch pitched his creation as a product to fill out a "Visi" product line for Personal Software. He called it VisiPlot/VisiTrend. Mitch went to work for Personal Software for a few months but wasn't happy when a new management team arrived. In place of equity in the company, Fylstra gave him $1.2 million for his software.

Mitch Kapor, ex–transcendental meditation teacher, didn't actually need $1.2 million, nor did he know quite what to do with it. Finally he decided to start a company. It wasn't what his father, a businessman who had always wanted his son to become a professor, wanted. For that matter, it wasn't terribly consistent with Kapor's own 1960s anticorporate values. He reasoned that having his own company would allow him to do what he wanted, while putting enough money in his pocket so that he wouldn't feel like a drifter.

He called the company Micro Finance Systems, and its first product was to be called Executive Briefing System. Its trick was to take a graph or plot and organize it into a presentation. It borrowed some of its look and feel from Kapor's VisiPlot. Mitch conceived and designed the product, but this time he got programming help: a teenaged hacker named Todd Agulnick coded Executive Briefing System. Kapor would later write cogently about his notion of the role of the software designer, as opposed to the role of the programmer, in the development of a software product, but in the early days of Executive Briefing System he was less clear on the concept. He did know, though, that he wanted a better programmer than himself writing his software.

Shortly thereafter, Kapor changed the company name to Lotus Development Corporation, in honor of his days as a transcendental meditation teacher. This was before Executive Briefing System ever shipped. In fact, the product barely shipped at all. Although some sales of Executive Briefing System apparently showed up on the balance sheet during second-round venture financing for Lotus, Kapor never made much effort to sell the product, soon dropping it altogether to put all the Lotus eggs into a different basket.

The inspiration for the second product was a chance meeting at an Apple II user group with a seasoned professional programmer named Jonathan Sachs.

Sachs had his own software company, Concentric Data Systems. Not long before, Sachs had been in charge of a team of programmers writing an operating system at Data General, a minicomputer company, and before that had spent more than a decade studying and developing software at MIT. Concentric was a tiny venture. It was a consulting firm that consisted of Sachs, who was trying to create products, and John Henderson, his former boss at Data General, who was bringing in the real money with contract programming. Together, they wrote a technically spiffy but strategically disastrous spreadsheet for Data General hardware that did nothing for Concentric's bottom line and contributed greatly to the breakup of their partnership. When they split, they held joint custody of the spreadsheet. Sachs hooked up with Kapor and set to work reimplementing the spreadsheet in the C programming language for a machine with a Z80 microprocessor.

It was soon clear that two things needed to change: programming in C was inefficient compared to working in assembly language, and the Z80 was not the platform of the future. When the IBM PC was released in August 1981, Kapor and Sachs had no doubt what the platform of the future was, and changed direction rapidly.

Out went the C code and the plans for the Z80 implementation. Out went the powerful embedded programming language that Sachs liked. And what had been a simple spreadsheet soon became a three-function program. Mere spreadsheets had been done, Kapor argued; integrated software was the trick. Their program would combine the functions of spreadsheet, graphics, and word processing in one integrated program. And because it did more, Kapor explained, they could charge more for it.

Making money was not the prime motivation behind the increasingly frenetic activity at Lotus, but somewhere along the way it occurred to Kapor that one could make a lot of money on this stuff, which, he decided, would be a "good thing." Somewhere around this time it also occurred to him that the marketing strategies of current software companies were a little on the quaint side. If personal computer software was going to be a serious business—and the $1.2 million Fylstra had paid him felt pretty serious to him—marketing strategies would have to change.

Meanwhile, Sachs coded. He worked furiously, and he worked at home, coming to the office once a week to run the latest accomplishments past Kapor and get feedback. They were up against a deadline, but they didn't know what it was. When IBM released its personal computer, whenever that happened, their window would open up. There was no telling how long it would be open.

As Sachs honed the program into a product with Kapor's design feedback, the original three functions of spreadsheet, graphics, and word processing changed into spreadsheet, graphics, and database management. The word processor component proved just a little too hairy to implement. That turned out to be a nice choice, though: the database capability fit better with the other capabilities. And it was still a three-function program, which Kapor thought was important. They decided to play up the three functions in the product's name, and called it Lotus 1-2-3.

Abruptly, in 1981, the window of opportunity for this product opened wide and the pace picked up. IBM introduced its PC, and Kapor immediately started talking up Lotus 1-2-3 to potential investors and buyers.

Kapor thought that one potential buyer would be Dan Fylstra, who had already bought his VisiPlot/VisiTrend. Fylstra knew Kapor well and had the money and the market position. Personal Software was at this point the largest personal computer software company, having just grossed $12 million that year. But Fylstra passed on the idea, wishing Mitch well.

One potential investor in Kapor's product was venture capitalist Ben Rosen. Kapor pitched Rosen on this integrated spreadsheet, database, and graphics program that could take advantage of the IBM PC's 640K RAM. He also pitched him the company. Lotus Development Corporation was going to be a serious software powerhouse.

Rosen didn't pass on the idea. He kicked in the $1 million seed capital in 1982 to get Lotus Development Corporation off the ground. In April 1982, Lotus was up and running, with eight employees and one product under development. Six months later, in October 1982, Lotus announced 1-2-3 at the Windows on the World restaurant in New York City's World Trade Center. There was major press attendance, and a story about it appeared in the next day's *Wall Street Journal*.

Rosen delivered another $3.8 million in December. This was unheard of. In terms of investment, in terms of rolling the dice and sheer chutzpah, they were all in unexplored territory here. Nobody had put that kind of money into a personal computer software company before. Certainly not into one whose entire sales record consisted of a few copies of Executive Briefing System sitting on a store shelf in West Hartford, Connecticut.

The selling of Lotus 1-2-3 was a remarkable gamble. It was hands-down the biggest marketing blitz to date in the short history of the personal computer industry. To run the campaign, Kapor hired consultants McKinsey & Company, and McKinsey & Company assigned a new hire by the name of Jim Manzi to the job.

Lotus 1-2-3 hit the stores in January 1983. It sold more than 200,000 copies in its first year. It took over the top of Softsel's best-seller list by April and held it for the rest of 1983. That year, the product brought in $53 million in sales to Lotus, making a nice return on Ben Rosen's $4.8 million investment.

Manzi, the campaign's hero, joined Lotus as marketing director in May. He took out ads in *The Wall Street Journal,* a radical move given the skepticism with which personal computers were greeted in corporate circles. In three years, sales went to $300 million. Lotus 1-2-3 took the spreadsheet concept right to its intended audience of business users. Businesses liked 1-2-3, and they liked the company that made it. Lotus Development Corporation, alone among personal software companies, looked to the business community like a real business, not a bunch of lucky hackers.

Along the way, the lucky hacker who invented it learned that what he was selling was a spreadsheet. Silly him; he thought it was integrated software.

IBM Discovers the
Woz Principle

Welcome, IBM. Seriously.

AN APPLE COMPUTER ADVERTISEMENT

WHEN, ON AUGUST 12, 1981, INTERNATIONAL BUSINESS MACHINES announced its first personal computer, it radically and irrevocably changed the world for microcomputer makers, software developers, retailers, and the rapidly growing market of microcomputer buyers.

In the 1960s, there was a saying among mainframe computer companies that IBM was not the competition, it was The Environment. Whole segments of the industry, known collectively as the plug-compatibles, grew up around IBM products, and their prosperity depended on IBM's prosperity. To the plug-compatibles, the cryptic numbers by which IBM identified its products, such as the 1401 or the legendary 360, were not the trademarks of a competitor, but familiar features of the terrain, like mountains and seas. When IBM brought out a personal computer, it too had one of those product numbers. But the IBM marketing people knew that they were dealing with a new kind of customer and that a number might not convey the right message. It isn't hard to guess what IBM thought the right message was. By naming its machine the Personal Computer, it suggested this device was the only personal computer. The machine quickly became called the IBM PC, or simply the PC. The operating system, originally SCP-DOS (for Seattle Computer Products), became MS-DOS under Microsoft, but

IBM referred to it as PC-DOS on its machine, and some users slipped into the habit of just calling it DOS.

The IBM PC itself was almost conventional from the standpoint of the industry at the time. Sol and Osborne inventor Lee Felsenstein got his hands on one of the first delivered IBM PCs and opened it up at a Homebrew Computer Club meeting.

"I was surprised to find chips in there that I recognized," he said. "There weren't any chips that I didn't recognize. My experience with IBM so far was that when you find IBM parts in a junk box, you forget about them because they're all little custom jobs and you can't find any data about them. IBM is off in a world of its own. But, in this case, they were building with parts that mortals could get."

The machine used an 8088 processor, which, although it was not the premier chip then available, put the IBM PC a notch above any other machine then sold. The PC impressed Felsenstein—not technologically, but politically. He liked to see IBM admitting that it needed other people. The open bus structure and thorough, readable documentation said as much. "But the major surprise was that they were using chips from Earth and not from IBM. I thought, 'They're doing things our way.' "

In addition to operating systems and languages, IBM offered a number of applications for the PC that were sold separately. Surprisingly, IBM had developed none of them. Showing that it had learned from Apple, IBM offered the ubiquitous VisiCalc spreadsheet (Lotus 1-2-3 would come later and would become must-have software for business), the well-known series of business programs from Peachtree Software, and a word processor called EasyWriter from Information Unlimited Software (IUS).

WordStar, from Seymour Rubinstein's MicroPro, was the leading word processing program, and IBM had wanted it. But Rubinstein, like the Kildalls, balked at accepting IBM's terms. They wanted MicroPro to convert WordStar to run on the IBM PC and then turn the product over to IBM, Rubinstein said. "They said I could build my own program after that, but I'd have to not do it the same way. They were setting themselves up to sue me later. They were going to grab control of my product. I had something to protect, so I didn't do the deal. I tried to negotiate a different deal, but they wouldn't." IBM turned to IUS.

The IUS deal may have been the ultimate culture shock for the IBM people. They had designed their machine with non-IBM components. They had released to the general public the sort of information they had always kept secret. They had bought an operating system instead of writing it; they had done and dealt with things that had always been utterly beyond IBM's pale. But they hadn't bargained for John Draper.

IUS was a small Marin County software firm with a word processor called EasyWriter. IBM had approached IUS about EasyWriter, and Larry Weiss of IUS contacted EasyWriter's author, John Draper, alias Captain Crunch, avowed enemy of bureaucracy and the king of the phone phreaks, those who specialized in breaking into long-distance phone lines to make free calls. Draper recalled, "Eaglebeak [Weiss] comes to me and he says, 'John, I got this deal that you're not going to believe, but I can't tell you anything about it.' And then we had this meeting at IUS. There were these people in pinstripes and me looking like me. This was the time that I realized we were dealing with IBM. I had to sign these things saying that I wasn't going to be discussing any technical information. I wasn't even supposed to disclose that I was dealing with IBM. They were coming out with a home computer and Eaglebeak said something to me about putting EasyWriter on it."

Draper had written EasyWriter years before out of frustration because the Apple had no satisfactory word processor and he couldn't afford an S100 system on which he could run Michael Shrayer's Electric Pencil. Draper liked Electric Pencil, the only word processor he'd seen, so he fashioned his own after it. Demonstrating it at the fourth West Coast Computer Faire, he ran into Bill Baker, a transplanted Midwesterner who had started IUS, and Baker agreed to sell EasyWriter for him. All that had led to this: Captain Crunch sitting down with IBM.

IBM gave IUS and Draper six months to convert EasyWriter to run on the PC, and Draper went right to work. "In order to keep from slipping and talking about IBM, we called it Project Commodore," Draper recalled. Soon, Baker was irritating Draper. "Baker comes down on me for not working 8 to 5, and that's bullshit. Look, man, I don't operate in that style. I operate in a creative environment. I don't go by the clock. I go by the way my mind works." Then IBM made changes in the hardware that Draper had to incorporate. The six months passed and the release program wasn't done. Draper found himself pressured to say that an earlier but completed version was adequate and that it could be released with the machine. With grave reservations he finally agreed, and IBM's machine was sold with Captain Crunch's word processor. The program did not receive rave reviews. IBM later offered free updates to the program.

A word processor was sober software, no matter who wrote it, but at the last minute IBM decided to add a computer game to its series of optional programs. Toward the end of the press release announcing the PC, the company declared, "*Microsoft Adventure* brings players into a fantasy world of caves and treasures." Corporate data processing managers around the country read the ad and thought, "This is IBM?"

The PC's unveiling received wide play in the national press. It was by far the least expensive machine IBM had ever sold. IBM realized that the personal computer was a retail item that consumers would buy in retail computer stores and could not, therefore, be marketed by its sales force. The company again departed from tradition and arranged to sell its PC through the largest and most popular computer retail chain, the IMSAI spin-off ComputerLand. This was a much bigger departure for IBM than it had been for Xerox. IBM didn't stop there; it also announced plans to sell the PC in department stores, just like any appliance.

Wherever it was sold, the purchaser had a choice of operating systems: PC-DOS for $40 or CP/M-86 for $240. If it was a joke, Gary Kildall wasn't laughing.

Software companies quickly began writing programs for PC-DOS. Hardware firms also developed products for the PC. Because PC sales started fast and increased steadily, these companies were easily convinced that PC-based products would find a market. In turn, the add-on products themselves spurred PC sales, because they increased the utility of the machine. IBM's open system decision was now paying dividends.

Apple Computer could not have been surprised by the IBM announcement, as it had predicted an IBM microcomputer several years earlier. Steve Jobs claimed that Apple's only worry was that IBM might offer a machine with highly advanced technology. Like Felsenstein, he was relieved that IBM was using a nonproprietary processor and an accessible architecture. Apple responded publicly to the PC announcement by asserting that it would actually help Apple because IBM publicity would cause more people to buy personal computers.

The world's largest computer company had endorsed the personal computer as a viable commercial product. Although innovative hobbyists and small companies had founded the industry, only IBM could bring the product fully into the public eye. "Welcome IBM," Apple said in a full-page advertisement in *The Wall Street Journal*. "Welcome to the most exciting and important marketplace since the computer revolution began 35 years ago. . . . We look forward to responsible competition in the massive effort to distribute this American technology to the world."

IBM's endorsement certainly did increase demand for personal computers. Many businesses, small and large, still balked at the idea of buying a personal computer. Many seriously wondered why IBM wasn't working in that area. Now the personal computer had arrived. Between August and December 1981, IBM shipped 13,000 PCs. Over the next two years, it would sell 40 times that number. The early microcomputers had been designed in the absence of software. When CP/M and its overlayer of applications software became popular, hardware designers built machines that would run those programs. Similarly, the success of the IBM Personal Computer caused programmers to write an array of software for its MS-DOS operating system. New hardware manufacturers sprang up to introduce computers that could run the same programs as the IBM PC, so-called "clones." Some offered different capabilities than those of the IBM machine, such as portability, additional memory, or superior graphics, and many were less expensive than the PC. But all served to ratify the PC operating system. And MS-DOS quickly became the standard operating system for 16-bit machines.

Microsoft benefited more than any other player, including IBM. Gates had encouraged IBM to use an open design and had managed to get a nonexclusive license for the operating system. The former ensured that there would be clones, if other companies could get their hands on the operating system. The latter ensured that they could, and that they would pay Microsoft for it. And IBM's pricing strategy ensured that Microsoft's operating system would be the only one that mattered.

Even DEC entered the fray a year later with a dual-processor computer called the Rainbow that could run both 8-bit software under CP/M and 16-bit software under CP/M-86 or MS-DOS.

All the companies in the industry had to cope with the imposing presence of IBM. ComputerLand was dropping the smaller manufacturers for IBM, and even Apple found that it had to respond to IBM's incursion into the ComputerLand stores. Apple terminated its contract with ComputerLand's central office where IBM was influential and started dealing directly with the outlet franchise stores.

It was the end of the beginning. A shakeout that had been only foreshadowed in the failures of MITS, IMSAI, and Processor Technology began to loom real in the eyes of the pioneering companies, and with over 300 personal computer companies in existence, many hobbyist-originated companies began to wonder if they would still be in business two years hence. IBM had forced even the big companies in the market to reappraise their situations.

Xerox, Don Massaro said, had carefully considered that IBM might produce a personal computer. "We did a worst-case scenario in getting approval for the [Xerox 820] program. We said, 'What could IBM do? How could we not be successful in this marketplace?' The scenario was that IBM would enter with a product that would make ours technically obsolete, they would sell it through dealers, and it would have an open operating system." It seemed an unlikely prospect. "You see, IBM had *never* done that, had never sold through dealers, and had certainly never had an open operating system. I thought IBM would have their own proprietary operating system for which they would write their own software, and that they would sell through their own stores." Instead, Xerox's worst fear came to life in painful detail, and "the whole world ran off in that direction. IBM just killed everybody."

Not everybody. But the circle of attention had narrowed. There were now two personal computer companies that everyone was watching: Apple and an IBM nobody knew; an IBM that had, in John Draper's words, "discovered the Woz Principle" of the open system.

The presence of IBM and the other big companies shook the industry to its hobbyist roots. Tandy, with its own distribution channels, was only modestly affected. Commodore was doing all right concentrating on European sales and sales of low-cost home computers.

But the companies that had pioneered the personal computer began dropping out of the picture. The shakeout was in earnest. The resurrected IMSAI was one of the first companies to go. Todd Fischer and Nancy Freitas supplied the IMSAI computer that figured prominently in the popular movie *War Games,* and it was effectively the company's last act. Shortly thereafter, Fischer and Freitas gave the pioneering microcomputer company a decent burial. (But not permanently: Fischer and Freitas would be selling IMSAI computers again in 1999, feeding a retrocomputing craze.)

By late 1983, even some of the most successful of the personal computer and software companies to spring up out of the hobbyist movement were hurt. North Star, Vector Graphic, and Cromemco all felt the pinch. There were massive layoffs, and some companies turned to offshore manufacturing to stop leaking profits. Chuck Peddle, who had been responsible for the PET computer and had been active throughout the industry in semiconductor design at MOS Technologies and in computers at Commodore and briefly at Apple, was now running his own company, Victor, with a computer similar to IBM's. In the face of the IBM challenge, Victor soon had to severely cut back its work force, hurt by softening sales. George Morrow's company Microstuf considered a stock offering, but then withdrew the idea in response to IBM's growing influence in the market.

On September 13, 1983, Osborne Computer Corporation declared bankruptcy amid a mountain of debt, accumulated when it tried to catch up with Apple and IBM. Of all the company failures in the history of the personal computer industry, none was more thoroughly analyzed. OCC had flown high and fast, and its fall was startling. At the height of their success, Osborne executives appeared on the television program *60 Minutes,* predicting that they would soon be millionaires. They were, on paper, but the company's financial controls were so lax that the figures were meaningless. The media coverage of the company's failure was intense, but the analyses were conflicting. Certainly there were problems with the hardware, but most companies have them, and Osborne dealt with them. Osborne executives made serious mistakes in the timing of product announcements and the pricing of new products.

In May, Osborne had announced its Executive computer. Its

improvements included a larger screen, but the company's new "professional" management priced it at $2,495 and stopped selling the original product. Sales immediately declined. "If we had left the Osborne 1 on the market, management would have seen the mistake because it would have kept on selling," said Michael McCarthy, a documentation writer at the firm. Instead, first-time buyers who liked the Osborne 1 for its packaging and price now looked elsewhere.

What seems clear is that Osborne grew so fast in its attempt to be one of the three major companies that Adam Osborne had predicted would dominate personal computing in a year or so, that its managers were unable to control it. As industry analyst John Dvorak put it, "The company grew from zilch to $100 million in less than two years. Who do you hire who has experience with growth like that? Nobody exists." Osborne was just too successful for its own good.

The last chapter of the Osborne story had a bittersweet irony for the employees. Coming to work one day, they were instructed to leave the premises. Money owed them was not paid. Security guards were posted at the doors to ensure that they took no Osborne property with them. But someone had failed to inform the guards that the company made portable computers, and the employees walked out carrying Osborne's inventory with them.

Others fell under IBM's shadow. Small software companies like EduWare and Lightning Software allowed themselves to be bought by larger ones, and all software companies learned to think of first doing "the IBM version" of any new software product. Even major corporations adjusted their behavior. Atari and Texas Instruments swallowed millions in losses in their attempts to win their way into the personal computer market through low-cost home machines. Atari suffered deep wounds. And although TI had more of its low-cost TI-99/4 computers in homes than almost any other computer, it announced in the fall of 1983 that it was cutting its losses and getting out of personal computer manufacturing.

IBM's entry also affected the magazines, shows, and stores. David Bunnell, who had left MITS to start *Personal Computing* magazine, responded to IBM's arrival by coming out with *PC Magazine,* a thick publication directed at users of the IBM machine. Soon major publishers were fighting over Bunnell's magazine. Wayne Green, having built *Kilobaud* into an empire of computer magazines by 1983, sold the lot to an East Coast conglomerate. Art Salsberg and Les Solomon rode out *Popular Electronics*'s transformation into *Computers and Electronics.* Jim Warren started an IBM PC Faire in late 1983 and then sold his show-sponsoring company, Computer Faire, to publishing house Prentice-Hall, claiming that the business was too big for him to manage. ComputerLand and the independent computer stores found themselves competing with Sears and Macy's as IBM opened new channels of distribution for personal computers.

Late in 1983, IBM announced its second personal computer. Dubbed the PCjr, the machine offered little technological innovation. Perhaps to prevent business users from buying the new and less-expensive machine in place of the PC, IBM equipped the PCjr with a poor quality "chicklet" keyboard, a style of keyboard unsuited to serious, prolonged use. Despite the PCjr's unimpressive technological design and chilly reception, by announcing a second personal computer, IBM demonstrated that it recognized a broad, largely untapped market for home computers. IBM intended to be a dominant force in that market.

Apple, in preparation for its inevitable head-to-toe battle with IBM, made several significant moves. In 1983, the firm hired a new president, former Pepsi Cola executive John Sculley, to manage its underdog campaign against IBM.

That Apple, no longer the dominant company in an industry still in its infancy, could attract the heir apparent to the presidency of huge Pepsico was a tribute to the persuasive powers of its cofounder, Steve Jobs. "You can stay and sell sugar water," he told a vacillating Sculley, "or you can come with me and change the world." Sculley came.

Then, in January 1984, Apple introduced its Macintosh computer.

IBM had chosen to emphasize its name—the best-known three letters in the computer industry. Apple decided to provide state-of-the-market technology. The Macintosh immediately received accolades for its impressive design, including highly developed software technology that used a mouse, an advanced graphical user interface, and a powerful 32-bit microprocessor in a lightweight package.

Inevitably, the money dealers had come to where the money was, and the financial success of the industry rooted in hobbydom severed the industry from its roots. But the computer-power-to-the-people spirit Lee Felsenstein and others had sought to foster had by no means disappeared. Even staunchly conservative IBM had bent to it in adopting an open architecture and an open operating system. IBM's corporate policy in the 1950s and 1960s had often been to lease computers and to discourage sales. For the room-sized computers made then, this method was appropriate. With proprietary architectures and software, the power of the machines really belonged not to the people who used them, but to the companies that had built them.

In 1984, it looked like the personal computer and all the growing power it harnessed belonged to the people.

▲ *Inside the original Byte Shop*

◄ *Stan Veit, who founded The Computer Mart, an early computer store, in New York*

▲ *Bill Gates at the World Altair Computer Convention, 1976*

▲ *Sign advertising World Altair Computer Convention, 1976*

▲ Bob Marsh (head on fist) and Gary Ingram (right) at their company's booth at an early trade show

▲ Bob Marsh of Processor Technology entertaining children at a computer show

▲ *Chuck Peddle, designer of the Pet Computer,*
at the Consumer Electronics Show in June 1978

▲ *Dan Bricklin (seated) and Bob Frankston, who invented VisiCalc, the first*
microcomputer spreadsheet software, in 1979

John Mauchley, cocreator of ENIAC, speaking at the 1976 Atlantic City Computer Festival

COURTESY OF DAVID H. AHL

Jim Warren, a watchdog of the early personal computer industry when he was editing Dr. Dobb's Journal, *and a cofounder of the* West Coast Computer Faire

COURTESY OF JIM WARREN

An exhibitor getting ready at the First West Coast Computer Faire, 1977

Early West Coast Computer Faire trade show

Lyall Morrill (wearing the trademark of his Computer Headware software company) and Bill Baker at the Second West Coast Computer Faire

Peter Jennings (left), who developed the early computer chess game Micro Chess in the mid-1970s, and Dan Fylstra, whose company published the historic VisiCalc, at the West Coast Computer Faire

Carl Helmers, first editor of Byte magazine, at the National Computer Conference

The IBM PC in 1981, which gave the computer industry the stamp of approval it needed, changing it forever

Philip Estridge, who headed
the IBM PC project for IBM

COURTESY OF IBM ARCHIVES

John Draper, creator of the first word processor for the IBM
PC, alias Captain Crunch, the famous phone phreak who built
"blue boxes" that made free long-distance calls

COURTESY OF BILL BAKER

▲ *Adam Osborne with the Osborne 1, the first popular luggable PC*

COURTESY OF DAVID CARLICK

▲ *Osborne 1 advertising campaign shot, illustrating that it could be taken on an airplane (fitting it under the seat was another story)*

COURTESY OF DAVID CARLICK

▲ *Seymour Papert, inventor of the Logo computer language*

COURTESY OF DAVID H. AHL

◄ *Steve Jobs (right) with Dan Kottke at the Apple booth at an early computer show*

COURTESY OF DAN KOTTKE

Robert Metcalfe at Xerox PARC in 1973, coinventor of Ethernet, which became the standard for networking computers

digital   **intel**   **XEROX**

From: dave of digital at DEC node BLUE

Message: where is dave liddle?

      ]

Sent at 3-MAY-1981 13:44:14 via the 10MB Ethernet.

Printout of first transmission sent outside the Xerox PARC facilities using Ethernet, which eventually became the technical standard for networking digital computers in an office environment. The message was sent from one company's booth to another at the National Computer Conference in 1981.

▲ *Andy Hertzfeld, early Macintosh software designer,*
who helped design some of the Macintosh's key software

▲ *Steve Wozniak and Steve Jobs in Jobs's garage, ca. 1975*

▼ *Original Apple I, 1976*

▶ *Steve Wozniak's Apple I schematic, which many engineers consider a work of art*

OUR FOUNDER

▲ *The original Apple I circuit board, framed and hung in the Apple offices with the legend "Our Founder"*

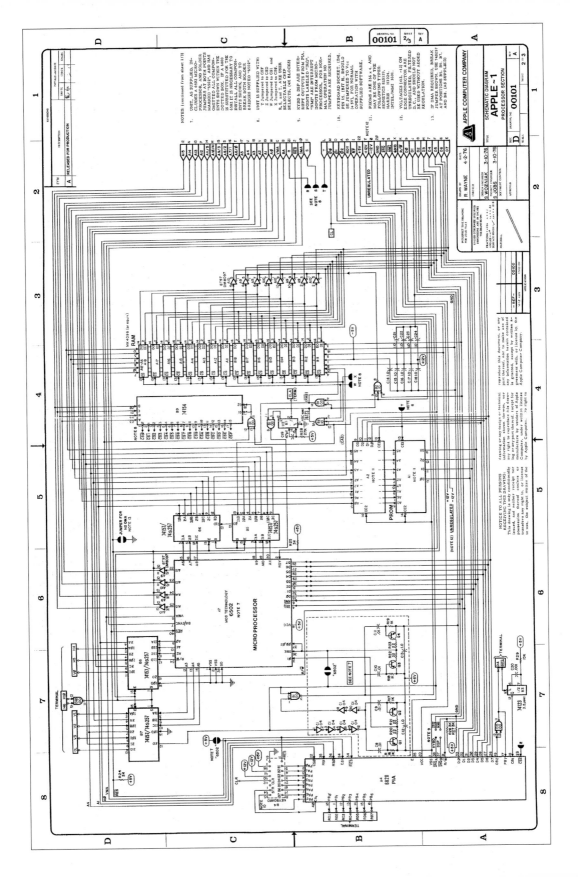

Regis McKenna (left) with Arthur Rock, venture capitalist and one of Apple Computer's first investors

COURTESY OF REGIS MCKENNA

Larry Tesler of Xerox PARC and Apple Computer

COURTESY OF LARRY TESLER

Rod Holt, Apple Computer's "everything-else guy"

COURTESY OF APPLE COMPUTER, INC.

CHAPTER 9

FIRE AND ASHES

*I think over the years Apple spent a long
time languishing on its laurels. Selling
computers but not advancing enough.
I hope we're getting back to [our roots] now.*

STEVE WOZNIAK
Cofounder of Apple Computer

Losing Their Religion

I never really get to see, except second hand, how abrupt he is with people. I couldn't be that way with people. But maybe that's what you need to run a business, to find things that are worthless and get rid of them. I don't know.

STEVE WOZNIAK, ON STEVE JOBS

AFTER THE RELEASE OF THE MACINTOSH IN 1984, STEVE JOBS FELT vindicated. Plaudits from the press and an immediate cult following assured him that the machine was, as he had proclaimed it, "insanely great." He had every right to take pride in the accomplishment. The Macintosh would never have existed if it hadn't been for Jobs. He had seen the light on a visit to Xerox PARC in 1979. Inspired by the innovations presented by the PARC researchers, he longed to get those ideas implemented in the Lisa computer. When Jobs was nudged out of the Lisa project, he hijacked a team of Apple developers working on a mildly interesting idea for an appliance computer and turned them into the Macintosh skunk works.

Jobs hounded the people on the Macintosh project to do their best work. He sang their praises, bullied them unmercifully, and told them they weren't making a computer, they were making history. He promoted the Mac passionately, making people believe that he was talking about much more than just a piece of office equipment.

His methods had all worked, or so it seemed. Early Mac purchasers bought the Jobs message right along with the machine, and forced themselves to overlook the little Mac's serious shortcomings. For about three months, Mac sales more or less matched Jobs's ambitious projections. For a while, reality matched the image in Steve Jobs's head.

Then Apple ran out of zealots.

The first Macintosh purchasers were what are called *early adopters*— technophiles willing to accept the inevitable quirks of new technologies for the thrill of being the first to use them. Those early adopters all bought Mac machines in the first three months of sales, and then the well dried up. In 1984 and 1985, the first two years of the Mac's life, sales routinely failed to reach the magnitude of Jobs's projections, sales projections that the company was counting on. For those two years, it was the old reliable Apple II that kept the company afloat. If Apple had had to depend on Mac sales alone, it would have folded before the 1980s were over.

All the while, the Mac team still got the perks, the money, the recognition, and the Apple II staff got the clear message that they were part of the past. Jobs told the Lisa team outright that they were failures and "C players." He called the Apple II crew "the dull and boring division."

Chris Espinosa came to the Mac division from the Apple II group. He had family and friends still on the Apple II side. The 20-year-old Espinosa had worked at Apple all of his adolescent and adult life. The us-versus-them syndrome he witnessed saddened him.

Customers, third-party developers, and Apple stockholders weren't all that happy, either. The Mac wasn't selling slowly for lack of an advertising budget. It deservedly failed in the market. It lacked some essential features that users had every reason to demand. Initially, it had no hard disk drive, and a second floppy disk drive was an extra-price option. With only a single disk drive, making backup copies of files was a nightmare of disk-swapping.

At 128K RAM, it seemed that the Mac's memory should have been more than adequate; 64K was the standard. But the system and application software ate up most of the 128K, and it was clear that more memory was needed. *Dr. Dobb's Journal* ran an article showing how anyone brave enough to attack the innards of their new Mac machine with a soldering iron could "fatten" their Mac to 512K, six months before Apple got around to delivering a machine with that much RAM.

But the memory limitations weren't a problem unless you had the software that used the RAM, and therein was the real problem. The Mac shipped with a collection of Apple-developed applications that allowed users to do word processing and draw bitmapped pictures. Beyond that, the application choices were slim, because the Mac proved to be a difficult machine to develop software for.

Jobs was entirely committed to his vision of the Macintosh, to the point that he continued to use the 10-times-too-large sales projections as though they were realistic. To some of the other executives, it began to look like Jobs was living in a dream world of his own. The Mac's drawbacks, such as the lack of a hard disk drive, were actually advantages, he argued, and the force of his personality was such that no one dared to challenge him.

Even his boss found it difficult to challenge Jobs. John Sculley, whom Jobs had hired from Pepsi to run Apple, concluded that the company couldn't afford to have its most important division headed up by someone so out of touch with reality. But could Sculley bring himself demote the founder of the company? The situation was getting critical: early in 1985, the company posted its first-ever quarterly loss. Losses simply weren't in the plan for Apple, which stood as an emblem of the personal computer revolution, a modern-day legend, and a company that had risen to the Fortune 500 in record time.

Sculley decided to take some drastic action. In a marathon board meeting that began on the morning of April 19, 1985, and continued into the next day, he told the Apple board that he was going to strip Jobs of his leadership over the Mac division and any management role in the company. Sculley added that if he didn't get full backing from the board on his decision, he couldn't stay on as president. The board promised to back him up.

For some reason, Sculley failed to act on his decision immediately. Jobs heard about what was coming, and in a plot to get Sculley out, began calling up board members to rally their support. When Sculley heard about this, he called an emergency executive board meeting on May 24. At the meeting he confronted Jobs, saying, "It has come to my attention that you'd like to throw me out of the company."

Jobs didn't back down. "I think you're bad for Apple," he told Sculley, "and I think you're the wrong person to run the company." The two men left the board no room for hedging. The individuals in that room were going to have to decide, then and there, between Sculley and Jobs.

They all got behind Sculley. It was a painful experience for everyone involved. Apple II operations manager Del Yocam, for one, was torn between his deep feelings of loyalty toward Jobs and what he felt was best for the future of the company. Yocam recognized the need for the grownup leadership at Apple that Sculley could supply, and that Jobs hadn't, and he cast his vote for maturity over vision.

Jobs was understandably bitter. In September, he sold off his Apple stock and quit the company he had cofounded, announcing his resignation to the press. The charismatic young evangelist who had conceived the very idea of Apple Computer, had been the driving force behind getting both the Apple II and the Macintosh to market, had appeared on the cover of every major newsmagazine, and was viewed as one of the most influential people in the computer industry was now out the door.

With Jobs gone, Sculley set to work saving the company from ruin. Under his direction, Apple dropped the Lisa computer, brought out a high-end Macintosh—the Macintosh II—along with new models of the original Mac, in particular a model called the Mac Plus that was introduced in January 1986.

The Mac Plus addressed most of the shortcomings of the original Mac and got the company back in the black. Sculley had stopped the financial bleeding and put the company back on its feet. The next few years were perhaps the best in Apple's history. Apple was golden.

Sculley had turned around the demoralization that followed Jobs's departure, got the Mac line moving, and made the company profitable again. Sculley eventually retired the Apple II line, but not without first giving the Apple II employees some of the credit they had been denied during the latter part of Jobs's tenure. As a sign of his support of the Apple II team, he promoted Del Yocam to chief operating officer.

With Jobs gone, Sculley began relying on two Europeans more than ever before. German Michael Spindler, savvy about technology and the European market, headed Apple's European efforts, while Jean-Louis

Gassée, a charismatic and witty Frenchman, got the job of inspiring and motivating the engineering troops.

Gassée, who had made Apple France the company's most successful subsidiary, was the one to alert Sculley that Jobs was plotting against him. "You destroy the company if you have that [situation], and this company is more important than any of us," he said. He quickly became the second most visible executive in one of the world's great corporate fishbowls. He had a penchant for metaphor and bold pronouncements; he once gave a speech called, "How We Can Prevent the Japanese from Eating Our Sushi." He won the respect and affection of Apple's engineers.

When alumni of Xerox PARC came up with a language for controlling printers and a program for designing publications, Apple released a laser printer and the desktop publishing market was born. Apple dominated the DTP market for years after that.

"We were in the catbird seat," Chris Espinosa recalled, with a product that was such a favorite among consumers that Apple could raise prices and get away with it, for the time being. "We were making 55 percent gross margins, on our way to becoming a $10 billion corporation. We were in fat city."

One portentous event took place that went unnoticed by the outside world: on October 24, 1985, Microsoft was threatening to stop development on crucial applications for the Mac unless Apple granted Microsoft a license for the Mac operating system software. Microsoft was developing its *graphical user interface* (the items and options a user sees and selects on-screen) for DOS, which they were calling Windows, and didn't want Apple to sue over the similarity between the Windows GUI and the Mac interface. Although Microsoft probably wouldn't have followed through with its threat to stop development on the applications, Sculley decided that Apple couldn't afford to take the chance. He granted Microsoft its license, a move that he would later regret, and try, unsuccessfully, to undo.

The company was prospering. Investors, customers, and employees were happy. But new and disturbing problems were developing for Apple.

Other companies had entered the personal computer market and were making machines that worked like the IBM PC and that ran all the same software. Prices for these IBM-compatibles or *clones* were dropping, and Apple's machines, already premium priced, were getting too far out of line. The Windows 3.1 operating system was released, and its user interface looked enough like the Mac's interface that it began taking market share from Apple.

Personal computers were becoming commodity items, with hardware mattering to consumers less than software. Third-party software (software developed by companies other than Apple or Microsoft) was being written first for Windows and then only occasionally for the Mac. The early message in some sections of the corporate world that the Mac was a toy, not a serious business machine, never was wholly refuted. And Apple retained its proprietary architecture which others could not replicate by building Mac clones, further limiting its potential market.

It seemed clear that Apple couldn't indefinitely go it alone against the whole IBM clone market. Apple appeared to have just two options: one was to rediscover the Woz principle—open the architecture so that other companies could clone the Mac, but do it under license so that Apple would make money on every clone sold; the other was to join forces with another company.

The licensing idea had been around since at least 1985 when Sculley got a letter from Bill Gates, of all people, detailing the reasons why Apple should license the Mac technology. At Apple, Dan Eilers, the director of investor relations, was a persistent proponent of licensing, both at that time and then for years after. Jean-Louis Gassée fought the idea, questioning whether Apple could really protect the company's precious intellectual property after they had released it. The question in Gassée's mind was, "How do you ensure that another company will only sell into a market that complements your own?"

A deal that may have worked to the benefit of Apple was close to completion in 1987. Apple would license its operating system to Apollo, the first workstation company, for use in high-end workstations, a market that seemed to nicely complement Apple's. But Sculley nixed the deal at the last moment.

Apple's waffling over the partnership may have helped to sink Apollo. Its workstation competitor, Sun, was pursuing an *open systems* model, licensing its operating system and swallowing up more and more of the workstation market.

The other option for Apple was a merger or acquisition. Early on, Commodore had tried to buy Apple, and came very close to a deal. Other merger or acquisition discussions were held over the years, and they grew more and more compelling as the PC-clone market grew. In the late 1980s, Sculley had Dan Eilers exploring the possibility of Apple buying Sun. A decade later, the relative fortunes of the two companies would be such that Sun would explore the possibility of buying Apple.

In 1988, Del Yocam got squeezed out as COO in a management reshuffling. Gassée and Spindler were immediate beneficiaries of the restructuring. "Reorgs" were routine at Apple by now. In a 1990 reorganization, Spindler was anointed COO, Sculley named himself chief technology officer (CTO), and Gassée was sidelined. Gassée soon resigned and left the company.

The Apple engineers were outraged. It wasn't just that this former sugar-water salesman Sculley had the gall to name himself CTO of Apple, but Gassée, whom they would have picked as CEO had they been asked, was being shown the door.

Apple employees exhibited a lot of so-called attitude about their status within the industry. They were paid extremely well—at least the engineers were—and they felt as if they were artists. They generally believed that Apple made forward progress only by innovative leaps. This meant that everyone wanted to work on the hot projects; nobody wanted to be in an equivalent of the Apple II division when an equivalent of the Mac was in the works.

One of those hot projects was Newton, a handheld computer with its own operating system and some groundbreaking new technology. As a demonstration of the achievements of the Apple research and development area it was wonderful, but it fell somewhat short as a successful consumer product. The Newton device had no keyboard; users were forced to enter information by handwriting. Unfortunately, the handwriting recognition didn't work all that well and resulted in some amusing mistranslation. Cartoonist Gary Trudeau lampooned the Newton's glitches repeatedly in his *Doonesbury* strip. Eventually the Newton's handwriting recognition software improved enough to be acceptable, but by then the damage was done. Newton never did turn into a killer product, and Apple eventually discontinued the line.

Another hot project was something called Pink. Pink was the internal Apple code name for the next-generation replacement operating system that could run on different machines, including IBM compatibles. The significant talent was placed on the Jaguar project, a new machine using all-new hardware technology, and Pink, a next-generation operating system.

On April 12, 1991, Sculley demonstrated Pink to IBM. The IBM executives were impressed by what looked like the Mac operating system running on IBM hardware. By October, Apple and IBM had agreed to work together on the operating system, now to be called Taligent, and on a new microprocessor for a new generation of computers to be developed by each company.

This wasn't a merger, or an acquisition, or a licensing deal—it was a collaboration with another company that had the potential to grab back a bigger chunk of the market for Apple. It was also evidence of the changing power structure of the industry: Apple could afford to work with its old nemesis IBM, because IBM wasn't the competition any more. Intel, which made the CPU for IBM and compatible computers, and Microsoft were the competition.

The deal with IBM was a bold move, and it may have been Sculley's last significant contribution to the company. Apple's longest-tenured CEO was getting burned out. He had already handed the presidency to Spindler, and now he was becoming distracted, ready to move on to something else.

That something else might have been a very different kind of job from running a personal computer company. Sculley was spending a lot of time with his new friends, Arkansas governor Bill Clinton and Hillary Rodham Clinton. It was 1992, and the Arkansas governor was running hard for President. There was talk of a cabinet position for Sculley, even talk that he was on Clinton's short list for the vice presidency. (He didn't get it, of course, but he did get to sit next to Hillary at the inauguration.) Little wonder he seemed a bit disconnected at marketing planning meetings.

He could always move to IBM. Not only were they recruiting him, but it looked as though he was going to be offered the top spot. IBM might not be as dynamic as Apple, but it was a lot bigger, and it would mean a move back to the East Coast, which appealed to Sculley.

That year he told Apple's board that he wanted to leave. April 1993 would be his 10-year anniversary, and that was long enough, he said. When they asked his advice for the company, he was blunt: sell Apple to a larger company such as Kodak or AT&T. The board asked him to stay until the sale happened.

But the sale didn't happen, and Apple's earnings per share dropped from a peak of $4.33 per share in 1992 to $0.73 per share in 1993 as competition mounted. On June 18, 1993, John Sculley was out the door and Michael Spindler was now the CEO of Apple.

Cloning Around

*Had Compaq or IBM changed in '88 or
'89, Dell would not have been a factor.
Now Dell is driving the industry.*

SEYMOUR MERRIN
Computer industry consultant

WHILE APPLE WAS LOSING ITS WAY IN THE WAKE OF IBM'S ENTRY INTO the market, IBM's own fortunes followed a strange path.

When IBM released its Personal Computer, very little about the machine was proprietary. IBM had embraced the Woz Principle of open systems, not at all an IBM-like move. One crucial part of the system was proprietary, though, and that part was, ironically, the invention of Gary Kildall.

Like Michael Shrayer, who had written different versions of his pioneering word processing program for over 80 brands of computers, Kildall had to come up with versions of his CP/M operating system for all the different machines in the market. Unlike Shrayer, however, Kildall found a solution to the problem. With the help of IMSAI's Glen Ewing, he isolated all the machine-specific code that was required for a particular computer in a piece of software that he called the basic input-output system, or BIOS.

Everything else in CP/M was generic, and didn't need to be rewritten when Kildall wanted to put the operating system on a new machine from a new manufacturer. Only the very small BIOS had to be rewritten for each machine, and that was relatively easy.

Tim Paterson realized the value of the BIOS technique and implemented it in SCP-DOS, from which it found its way into PC-DOS.

The BIOS for the IBM PC defined the machine. There was essentially nothing else proprietary in the PC, so IBM guarded this BIOS code and would have sued anyone who copied it.

Not that IBM thought it could prevent others from making money in "its" market. That was a given. In the mainframe market, people spoke of IBM as The Environment, and many companies existed solely to provide equipment that worked with IBM machines. When IBM moved into the personal computer market, many companies found ways to work with the instant standard that the IBM PC represented.

Employees of Tecmar were among the first in the doors of the Chicago Sears Business Center the morning the IBM PC first went on sale. They took their PC back to headquarters and ran it through a battery of tests to determine just how it worked. As a result, they were among the first companies to supply hard disk drives and circuit boards to work with the PC. These businesses took advantage of the opportunity to compete in this market with price, quality, or features. These "parasites" had done something similar with Ed Roberts's Altair six years earlier.

And just as IMSAI had produced an Altair-like machine to compete with MITS, many microcomputer companies came out with "IBM workalikes," computers that used MS-DOS (essentially PC-DOS but licensed from Microsoft) and tried to compete with IBM by offering a different set of capabilities, perhaps along with different marketing or pricing. Without exception, the market resoundingly rejected these IBM workalikes. Consumers might buy a computer that made no pretense of IBM compatibility—Apple certainly hoped so—but they weren't going to put up with any almost-compatible machine. Any computer claiming IBM compatibility would have to run all the software that ran on the IBM PC, support all the PC hardware devices, and accept circuit boards designed for the IBM PC, including boards not yet designed. But IBM's proprietary BIOS made it very hard for other manufacturers to guarantee total compatibility.

Yet the potential reward of creating a 100-percent IBM PC-compatible computer was so great that it was to be assumed that someone would find a way. In the summer of 1981, three Texas Instruments employees were brainstorming in a Houston, Texas, House of Pies restaurant about starting a business. Two options they considered were a Mexican restaurant and a computer company. By the end of the meal, Rod Canion, Jim Harris, and Bill Murto had deep-sixed the Mexican restaurant and sketched out, on the back of a House of Pies placemat, a business plan for a computer company, detailing what the ideal IBM-compatible computer would be like. With venture capital supplied by Ben Rosen, the same investor who had backed Lotus, they launched Compaq Computer and built their IBM-compatible. It was a portable or, at 28 pounds, more of a "luggable," had a nine-inch screen and a handle, and looked something like an Osborne 1.

Unlike the workalikes, the key to their machine was that it was 100 percent IBM compatible. Compaq had performed a so-called "clean-room" re-creation of the IBM BIOS, meaning that engineers reconstructed what the BIOS code had to be, based solely on the IBM PC's behavior and on published specifications, without ever having seen the IBM code. This gave Compaq the legal defense it needed for the lawsuit that they knew they would face from IBM.

Compaq marketed aggressively. It hired away the man who had set up IBM's dealer network, sold directly against IBM through dealers that IBM had approved to sell its PC, and offered those dealers better margins than IBM did. The plan worked. In the first year, Compaq's sales totaled $111 million. There were soon thousands of offices where a 28-pound "portable" from Compaq was the worker's only computer.

The expected lawsuit came and went, and the idea of a clean-room implementation of the IBM PC BIOS was vindicated. In theory, any other company could do what Compaq had done.

Few companies had the kind of financial backing that Compaq could call on to compete head-to-head with IBM, even if they had their own clean-room re-creations of the IBM BIOS. However, one did have enough savvy to sell the technology to others. After Phoenix Technology performed its clean-room implementation of the BIOS, it licensed its technology to others, rather than build its own machine. Now anyone who wanted to build fully IBM-compatible machines without risk of incompatibility or lawsuit could license the BIOS from Phoenix. Consumers and computer magazines tested the 100 percent compatibility claim, often using the extremely popular Lotus 1-2-3: if a new computer couldn't run the IBM PC version of 1-2-3, it was history. If it could, it usually could run other programs, also. The claims, generally, held up.

Soon there were dozens of companies making IBM-compatible personal computers. Tandy and Zenith jumped in early, as did Sperry, one of the pioneering mainframe companies. Osborne built a PC-compatible just before going broke. ITT, Eagle, Leading Edge, and Corona were some of the less-familiar names that became very familiar as they bit off large chunks of this growing PC-compatibles market.

Suddenly, IBM had no distinction but its name. Until now, that had always been enough. IBM had been The Environment, but now it had leaped into a business environment that it apparently didn't control. The clone market had arrived.

Apple stood virtually alone in not embracing the new IBM standard, initially with its Apple II and Apple III, and soon thereafter with the Macintosh. Although user loyalty and an established base of software kept the Apple II alive for years, it was not really competitive with the PC and compatibles, particularly when IBM began introducing new models based on successive generations of Intel processors and the Apple II was locked into the archaic 6502. But the Macintosh graphical user interface, or GUI, gave Apple the edge in innovation and ease of use, and kept it among the top personal computer companies in terms of machines sold. Jobs's prediction that it would come down to Apple and IBM was initially borne out, although the clones were not to be overlooked.

Software was growing increasingly important, too. With the advent of the clone market, the choice of a personal computer was becoming a matter of price and company reputation, not technological innovation. And because machines were being bought specifically to run certain programs, such as Lotus 1-2-3, Apple started to be marginalized. Even if Apple was selling as many machines as IBM or Compaq, its platform was a minority player, while computers using the magic combination of IBM's architecture, Intel's microprocessor, and Microsoft's operating system increasingly became the dominant platform.

Why didn't anyone clone the Mac? There was no Mac equivalent of Kildall's BIOS—what made the Mac unique was many thousands of lines of code. It was, in short, much harder to clone the Macintosh. In fact, it couldn't be done without Apple's approval, which was invariably withheld. But while there couldn't be Mac clones, there could be attempts to clone its graphical user interface. Alternative GUIs were a threat to Apple, undermining its advantage of uniqueness and ease of use, while not expanding the market share for the platform. And between 1983 and 1985, in addition to Apple's, several GUIs were in the works. IBM had its TopView; Digital Research its GEM; DSR, a small company run by a programmer named Nathan Myhrvold, had something called Mondrian; and VisiCorp (née Personal Software) had VisiOn.

These GUIs were designed to be pasted on top of MS-DOS or PC-DOS. Microsoft, though, was perhaps the only company that could write such a program and have it work really well, because Microsoft defined and controlled DOS. IBM saw that this was the case when it released TopView, which performed poorly and sold no better. However, IBM also recognized the limitations of DOS and contracted with Microsoft to develop a new operating system with the best features of mainframe and minicomputer operating systems of the day, plus a GUI. It was to be called OS/2.

Microsoft was working on Windows, its own GUI for DOS. Apple's Macintosh had shown that GUIs were the future of the user experience on personal computers, and Microsoft wanted in on that. There was clearly a fortune to be made by giving computer users a popular, easy-to-use GUI.

In developing Windows, Microsoft had another advantage. As a key Apple developer, it had had access to the Mac OS code, and as it developed successive versions of Windows, Microsoft somewhat belatedly licensed certain key elements of the Mac OS from Apple to protect itself from legal challenges. Windows was announced before the Mac, in 1983, but not released until 1985. The early versions were more proof of concept than product, but in 1988 version 2.01 showed that the product was moving closer to the look and feel of the Mac GUI. It was soon a serious threat to Apple's very existence.

As companies tried to outdo each other to create better and more refined graphical user interfaces, new clone makers were entering the market to design cheaper systems for those GUIs to run on. One notable success story was Dell Computer, started in 1984 by Michael Dell in his college dorm room. Five years later, Dell Computer had revenues of a quarter billion dollars.

Sticking Around for Apple's Endgame

We found ourselves a big company,
glutted from years of overspending. Then
the money supply dried up, and that
caused the first of a series of convulsions.

CHRIS ESPINOSA
Employee no. 8 at Apple Computer

AS APPLE COMPUTER STRUGGLED TO SURVIVE IN A MICROSOFT Windows–dominated market, Steve Jobs was learning to live without Apple. When he left, he gathered together some key Apple employees and started a new company.

That company was NeXT Inc., and its purpose was to produce a new computer with the most technically sophisticated, intuitive user interface based on windows, icons, and menus, equipped with a mouse, running on the Motorola 68000 family of processors. In other words, its purpose was to show them all—to show Apple and the world how it should be done. To show everyone that Steve was right.

NeXT and Steve Jobs were quiet for three years while the NeXT machine was being developed. Then, at a gala event at the beautiful Davies Symphony Hall in San Francisco, Steve took the stage, dressed all in black, and demonstrated what his team had been working on all those years. It was a striking, elegant black cube, 12 inches on a side. It featured state-of-the art hardware and a user interface that was, in some ways, more Mac-like than the Mac. It came packaged with all the necessary software and the complete works of Shakespeare on disc, and it sold for less than the top-of-the-line Mac. It played music for the audience and talked to them. It was a dazzling performance, by the machine and by the man.

Technologically, the NeXT system did show the world. While the Mac had done an excellent job of implementing the graphical user interface that Steve had seen at PARC, the NeXT machine implemented much deeper PARC technologies. Its operating system, built on the Mach Unix kernel from Carnegie-Mellon, made it possible for NeXT engineers to create an extremely powerful development environment called NeXTSTEP for corporate custom software development. NeXTSTEP was regarded by many as the best development environment that had ever been put on a computer.

Jobs had put a lot of his own money into NeXT, and he got others to invest, too. Canon made a significant investment, as did computer executive and occasional Presidential candidate Ross Perot. In April 1989, *Inc.* magazine selected Steve Jobs as its "entrepreneur of the decade" for his achievements in bringing the Apple II and Macintosh computers to market, and for the promise of NeXT.

NeXT targeted higher education as its first market, because Jobs realized that the machines and software that graduate students use are the machines that they will ask the boss to buy them when they leave school. NeXT made some tentative inroads into this target market. It made sense to academics to buy machines for which graduate students, academia's free labor force, could write the software. NeXTSTEP meant that you could buy the machine and not have to buy a ton of application software. Good for academic budgets, but not so good for building a strong base of third-party software suppliers.

The company had some success in this small market, and at least one moment of fame: the World Wide Web was invented on a NeXT machine. But after its proverbial "15 minutes' worth," the black box was ultimately a commercial failure. In 1993, NeXT finally acknowledged the obvious and killed off its hardware line, transforming itself into a software company. It immediately ported NeXTSTEP to other hardware, starting with Intel's.

In the early days of microcomputers, there had been a friendly rivalry between the sixers—users of microprocessors from Motorola, Mostec, and others, which typically had sixes in their model numbers—and the eighters—users of Intel chips, which typically had eights in their model numbers. If this was another sixers versus eighters contest, Jobs was defecting from the sixers' camp to the eighters' camp. By this time, all five of the Apple employees that Jobs had brought along to NeXT had left. Ross Perot, too, resigned from the board, saying it was the biggest mistake he'd ever made.

The reception given to the NeXT software was initially heartening. Even conservative CIOs who perpetually worry about installed bases and vendor financial statements were announcing their intention to buy NeXTSTEP. It got top ratings from reviewers, and custom developers were citing spectacular reductions in development time from using NeXTSTEP, which ran "like a Swiss watch," according to one software reviewer.

But for all the praise, NeXTSTEP did not take the world by storm. Not having to produce the hardware its software ran on made NeXT's balance sheet look less depressing, but NeXTSTEP was really no more of a success than the NeXT hardware. While custom development may have been made easy, commercial applications of the "killer app" kind, which could independently make a company's fortune, didn't materialize. NeXT struggled along, continuing to improve the operating system and serve its small, loyal customer base well, but it never broke through to a market share that could sustain the company in the long run without Jobs's deep pockets.

Meanwhile, at Apple, Michael Spindler's first act as CEO was to cut 16 percent of the staff. It was necessary. Apple was running an aging operating system on a dead-end microprocessor line. The Motorola 68000 line was nearing the end of its life, and Apple was committed to move to a new processor, the PowerPC chip being codeveloped with IBM and Motorola.

Spindler presided over the transition to PowerPC, which was itself an impressive technical achievement. Apple had produced some 70 models of Macs on the 68000 family, and its operating system was written for the 68000 chip. Moving to the PowerPC meant rethinking both hardware and software, basically rebuilding everything the company was doing, plus asking all third-party developers who wrote programs for Macintosh to rewrite their software, too. It was like rebuilding a car while driving it in the passing lane on the freeway.

Apple pulled it off, but not without some help. A company named MetroWerks came through at the last minute with the development software that third-party developers needed to convert their software to the PowerPC. Apple hadn't managed to get a decent development system together in time. In March 1994, Apple began selling PowerPC machines, and they were immediately successful.

The other part of the formula for getting Apple back in shape—namely, the new operating system—was in trouble. The Taligent effort (Apple's joint venture with IBM) was failing; it was a $300 million casualty of committee design and lack of focus. Moreover, Apple was still pursuing all the visionary R&D projects that had been launched in Sculley's golden years, but only allocating two or three programmers when there had been dozens before. Those projects ate resources with little chance of ever producing results.

Merger talks went on, including talk of joining Compaq, but they went nowhere.

The ever contentious push to license the Mac operating system finally bore fruit in 1995. The first licensee was Power Computing, a company started by Steve Kahng, who had designed a top-selling PC clone—the Leading Edge PC—10 years before. Unfortunately, it was too late. Apple's fruit had dried up. The Mac clone market didn't take off as it might have earlier. The Mac operating system appeared to be on its last legs. Power Computing did all right for itself, but it wasn't helping Apple's bottom line.

Christmas was a sales disaster. Fujitsu edged in on the Japanese market, formerly a reliable income source for Apple. By January 1996, it was time for more layoffs.

Apple had been aggressively pursuing a buyer since 1992; now Sun Microsystems stepped in with an offer. At two-thirds the stock valuation, it was a slap in the face, but it was also probably an accurate assessment of Apple's real worth.

A lot had gone out of the company. Jobs was gone. Woz was technically an employee but hadn't been involved in years. Chris Espinosa, who had been there virtually from the beginning, who had ridden his moped to the Apple offices at age 14 and written the first user manual for the Apple II while in college, was in his thirties now, married, with children. He could remember Apple as no one else in the company had known it, and it pained him to see it dying. He had never had another job, and wasn't eager to go looking for one. He decided just to hang on for the endgame. "I might as well stick around to turn out the lights," he told himself.

The endgame was about to begin, apparently. Spindler was fired on January 30, and Apple board member and reputed turnaround artist Gilbert Amelio was named CEO. Apple needed a turnaround artist, all right. The company was in serious trouble.

Big Business

*We were going to change the world. I
really felt that. Today we're creating
jobs, benefiting customers. I talk in
terms of customer benefits, adding
value. Back then, it was like pioneering.*

GORDON EUBANKS
Software pioneer

ON OCTOBER 17, 1989, THE 7.1-MAGNITUDE LOMA PRIETA EARTH-quake that hit the San Francisco Bay Area also rocked Silicon Valley. When systems came back online, this was the state of the industry:

There was a renewed rivalry between the sixers, users of microprocessors from the Motorola/Mostec camp, and the eighters, users of Intel microprocessors. Intel had released several generations of processors that upgraded the venerable 8088 in the original IBM PC, and IBM and the clone makers had rolled out newer, more powerful computers based on them. Motorola, in the meantime, had come out with newer versions of the 68000 chip it had released a decade earlier. This 68000 was a marvel, and the chief reason why the Macintosh could do processor-intensive things such as displaying dark letters on a white background and maintaining multiple overlapping windows on the screen without grinding to a halt. Intel's 80386 and Motorola's 68030 were the chips that most new computers were using, although Intel had recently introduced its 80486 and Motorola was about to release its 68040. The two lines of processors battled for the lead in capability.

Intel, though, held the lead in sales quite comfortably. Its microprocessors powered most of the IBM computers and clones, whereas Motorola had basically one customer for its processors—Apple.

Intel cofounder Gordon Moore had formulated a "law" in the early 1970s that has proven remarkably accurate over the years, and in 1989 it was the best definition available for what was happening in the industry. Moore's Law holds that memory chip capacity doubles every 18 months. Variations on it have been formulated for microprocessor power and for capacity of other chips, and the law has proved reliable for decades. Its implications, though, extend far beyond semiconductor capacity. Memory capacity and processor power determine the limits of the capabilities of the computers and the software written for them. Even the spread of personal computers through the general population seemed to follow some function of these variables. In 1989, the industry grew apace with Moore's Law.

The best-selling software package in 1989 was Lotus 1-2-3; its sales were ahead of WordPerfect, the leading word processor, and MS-DOS. The top 10 best-selling personal computers were all various models of IBM, Apple Macintosh, and Compaq machines. Compaq was no mere clone maker; it was innovating, pushing beyond IBM in many areas. It introduced a book-sized PC-compatible computer in 1989 that changed the definition of portability. Compaq also introduced a new, open, nonproprietary bus design called EISA, which was accepted by the industry, demonstrating the strength of Compaq's leadership position. IBM had unsuccessfully attempted to introduce a new, proprietary bus called MicroChannel two years earlier. IBM was fast losing control of the market, and it was losing something else—money.

By the end of 1989, IBM would announce a plan to cut 10,000 employees from its payroll and within another year Compaq and Dell would each be taking more profits out of the personal computer market than IBM. In another three years, IBM would cut 35,000 employees and suffer the biggest one-year loss of any company in history.

ComputerLand's dominance of the early computer retail scene was short-lived. During ComputerLand's heyday, consumers wanting to buy a particular brand had to visit one of the major franchises and distribution was restricted to a few chosen chains, the largest of which was ComputerLand. But in the late 1980s, the market changed. Price consciousness took precedence over brand name, and manufacturers had to sell through any and all potential distributors. The cost of running a chainstore such as ComputerLand was higher than competitive operations, which could now sell hardware and software for less.

Another line of computer stores, called BusinessLand, gained a foothold and for a time became the nation's leading computer dealer in the late 1980s by concentrating on the corporate market and promising sophisticated training and service agreements. But consumers were more comfortable with computers and no longer willing to pay a premium for hand-holding. Electronics superstores such as CompUSA, Best Buy, and Fry's, which offered a wide range of products and brands at the lowest possible prices, eclipsed both ComputerLand and BusinessLand. Computers were becoming commodities, and low prices mattered most.

Bill Gates and Paul Allen were billionaires by 1989; Gates was the richest executive in the computer industry. In the industry, only Ross Perot and the cofounders of another high-tech firm, Hewlett-Packard, had reached billionaire status, but most of the leaders of the industry had net worths in the tens of millions, including Compaq's Rod Canion and Dell Computers' Michael Dell. In 1989, *Computer Reseller News* named Canion the second most influential executive in the industry, deferentially placing him behind IBM's John Akers. But perspective matters: in the same year, *Personal Computing* asked its readers to pick the most influential people in computing from their list, which included Bill Gates, Steve Jobs, Steve Wozniak, Adam Osborne, and the historical Charles Babbage. Only billionaire Bill made everyone's list.

There was a lot of money being made, and that meant lawsuits. Like much of American society, the computer industry was becoming increasingly litigious. In 1988, Apple sued Microsoft over Windows 2.01, and extended the suit in 1991 after Microsoft released Windows 3.0. Meanwhile, Xerox sued Apple, claiming that the graphical user interface was really its invention, which Apple had misappropriated. Xerox lost, and so, eventually, did Apple in the Microsoft suit, although it was able to pressure Digital Research into changing its GEM graphical user interface cosmetically, making it look less Mac-like.

GUIs weren't the only contentious issue. A number of lawsuits over the "look and feel" of spreadsheets were bitterly fought at great expense to all and questionable benefit to anyone. The inventors of VisiCalc fought it out in court with their distributor, Personal Software. Lotus sued Adam Osborne's software company, Paperback Software, as well as Silicon Graphics, Mosaic, and Borland, over the order of commands in a menu. Lotus prevailed over all but Borland, where the facts of the case were the most complex, but the Borland suit dragged on until after Borland had sold the program in question.

Borland was also involved in two noisy lawsuits over personnel. Microsoft sued Borland when one of its key employees, Rob Dickerson, went to Borland with a lot of Microsoft secrets in his head. Borland didn't sue in return when its key employee, Brad Silverberg, defected to Microsoft, but it did when Gene Wang left for Symantec. After Wang left, Borland executives found e-mail in its system between Wang and Symantec CEO Gordon Eubanks—e-mail that they claimed contained company secrets. Borland brought criminal charges, threatening not just financial pain but also jail time for Wang and Eubanks. The charges were eventually dismissed.

Through essentially the whole of the 1980s, Intel and semiconductor competitor Advanced Micro Devices (AMD) were in litigation over what technology Intel had licensed to AMD.

Meanwhile, in the lucrative video game industry, everyone seemed to be suing everyone else. Macronix, Atari, and Samsung sued Nintendo; Nintendo sued Samsung; Atari sued Sega; and Sega sued Accolade. In 1989, the Beatles sued Apple Computer over the name Apple and settled out of court. "It's been," the Beatles' lawyer said later, "a long and winding road."

As their market eroded, it was becoming a tough haul for the traditional minicomputer companies. *Forbes* magazine wrote, "1989 may be remembered as the beginning of the end of the minicomputer. Nowhere were the effects felt more severely than outside Boston on Route 128, where minicomputer makers Wang Laboratories, Data General, and Prime Computer incurred staggering losses."

Minicomputers were being squeezed out by workstations. These workstations were, in effect, the new top of the line in personal computers, equipped with one or more powerful, possibly custom-designed processors, running the Unix minicomputer operating system developed at AT&T's Bell Labs, and targeted at scientists and engineers, software and chip designers, graphic artists, movie makers, and others needing high performance. Although they sold in much smaller quantities than ordinary personal computers, they sold for significantly higher prices.

The Apollo, which used a Motorola 68000 chip, had been the first such workstation in the early 1980s, but by 1989 the most successful of the workstation manufacturers were Sun Microsystems, one of whose founders, Bill Joy, had been much involved in developing and popularizing the Unix operating system, and Silicon Graphics, which marketed machines for video and audio editing.

During the 1990s, Moore's Law and its corollaries continued to describe the growth of the industry. IBM had become just one of the players in what originally had been called the "IBM-compatible market," then was called the "clone market," and later was called just the "PC market."

By 1989 the pattern was clear, and it persisted into the next decade—personal computers were becoming commodities, increasingly powerful but essentially the same. They became obsolete every three years by advances in semiconductor technology and software, where innovation proceeded unchecked. Personal computers were becoming accepted and spreading throughout society; the personal computer industry had become big business, with ceaseless litigation and the focused attention of Wall Street; and this technology, pioneered in garages and on kitchen tables, was driving the strongest, most sustained economic growth in memory.

Big business? Within two decades the personal computer market launched in 1975 with the *Popular Electronics* cover story on the Altair surpassed the combined market for mainframes and minicomputers. As if to underscore this, in the late 1990s, Compaq bought Digital Equipment Corporation, the company that had created the minicomputer market. Those still working on mainframe computers demanded Lotus 1-2-3 and other personal computer software for these big machines. Personal computers had ceased to be a niche in the computer industry. They had become the mainstream.

In the process, the personal computer industry became a commodity business, something that some of the pioneers were unwilling to accept.

A Different Set
of Rules

*It was Gary's bad luck that put him up
next to the most successful businessman
of a generation. Anyone is a failure
standing next to Bill Gates.*

ALAN COOPER
Software designer and entrepreneur

AT THE HEIGHT OF DIGITAL RESEARCH'S SUCCESS, GARY KILDALL HAD moments of doubt about whether coping with the competitiveness and politics of business was what he wanted to be doing with his life. What had been fun in the beginning had become an albatross around his neck. Running a business wasn't what he had had in mind when he began writing software for those early Intel chips. In one of the darkest of those moments in the late 1970s, Gary passed the parking lot on his way to work and continued around the block, realizing that he just couldn't bring himself to go in the door. He circled the block three times before he could force himself to confront another day at DRI.

Later, in frustration, he offered to sell the company to his friends Keith Parsons and Alan Cooper. Parsons and Cooper were running one of the first companies to deliver business software for microcomputers, a kitchen-table startup named Structured Systems Group. Gary was fed up with what he saw as the pointless games and distractions of business. They could have the whole operation for $70,000, he told them. As for him, he would go back to teaching.

It was ridiculous; there was no way it could have happened. Parsons and Cooper had little hope of coming up with $70,000. Moreover, Dorothy McEwen would never have okayed the deal. She knew that

DRI was worth a lot more. By 1981, it was obvious to the dullest wit that she was right. In that year, there were some 200,000 microcomputers running CP/M, in more than 3000 different hardware configurations, a spectacular testament to the portability that Gary had designed into CP/M. Digital Research employed 75 people in various capacities. That year, the company took in $6 million. It had come a long way since its start only seven years earlier in Gary and Dorothy's house. Most of the time Gary was having a ball.

Then came the deal that didn't happen with IBM, and Microsoft's usurpation of the lead in operating systems on the strength of code that Gary considered had been stolen from him. From that point on, a lot of the fun had gone out of the business.

DRI was one of the first personal computer companies to seek venture capital funding to go public. The venture capitalists were willing, but they insisted that strong management be brought in to get the business under control. Gary was thrilled at the idea of bringing in someone on whom he could unload all the annoying business decisions. John Rowley got that job.

Personable, bright, and enthusiastic, Rowley nevertheless struck some around him as a bit unfocused. "He thought focus meant paying attention to his strategy," according to Alan Cooper. But if there was an overall strategy to his actions, it wasn't obvious.

In part, Rowley was responding to customers, some of whom were not happy. Tom Lafleur, DRI's director of R&D, recalled that Rowley would "tell internal people that we weren't going to do something, and then he'd tell a customer we were doing it, and then he'd call the internal people and say we need this right away. It was last in, first out."

To give him credit, Rowley may have had a tougher job than anyone realized. The company remained Gary's, and any actions Gary took or authorized could drive the company into one market or another. And they did.

Gary decided to write a version of the programming language LOGO for his son Scott, thinking merely that it would be fun and that Scott could learn about programming and logic from it. Having finished this gift to his son, he handed the result to John Rowley, and LOGO became a full-fledged DRI product. A project like this would add to the company workload and spread the company's resources thin because the software required its own marketing and sales support.

Gary was also intrigued by the Lisa/Mac user interface, and along with DRI employee Lee Lorenzen, began experimenting with DRI's own GUI. The company's focus was supposed to be operating systems, but the result of Gary's interest in user interfaces was that one of the many varieties of CP/M then under development got sidetracked into a user interface shell that would sit atop an operating system. That was Lorenzen's GEM, a Mac-like user interface for non-Mac computers. GEM was well crafted and technically superior to IBM-developed TopView. Apple, though, thought it was a little too Mac-like and threatened to sue. DRI caved. It couldn't have been lost on Gary that Microsoft, which also had a Mac-like user interface called Windows, did not (at least then) get threatened with a lawsuit, nor did IBM. It was cold, cynical business logic: Microsoft and IBM were too powerful, and Microsoft, with its Mac application programs, was too important to Apple. Digital Research was an easier target. The technical merits of GEM or the fairness of the situation didn't enter into it.

The company was still making lots of money, but it was also making some serious mistakes. Not keeping customers happy was one of the worst. DRI just wasn't sufficiently responsive to customers' complaints and requests.

Although Gary wasn't in charge of dealing with customer requests, it was understood that any significant change in the way CP/M worked had to receive his approval, and that was hard to get. If anyone proposed a change, Cooper recalled, "Gary would try to argue you out of it." He didn't want to pollute good code with kludged-on features.

The PIP command, for example, exemplified this attitude. In CP/M, you typed **PIP B: A:** to copy a file from disk drive A to drive B. In MS-DOS, you typed **COPY A: B:** to do the same thing.

PIP? What did that mean? It didn't matter; Gary thought that any halfway intelligent person could learn that PIP was the command you used to copy, and that you copied (or "pipped") from right to left, not left to right. No matter that this was arbitrary, confusing, and counterintuitive, or that customers complained about it.

Bill Gates listened to his customers. "That difference in attitude,"

Cooper said, "is worth twenty million dollars." Gary wasn't really all that interested in what customers wanted. Gary was only interested in inventing.

On Cooper's first day at DRI in May 1982, Gary took him to a high-level industry conference in Palm Springs, California, hosted by influential industry watcher and analyst Esther Dyson. Gary gave him John Rowley's name badge, and they climbed into his Aerostar and flew south. All the top executives of the major companies were at the conclave (though, apparently, not John Rowley), and Cooper ran into Bill Gates. He bragged that he had just joined Gary Kildall in research and development. Gates chuckled. Gary had set up an R&D department! It was such an academic thing to do. In Gates's view, R&D was just part of doing business; it didn't warrant a separate department.

Gary, however, wanted to segregate R&D from the mundane concerns of the business. He wanted a skunk works, a small crew that pursued projects on the basis of interest, just as pure academic researchers follow a beguiling idea rather than worrying about someone's bottom line.

Some ideas came out of the skunk works, although most of the best came from Gary himself. He did groundbreaking work on CD-ROM software and on interfacing computers and videodiscs. A company, KnowledgeSet, spun off from that work. So did CD-ROM-based Grolier's Encyclopedia, which showed everyone how to do CD-ROM content right. Microsoft's later enviable position in the CD-ROM content market owed a lot to Gary Kildall's good ideas and Bill Gates's ability to spot a smart idea and pounce on it.

"Gary never did have the ruthless, go-for-the-jugular business sense," said Tom Rolander, one of Kildall's closest friends. "If it hadn't been Bill Gates, the next aggressive businessman might have won the business war."

In the midst of the confusion that was life at DRI, Gary and Dorothy split up. The atmosphere grew even tenser.

As Digital Research flailed, bachelor Gates's Microsoft flourished—sometimes on ground cleared by Gary Kildall, as in the case of MS-DOS (which trounced his CP/M) and multimedia/CD-ROM technology. The legend of Bill Gates grew, while a dwindling percentage of computer users had even heard of Gary Kildall. Kildall was always publicly gracious about his fading celebrity, yet he hid a distress that few ever saw. One day in 1983, Cooper caught a glimpse of it.

Gary took him aside and started discussing Apple Computer. "He opened this door and I saw the bitterness: 'Steve Jobs is nothing. Steve Wozniak did it all, the hardware and the software. All Jobs did was hang around and take the credit.' " Cooper understood that Gary wasn't talking about Apple so much as Microsoft. Kildall hated the fact that Gates, this *dropout*, this *businessman*, was winning the acclaim for his own inventions. "All of a sudden, there was this cauldron of resentment. It must have tortured Gary that Bill Gates got all the credit."

Kildall took great pride in programming well. His code was like Japanese carpentry—everything fit together without nails. In Gary's eyes, Bill Gates did gawky work. He couldn't bring himself to respect that ungainly code, or the man who created it.

It was an academic perspective, perhaps, and Gary was certainly an academic, although he never went back to it; he stayed with DRI until the end in 1991, when Novell bought the firm. At Novell, all traces of DRI products and projects quickly dissolved and were absorbed like sutures on a healing wound.

No one could pity Kildall financially. The Novell deal made him a very wealthy man. He had always enjoyed toys, treating work like play, and now that he was rich, he played with rich people's toys. He moved to the West Lake Hills suburb of Austin, Texas, where he kept a stable of 14 sports cars and a video studio in the basement. He owned and flew his own Lear Jet. In California, he maintained a second house, a mansion with a spectacular ocean view on legendary 17 Mile Drive in Pebble Beach. His friends may have felt that he would have been happier as a poor programmer, but his story ends differently. Kildall died ignominiously in 1994 at the age of 52 after falling and hitting his head one night when he had drunk too much. He died a rich, but dissatisfied, man.

Yet he left a remarkable legacy. Gary Kildall created the first microprocessor disk operating system, which eventually sold a quarter million copies. He defined the first programming language and wrote the first compiler specifically for microprocessors. He developed the file system and data structures for the first consumer CD-ROM. He created the first computer interface for videodiscs that allowed automatic nonlinear playback, presaging today's interactive multimedia. He created the first successful open-system architecture by segregating system-specific hardware interfaces in a set of BIOS routines, an innovation that made the whole third-party software industry possible.

Finally, he personified an approach to work that was widespread during the first decade of the personal computer revolution. The belief that science and technology advance through the open sharing of discoveries, that it's more important to create the next invention than protect the last one—these were Kildall's values. "He had such an enthusiasm for technology; it was infectious," said Rolander.

When litigation and guarding one's flanks became the order of the day, Kildall lost interest. For other pioneers in the industry, however, this new atmosphere was heady and invigorating.

WEALTH AND WAR

We want to take our success in one area
and have it help us in another area. . . .

BILL GATES
Articulating in 1983 a strategy that would
get the company in trouble in 1997

"Billg" and
the Bill Clones

You have to think it's a fun industry.
You've got to go home at night and open
your mail and find computer magazines
or else you're not going to be on the same
wavelength as the people [at Microsoft].

BILL GATES, 1983

As 1981 began, Microsoft and Bill Gates were only known within the tight community of personal computer companies. Outside that community, both the company and the man were inconsequential.

The company's business focused on programming languages, with some application software and a lone hardware product thrown in—Paul Allen's brainchild, the SoftCard, which let people run CP/M programs on an Apple computer. DOS, which would begin the company's rise to prominence, was under development, but did not come out until months later, when the IBM PC was released.

Although Gates had insisted that Microsoft should not sell directly to end users, an aggressive salesman named Vern Raeburn convinced him otherwise, using the now-standard method of impressing Bill: he challenged him, had his facts straight, and didn't back down. After winning his argument with Gates, Raeburn became president of a new Microsoft subsidiary, Microsoft Consumer Products, which began selling both Microsoft-developed products and other licensed products, including some applications, in computer stores and anywhere else

Raeburn could find shelf space. But in 1981, this operation was just beginning, and the company wasn't a major player, even in the young computer industry.

Microsoft's total revenues for 1981 were about $15 million. It seemed like a lot of money to Gates, but by way of contrast, Apple's annual gross revenues were running just about 20 times as high, and IBM was in another league altogether.

Microsoft converted from a partnership to a corporation in June 1981. Almost all the stock was held by three people: Bill, his boyhood friend and long-time partner Paul Allen, and the Harvard-educated friend from Bill's brief college stint, Steve Ballmer. A clear majority of the stock was in the hands of the unkempt, squeaky-voiced president, who new employees sometimes mistook for some teenaged hacker trespassing in the president's office.

Such new employees soon learned that the 26-year-old president, who looked 18 years old, was a force to be reckoned with. And they learned that the company they had come to work for was, in many ways, as unusual as its young president. The company was, in fact, a lot like Bill Gates.

This was not surprising because Gates made it a point to hire people who were like himself—bright, driven, competitive, and able to argue effectively for what they believed in. A small but influential number of the new employees came from fabled Xerox PARC, the research lab where Steve Jobs saw the vision that would become the Macintosh.

Gates invited employees to argue with him about important technical issues. He hardly gave what could be called positive feedback; he frequently characterized work or ideas as "brain damaged" or "the stupidest thing I ever heard." But he prided himself on being open to good ideas from any source, and even when he delivered one of his devastating denouncements, it was always the idea he attacked, not the individual. Because Gates was such a demanding critic, employees who impressed him gained credibility and influence. It was the key to the executive washroom, the prime parking place in a company that had no executive washroom and no reserved parking places.

The easy access to the president and his willingness to listen to good arguments from any employee gave the appearance of democracy to the company culture. Even if you couldn't nail him down in the hall, anyone could send an e-mail message directly to *billg* and know that Bill G. himself would read it. But Microsoft was far from a democracy. The flattened communication structure was a two-edged sword. Although displeasing Bill Gates was death, getting positive feedback from *billg* on your work or ideas was money in the bank. Those who were most favored tended to see Microsoft as a meritocracy.

In a meritocracy, the real power resides in the authority to judge merit. At Microsoft, Bill's judgment was the final word.

One competent employee who just didn't fit the Bill mold was Jim Towne. Towne was hired from Tektronix in July 1982 to serve as president of Microsoft. Gates was conscious that a lot of early microcomputer companies had failed because they didn't know when to bring in more experienced managers. "Entrepreneur's disease" it was called, and it was at least part of what had killed MITS, IMSAI, and Proc Tech. Bill was juggling a lot of balls, and he brought Towne in to lighten his load and take the official title of president. Towne served about a year, but Gates never thought he had the right feel for the company. There was no real problem with his management; ultimately, Towne failed to "take" at Microsoft because he wasn't Bill. It began to appear that what Bill wanted was not a president but a way to clone himself.

Through the early 1980s, the IBM deal and its aftermath gave the company a huge boost, particularly when Compaq and Phoenix Technologies created a clone market for Microsoft to sell MS-DOS to.

By the end of 1981, Microsoft had grown to 100 employees and had moved to new offices in Bellevue, Washington. The stresses of the IBM deal and the company's growing pains were getting to some employees. Soon after, some long-timers left, including Bob Wallace, who had been a mainstay since Albuquerque days. But Wallace's leaving was a blip compared to the departure of Paul Allen, Bill's lifelong friend and partner. Although Allen's departure was a health issue (he had Hodgkin's disease) and not stress-related, it increased Gates's own level of stress. Now the company was totally his to run.

Pam Edstrom, Microsoft's PR chief, was pushing an image of Bill as the nerd who made good. Another story was equally true, however: the privileged child of comfortable affluence, weaned on competition and the importance of winning, who read *Fortune* magazine in high school and became a ruthless cutthroat businessman determined to dominate markets and crush the competition. But the general press could only handle one image of Gates, and Edstrom made sure they got the "right" one—right for Microsoft, that is. Journalists certainly had no trouble believing the official tale; a few minutes with Gates would convince anyone that he was a nerd, and the balance sheet made the case for his having done well.

Gates, meanwhile, was presenting an image of Microsoft that stuck in the craw of industry insiders. He insisted that Microsoft produced quality products, whereas the reality was that the general run of stuff was less than top-notch work. Microsoft's software was of varying quality, sometimes buggy, sometimes slow. And within the company the image of quality and professionalism was a joke. Internal systems were a disaster. There were not enough computers. The huge plastic boxes in which Microsoft was packaging its products were a warehouse nightmare and one more indication that all was not rosy inside Bill's empire. If Microsoft reflected Bill Gates's personality and values, its organization could have been modeled on Bill's personal life. He ate fast food, neglected to shower, had trouble remembering to pay his bills. Microsoft paid its bills, but otherwise its internal systems looked a lot like Bill. The second try at getting somebody in to clean up the mess made Radio Shack's Jon Shirley the new president of Microsoft.

There was another way in which the image of Microsoft didn't match the reality. Microsoft would have people believe that its OEM customers bought its products solely for their quality, not because of Microsoft's aggressive business dealings. (OEM, or original equipment manufacturer, refers to the computer companies who licensed software from Microsoft to include with their machines.) Microsoft's cutthroat tactics with its OEMs were most evident in Microsoft's efforts to win the GUI market.

The early 1980s saw the emergence of the graphical user interface (GUI) for personal computers. Apple released the Lisa in 1983 and the Macintosh in 1984. VisiCorp (formerly Personal Software) had VisiOn, a windowing environment that put all the Visi products, including the popular VisiCalc, in easy-to-use windows. Bill was impressed by VisiOn. Digital Research had more or less cloned the Mac user interface with a snappy product called GEM, which it was about to ship. IBM was promoting a GUI called TopView that Bill considered brain damaged. And Microsoft had something in the works that it called Windows.

Microsoft was one of the first companies to develop software for the Mac, and had been briefed on Apple's project for months before the release. So closely did Microsoft work with Apple that its programmers were making suggestions about the operating system as it was being refined. Microsoft Windows was based on what Microsoft learned during that process.

On November 10, 1983, Microsoft staged an impressive media blitz for its upcoming Windows product that trumpeted to the industry the scores of vendors who had signed on to develop application software that would be Windows compatible. Some of these had also signed on with VisiOn and were wavering in their commitment to Microsoft, so the message was a little disingenuous—plus Windows wasn't anywhere to be seen.

According to one OEM customer, Microsoft agreed to give its OEMs an early beta version of Windows—absolutely necessary if the OEM wanted to have a Windows-compatible application out when Windows itself came out—but only if the OEM agreed not to develop for a competing product such as VisiOn. The Justice Department might have considered such tactics—and other tactics Microsoft was engaging in at the time—as restraint of trade or unfair business practices, but nobody was talking about these backroom deals. (Later there would be charges of "undocumented system calls"—code in Windows or DOS that Microsoft reserved for its own use to give its application software an advantage over any competitor's. Microsoft was engaging regularly in behavior that would eventually lead the Justice Department to its door.)

Windows was finally released in 1985. After an initial burst of good press, the actual reviews began to come in—and they were not kind.

Given the wide variety of hardware configurations that MS-DOS had to support, cloning the Mac GUI to run snappily on top of it was a tough problem, and Microsoft hadn't adequately solved it. And yet Windows did have to run on top of MS-DOS. The MS-DOS operating system was installed in all the IBM and clone machines, which made up most of the market. Microsoft had to maintain compatibility with all those machines when it released this Mac-like user interface, and the only way to do that was to make Windows merely an interface between the user and the real operating system. Underneath, it had to be MS-DOS, dealing with application programs, and data files, and printers, and disk drives, just as MS-DOS always had.

But Microsoft continued to prosper, with MS-DOS making up a larger and larger share of the company's revenues. The company's March 1985 initial public offering of stock was eagerly anticipated in the financial community. When the numbers were tallied after the IPO, Bill's 45 percent of the company was worth $311 million. Microsoft had grown to over 700 employees, and it had moved to larger headquarters.

The Richest Man
in the World

*[It's] like parts of an airplane. When you
really get down to wanting to fly from one
place to another, it's not very much a free
marketplace. You don't get to bid for the
tail and the wing. Somebody puts it
together and says, this is an airplane,
I guarantee it, and let's go fly.*

BILL GATES, 1983

BY 1987, MICROSOFT PASSED LOTUS AS THE TOP SOFTWARE VENDOR. This remarkable ascendancy came about in large part due to its control over the MS-DOS operating system used on nearly all non-Apple PCs. But Microsoft had increasingly developed ambitions to offer products for most software categories, including spreadsheets, word processors, presentation programs, and educational tools. There were now some 1800 Microsoft employees worldwide.

Meanwhile, IBM, beginning to face real competition from the clone manufacturers, decided to replace DOS (and the unsuccessful Top-View) with a new, powerful operating system with a graphical user interface. The new operating system would be called OS/2.

Microsoft was commissioned once again to work on the operating system, but the arrangement was rocky from the start. By 1990, the final split with IBM was imminent.

Microsoft had committed a lot of resources to OS/2, as had IBM.

But it appeared that neither party was entirely faithful in this software development marriage.

Microsoft was alarmed when IBM seemed to be hedging its bets by leading an industry effort to standardize the Unix operating system and by licensing NeXTSTEP, the operating system from Steve Jobs's NeXT Inc. This was normal behavior; IBM typically had a number of alternate plans in the works, with different divisions of the company competing with one another to see whose project would actually be chosen to ship. But that was hardly a comfortable position for Microsoft, which would be in trouble if OS/2 was scrapped in favor of Unix or NeXTSTEP while Microsoft had spent years developing an operating system that IBM decided it didn't want to support.

And, of course, at the same time Microsoft was developing Windows. Windows wasn't actually an operating system, but Windows plus DOS was, so Microsoft had its own hedge. At first, the plan was to make Windows and the graphical interface of OS/2 work alike. Microsoft started telling programmers that if they developed software for Windows they would be ready for OS/2 when it came out. This grew less plausible as time went on.

Before long, Microsoft programmers working on OS/2 weren't talking to IBM OS/2 programmers and vice versa. The companies officially denied the friction, but the marriage was on the rocks. IBM was convinced that Microsoft had shifted its efforts to Windows, that Microsoft was only pretending to be concentrating on OS/2, and that Microsoft was claiming that Windows would not compete with OS/2 when that was exactly the plan. That was all true, eventually.

IBM announced that OS/2 would be released in two versions, the more sophisticated of which would be sold exclusively by IBM. That wasn't news Bill Gates wanted to hear.

Finally, Gates told Steve Ballmer that they were going to go for broke on Windows and that he wasn't worrying about what IBM thought about it. Then a Gates memo that called OS/2 "a poor product" was made public. The arrangement fell apart, IBM took over OS/2, and Microsoft indeed went for broke on Windows.

Windows 3.0 rolled out in 1990, which was the first adequate release of the GUI product. Jon Shirley also departed from Microsoft in 1990. Although things had worked out all right, the Texan just figured it was time to move on. In six weeks, Gates had hired ex-IBMer Mike Hallman as the new president. Although he only lasted into 1992, it hardly mattered to the direction and atmosphere of the company. Microsoft was Bill Gates's baby.

As Gates approached 40, neither he nor Microsoft seemed to lose any vitality. The break with IBM invigorated Microsoft and left IBM floundering. Windows was finally getting positive reviews while IBM's OS/2 and Presentation Manager were not. Computer companies and software developers believed that Microsoft was in charge and followed its lead. In the mid-1990s, Microsoft's stock valuation made Bill Gates the richest person in America. At the end of the decade he was the richest person in the world.

Microsoft continued to push into new areas. When the OS/2 deal fell apart, an operating system project that had been quietly in development since 1988 was pulled to center stage, given serious funding, and dubbed "Windows NT." NT would be sold into "corporate mission-critical environments"—chiefly the server market, which was then dominated by the venerable Unix operating system.

Server computers provide resources to—or "serve"—computers connected to them on a network. File servers are like libraries, holding shared files; application servers hold application programs used by many machines; mail servers manage electronic mail for offices. Servers are often used in business and academia, tend to be more expensive than individual users' computers, and, because many users depend on them, are typically maintained by technically sophisticated personnel, which explains why they so often run Unix.

Unix came on the scene in 1969. Invented by two Bell Labs programmers, Ken Thompson and Dennis Ritchie, it was the first easily portable operating system, meaning that it could be run on many different types of computers without too many modifications. As Unix was stable, powerful, and widely distributed, it quickly became the operating system of choice in academia, with two results: lots of people wrote utility programs for it, which they distributed free of charge, and virtually all graduating computer scientists knew Unix inside and out. On the job, they typically had control of a server, and they preferred to run the familiar Unix, with its large, loose collection of utility programs, on it.

Microsoft hoped to supplant Unix and take over the server market.

In addition to its NT project, Microsoft continued to exert a powerful influence over its MS-DOS and Windows OEMs. The control extended to dictating what icons representing third-party programs could appear on the user's desktop when the computer first started up.

In 1994, Compaq, by then the leading personal computer maker, decided to install a program on all its machines that would run "in front of" Microsoft Windows. This small "shell" program would display icons that let the user start selected programs. Although this shell program was very simple and wouldn't supplant Windows, it would have undermined the gatekeeper role that Windows was coming to play, and thus undermine Windows' control of the user's desktop.

"We've got to stop this," Gates said.

And he did. What was said, what was intimated, may never be known, but Compaq removed the program.

Compaq also backed down two years later, when Microsoft threatened to stop selling it Windows unless Compaq included Microsoft's Internet browser on its machines.

It looked as though the Justice Department would soon take action against the company over its alleged anticompetitive practices, possibly breaking it up as it had broken up AT&T. But Gates and Microsoft weathered that challenge without damage, although it would not be the last such threat.

In the 1980s, online systems had become a big thing. These were an outgrowth of the early computer bulletin board systems (which offer a public area for posting messages to other users much like a typical "corkboard" bulletin board found in an office), or BBSs. BBSs provided content, such as news services, discussion groups, stock quotes, and electronic mail, to their subscribers. CompuServe, Prodigy, America Online, and others maintained their own proprietary systems, which users could access with a local telephone call.

When the Internet blossomed in popularity with the invention of the World Wide Web in 1994, the online systems began having trouble justifying their existence independent of the Internet, and all began offering Internet access. The sudden popularity of the Internet and the World Wide Web began changing the whole nature of computing, shifting the emphasis away from the operating system and the individual desktop to the network.

Every company struggled to forge an Internet strategy. New companies emerged to take advantage of this shift in the market. Amazon.com and others exploited radical new forms of electronic commerce. Cisco Systems provided the networking infrastructure for this new market.

Microsoft responded promptly, trying several approaches to carve out its profits from the phenomenon, and just as promptly cutting these attempts short when the market moved in a different direction. The company hadn't settled on an Internet strategy, but it responded quickly to the rapidly changing landscape, more easily than most large companies could.

Perhaps it was because of the structure Gates installed when Hallman left.

In 1992, Gates set up an organizational arrangement that he could live with: the Office of the President. It was also known as BOOP—Bill and the Office of the President. It consisted of Bill and three close friends: Steve Ballmer, Mike Maples, and Frank Gaudette. By this time these friends had been influenced by Gates, and had arguably influenced him to the extent that he could trust them to make decisions he'd approve of.

He had succeeded in spreading himself thinner.

For so large a company as Microsoft to be able to change directions so quickly was impressive. The biggest fish in the pond and maneuverable, too: Microsoft in the mid-1990s dominated the personal computer industry and seemed utterly invincible.

Back from the Dead

*Finally in Steve we have a leader whom
the people at Apple are willing to follow.
All he has to do is bend his eyebrow the
wrong way and people do what he wants.*

CHRIS ESPINOSA
Employee no. 8 at Apple Computer

MEANWHILE, JOBS WAS FINDING A USE FOR SOME OF THE MILLIONS
that he hadn't put into NeXT.

This portion of Jobs's story casts its roots back to 1975, the same
year that the Altair was announced. When Paul Allen was spotting the
Popular Electronics cover in Harvard Square and rushing to tell Bill
Gates that they had better do something or they would be left out,
some computer graphics experts at the New York Institute of Technology were getting together to see what they could come up with in computer animation. They worked hard, and by 1979, Edmund Catmull,
Alvy Ray Smith, and their team had come up with some nifty tricks and
moved to Marin County, California, to work for George Lucas at Industrial Light and Magic, which became the premiere special-effects
house and changed the way movies are made.

Seven years later, frustrated that Lucas's ambition did not match
theirs, they began looking for a way out. Lucas gave it to them when he
sold their division to Steve Jobs, who had recently sold his Apple stock
and had a spare $10 million to invest. The resulting company was
called Pixar.

Pixar ate another $50 million of Jobs's money over the next five years, as Jobs encouraged the Pixar employees to push the state of the art as far as possible. That was exactly what Catmull and his team had in mind; during these years, Pixar employees published seminal articles on computer animation, won awards, and invented most of the cutting-edge techniques that made it possible to do computer-animated feature films.

Jobs had once again placed himself among bright people and new technologies, and he was pushing the crew at Pixar to do the best they could. If building computers had become a boring commodity business, computer animation was a field hot with creative fire.

In 1988, Pixar's *Tin Toy* became the first computer-animated film to win an Academy Award. Then, in 1991, Disney signed a three-picture deal with Pixar, including a movie called *Toy Story.*

The Pixar team put everything they had into *Toy Story.* By the time the box office receipts had been counted in 1995, *Toy Story* was a major success, Pixar was a player in the movie industry, and Jobs himself had become a billionaire. He promptly went to Hollywood and, over lunch with Disney head Michael Eisner, negotiated a new contract that was much more favorable to Pixar.

Jobs, the newest movie-industry billionaire, was now dealing with the biggest names in Hollywood. Compared to that, NeXT was small change, and Apple, his first company—well, it was floundering badly.

Gilbert Amelio had been named the new CEO at Apple, as well as chair of the board; Mike Markkula accepted a demotion to vice chair.

The operating system was the biggest problem Apple had to solve. Taligent, the joint venture with IBM, had fallen apart and Copland, the in-house operating system project, was going nowhere fast. Amelio's chief technologist, Ellen Hancock, recommended that Apple buy or license an operating system from someone else.

There were at least three options on the table: license Sun's operating system and put a Mac face on it; do the same with Microsoft's NT operating system; or purchase Jean-Louis Gassée's BeOS. Gassée, Apple's ex-head of engineering, had formed a company called Be when he left Apple, and it had come up with a highly regarded, albeit not quite finished, operating system.

The press was having fun guessing which way Apple would turn.

BeOS looked like the best fit. But Hancock told the press cryptically, "Not everyone who is talking to us is talking to you."

Meanwhile, Oracle's unpredictable founder Larry Ellison, now a member of the Silicon Valley billionaire boys club, was stirring things up by hinting that he would buy Apple and let his good friend Steve Jobs run it. Jobs gave no credence to Ellison's hints, and no one took Ellison too seriously, but Jobs did at one point call Del Yocam, Apple's COO from the company's best days and now CEO of a restructured and renamed Borland (to Inprise), to bend Yocam's ear about their running Apple together.

When Apple's decision was announced, hours after it was made, it caught the industry by surprise. Apple would acquire NeXT Inc., lock, stock, and barrel, and use its technology to build a next-generation operating system for its computers. Apparently when Hancock had said that not everyone talking to Apple was talking to the press, she was talking about NeXT.

One detail of the announcement overshadowed the rest for sheer drama: Steve Jobs was coming back to Apple.

The deal made Jobs a part-time consultant, who reported to CEO Gilbert Amelio, and who was charged with helping to articulate Apple's next-generation operating strategy, but with no one reporting to him, no clearly articulated responsibilities, no seat on the board, and no power.

No power? Amelio didn't know Steve Jobs.

Apple unquestionably needed saving. After four profitable quarters in fiscal 1995, it had lost money quarter after quarter, gone through major restructuring and layoffs, and was losing market share rapidly. Third-party software developers were choosing almost routinely to develop for Windows first, and then, maybe, to port their products to the Mac. Apple stock was falling and brokerage firms were recommending not to buy Apple. The press was sounding its death knell.

People weren't buying Apple's computers, either, at least not enough to maintain Apple's market share, because they didn't see any advantage in the Macintosh over Windows machines. This was partly because of the aggressive marketing of the Windows 95 release by Microsoft, which included purchasing the rights to the Rolling Stones'

"Start Me Up" for $10 million, but mostly because of Apple's demonstrated inability to deliver a long-delayed overhaul of the Mac operating system.

By the end of 1996, Apple's future was in question, but some observers thought that the company could be turned around if it got three things: focused management, a better public image, and a next-generation operating system. And it needed all of them right away.

Some thought that Amelio and the team he had put together were that focused management. And NeXTSTEP really was a next-generation operating system, not an implausible idea. Even though it was more than half the age of the doddering Macintosh operating system, it had everything a modern operating system should have. Things like the capability of running more than one program at a time, and to have the computer keep running even if one of the programs crashes. The NeXT team had designed well, and NeXTSTEP was field-tested. As for the change in Apple's public image. . . .

Three weeks after the announcement, Amelio took the stage for his keynote address at the Macworld Expo in San Francisco, the biggest Macintosh event of the year, the place where Apple often laid out its plans for the coming year. The room was jammed, and attendees had to find sitting or standing room in the aisles. The word was out that Apple had bought NeXT and that Steve Jobs was back, but little more was known. The news was dramatic, but the unknowns were even more of a draw.

Amelio laid out the essence of the plan plainly: Apple would produce a new operating system, based very closely on NeXTSTEP, to run on its PowerPC hardware. The operating system would be able to run existing Macintosh applications in a segregated section of the software referred to as "the blue box." It would also run NeXT-based applications in a different "yellow box." The Mac operating system, which would now live in the blue box, would continue to be enhanced over the next few years at least, but the NeXTSTEP side of the new operating system was really the future.

In other words, Apple was gently retiring the Mac. It would live on for some time, but in an incorporeal state, like a deceased character in a science fiction story whose personality is recorded on disk and played back when someone wants to talk to it. NeXTSTEP, modified with elements of the Mac user interface and some other Apple technologies, was Apple's future.

Then he introduced Steve Jobs. The crowd jumped to its feet and applauded wildly. When things finally quieted down, Jobs described NeXTSTEP and his view of the challenges facing Apple. He could have said anything. He had the crowd in his hand.

Later, Amelio called Jobs back to the stage, along with cofounder Steve Wozniak. The packed house rose to its feet again, and again there was thunderous applause.

It was a moment.

For Steve Jobs it was also a symbol of some kind of a homecoming, and like all homecomings, this one was remarkable for what had changed as well as for what had not. A great deal had changed for Steve Jobs since he left Apple more than a decade earlier. He was married now and had a family. The lack of success at NeXT would have been humbling to anyone else, and probably was even to Jobs. But by selling NeXT he had finally paid his debt to its long-suffering employees (and had stock options that were now worth real money). And both Jobs and Apple were simply older; the company was now as old as the man was when he and Steve Wozniak founded it.

What followed was not quite what Amelio expected. The correct word for it is *coup*. Within weeks, Jobs had his chosen managers in place. NeXT veterans Jon Rubenstein and Avi Tevanian were now totally in charge of Apple's hardware and software divisions. By midyear, Jobs had eased Amelio out of the company entirely, engineered a new board of directors entirely loyal to himself, and was appointed *interim* CEO with unchallenged authority over every aspect of the company's business. Months later, Amelio was still trying to put a favorable spin on the coup.

And so began the turnaround year. Most of the changes Jobs implemented had been planned on Amelio's watch, and many had been the ideas of CFO Joseph Graziano, but Jobs made them happen. He shut down the licensing program, which had come too late and had produced the effect of letting clonemakers cut into Apple's own sales as Gassée had feared. He laid off employees, dropped 70 percent of the projects, radically simplified the product line, instituted direct sales on the Web, and stripped down the sales channel.

Most of the decisions ruffled at least some feathers, but one move shocked the Apple faithful and drew boos from the crowd when it was announced at the next Macworld Expo. As Jobs stood on stage, the face of Bill Gates appeared on the enormous screen behind him, looking down like Big Brother in the movie version of George Orwell's *1984*. Jobs announced that Microsoft was investing $150 million in Apple. Jobs recovered by assuring the crowd that it was a *nonvoting* stake. The investment gave Apple an infusion of needed capital and the good public relations of the endorsement of Microsoft, but Microsoft exacted a heavy price: the rights to many Apple patents and the agreement that Apple would make Microsoft's Internet browser—a program for accessing the World Wide Web—its browser of choice. Microsoft was enlisting Apple in its war to control the key software used to browse the Internet.

Despite the plan laid out in the earlier Macworld keynote address, Jobs didn't retire the Mac operating system. Instead, he folded the NeXT technology into an improved OS that was still Macintosh.

It would be easy to think, knowing Jobs, that the whole NeXT acquisition had been a Machiavellian scheme, but it wasn't that simple. Jobs was not at all convinced that Apple could be saved when he sold NeXT. He unloaded the 1.5 million Apple shares he got in the NeXT deal cheaply, convinced that the stock wasn't going up. "Apple is toast," he said to a friend in an unguarded moment. But within months Apple had gone from a zero to a one in Jobs's mind, and he threw himself into saving it. The board was willing to give him anything he wanted, repeatedly offering him the CEO job and chairmanship. He turned them down, but still ran the company dictatorially, inserting himself into any department at any level he thought necessary, under the title of interim CEO. He wasn't getting any significant compensation and, having sold his Apple stock almost at its lowest point, wasn't getting any financial benefit from Apple's success. But he was being rewarded.

Conceding that personal computers had become commodities, Jobs embraced that model and used commodity features to sell computers. The iMac and the new desktop Mac computers that came out in 1998 and 1999 brought color and a sense of style to computers to a degree that had never been attempted before. The market ate them up. The iMac not only sold well, it became the best-selling computer on the market for several months running. Apple began making consistent profits again, and analysts pronounced that the slide had been halted and Apple was a good investment again.

Jobs was re-creating Apple into a company that had at least a chance of surviving in a market heavily commoditized and dominated by Microsoft.

Some Bright Young Hacker

*There was no particular reason why it
took two guys at the University of
Illinois to do it, any more than it should
have taken two guys in Sunnyvale to do
the Apple I. It's just that sometimes the
establishment needs a kick in the pants.*

MARC ANDREESSEN
Cofounder of Netscape

BILL GATES MAY HAVE BEEN A BILLIONAIRE IN 1994, BUT HE WAS DRIVEN by fear.

No matter that he was the richest person in America, viewed by most people as the symbol, and possibly the inventor, of the personal computer revolution. Nor did it matter that he was the founder and leader of the company whose products dominated most of the industry. Gates truly believed that he and Microsoft held their position only by virtue of constant vigilance, aggressive competition, and tirelessly applied intelligence. He was convinced that some bright young hacker somewhere could knock out a few thousand lines of clever code in a couple of months that would change the rules of the game, marginalizing Microsoft overnight.

Gates knew about these hackers because he had been one. He had known the thrill of proving your mettle by outsmarting a giant corporation. Now he was on the other side, and somewhere out there he could picture the bright young hacker who would one day succeed in outsmarting *him*.

Some bright young hacker like Marc Andreessen, maybe.

Andreessen's feat was accomplished in the milieu of the World Wide Web, but to understand its significance, one has to cast back further.

Electronics enthusiasts in Albuquerque and Silicon Valley didn't invent the World Wide Web, but its origin owes much to that same spirit of sharing information that fueled the first decade of the personal computer revolution. In fact, it could be argued that the Web is the realization of that spirit in software.

The genesis of the Web goes back to the earliest days of computing, to a visionary essay by Franklin Delano Roosevelt's science advisor, Vannevar Bush, in 1945. Bush's essay, which envisioned information-processing technology as an extension of human intellect, inspired two of the most influential thinkers in computing, Ted Nelson and Douglas Engelbart, who each labored in his own way to articulate Bush's sketchy vision of an interconnected world of knowledge. Key to both Engelbart's and Nelson's visions was the idea of a link; both saw a need to connect a word *here* with a document *there* in a way that allowed the reader to follow the link naturally and effortlessly. Nelson gave the capability its name: hypertext.

Hypertext was merely an interesting theoretical concept, glimpsed by Bush and conceptualized by Nelson and Engelbart, without a global, universal network on which to implement it. Such a network was not developed until the 1970s, at the Defense Advanced Research Projects Agency, or DARPA, and at several universities. The DARPA network (DARPAnet) didn't just link individual computers; it linked whole networks together. As the DARPAnet expanded, it came to be called the Internet, a vast global network of networks of computers. The Internet finally brought hypertext to life. And by the DARPA programmers having developed a method for passing data around the Internet, and the personal computer revolution having put the means of accessing the Internet in the hands of ordinary people, the pieces of the puzzle were all on the table.

Tim Berners-Lee, a researcher at CERN, a high-energy research laboratory on the French-Swiss border, invented the Web in 1990. Berners-Lee created the World Wide Web in 1989, by writing the first Web *server,* a program for putting hypertext information online, and by writing the first Web *browser,* a program for accessing that information. The information was displayed in manageable chunks called *pages.*

It was a fairly stunning achievement, and it impressed the relatively small circle of academics who could use it.

The circle was small because hardly anyone had the right kind of machine—this browser was not implemented on machines that mere mortals owned (Berners-Lee did his development on one of those hot new black cubes from NeXT), and it deliberately restricted communications to text. Nelson, Engelbart, and Bush had never meant hypertext to be just linked text; hypermedia was a more descriptive term.

One of the places where Berners-Lee's achievement was fully appreciated was at the NCSA (National Center for Supercomputing Applications) at the University of Illinois' Urbana-Champaign campus. NCSA had a large budget, a lot of hot technology, and a large staff with "frankly, not enough to do," according to one of the bright young hackers privileged to work there.

Even at $6.85 an hour, Marc Andreessen saw it as a privilege to work at NCSA. He was a sharp undergraduate programmer who loved being in an environment where he could talk about Unix code. Andreessen looked at what Berners-Lee had done and saw the potential of the Web, but he also saw that potential being restricted to a few academics, accessed on expensive hardware through archaic, arcane software. The opportunity to open up the Web to everyone looked to him like "a giant hole in the middle of the world."

Riding in friend Eric Bina's car one night late in 1992, Andreessen put the challenge to Bina: "Let's go for it," he said. *Let's fill that hole.*

They coded like mad. Between January and March of 1993, they wrote a 9000-line program called Mosaic. It was a Web browser, but not like Berners-Lee's. Mosaic was a browser for the GUI generation, a Web browser for everyone. It displayed graphics, it let you use a mouse and click on buttons to do things—no, to *go places.* Mosaic completed the process of turning abstract connection into place; using Mosaic, one had a compelling sense of going from one location to another in some sort of space. Some called it cyberspace.

This was exactly what Bill Gates had feared: some bright young hacker—well, two—had knocked out a few thousand lines of clever code in a couple of months that would change the rules of the game forever, putting the biggest software company in the world on the defensive, and threatening everything Gates had built.

Andreessen and Bina released Mosaic on the Internet. They signed on other NCSA kids to port Mosaic from the Unix operating system to other platforms, and released those on the Internet, too. Millions of people downloaded it. No piece of software had ever got into so many hands so quickly.

This thing let you travel the planet, virtually. It was amazing. It let you read about Shakespeare on a computer in a New York library, click once to zip across the ocean to England to look at a picture of the Globe Theater, click again to return to the stacks to read *Hamlet*— except that they're different stacks. This copy of *Hamlet* happens to be on a Web site in Uzbekistan. Doesn't matter; terrestrial geography isn't relevant in cyberspace. You can browse a world of information without leaving your chair. None of this could happen until people had created the Web sites, but this happened in tandem with the spread of Mosaic. Everyone who tried it "got it"; Mosaic was a hit and Andreessen was a hero.

In December 1993, Andreessen graduated from college, wondering what to do for an encore. Gravitating to Silicon Valley, he met Jim Clark, founder of Silicon Graphics. Clark was impressed by Mosaic and by Andreessen's grasp of the potential of the Web. By April 1994, the two had founded a company, first called Electric Media, then Mosaic Communications, and finally Netscape Communications. They were going to produce software in support of this new thing, this World Wide Web.

They were not alone. By midyear there were dozens of Web browsers: some free, some commercial; some available for Windows and the Macintosh and Unix, some platform-specific; some stripped-down, some festooned with bells and whistles. In addition to Mosaic, there were MacWeb, WinWeb, InternetWorks, SlipKnot, Cello, NetCruiser, Lynx, Air Mosaic, GWHIS, WinTapestry, WebExplorer, as well as others.

Creating personal Web pages became a fad. So did new uses of the Web such as ordering pizza via the Web. Webcams were another fad— digital cameras feeding a continuous stream of pictures to a Web site. You could visit a Web site and watch coffee perk at MIT, check the commute traffic on Highway 17 coming up from the Santa Cruz beaches into Silicon Valley, or monitor the waves along the California coast. Steve Wozniak set up a Wozcam so friends could watch him work. The Web was a wave and Clark and Andreessen were riding it.

They hired Eric Bina and other NCSA kids from the Mosaic effort, wrote a new browser from scratch, and made it as bulletproof and nifty as they knew how. By October 1994, they had a beta version out on the Internet. By December, they were shipping the release version of Netscape Navigator, along with other Web software products. By the end of 1996, 45 million copies of Navigator were in people's hands. The company was growing at a delirious rate, and Clark brought in industry veteran Jim Barksdale, who was widely respected for his management of McCaw Cellular Communications, as president.

Netscape was perceived in the industry, and on Wall Street, as a hot property. One admirer was Steve Case of America Online (AOL), the premier online service. He offered to put up money for Netscape's first round of financing, but Clark turned him down, concerned that AOL's involvement might put off potential customers who considered AOL to be competition. On August 9, 1995, Netscape filed its initial public stock offering (IPO) of 5 million shares at $28 each. Its stock doubled by the end of the day, and Netscape was suddenly worth $3 billion.

That year, Microsoft responded.

In May 1995, Gates had already described the Internet to his staff as "the most important single development to come along since the IBM PC in 1981." In December, he announced publicly that the Internet was to be pervasive in all that Microsoft did. Netscape's stock immediately dropped 17 percent and never recovered. Microsoft was going to enter the browser market. It did that, rapidly and impressively, licensing some browser technology and developing its own browser, Internet Explorer, to compete with Netscape's browser. The company launched by the bright young hacker and the industry veteran was, in Gates's opinion, a threat to Microsoft's existence, and it needed to be snuffed.

Gates was not alone in seeing the Internet as a threat to Microsoft's dominance in the PC market. Bob Metcalfe, the networking guru who had developed the Ethernet protocol, wrote a weekly column for the industry magazine *InfoWorld*. In February 1995, he predicted that the browser would in effect become the dominant operating system for the next era. The dominant operating system for the current era was, of course, Microsoft's Windows. Metcalfe was predicting that the Windows' dominance was on the verge of ending.

How, exactly, could a browser replace an operating system? Partly by providing the same capabilities; Netscape Navigator could launch application programs, display directories of files, and do most of the things an operating system did. Partly by making the choice of operating system invisible and irrelevant—Navigator ran on Macs and PCs and workstations and looked and acted the same on all of them—and partly by moving the center of the computing universe. Sun Microsystems had a slogan, "The network is the computer." With Navigator, it didn't matter if an application program or a data file was on your hard disk, on a server in the next office, or on a computer in another country. It didn't matter what computer—Mac, PC, or Amiga—it was on; it just mattered whether you could get to it with your browser.

If the network was the computer, the browser was the operating system, and single-computer-based operating systems were irrelevant. Gates wasn't going to let Windows become irrelevant.

Over the next few years, Microsoft, Netscape, and certain other companies whose interests intersected at the Internet crossroads performed a complex dance. Mostly it was Microsoft against everybody else, but there were complications.

One of the most significant of those other companies was Sun Microsystems.

The Joy of
Computers

At least I graduated.

SCOTT MCNEALY
Cofounder of Sun Microsystems

ON APRIL 1, 1988, ENGINEERS AT SUN MICROSYSTEMS KNOCKED DOWN a wall between the offices of company president Scott McNealy and executive vice president Bernie Lacroute and built a 40-foot golf hole, complete with sand trap, water hazard, ball washer, and golf cart. April Fool's pranks were a tradition at Sun and always earned the company lots of ink.

McNealy took the joke in stride, for he had already become extremely successful. Since its founding in 1982, Sun had pushed the technological envelope and employed some techniques of the personal computer companies to win the business of technical and scientific users previously in the minicomputer and mainframe camps.

But Sun was different from Apple and all the PC companies. Scott McNealy grew up in the Rust Belt and was the son of the vice chair of American Motors. As a child he used to open his father's briefcase and read confidential business documents in order to understand what his father did. He scored a perfect 800 on his math SATs and attended Harvard at the same time as Bill Gates.

A few other key individuals went into the Sun mix. One was Bill Joy, who, like McNealy, came from Michigan. Joy was a child prodigy, an early math whiz who could read by age 3, skipped several grades, and became a National Merit Scholar. He obtained a B.S. in electrical engineering at the University of Michigan, and while both Stanford and Caltech accepted him for graduate work, he chose UC Berkeley instead. At Berkeley he took on the Herculean task of rewriting the Unix operating system. His Berkeley Unix became ubiquitous in research and technical communities.

A second was Andreas Bechtolsheim, who came to the United States from West Germany in 1975 to study computer science. He obtained his Master's degree from Carnegie-Mellon University a year later and then transferred to Stanford. There, Bechtolsheim took on the project of designing the computer he desired for himself, much as Steve Wozniak had done earlier. He wanted it to be as powerful as a technical workstation, to use off-the-shelf components, and to connect to the Stanford network.

And the man who stirred these ingredients together was Vinod Khosla. Born in New Delhi in 1956, he had dreamed of working in Silicon Valley as a teenager reading American engineering magazines. He earned a B.A. in electrical engineering at the Indian Institute of Technology, a Master's degree in biomedical engineering at Carnegie-Mellon University, and was working on his Stanford MBA when he became avid for entrepreneurship. He helped found Daisy Systems, which built computers used mostly to design other computers. Khosla was convinced that the future lay in a less costly and more all-purpose workstation. A computer like Andy Bechtolsheim's SUN (short for "Stanford University Network").

In 1982, Khosla formed this impressive team, helped raise venture capital, and launched Sun Microsystems. The company went public in 1986, exceeded $1 billion in sales in six years, and became a Fortune 500 company in 1992. In the process, it displaced minicomputers and mainframes, and made *workstation* an everyday term in the business world.

But one victory eluded Sun. By the 1990s, the price of workstations had fallen below $5,000. That was low enough for Sun to sell them to mainstream consumers. Yet Sun failed to thrive in the personal computer field, even when it offered machines built around the same Intel microprocessors used by IBM, Compaq, and others. Because of Sun's history and target market, it had a deep commitment to one operating system, and it wasn't MS-DOS. Sun's computers and software used the Unix operating system, which it had customized for its own purposes, and its focus on products for technical professionals kept it from marching into the popular market.

McNealy believed that Sun's big enemy was Microsoft. In the 1990s, Gates's firm had a new operating system called Windows NT, which was intended to give business PCs all the power of workstations. McNealy decided to wage not only a technical war but also a public-relations war. In public talks and interviews, he ridiculed Microsoft and its products. Along with Oracle CEO Larry Ellison, he tried to promote a new kind of device, called a network computer, which would get its information and instructions from servers on the Internet. This device did not immediately catch on.

But Sun had a hidden advantage in the consumer market—its early, foursquare advocacy of networks. People were repeating its slogan, "The network is the computer," and it seemed prescient as the Internet emerged.

Sun was a magnet for talented programmers who enjoyed the smart, free-spirited atmosphere of the Silicon Valley firm. In 1991, McNealy gave one of its star programmers, James Gosling, carte blanche to create a new programming language. Gosling realized that almost all home electronics products were now computerized. But a different remote device controlled each, and few worked in the same way. The user grappled with a handful of remotes. Gosling sought to reduce it to one. Patrick Naughton and Mike Sheridan joined him, and they soon designed an innovative handheld device that let people control electronics products by touching a screen instead of pressing a keyboard or buttons.

The project, code-named Green, continued to evolve as the Internet and World Wide Web began their spectacular bloom. But more than the features evolved; the whole purpose of the product changed. The team focused on allowing programs in the new language to run on many platforms with diverse central processors. They devised a technical Esperanto, universally and instantly understood by many types of hardware. With the Web, this capacity became a bonanza.

Although the project took several years to reach market, Sun used the cross-platform programming concepts from Green, which became known as Java, to outmaneuver its competition. Sun promoted Java as "a new way of computing, based on the power of networks." Many programmers began to use Java to create the early, innovative, interactive programs that became part of the appeal of Web sites, such as animated characters and interactive puzzles.

Java was the first major programming language to have been written with the Web in mind. It had built-in security features that would prove crucial for protecting computers from invasion now that this electronic doorway—the Web connection—had opened them up to the world. It could be used to write programs that didn't require the programmer to know what operating system the user was running, which was typically the case for applications running over the Web.

Java surprised the industry, and especially Microsoft. The software titan was slow to grasp the importance of the Internet, and as a result Netscape flourished early on. But once in the fray, Gates made the Internet a top priority.

At the same time, Gates was initially skeptical about Java. But as the language caught on, he licensed it from Sun, purchased a company called Dimension X that possessed Java expertise, and assigned hundreds of programmers to develop Java products. Microsoft tried to slip around its licensing agreement by adding capabilities to its version of Java that would only work on Microsoft operating systems. Sun brought suit. Gates saw Sun and its new language as a serious threat. Why, if Java was a programming language, and not an operating system? Because the ability to write platform-independent programs significantly advanced the possibility for a browser to supplant the operating system. It didn't matter if you had a Sun workstation, PC, Macintosh, or what-have-you; you could run a Java program through your browser.

And Sun was serious about challenging Microsoft's hegemony in the "post-PC" era. In 1998, it agreed to work with Oracle on a line of network server computers that would use Sun's Solaris operating system and Oracle's database so that desktop computer users could scuttle Windows. Moreover, Sun began to sell an extension to Java, called Jini, which let people connect a variety of home electronics devices over a network.

In a speech at an Internet conference, Bill Joy called Jini "the first software architecture designed for the age of the network." Several dozen companies signed up to license Jini, including major software companies and consumer electronics firms. Sun's ambition was also evident in another move it made involving Netscape and AOL.

The Browser Wars

*There is nothing about the Internet that
repeals the normal laws of business.*

MARC ANDREESSEN
Cofounder of Netscape

AOL WAS CONTINUING A COURTSHIP WITH NETSCAPE AND A BATTLE
with Microsoft.

When Jim Clark rebuffed AOL's offer to buy into Netscape, AOL had
purchased a browser from another source—grabbing the other browser
just before Microsoft could—but Steve Case was still interested in both
Netscape and its browser. The browser was regarded as the best available, and the company was a hot property. But there was another reason for his interest in Netscape: most AOL executives viewed
Netscape's team as people they could relate to. At AOL, Netscape was
viewed as a natural ally in the war against Microsoft.

Microsoft had been steadily moving into AOL's territory, online systems, for years. Although AOL was enabling people to get on the Internet with its Web browser, its business was primarily as an online
service. Since the 1980s, online services provided Internet connections
to paying subscribers, hosted electronic discussion groups for them,
and gave them e-mail. All these services were also available on the
Internet, but online services were a lot easier to work with—and familiar. Microsoft had entered this market with its Microsoft Network,
MSN. AOL was still the unchallenged leader of the online companies,
but it was worried.

*Apple Computer's first
ad as a company*

"A is for Apple" ad

▲ Scientific American
ad on Steve Jobs

▶ *Apple Computer's
original "Newton" logo*

from altair™ to zaltair™

Predictable refinement of computer equipment should suggest online reliability. The elite computer hobbiest needs one logical optionless guarantee, yet.

Ed Roberts
President, MITS, Inc.

Imagine a dream machine. **Imagine** the computer surprise of the century, here today. **Imagine** Z80 performance plus. **Imagine** BAZIC in ROM, the most complete and powerful language ever developed. **Imagine** raw video, plenty of it. **Imagine** autoscroll text, a full 16 lines of 64 characters. **Imagine** eye-dazzling color graphics. **Imagine** a blitz fast 1200 baud cassette port. **Imagine** an unparalleled I/O system with full **ALTAIR-100** and **ZALTAIR-150** bus compatibility. **Imagine** an exquisitely designed cabinet that will add to the decor of any living room. **Imagine** the fun you'll have. **Imagine ZALTAIR,** available now from MITS, the company where microcomputer technology was born.

bazic™

Without software a computer is no more than a racing car without wheels, a turntable without records, or a banjo without strings. BAZIC is the language that puts ZALTAIR's powerful hardware at your fingertips. For example, you can test the entire memory with the MEMTEST statement. Or read the keyboard directly with the KBD function. If you like to keep time the CLCK function will really please you. And in case you're in a hurry, you'll be glad to know that BAZIC runs twice as fast as any BASIC around. The best thing of all about BAZIC is the ability to define your own language...a feature we call perZonality.™ And ZALTAIR's BAZIC language comes standard in ROM, to insure 'rip-off' security.

hardware

We really thought this baby out before we built it. Two years of dedicated research and development at the number ONE microcomputer company had to pay off, and it did. A computer engineer's dream, all electronics are on a single pc card, **EVEN THE 18-SLOT MOTHERBOARD.** And what a motherboard. The ZALTAIR-150 bus is fully ALTAIR-100 compatible with 50 extra connectors. In addition, with ZALTAIR's advanced I/O structure called verZatility,™ access to peripherals is easier than ever before. And of course, our complete line of ALTAIR peripherals is directly compatible with the ZALTAIR 8800.

don't miss out

Weighing just 16 pounds, the ZALTAIR 8800 is a **portable** computer. The highly attractive enclosure was designed by an award winning team, and is fabricated from high-impact, durable ABS Cycolac® plastic. In the MITS tradition, nothing is compromised. Because of its superior design we were able to price the ZALTAIR 8800 far below the competition for this special introductory offer only. **You will not find the ZALTAIR in any store.** We want to bring this incredible offer to you directly, and avoid the retail mark-up of a middle man. Already, over 100 ZALTAIR's have been delivered to 75 satisfied customers. Don't miss out, order your ZALTAIR before April 30, 1977, and get immediate delivery.

▲ *One of Steve Wozniak's practical jokes, a 1977 brochure describing the "Zaltair," which poked fun at the Altair and all the new firms that were starting to boast about their products at that time*

Original Apple II, 1977

Mike Markkula presenting Steve Jobs with a check for $92 million from his stock offering after Apple Computer went public in December 1980

Steve Jobs and Mike Markkula

Apple Computer's product description when it released the Lisa, which proved not to be a commercial success: "Lisa, a personal computer for the office, was introduced by Apple Computer, Inc., in January 1983. The 32/16-bit computer, aimed at revolutionizing the way work is done in the office environment, features six integrated software applications that cover the core functions of today's office. Lisa incorporates the latest software and hardware technology in a system that's powerful and advanced, yet is so easy to learn that a first-time user can put it to work in less than 30 minutes."

Wendell Sander, designer
of the Apple III

COURTESY OF APPLE COMPUTER, INC.

Apple Computer's product description when it released the vastly more successful Apple
II Plus: "The Apple II Plus personal computer system equipped with a Monitor III, a Disk II
floppy disk drive, and Apple Writer software provides a powerful text editing capability that
enables users to write, revise, edit, and print a wide range of documents quickly and easily."

COURTESY OF APPLE COMPUTER, INC.

▲ *Regis McKenna (left), Apple Computer's public relations advisor,
and Andy Grove of Intel Corporation*

▲ *John Sculley, then CEO of Apple Computer, with colleagues at the computer industry's
prestigious Agenda conference*

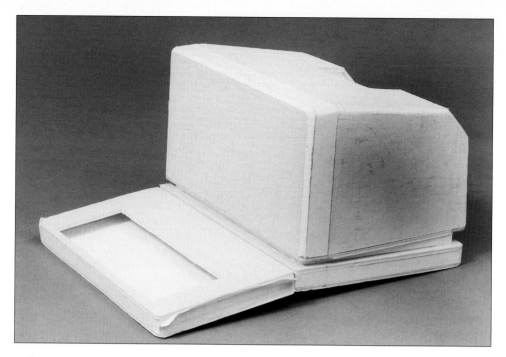

▲Apple Macintosh prototype, an essential component of successful computer design and manufacturing

▲Members of the Macintosh design team

▲ *Apple Computer's original Macintosh, 1984*

▲ *President Ronald Reagan honoring Apple cofounders Steve Wozniak and Steve Jobs with the Medal of Honor at the White House in 1984*

▲ *Steve Jobs and John Sculley at a 1984 shareholders meeting*

▲ *Paul Allen and Bill Gates surrounded by personal computers on October 19, 1981, shortly after signing a contract with IBM to write software for the IBM PC*

▲ *Charles Simonyi and Bill Gates of Microsoft*

▲ *Bill Gates giving a software demo to computer magazine entrepreneur David Bunnell in 1981*

Steve Ballmer and Bill Gates

COURTESY OF SARAH HINMAN,
MICROSOFT MUSEUM

Mitch Kapor, Lotus 1-2-3 coinventor and company founder, 1982

COURTESY OF MITCH KAPOR

Philippe Kahn, programmer, founder of
Borland International and Starfish Corp.,
and accomplished jazz musician

Vinod Khosla, Bill Joy, Andy Bechtolsheim, and Scott McNealy,
founders of Sun Microsystems in 1982

Tim Berners-Lee, inventor of the World Wide Web and creator of HTTP and HTML in 1990

Marc Andreessen, cofounder of Netscape and developer of the Mosaic Web browser that popularized the Internet

▲ The North Star staff in front of their Berkeley headquarters

PHOTO BY MARTIN J. COONEY STUDIO,
COURTESY OF NORTH STAR

◀ Dan Fylstra of Personal Software (later VisiCorp), which published the first electronic spreadsheet software VisiCalc

PHOTO BY LIANE ENKELIS

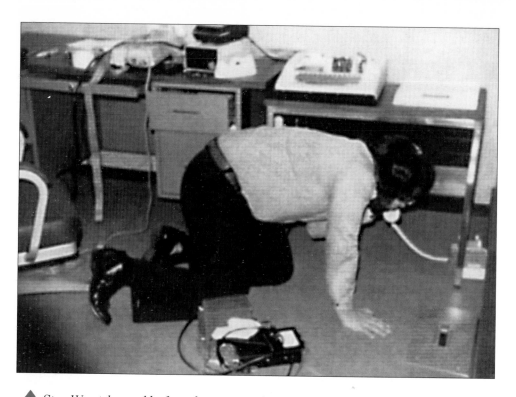

▲ *Steve Wozniak scrambles for a phone in one of Apple's original offices*

▲ *Steve Jobs (left) and Steve Wozniak looking over an early Apple circuit board*

The future of online companies was becoming cloudy as browsers made the Internet easier to navigate. That was why AOL needed a browser and why it was interested in Netscape, and it was why Microsoft was willing to undercut its own MSN in order to beat Netscape.

In 1995, Microsoft committed itself publicly to the Internet. What that meant was soon evident. After licensing browser technology from a small company and then developing its own browser, Internet Explorer, Microsoft approached AOL.

Getting AOL's browser replaced by Microsoft's would be a huge blow to the stellar public image of Netscape. By this time, AOL had millions of subscribers; if every one of them began using Microsoft's browser, Netscape would be well on its way to second place behind Microsoft in the browser wars.

To get its browser on AOL subscribers' screens, Microsoft was willing to make a very sweet deal. In exchange for AOL's licensing Internet Explorer, Microsoft would put an icon for AOL on the Windows desktop. This amounted to free advertising and an endorsement from Microsoft appearing on every Windows user's computer screen every time they started up their machines. This was a major sellout of Microsoft's own online service, MSN, but that didn't matter. What mattered to Microsoft was crushing Netscape. And the price made the sweet deal even harder for AOL to turn down—AOL could have the browser for free.

Incredibly, AOL *still* considered turning down the offer. Microsoft was the enemy. In the end, AOL cut deals with both Netscape and Microsoft, but Microsoft's browser was promoted as the preferred browser. Netscape got the short end of the deal.

During the negotiations with Netscape, Case emphasized the importance of Netscape's Web site. This was an immensely popular area on the Web, and Netscape could easily sell advertising on it. Millions of people were visiting Netscape's site on a daily basis. Case pointed out that it was analogous to the presence that the online services were able to have with their subscribers. Microsoft understood this and was already evolving its MSN into its own Web site. Case didn't think that Netscape understood what a treasure it had.

At the same time, AOL was negotiating with Sun regarding Java, and

Netscape was working with Sun on a simple language, unrelated to Java but called JavaScript, that would let people add interactive features to Web pages without the need to learn a full programming language like Java. All three companies saw Microsoft as the enemy and had reason to work together.

Now everyone was threatening Microsoft. At least that was the view from Microsoft's headquarters. Sun had ideas about a Java-based operating system. Netscape was developing the browser as an alternative to an operating system, in a sense. And Oracle jumped into the fray by pushing these stripped-down machines that wouldn't run Windows.

In October 1996, Oracle and Netscape announced that they would be working together on an NC, a network computer. This announcement showed how fear of Microsoft could drive companies together; two months earlier, Marc Andreessen had ridiculed the NC and Larry Ellison had derided Netscape's technology as "very, very thin."

The anti-Microsoft contingent got a heavy hitter in the late 1990s when IBM made a heavy commitment to Java. But Microsoft continued to make inroads into the Internet and online spaces. By the end of 1997, Internet Explorer had passed Netscape's browser in popularity, and by the end of 1998 MSN had passed Netscape's Netcenter site in the number of visitors and had become a major *portal*, a place that millions of people used as a sort of home base from which to conduct their explorations of the Web. Netscape was rapidly losing ground. It wasn't clear what its future would be.

Early in 1998, fighting for survival in the market Andreessen had launched just five years earlier, Netscape did something that made jaws drop in corporate boardrooms and cheers rise from programmers. It freed the source code for its browser.

The source code for its products are a software company's crown jewels, to be protected against prying eyes and thieving hands. Legal wars had been fought over such intellectual property, so bitterly that in some cases the warring companies were damaged beyond recovery. Borland was deeply wounded by the cost of such litigation; Digital Research had lost its chance to recover from the IBM disaster when Apple threatened to sue over GEM; and Software Arts was driven out of business by protracted litigation with Personal Software.

But Netscape was proposing to put its source code on the Internet for all to see. And not just see. Programmers would be free to use the code to develop new products. But what they developed would also have to remain open to other developers. This meant that Netscape could use enhancements written by other programmers in its browser. The company was inviting the entire software community to help develop its software. The project and its Web site were called Mozilla, the original code name for Netscape's browser.

Andreessen and Clark knew that there were risks in doing this, but they also knew the benefits of open systems. The personal computer industry had been built on the free sharing of information. Where progress was rapid, it made sense to share, they believed. In fast-growing areas like the Internet, it didn't make sense to protect technology that was growing rapidly obsolete anyway. It was a bold plan.

But not without precedent. Most of the software underlying the Internet had been developed in this open way. Also, the Unix operating system had often advanced in this open manner. In the mid-1990s a new variant of the Unix kernel (the part of an operating system that handles basic operations such as memory, files, and peripheral interfaces) was developed by a bright young hacker in Finland named Linus Torvalds. Torvalds called his operating system *Linux,* and he made the source code public, inviting the programming community to contribute to its enhancement. The response was electrifying: in six years, Linux had come from a hobby project at the University of Helsinki to become the dominant version of Unix. It was ported to Intel PCs and the Mac and spread like a virus through the software development community. Before long, competition from Linux was forcing Microsoft to rethink NT, the high-end operating system that it had hoped would supplant Unix in the server market. With apparently thousands of talented programmers contributing to the development of Linux, it was questionable that even Microsoft could keep up.

Web professionals, in particular, understood and appreciated the open-source model. Apache, the leading Web server program, was a free, open-source product, as were many other must-have Internet tools. The Internet and the Web had emerged in academic environments where this was the natural model. It may not have been the most obvious commercial model, but that was deceiving. Linux companies were making money, attracting investors. And *open* is not the same as free.

Meanwhile, on May 18, 1998, the U.S. Justice Department and the attorneys general of some 20 states filed an antitrust suit against Microsoft, alleging, among other things, that Microsoft abused its monopoly position in operating systems to thwart competition, particularly in the case of Netscape.

Netscape was thwarted, all right. The company was thrashing about, trying to decide whether its future, if it had one, was in browsers, in other Web software, in services, or in promoting its Web site as a source of advertising revenue. The fate of Mozilla was uncertain.

Then, on November 24, 1998, AOL announced that it had concluded negotiations to buy Netscape Communications in a stock swap valued at some $4.2 billion. Case finally got the company he thought would complement AOL. Sun Microsystems figured in the deal, too, with Sun promising to market the Netscape software that AOL didn't need in return for a cut of its earnings on the products and some Sun-developed technology. Netscape's assets were carved up and served to the parties most likely to be capable of exploiting them.

Microsoft pointed to the deal as evidence that the playing field had been leveled and that the lawsuit should be dropped. The court didn't see it that way, and as this book goes to press, the case continues.

Meanwhile, the Mozilla project, by enlisting the help of hundreds of programmers outside the company, finished a new version of the browser. Although AOL announced continued support for Mozilla, it hardly mattered. Now that it was an open-source product, the browser had, as one journalist put it, "gone directly from the Internet's endangered species list to virtual immortality." No longer tied to one company, it would be around as long as programmers saw value in maintaining it. But immortal or not, it had been marginalized by Microsoft.

Had Microsoft won? Had it crushed the threat from Netscape? Or did this open-source thing change the rules of the game?

Some have predicted that open-source programs will dominate the software market. Supporters say that open-source software is often better than the commercial kind, because everyone is invited to find and fix its bugs. They claim that in an open-source world, a kind of natural selection will ensure that only the best software survives. Eric S. Raymond, an open-source proponent and author, believes that in open source we are seeing the emergence of a new nonmarket economy, with similarities to medieval guilds.

But is it really new? This open-source idea, what John Draper had called the Woz Principle, is really just an elaboration of the sharing of ideas that Gary Kildall had enjoyed in academia, and that scientifically trained people such as Engelbart understood as the key to scientific advance. It was older than Netscape, older than Apple, older than the personal computer revolution. As an approach to developing software, it began with the first computers in the 1940s and has been part of the advance of computer software technology ever since. It had been important in the spread of the personal computer revolution, and now, with the Internet, it was moving a new revolution forward.

Programmer and editor Andrew Flugelman came up with the idea of sharewares—users could try the software and pay him if they found it useful.

The particular technological revolution that produced the personal computer is over. It grew out of a unique mixture of technological developments and cultural forces, took off with the announcement of the Altair computer in 1975, and came to fruition in 1984, with the release of the Apple Macintosh, the first computer designed for the masses and delivered to the mass market.

But revolutions don't really end with the seizing of the palace. Since 1984, we have witnessed the 15-year dénouement: the development of increasingly more powerful machines and software, innovations in the way computers interact with people; the widespread acceptance of the personal computer as an indispensable tool for business and as an increasingly ubiquitous home appliance; and the empowering of a broader spectrum of people through computer technology.

This technology is now the driving force of the economies of most developed countries, and is contributing to the development of the rest. It is changing the world.

Changing the world.

In 1975, that had been a crazy dream.

Time and again, crazy dreamers had run up against resistance from accepted wisdom and had prevailed to realize their dreams. David Ahl, trying to convince Digital Equipment management that people would actually use computers in the home; Lee Felsenstein working in post-1960s Berkeley to turn technology to populist ends; Ed Roberts looking for a loan to keep MITS afloat so it could build kit computers; Bill Gates dropping out of Harvard to get a piece of the dream; Steve Dompier flying to Albuquerque to check up on his Altair order; Dick Heiser and Paul Terrell opening stores to sell a product for which their friends told them there was no market; Mike Markkula backing two kids in a garage. Dreamers all. And Ted Nelson, the ultimate crazy dreamer, envisioning a new world and spending a lifetime trying to bring it to life. In one way or another, they were all dreaming of one thing: the personal computer, the packaging of the awesome power of computer technology into a little box that anyone could own.

Today, changing the world is the little machine's *job*. The personal computer, once a truly revolutionary idea, has become a commonplace tool. But it's a revolutionarily empowering tool, and a tool that can empower revolutions. Just as the World Wide Web was invented on a NeXT cube, it is likely that the *next* technological revolution will be invented on a personal computer.

Probably by some bright young hacker.

She may even be reading this book right now.

AFTER THE REVOLUTION

We were young. It was a very lucky point in time. [That] something so huge and successful sprang out of it . . . was a huge surprise.

STEVE WOZNIAK
Apple Computer cofounder

Taming the Electronic Frontier

It was awful. So I left.
I just walked away one day.

MITCH KAPOR
Former CEO of Lotus Development Corporation

A**T THE HEIGHT OF HIS POWER AND INFLUENCE AT** LOTUS DEVELOP-ment Corporation, Mitch Kapor walked away from it all.

Lotus had grown large very quickly. The first venture capital arrived in 1982, Lotus 1-2-3 shipped in January of 1983, and that year the company made $53 million in sales. By early 1986, some 1300 people were working for the company.

Working for Mitch Kapor.

It had grown too fast. It was out of control, and it was overwhelming. Rather than feeling empowered by success, Kapor felt trapped by it. It occurred to him that he didn't really like big companies, even when he was the boss.

Then came a day when a major customer complained that Lotus was making changes in its software too often. That it was, in effect, innovating too rapidly. So what were they supposed to do, slow down the pace of innovation? Exactly. That's what they did. It was perfectly logical, and met the needs of that customer—and probably of other customers. Kapor didn't really fault it as a business decision. But what satisfaction was there in dumbing down your company?

Lotus just wasn't fun any more. So Kapor resigned. He walked out the door of Lotus and never looked back.

This act left him with the question: what now? After having helped launch a revolution, what should he do with the rest of his life? He didn't get away from Lotus clean. He spent a year completing work on a Lotus product called Agenda while serving as a visiting scientist at MIT. After that, he jumped back in and started another firm, the significantly smaller On Technology, a company focusing on software for workgroups.

And in 1989, he began to log on to an online service called The Well. The Well, which stood for Whole Earth 'Lectronic Letter, was the brainchild of Stewart Brand, who had also been behind *The Whole Earth Catalog*. The Well was an online community of bright, techno-savvy people.

"I fell in love with it," Kapor said later, because "I met a bunch of people online with similar interests who were smart that I wanted to talk to." He plunged headlong into this virtual community.

One day in the summer of 1990, he even found himself on a cattle ranch in Wyoming talking computers with a former lyricist of the Grateful Dead.

What led to that unlikely meeting was a series of events that bode ill for civil liberties in the new wired world. A few months earlier, some anonymous individual, for whatever motive, had "liberated" a piece of the proprietary, secret operating system code for the Apple Macintosh and had mailed it on floppy disks to influential people in the computer industry. Kapor was one of these people. John Perry Barlow—the former Grateful Dead lyricist, current cattle rancher, and computer gadfly—was not. But apparently because Barlow had attended something called The Hacker's Conference, the FBI concluded that Barlow might know the perpetrator.

This Hacker's Conference was a gathering of gifted programmers, industry pioneers, and legends, organized by the same Stewart Brand who had launched The Well. *Hacker* in this context was a term of praise, but in society at large it was also coming to mean "cybercriminal"—that is, one who illegally breaks into others' computer systems.

An exceptionally clueless G-man showed up at Barlow's ranch. The agent demonstrated his ignorance of computers and software, and Barlow attempted to educate him. Their conversation became the subject of an entertaining online essay by Barlow that appeared on The Well.

Soon after, Barlow got another visitor at the ranch. But this one, being the founder of Lotus Development Corporation, knew a lot about computers and software. Kapor had received the fateful disk, had had a similar experience with a couple of clueless FBI agents, had read Barlow's essay, and now wanted to brainstorm with him over the situation.

"The situation" transcended one ignorant FBI investigator or a piece of purloined Apple software. The Secret Service, in an operation they called "Operation Sun Devil," had been waging a campaign against computer crime, chiefly by storming into the homes of teenaged computer users at night, waving guns, frightening the families, and confiscating anything that looked like it had anything to do with computers.

"The situation" involved law enforcement agencies at various levels responding often with grotesquely excessive force to acts they scarcely understood. It involved young pranksters being hauled into court on very serious charges in an area where the law was murky and the judges as uninformed as the police.

Barlow was eager to brainstorm with Kapor about the situation. It did not escape their notice that they were planning to take on the government, to take on guys with guns.

What should they do? At the very least, they decided, these kids need competent legal defense. They decided to put together an organization to provide it. As Kapor explained it, "There was uninformed and panicky government response, treating situations like they were threats to national security. They were in the process of trying to put some of these kids away for a long time and throw away the key, and it just felt like there were injustices being done out of sheer lack of understanding. I felt a moral outrage. Barlow and I felt something had to be done."

In 1990, they cofounded the Electronic Frontier Foundation (EFF). They put out the word to a few high-profile computer industry figures they thought would understand what they were up to. Ex–blue boxer Steve Wozniak kicked in a six-figure contribution immediately, as did Internet pioneer John Gilmore.

Merely fighting the defensive battles in the courts was a passive strategy. EFF, they decided, should play an active role. It should take on proposed and existing legislation, guard civil liberties in cyberspace, help open this new online realm to more people, and try to narrow the gulf between the "info-haves" and the "info-have-nots."

The pace picked up when they hired Mike Godwin to head their legal efforts. "Godwin was online a lot as he was finishing law school at the University of Texas," Kapor remembers. "I was impressed by him."

EFF evolved quickly from a legal defense fund for some kid hackers to an influential lobbying organization. "In a way it was an ACLU of cyberspace," Kapor now says. "We quickly found that we were doing a lot of good raising issues, raising consciousness [about] the whole idea of how the Bill of Rights ought to apply to cyberspace and online activity. I got very passionate about it."

By 1993, EFF had an office in Washington and the ear of the Clinton administration, especially Vice President Al Gore, who dreamed of an information superhighway analogous to his father's (Senator Albert Gore, Sr.) favorite project, the interstate highway system. Other organizations were also addressing the issues, such as Computer Professionals for Social Responsibility, which EFF was now partly funding.

Despite EFF access, Clinton administration policy often proved a mere shadow of activists' expectations, or flouted them altogether. The activists began saying that EFF had sold out.

Kapor may have agreed. "The first major change was when we opened the Washington office and decided to get involved in advocacy work inside the Beltway. That was an educational, if unsuccessful, experience. We wound up being co-opted by Beltway politics rather than changing it."

The Digital Telephony Act, for example, was not in line with the principles of the organization or what the board wanted. "*Wired* [magazine] ran a piece about how EFF blew it. On reflection, I agree that we weren't skillful enough to maintain our principles and be effective. And as a result, we neither kept our principles nor were effective."

So EFF moved out of Washington and did some soul-searching.

Today, Kapor says, "It's a little street theater, a little advocacy, a little consciousness raising. And in projects like [those] it continues to be effective."

He himself moved on to other things. He chaired a commission to investigate and report on the problem of computer crime in Massachusetts. He served on the Computer Science and Technology Board of the National Research Council and the National Information Infrastructure Advisory Council. And he taught classes about software design, democracy and the Internet, and digital community at MIT.

But Kapor hasn't lost interest in the human issues raised by technological change. As more and more of humanity's work, play, and intellectual activity move onto the Net, the key issues have become privacy, freedom of speech, security, access, and the locus of political decision making.

"We have to figure out as a culture how to make [the Internet] a place where one would want to spend one's time. What are the rules of the road? Where's the power? Classical issues about free speech. What's the appropriate role for state action? What ought the boundaries be? Those are issues we've faced for hundreds of years, and we'll continue to face in changing circumstances." They are the issues that engage Kapor these days.

At the same time, he's back in the business, this time as an investor. "I have reentered the industry in another role as a venture capitalist at Accel Partners. That's a different direction from Woz. . . ."

Woz's Way

*Woz has life all figured out: design
a product you love, make a lot of money,
retire young, and do something
for people.*

GUY KAWASAKI
Apple Computer's first software evangelist

I N JANUARY 1997, APPLE CEO GILBERT AMELIO CLOSED HIS MACWORLD conference keynote speech with a surprise. It was Apple's twentieth anniversary. The company was now almost as old as its founders had been when they started it back in the late 1970s. A lot had changed in the two decades since the wild days of the revolution. Among the changes was this little detail of Apple history: its founders, Steven Paul Jobs and Stephen Gary Wozniak, had been absent from the company they founded for the second of those decades.

In celebration of Apple's twentieth anniversary, Amelio brought Jobs and Woz onstage. It was a dramatic moment, and an emotional one for many of the Apple fans in the audience, for this was still a company that had fans.

One could hardly help noticing the contrast between the two founders, however.

Jobs was now a billionaire and the CEO of Pixar, one of the hottest companies in the convergence of computer technology and entertainment. He was nattily dressed, trim, and poised, a long way from the unkempt college dropout in ragged jeans who had conceived of Apple a generation earlier.

Jobs had just cut a $400 million deal with Amelio. Apple was buying

NeXT, the company Jobs had started when he left Apple. Apple was in dire need of a new operating system, and that was just what NeXT had to offer. The message was clear: Jobs's operating system was going to save Apple's corporate life.

In addition, he himself was coming back to Apple as an advisor to Amelio, at a time when the industry, the customers, and the stock market all felt that Apple desperately required good advice. Jobs had helped guide Apple in its rocket ride to prominence; he had been one of the two guys in a garage who had made it all happen. And he had been far away during the company's recent troubles. A movie director could hardly have arranged things better to display Jobs as a corporate savior.

On stage, Jobs was mesmerizing. After Amelio rambled on for three hours about Apple's technology, Jobs delivered a one-sentence mission statement that seemed to articulate what Apple had to do to solve its problems more clearly than anything any Apple CEO had said in 10 years.

Even before he left the stage, rumors were starting that he would be more than just an advisor. With Apple's stock price dropping daily, one route to a major role for Jobs was clear. His friend Larry Ellison, billionaire CEO of network giant Oracle, had stated publicly that he was ready and willing to buy Apple himself and install Jobs as CEO. All Steve had to do, he said, was ask.

When Jobs finished onstage, Steve Wozniak stepped up. Next to Amelio and Jobs, he looked dumpy and uncomfortable. He wore a fuzzy sweater and fidgeted. It was easy to see the computer nerd of 20 years earlier in this older, unlikely looking multimillionaire. Woz was just there to take a bow and say a word or two on the occasion of the company's twentieth anniversary. He had no $400 million deal in the works, no well-crafted image to project. He looked small and inconsequential.

He was anything but that. Some people, like Gary Kildall, had always thought that Woz was the Steve who counted, the one who had actually enriched the world, and that Jobs was just a pitchman. Perhaps. But if so, why did Woz look like Amelio had pulled him out of mothballs for the occasion? Where had he been, and what, if anything, was he doing these days?

He hadn't been idle.

Since ceasing active involvement at Apple a decade earlier, Woz had started several firms, although none memorable or profitable. He took some ribbing in the industry and the press over his companies, but he has no regrets about them.

He had funded nonprofits that he believed in, including the EFF. His Web server was hosting sites for friends, including Joan Baez. He had donated computers to schools. He was giving away a lot of money. The city of San Jose honored some of his contributions when it named a street after him. Don't look for "Stephen G. Wozniak Boulevard," though; the street, which runs past the Children's Discovery Museum of San Jose (which he funded), is named Woz Way. He was still The Woz.

He was still on Apple's payroll, too—basically retired but drawing a token salary because, he said, "That's where my loyalty should be forever." He was living his life. He went to rock concerts and Golden State Warriors games, and he took the family to Disney World.

He conceived and funded a rock concert called the US Festival, his version of Woodstock. Woz had never been to Woodstock, and when he read a book about it, he wondered if he should proceed with the festival. Woz's vision of Woodstock was more innocent than the real thing. He did two, in 1982 and 1983, and as investments they weren't particularly successful. But Woz was pleased. "More people thank me for those festivals than thank me for Apple."

He had been teaching, too. "In the sixth grade," he once told a friend, "I decided I was going to be an engineer, and then an elementary school teacher." Strip away the extras of launching a high-tech start-up and becoming a high-profile multimillionaire, and that's exactly what he did: he became an engineer and then a teacher.

Since leaving Apple, Woz has devoted much of his time teaching fifth- to eighth-graders how to use computers. Many of his pupils probably don't realize that this enthusiastic, roly-poly teacher is a millionaire many times over, or that he invented the predecessor of the computer they are typing on, or that he may have given the school all the computers in the classroom.

His students are public school kids, and he teaches them the basics. He introduces them to the Internet and Web page design. Advanced students from prior years come to his office after school for their lessons. He teaches programming to older kids.

Teaching is not a hobby to Woz. It's a passion. He doesn't see much use in traditional math problems, like calculating where two canoes going at certain speeds will meet in the middle of a lake. Those problems just don't come up that often in real life, he explains. Computer logic is much more important. Computer science, he says, is the most important scientific discipline to teach kids.

He wishes that more of the kids he teaches wanted to learn programming. "It's a little disappointing, because I loved computers, how they worked and how they're programmed. When you program, you're the master. Now, you follow the way someone else tells you to do it. You're a slave, almost, to computer programs. I don't see creativity in that; not much more than in driving a car."

He looks back on the early days of the personal computer revolution as a magical time, but he also feels sadness for a spirit lost. "I always, my whole life, believed in openness and the open sharing of ideas." You share what you've learned with someone and "they sit down and go a little farther than you did." Although that ideal persists, notably in the open-source software movement, it's no longer relevant, he thinks, to building and selling computers. "Once it is big business, it's hard to do something really significant without an awful lot of money. The Homebrew approach can't sell anymore.

"We were young. There were not that many dollars visible in this industry. It was as open as ham radio—just hobbyist groups. It was a very lucky point in time. And something so huge and successful sprang out of it. That such [a thing] happened was a huge surprise.

"That open and truthful period is rare, and it's great to be near it and feel it. It's beyond us now."

To those who understand what they're looking at when they open up a computer, the Apple II remains a work of art. In 1977, maybe a handful of people in the whole world had the knowledge—of hardware and software, electronics, and circuit board layout—as well as the skill, the artistry, and the passion for excellence to have designed the Apple II. Or maybe only one. Steve Wozniak is deservedly a legend.

It's hard for some people to connect this mythic figure with the anonymous fifth-grade teacher, but Woz has no regrets about stepping out of the limelight. "What I admire about Woz," Mitch Kapor says, "is that he has found himself, and is happy doing things that are meaningful, working with kids. He doesn't really give a rat's ass about what other people might think, or what it might look like. As in, 'a genius like you wasting your life on this?' More power to him."

Woz is clearly doing what he enjoys. The personal computer revolution wrested power away from the white-coated priesthood and put it in the hands of ordinary people, and Woz fought in the front lines of that war. Now it's over, and he's content to show a new generation of computer users how to use the gift he and others crafted for them. Seeing him working with children, conveying his excitement over the semi-magic powers of the technology, his choice seems perfectly reasonable. After all, isn't this what it was all about?

While some, like Woz and Kapor, were facing the question of what to do after the revolution, others were waiting for a revolution that still hadn't happened.

Engelbart

*I don't know what Silicon Valley will do
when it runs out of Doug's ideas.*

ALAN KAY
Fellow, Walt Disney Imagineering

IN THE 1970S, XEROX PARC IMPLEMENTED DOUG ENGELBART'S IDEAS of networked computers, windowing, and his patented device, the mouse, on Xerox computers that the general public never saw. Xerox PARC was where the great ideas about personal computer technology got turned into actual metal and plastic sitting on people's desks. Mostly Xerox PARC engineers' desks.

The bulk of these technologies eventually did reach the market, some at Xerox, many at Apple, and later in many other places. Engelbart remains the source of some of the most powerful ideas in user interface design in computers today. In addition to the mouse, e-mail, and the first fully integrated two-way computer/video teleconference, he pioneered multiple-window computer displays, hypermedia, groupware, and electronic publishing.

Recently, he began receiving the recognition he deserves.

In 1997, Engelbart won the $500,000 Lemelson-MIT Prize, the world's largest cash award for American invention and innovation. The prize is given upon the recommendation of three review panels of leading experts representing scientific, engineering, and medical disciplines in academia and industry.

In 1998, his peers and fans honored him in "Engelbart's Unfinished

Revolution," a day-long *Festschrift* commemorating the thirtieth anniversary of "The Mother of All Demos," his presentation at the 1968 Fall Joint Computer Conference in San Francisco where he demonstrated his mouse and many of the precursors of today's computer necessities. Industry leaders praised him and, in a repeat performance of that presentation, the 1500 audience members gave him a standing ovation.

Ted Nelson said, "This prophet-without-honor thing is all completely true. The lack of appreciation of Doug is like you stand next to the Empire State Building and you don't know how tall it is. You just know it's taller than you and a lot of people resent that."

Although moved by the show of support, Engelbart couldn't help reflect that he had not yet solved the problem he set for himself back in 1951: augmenting human intellect to deal with the complexity of life.

Back in 1977, when the Xerox PARC researchers began honing some of his ideas, Engelbart kept working on the ideas behind these ideas. His computer devices were only part of the message, and that real message, more revolutionary than his inventions, was about developing new systems to expand mental scope. These systems didn't have to be technological. The key to getting more intelligence out of any organization, Engelbart believes, is sharing information and techniques.

Although companies tend to guard information and techniques closely, treating them as intellectual property to shield from competitors, Engelbart draws distinctions among kinds of information, based on types of work.

A-work is the primary mission of an organization, like building cars. It requires knowledge that is widespread and common in an industry.

B-work includes techniques for improving A-work. The problems here are the same for all companies and the solutions give a competitive edge, so firms usually protect them as proprietary information.

C-work is knowledge about improving the improvement process itself, such as systems for responding to customer complaints. Engelbart believes in sharing this kind of knowledge, and because it is widely useful and high-level knowledge, its spread can enormously benefit society as a whole.

Having identified his target, he moved on to identifying methods for sharing it. Actually, he began *inventing* methods for sharing it. E-mail, hypertext documents, and shared-screen teleconferencing were remarkable breakthroughs, but to Engelbart they were merely tools for achieving the real goal: sharing C-work knowledge.

Much of what's gone on in the personal computer revolution, Engelbart thinks, doesn't do much to advance that cause. The concept of groupware, for example, is really just about sharing a *document*. It doesn't get into how people can work together within a complex hypertext-linked repository of documents. The personal computer has delivered a lot of power to the individual, but hasn't done very much to help people work together in new ways.

In Engelbart's view, the tragedy of the personal computer revolution was this decade-long detour away from the crucial goal of connecting people in new, more empowering ways. He had hoped to see the computer change the very nature of collaborative work, with work happening in shared virtual spaces like electronic whiteboards that everyone could write on and annotate in parallel. But everywhere he looked he saw office workers grinding away in the relative seclusion of their offices or cubicles, limiting their information sharing to e-mailed messages and static files.

Today, though, the trend has shifted toward sharing information and technology. The recent phenomenal spread of the Java programming language, with its more secure programming model, may be the key to businesses letting their software work together without risking company secrets or security. The Internet and the World Wide Web are bringing people together in unexpected ways, hinting at new modes of collaboration, new models of wall-less libraries open to all. Open-source software development is both a model of how people can work together productively and a test bed for collaborative techniques.

But will they be the techniques Engelbart thinks we need? He believes that corporations in the same market niche should work together on pilot projects in which high-performance teams can experiment with ways to get bootstrapping processes started. Is this naive? Does Engelbart underestimate the pressures to compete?

Possibly so, but his principles have an interesting resonance with the open-source software movement. When proponents of the free sharing of software ideas and code talk about how quickly problems can be fixed in this open atmosphere and how rapidly technology can advance when anyone is free to contribute to the most promising projects, what are they talking about but bootstrapping?

The goal that Engelbart set for himself nearly 50 years ago still eludes him. There have been many quiet successes, a few moments of acknowledgment, off-again-on-again funding, and much disappointment. But with the embracing of the Internet by businesses, we may be moving toward the future that Engelbart envisioned so long ago. He is guardedly hopeful, but he continues to work 12 hours a day at his Bootstrap Institute, seeking ways technology can make people smarter.

Citizen Nelson

I thought there would be a real
computer revolution; I see
complete betrayal.

TED NELSON
The Thomas Paine of the personal
computer revolution

WHEN THE COMPUTER INDUSTRY CAME TOGETHER IN 1998 TO HONOR Doug Engelbart at the "Engelbart's Unfinished Revolution" event, it was only fitting that Ted Nelson be there. Not because he had built any machines or based any software on Engelbart's ideas. He had not. Nelson was, in fact, a seer in his own right, the begetter of a vision every bit as grand and detailed as Engelbart's. With Engelbart and Nelson on stage, the audience was viewing the prophets of two rival religions.

Although he praised Engelbart lavishly, Nelson also identified the key difference in their philosophies. "I visited Doug in the spring of 1967," he told the audience. To him, Engelbart's emphasis on collaboration "seemed completely naive. I've always been sensitive to conflict: agreement among people is a miracle. One of the things that moves me greatly is seeing this audience here because it shows that [Engelbart's] emphasis on collaboration, on working together, does have meaning."

Nelson, though, has always been more interested in how to empower the dissenter. This is not surprising, since he is often described as the Thomas Paine of the personal computer revolution.

The son of Academy Award–winning actress Celeste Holm and director Ralph Nelson, Ted Nelson felt the lure of show business early on, yet was always deeply impressed by the potential of computers. Like Ada Byron, Lady Lovelace, he sought a synthesis of art and technology.

In 1974, before the Altair was announced, before there was anything that could be accurately called a personal computer, he self-published *Computer Lib,* in which he explained computers to the lay reader in clear and witty prose and laid out the political agenda for the personal computer revolution.

"You can and must understand computers NOW," the book trumpeted. "Computer power to the people! Down with cybercrud!" Also, "If computers are the wave of the future, displays are the surfboards." Along with the bumper-sticker slogans were many essays, jokes, thoughts, and anecdotes, all stitched together in a style blatantly imitative of Stewart Brand's underground classic *The Whole Earth Catalog.*

The book somehow reached all the right people. It influenced Steve Wozniak. Ed Roberts had it on his desk while MITS was building the Altair. *Computer Lib* was Thomas Paine's *Common Sense* for the computer hobbyist. Lee Felsenstein wrote, "Ted succeeded with *Computer Lib* to rally a rabble of latent crackpots into an anarchistic army which breached the sanctum of Official Computerdom and brought computers to everyone."

The book was fiercely individualistic in style and in philosophy. Because there were no personal computers, Nelson urged people to turn what technology was available to their personal use. "Maybe you should consider buying your own minicomputer [or] chipping in with several other families to get one." He gave contrarian business advice that served the early personal computer makers well: "This is . . . a field where individuals can have a profound influence. But the wrong way to try it is through conventional corporate financing. [D]o it in a garret, and *then* talk about ways of getting it out to the world."

Nelson spoke as provocatively and as entertainingly as he wrote, and was much in demand as a speaker at computer conferences. In April 1977, he addressed the West Coast Computer Faire on the subject of "Those Unforgettable Next Two Years." In the speech, he correctly predicted that major technology companies would enter the field, but would have trouble because of their cumbersome decision-making processes; that standards like the S100 bus would dictate which computers succeeded and which didn't; that small programs would give way to large, complex programs requiring more memory; and that the legendary and unassailable IBM would run into big problems, leading to massive layoffs and reorganization.

He was just continuing a record of prescience: in *Computer Lib* he had predicted the arrival and the amazing spread of personal computers, and the transfer of most office work from paper on desks to computer desktops.

With the arrival of the revolution he had predicted and fomented, however, Nelson had little patience with the pace of progress or the actual systems.

He rebelled at things as fundamental as the structure of files on a computer, even the concept of files. To him, file structures impose a hierarchical mindset that has nothing to do with reality. You put away the current item neatly and pry open the packing crate in which the next is stored. "Today's software is designed for clerks and engineers," he said, "not for people who think."

Software applications also ticked him off. "Word processing" is not a category of human activity, he fumed, but a label for the artificial boundaries imposed by inadequate programs. He found most application programs disappointing, but he was more offended by the very concept of application categories such as word processing. The idea that one should be boxed into these tight categories of computer use angered him.

The acronym WYSIWYG, for What You See Is What You Get, was supposed to convey the boons of new printing technology in the 1980s. "What it really means," Nelson complained, "is What You Get When You Print It Out. In other words, we are using the computer as a paper simulator, which is like tearing the wings off a 747 and driving it as a bus on the highway."

Nor did he believe the Macintosh was the panacea some claimed. He called it "an Application Prison, distracting its inmates with bread and circuses (Fonts and Graphics) from the fact that there was no structural support for organization of projects. And it gave us the Abominable Hidey-Hole—called 'The Clipboard'—except that you can't see it, it holds only one item, and each item destroys the previous; in ALL other respects like a regular clipboard, except there aren't any [other aspects]. This is called a 'metaphor,' meaning a stupid scrap of resemblance on which bad software is built."

The whole software development process was wrong, he was convinced. His take on the writing of Lotus Symphony: "Mitch said, 'Here's the Lotus wish list, will you implement exactly as stated?' [The programmer] programmed it and got backing to develop Lotus Notes and the list was released as Lotus Symphony." The tale may be apocryphal, but it did have the ring of truth.

Software, Nelson was sure, should be "designed according to an auteurist approach—an approach already working quite well in video games—integrated virtuality unified by the hand of a movie director, who trades off, polishes, and edits all the effects. The incredible clunkiness of today's office software begs for huge speedup and a new silky feel.

"Why are video games so much better designed than office software? Video games are designed by people who love to play video games. Office software is designed by people who want to do something else on the weekend."

He's serious about the movie director analogy. "Interactive software is a branch of moviemaking. And most computer science is irrelevant. What is relevant is studying your Orson Welles, studying your Alfred Hitchcock, [and] studying your good documentaries. Because right now we are in the stage of software which compares to the movie business before 1904, where movies were made by the cameraman because he understood the equipment. In 1904, they invented the director. He had to know how to make those parts come together."

As the son of a movie director, Nelson tried his own hand at software design. As a college student at Harvard, Nelson generated huge amounts of notes and began to despair of ever getting them all organized. Then in 1960, he discovered computers and had an immediate epiphany. I'll just write a program to keep track of all my notes, he thought. Nearly 40 years later, he's still working on it.

Certain features seemed necessary. The program should reflect the way thoughts are organized. For one thing, thinking is parallel, not linear. Furthermore, he didn't want to throw away old versions of a document when he produced a new one; he wanted the various versions linked together. Footnotes are a feeble way to tie ideas together, no more helpful than a fingerpost. Surely in moving from paper to electronic storage, one could find a better approach. But links should go in both directions, so that he could see what documents referred to this document, as well as what documents it referred to. He called the system "hypertext."

With the help of many programmers over several decades, these ideas evolved into a massive project called Xanadu.

Xanadu would be a world of interconnected text, graphics, sound, and video, like the World Wide Web, but unlike the Web it would provide version management, links that worked both ways and didn't break, transparent compensation for authors, and support for expression that recognized the nonlinearity of thought. In short, the World Wide Web done right (and conceived long before).

For years, Nelson and his programmers labored to bring Xanadu to life. They worked generally without adequate funding, pursuing a goal that, like Engelbart's plans, kept moving further off. For a while, Autodesk, a successful public software firm in San Rafael, north of the Golden Gate Bridge, backed the project, and it looked like it was going to happen. Then a few years later, the Web sprang to life and popularity. Like the Samuel Taylor Coleridge poem for which it was named, Xanadu remains unfinished.

"Getting [financial] backing," he explains, "especially to do things *way* differently, is exactly like trying to get backing for a movie. It's complicated politics, everybody thinks he can direct, and that's what Hollywood sorts out—the politics of Getting to Direct." He hasn't gotten to direct yet; like Engelbart, he hasn't realized his grand design.

In September 1999, Nelson either admitted defeat or took a logical and fitting step in the evolution of Xanadu: he released its unfinished code under an open-source license. In the future the implementation of the Xanadu dream would be something to which anyone, rather than just the small team of programmers for whom Nelson was able to find funding, could contribute. For better or worse, its future was now out of Ted Nelson's hands.

Speaking of Engelbart, he said, "We both made the same fundamental error, I think—what each of us was trying to do required the existence of the system we were building in order to build it. He seems to want his 'high-power teams' on hand to recognize and choose the structures to be created in order to create and empower high-power teams. Similarly, I have assumed the existence of [my kind of hypertext] literary systems in order to manage the versions of trying to build them."

The computer systems that exist today, as well as the World Wide Web, represent a failure to Nelson, who holds firm to his more ambitious vision.

"I see a completely different computer world, of empowerment and putting real computer power in people's hands. Forms of publication that are orders-of-magnitude richer in structure and comparison, rather than dumb special effects. So what I still intend to do: the same, retrofitted to the Web. Another day will dawn, I tell you. And it will NOT be stupid Talking Agents on a screen." Like Douglas Engelbart, Ted Nelson is still working to bring about the *real* computer revolution that he sees so clearly and that *still* hasn't happened. Like Mitch Kapor, he has always been keenly aware that technological decisions have political consequences. Like Steve Wozniak, he believes that the goal must be the empowerment of the individual human being.

From Nelson's impassioned "Computer power to the people!" in *Computer Lib* and David Ahl's earnest pitch to DEC management to build a personal computer, through the wild enthusiasm that greeted the announcement of the Altair, to the ubiquity of personal computers in homes, schools, and offices today, and the ongoing transformation of business and society by the Web, empowering the individual has been a powerful motivator. Indeed, for many who wrought the revolution, that was what it was all about. Taking that as the goal, it is clear that we have come a long way. And we have a long way to go.

The revolution is over, and it has only begun.

I was sitting like a spider in the middle of a web. This magazine was the only outlet these guys had. There was nothing else. And I was crazy enough to talk to them.

LES SOLOMON, DESCRIBING THE WRITERS AND ENGINEERS HE WORKED WITH AT POPULAR ELECTRONICS

I knew the Altair was an exciting project, and it really turned me on. But it was much more a labor of love.

ED ROBERTS

We were called computer nerds. Anyone who spends their life on a computer is pretty unusual.

BILL GATES

We didn't do three years of research and come up with this concept. What we did was follow our own instincts and construct a computer that was what we wanted.

STEVE JOBS

Starting a company didn't mean that much to me. I can design computers. I know I can.

STEVE WOZNIAK

*You were dealing with entrepreneurs
mostly. Egos, a lot of egos.*

ED FABER

*I always enjoyed computer games, and
when there weren't any to play,
I had to write them.*

SCOTT ADAMS

A year was a lifetime in those days.

LEE FELSENSTEIN

INDEX